W9-CFA-733

Dream Chasers

COVER
ILLUSTRATOR

SPOTLIGHT

MICHAEL MCGURL

▼ The use of form, shape, and bold color to represent images are hallmarks of artist Michael McGurl's work. His unique graphic style, as shown on the cover of *Dream Chasers*, developed from his wish to "do something different." One of the things the Santa Fe resident enjoys most about being an artist is the challenge of "making something interesting and creative" out of seemingly impossible jobs.

Acknowledgments appear on pages 558–560, which constitute an extension of this copyright page.

© 1993 Silver Burdett Ginn Inc.
Cover art © 1993 by Michael McGurl.

All rights reserved. Printed in the United States of America. This publication, or parts thereof, may not be reproduced in any form by photographic, electrostatic, mechanical, or any other method, for any use, including information storage and retrieval, without written permission from the publisher.

ISBN 0–663–54659–1

2 3 4 5 6 7 8 9 10 RRD 98 97 96 95 94 93

New Dimensions
IN THE
WORLD OF READING

Dream Chasers

PROGRAM AUTHORS

James F. Baumann   Roselmina Indrisano   P. David Pearson
Theodore Clymer   Dale D. Johnson   Taffy E. Raphael
Carl Grant   Connie Juel   Marian Davies Toth
Elfrieda H. Hiebert Jeanne R. Paratore   Richard L. Venezky

SILVER BURDETT GINN

NEEDHAM, MA   MORRISTOWN, NJ

ATLANTA, GA   DALLAS, TX   DEERFIELD, IL   MENLO PARK, CA

Unit 1 Theme
A Job Worth Doing

Unit 2 Theme
The Land of the Free

7

Unit 3 Theme

Imagine a Place . . .

Unit 4 Theme
The HOME of the BRAVE

11

A Job Worth Doing

Building bridges or starting a business—why is work worth doing also worth reading about?

LES CONSTRUCTEURS, *oil on canvas by Fernand Léger, French, 1950*

Theme Books for
A Job Worth Doing

*H*ave you discovered what your special talent is? When you are especially good at something you enjoy doing, then you gain a special pleasure from the work you do.

✦ Read about how Jane Goodall's special love for animals developed into a lifetime career in *My Life With the Chimpanzees* by Jane Goodall.

✦ In *Hero Over Here* by Kathleen V. Kudlinski, Theodore wishes that he could be a war hero like his father and brother. But when his mother and sister come down with the deadly Spanish flu, he must rely on his own talents to help them survive.

✦ "Fraidycat" Addie is moving to the Dakota Territory. Does she have what it takes to live in a wild and dangerous land? Find out in *Addie Across the Prairie* by Laurie Lawlor.

✦ Mary didn't understand why white children could go to school, but she, an African-American, could not. Read about how Mary's desire to learn led her to become an influential educator in *Mary McLeod Bethune: Voice of Black Hope* by Milton Meltzer.

More Books to Enjoy

The High King by Lloyd Alexander
The Pushcart War by Jean Merrill
Ordinary Jack by Helen Cresswell
Mysteriously Yours, Maggie Marmelstein
  by Marjorie Sharmat

AWARD
WINNING
AUTHOR

16

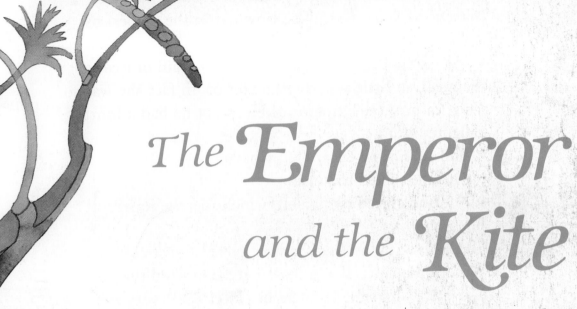

The Emperor and the Kite

by Jane Yolen

Once in ancient China there lived a princess who was the fourth daughter of the emperor. She was very tiny. In fact she was so tiny her name was Djeow Seow,[1] which means "the smallest one." And, because she was so tiny, she was not thought very much of—when she was thought of at all.

Her brothers, who were all older and bigger and stronger than she, were thought of all the time. And they were like four rising suns in the eyes of their father. They helped the emperor rule the kingdom and teach the people the ways of peace.

Even her three sisters were all older and bigger and stronger than she.

They were like three midnight moons in the eyes of their father.

They were the ones who brought food to his table. But Djeow Seow was like a tiny star in the emperor's sight.

She was not even allowed to bring a grain of rice to the meal, so little was she thought of. In fact she was so insignificant, the emperor often forgot he had a fourth daughter at all.

And so, Djeow Seow ate by herself.

And she talked to herself.

And she played by herself, which was the loneliest thing of all.

Her favorite toy was a kite of paper and sticks.

Every morning, when the wind came from the east past the rising sun, she flew her kite. And every evening, when the wind went to the west past the setting sun, she flew her kite. Her toy was like a flower in the sky. And it was like a prayer in the wind.

In fact a monk who passed the palace daily made up a poem about her kite.

> My kite sails upward,
> Mounting to the high heavens.
> My soul goes on wings.

But then, he was a monk, and given to such thoughts.

As for Princess Djeow Seow, she thanked him each day for his prayer.

Then she went back to flying her toy.

But all was not peaceful in the kingdom, just as the wind is not always peaceful.

For the wind can trouble the waters of a still pond.

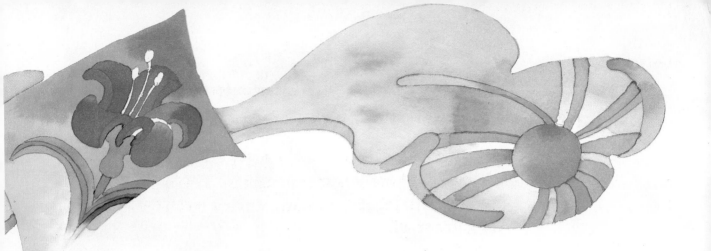

And there were evil men plotting against the emperor.

They crept up on him one day when he was alone, when his four sons were away ruling in the furthermost parts of the kingdom and his three daughters were down in the garden. And only Princess Djeow Seow, so tiny she seemed part of the corner where she sat, saw what happened.

The evil men took the emperor to a tower in the middle of a wide, treeless plain. The tower had only a single window, with an iron bar across the center. The plotters sealed the door with bricks and mortar once the emperor was inside.

Then they rode back to the palace and declared that the emperor was dead.

When his sons and daughters heard this, they all fled to a neighboring kingdom where they spent their time sobbing and sighing. But they did nothing else all day long.

All except Djeow Seow. She was so tiny, the evil men did not notice her at all.

And so, she crept to the edge of the wide, treeless plain.

And there she built a hut of twigs and branches.

Every day at dawn and again at dark, she would walk across the plain to the tower.

And there she would sail her stick-and-paper kite.

To the kite string she tied a tiny basket filled with rice
and poppyseed cakes, water chestnuts and green tea. The
kite pulled the basket high, high in the air, up as high as
the window in the tower.

And, in this way, she kept her father alive.

So they lived for many days: the emperor in his tower
and the princess in a hut near the edge of the plain.

The evil men ruled with their cruel, harsh ways, and
the people of the country were very sad.

One day, as the princess prepared a basket of food for
her father, the old monk passed by her hut. She smiled
at him, but he seemed not to see her.

Yet, as he passed, he repeated his prayer in a loud
voice. He said:

> *My kite sails upward,*
> *Mounting to the high heavens.*
> *My emperor goes on wings.*

The princess started to thank him. But then she
stopped. Something was different. The words were not
quite right.

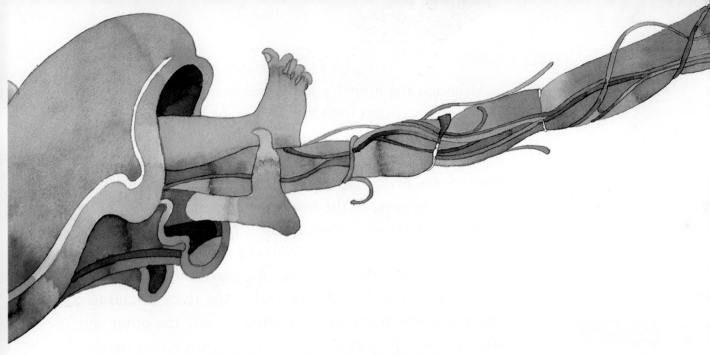

"Stop," she called to the monk. But he had already passed by. He was a monk, after all, and did not take part in things of this world.

And then Djeow Seow understood. The monk was telling her something important. And she understood.

Each day after that, when she was not bringing food to her father, Djeow Seow was busy. She twined a string of grass and vines, and wove in strands of her own long black hair. When her rope was as thick as her waist and as high as the tower, she was ready. She attached the rope to the string of the stick-and-paper kite, and made her way across the treeless plain.

When she reached the tower, she called to her father.

But her voice was as tiny as she, and her words were lost in the wind.

At last, though, the emperor looked out and saw his daughter flying her kite. He expected the tiny basket of food to sail up to his window as it had done each day. But what should he see but the strand of vines and grass and long black hair. The wind was raging above, holding the kite in its steely grip. And the princess was below, holding tight to the end of the rope.

Although the emperor had never really understood the worth of his tiniest daughter before, he did now. And he promised himself that if her plan worked she would never again want for anything, though all she had ever wanted was love. Then he leaned farther out of the tower window and grasped the heavy strand. He brought it into his tower room and loosened the string of the kite. He set the kite free, saying, "Go to thy home in the sky, great kite." And the kite flew off toward the heavens.

Then the emperor tied one end of the thick strand to the heavy iron bar across the window, and the other end stretched all the way down to Djeow Seow's tiny hands.

The emperor stepped to the window sill, slipped under the iron bar, saluted the gods, and slid down the rope. His robes billowed out around him like the wings of a bright kite.

When his feet reached the ground, he knelt before his tiny daughter. And he touched the ground before her with his lips. Then he rose and embraced her, and she almost disappeared in his arms.

With his arm encircling her, the emperor said, "Come to thy home with me, loyal child." He lifted the tiny princess to his shoulders and carried her all the way back to the palace.

At the palace, the emperor was greeted by wild and cheering crowds.

The people were tired of the evil men, but they had been afraid to act.

With the emperor once again to guide them, they threw the plotters into prison.

And when the other sons and daughters of the emperor heard of his return, they left off their sobbing and sighing, and they hurried home to welcome their father. But when they arrived, they were surprised to find Djeow Seow on a tiny throne by their father's side.

To the end of his days, the emperor ruled with Princess Djeow Seow close by. She never wanted for anything, especially love.

And the emperor never again neglected a person— whether great or small.

And, too, it is said that Djeow Seow ruled after him, as gentle as the wind and, in her loyalty, as unyielding.

Reader's Response ⁓ Do you think Djeow Seow was just "too good for words"? Explain.

Kites Aloft

Kites have had many different uses since their invention in ancient times. Djeow Seow used a kite to fly her father to freedom. Alexander Graham Bell had a similar idea around the turn of the century. He connected huge kites together to see if he could lift people off the ground! Do you think he was successful?

Kites have been used for scientific experiments for a long time. One of the most famous experiments involved Ben Franklin, a storm, and a key. Ben Franklin wanted to prove that there was electricity in storm clouds. One stormy day he flew his kite. Lightning struck the kite, then traveled down to a brass key and caused a spark—he knew that he was right!

In 1901, Italian inventor Guglielmo Marconi received the first transatlantic wireless communication (from Britain to Canada) via an aerial antenna hoisted aloft by a large kite.

Before Wilbur and Orville Wright flew their first plane in 1903, they flew box kites to find out how to make wings that would keep their plane in the air.

The U.S. Weather Bureau (now the National Weather Service) relied on kites for many years to carry thermometers and other measuring instruments into the air. Airplanes eventually took the place of those kites.

The Toothpaste Millionaire

from the book by Jean Merrill

Twelve-year-old Rufus Mayflower is a math whiz and inventor. With the help of his friend and fellow sixth–grader, Kate MacKinstrey, he stumbled on an idea that would make him a millionaire by eighth grade.

I remember the morning Rufus got the idea for toothpaste. He had to do some shopping for his mother, and I went along with him. We were in the Cut-Rate Drugstore, because toothpaste was one of the things on Rufus's list.

I was looking at some name-brand eye shadow that was on sale, when I heard Rufus say, "79¢! 79¢ for a six-inch tube of toothpaste. That's crazy!"

"It's better than 89¢," I said. I pointed to some 89¢ tubes farther down the shelf.

"That's even crazier," Rufus said. "What can be in those tubes anyway? Just some peppermint flavoring and some paste."

"Maybe the paste is expensive to make," I said.

"Paste!" Rufus said. "You don't need powdered gold to make paste. Paste is made out of everyday ordinary stuff. Didn't you ever make paste?"

"Toothpaste?" I said.

"I mean just plain paste for pasting things together," Rufus said. "My Grandma Mayflower showed me how to make paste when I was four years old."

"How do you do it?" I asked.

"Simple," Rufus said. "You just take a little flour and starch and cook them with a little water till the mixture has a nice pasty feel. Then you can use it to paste pictures in a scrapbook. Or paste up wallpaper."

"But you couldn't brush your teeth with *that*," I said.

"Well, I don't know," Rufus said. "I never tried. But I bet toothpaste isn't any harder to make. Anyway, I'm not paying any 79¢ for a tube of toothpaste."

Rufus crossed toothpaste off his mother's shopping list.

"But your mother said to get toothpaste," I said. "You can't help it if it's expensive."

"I'll make her some," Rufus said. "I bet I can make a gallon of it for 79¢."

"Maybe even for 78⅛¢," I said.

Rufus laughed. "Maybe," he said.

"Hey," I said. "Do you think you could make eye shadow, too?"

It suddenly struck me that 69¢ for a smidge of eye shadow about as big as a nickel—and that was the cut-rate sale price—was a little bit expensive, too.

"Eye shadow's a kind of pasty stuff," I told Rufus. "Maybe if you just added coloring to toothpaste…"

"Maybe," Rufus said. "But what's the point? Nobody really needs eye shadow. If anybody's crazy enough to pay 69¢ for something he doesn't *need*, I can't be bothered about him. But everybody needs to brush his teeth. If I could make a good, cheap toothpaste, that would be worth doing."

I decided not to buy any eye shadow. Rufus was right. Who needed it?

In addition to which, I didn't even *like* eye shadow. I had tried it, and I didn't like the feel of it or the bother of putting it on. But some of my friends were buying eye shadow and trying out new shades and talking about which brand was the best, and I just got into the habit of going along with them.

"Rufus," I said, as we rode our bikes home. "I'm going to tell you something I've never told anyone before. I hate eye shadow. I really *hate* it."

"I don't care too much about it one way or the other myself," Rufus said.

"And it just occurred to me," I said, "that if I never buy any eye shadow for the rest of my life, I'll probably save at least $10 a year. If I live till I'm 80, that's $700."

"Great!" Rufus said.

"And if I could save money on toothpaste, too…" I said. "Wow!" I was thinking about how easy it would be to get rich just by not buying things the stores want you to buy.

"How much do you think it would cost us to make our own toothpaste?" I asked Rufus.

"I don't know," Rufus said. "But I just thought of something else. You know what I used to brush my teeth with when I stayed at my Grandma Mayflower's in North Carolina? You know what my Grandma uses to brush her teeth?"

"What?" I asked.

"Bicarbonate of soda," Rufus said. "Just plain old baking soda. You just put a little of the soda powder on your toothbrush."

"*Bicarb*?" I said. "That's the stuff my mother tries to give me when I feel sick to my stomach. Bicarbonate of soda in water. I can't *stand* the taste."

"Really?" Rufus said. "To me bicarb has a nice refreshing taste. Sort of like 7-Up without the lemon-lime flavor."

"But who wants to drink 7-Up without the lemon-lime flavor?" I said. "That's the whole *point* of 7-Up."

"I guess you're right," Rufus said. "I guess that's why more people don't brush their teeth with bicarb."

The next afternoon when I stopped by Rufus's house to borrow his bike pump, he had about fifty bowls and pans scattered around the kitchen.

"What are you making?" I asked.

"I already made it," Rufus said.

He handed me a spoon and a bowl with some white stuff in it. I took a spoonful.

"Don't eat it," Rufus said. "Just taste it. Rub a little on your teeth."

I tried a little.

"How does it taste?" Rufus asked.

"Not bad," I said. "Better than the kind my mother buys in the pink-and-white striped tube. How'd you get it to taste so good?"

"A drop of peppermint oil," Rufus said, "But I've got other flavors, too."

He pushed three other pots of paste across the table. The first one had a spicy taste.

"Clove-flavored," Rufus said. "You like it?"

"I don't know," I said. "It's interesting."

"Try this one."

The next sample had a sweet taste. "Vanilla," I guessed.

"Right," Rufus said.

"I like vanilla," I said. "In milkshakes. Or ice cream. But it doesn't seem quite right in toothpaste. Too sweet."

"This one won't be too sweet," Rufus said, handing me another sample.

"*Eeegh*," I said and ran to the sink to wash out my mouth. "What did you put in *that?*"

"Curry powder," Rufus said. "You don't like it? I thought it tasted like a good shrimp curry."

"Maybe it does," I said, "but I don't like curry."

Rufus looked disappointed. "I don't suppose you'd like it almond-flavored, either," he said. "I made some of that, too, but I decided not too many people would take to almond."

"What flavor is in that big plastic pan?" I asked. "You've got enough of that kind to frost twenty-seven cakes."

"That's no-kind yet," Rufus said. "That's just 79¢ worth of the stuff that goes in the paste. I didn't want to flavor it till I figured out the best taste."

"What does it taste like plain?" I asked.

"Well," Rufus said, "mostly you taste the bicarb."

"Bicarb!" I said. "You mean all this stuff I've been tasting has got bicarbonate of soda in it?"

Rufus grinned. "Yeah," he said. "It's probably good for your stomach as well as your teeth."

Know what I did when I got home that night? I mixed up some bicarbonate of soda in water. It wasn't that I was feeling sick. It was just that Rufus gave me this inspiration.

What I did was to add a few drops of vanilla and a little sugar to the bicarb water. And you know what? It tasted something like cream soda. You'd never know you were drinking bicarb.

And I like cream soda even better than 7-Up.

I forgot to mention another nice thing about Rufus. The afternoon Rufus let me sample his first batch of toothpaste, he was trying to figure out how many tubes of toothpaste it would make.

We looked at a medium-sized tube of toothpaste.

"You must have enough for ten tubes in that plastic bowl," I guessed.

"More, I bet," Rufus said.

"Why don't you squeeze the toothpaste in the tube into a measuring cup and then measure the stuff in the bowl," I suggested.

"That would be a waste of toothpaste," Rufus said. "We couldn't get it back in the tube." Rufus hates to waste anything.

"I have a better idea," he said. "I'll pack into a square pan the toothpaste I made. Then I can figure out how many cubic inches of toothpaste we have. And you can figure out how many cubic inches of toothpaste are in the tube."

"But the tube is round, Rufus," I said. "I can't measure cubic inches unless something is cube-shaped."

Rufus thought a minute. "Maybe we can squeeze the tube into a cube shape," he said.

I thought that was brilliant. But then I had another idea.

"Rufus," I said. "It says on the tube that it contains 3.25 ounces of toothpaste. Why couldn't we just weigh your paste and divide by 3.25 to see how many tubes it would make?"

"Hey—we could!" Rufus said. "You are *smart*, Kate. I'm always doing things the hard way."

That's what is really so nice about Rufus. It's not just that he gets great ideas like making toothpaste. But if *you* have a good idea, he says so.

I was pleased that I had thought of a simpler way of measuring the toothpaste, but I told Rufus, "I wish I was smart enough even to *think* of a hard way of doing something."

I *never* would have thought of measuring toothpaste in cubic inches. Partly because I never can remember exactly how to figure cubic inches. And I certainly wouldn't have thought of making a round tube cube-shaped. Would you?

Anyway it turned out Rufus had made about forty tubes of toothpaste for 79¢.

Before I finished breakfast the next morning, there was a knock on the door. It was Rufus. He was very excited.

"Kate!" he said. "Do you know what the population of the United States is?"

"No," I said. I never know things like that.

My father looked up from his paper. "According to the most recent census—over 200,000,000," he said to Rufus. My father always knows things like that.

"You're right," Rufus said. "And by now, it must be even bigger."

"Probably," my father said. "The growing population is a very serious matter. Have you thought much about that problem, Rufus?"

"Not yet, Mr. MacKinstrey," Rufus said. "At the moment, I was thinking mainly about toothpaste. I was thinking that everybody in the United States probably uses about one tube of toothpaste a month."

"Probably," my father said.

"And if they do," Rufus said, "how many tubes of toothpaste are sold in a year?"

My father thought for a second. "Roughly two-and-a-half billion tubes."

"Right!" Rufus said.

I hate people who can multiply in their heads. Except that my father and Rufus are two of the people I like best in the world. How do you explain that?

I really don't like math at all, even when I have a paper and pencil and all the time in the world to figure something out.

And at the same time I look forward every day to Mr. Conti's math class. And how do you explain that, since that's the class where I'm always getting in trouble?

For example, the same day my father brought up the population explosion, there's Mr. Conti in math class saying:

"Kate MacKinstrey, would you please bring me that note."

"Well, it isn't exactly a note, Mr. Conti."

"I see," says Mr. Conti. "I suppose it's another math problem."

"It looks like a math problem, Mr. Conti."

The message from Rufus that Mr. Conti got to read that day said:

If there are 2 ½ billion tubes of toothpaste sold in the U.S. in one year, and 1 out of 10 people switched to a new brand, how many tubes of the new brand would they be buying?

The right answer is 250 million. It took the class a while to figure that out. Some people have trouble remembering how many zeros there are in a billion.

Then there was a second part to the note:

If the inventor of the new toothpaste made a profit of 1¢ a tube on his toothpaste, what would his profit be at the end of the year?

And it turns out that the inventor of this new toothpaste would make a two-and-a-half million dollar profit!

Well, that's how Rufus's toothpaste business started. With Rufus figuring out that if he sold the toothpaste for only a penny more than it cost him to make—it cost him about 2¢ a tube—that he'd soon have millions of customers.

He had to start in a small way, of course. When he started his business, Rufus packed the toothpaste in baby food jars.

A baby food jar holds about as much as a big tube, and the jars didn't cost him anything.

People with babies were glad to save jars for Rufus, as nobody had thought of a way of instantly recycling baby-food jars before. When Rufus put a sign on the bulletin board at school saying he could use the jars, kids brought us hundreds of them.

We sterilized and filled the jars. When we had about five hundred jars, Rufus and I stuffed our saddlebags with as many as they would hold and rode our bikes around the neighborhood selling the toothpaste.

We sold quite a few jars. At only 3¢ a jar, most people felt they could afford to give it a try, and most of the customers said it was good toothpaste.

Still, I could not see how Rufus was going to get rich on 3¢ toothpaste unless millions of people knew about it. Then I had this idea about how he could get some free advertising.

Everybody in Cleveland watches a program called the "The Joe Smiley Show." On the show, Joe interviews people who have interesting hobbies.

I wrote Joe Smiley a letter telling him I had this friend who has a hobby of making toothpaste and could make about two years' supply for the price of one tube. And Joe Smiley called up Rufus to ask if he would be on the show.

Rufus was very good on the show, though I was afraid that he never would get around to talking about the toothpaste. I was worried because when Joe Smiley asked Rufus how he had learned to make toothpaste, Rufus started telling about his Grandmother Mayflower.

He not only told about the scrapbook paste, but about how his Grandma Mayflower had made her own furnace out of two 100-gallon oil barrels. Joe Smiley was so interested in that furnace that it was hard to get him off the subject of Rufus's grandmother.

Rufus told about his grandmother taming raccoons, woodchucks, mice, chipmunks, and catbirds. And, of course, about her brushing her teeth with plain baking soda. But the story I liked best was about his grandmother's name.

It seems Mayflower was his grandmother's *whole* name. She didn't have any last name till she got married. Then she took her husband's name which was Proctor and was known as Mrs. Mayflower Proctor.

But Rufus's grandmother never did like the name Proctor, because it was a slave name. (Rufus explained that back when there were slaves, a black man was sometimes called by the name of the white family who owned him.)

So when Mayflower's husband died, she dropped the Proctor part of her name, and she and her children went back to being Mayflowers. Then Social Security came along and said she had to have a first name and a last name on her Social Security card. But rather than let the government put her down with a slave name, Mrs. Mayflower wrote the Social Security people and signed herself Mrs. May Flower, with a space between the "May" and the "Flower."

I love that story. In fact, I'm seriously thinking about changing my name to Mac Kinstrey, as I don't care too much for Kathryn. Mac sounds like a boy's name, and boys' names usually sound a lot more forceful than girls' names to me.

But I'm getting off the subject of toothpaste, just as Rufus did on "The Joe Smiley Show." You wouldn't think all that stuff about Rufus's grandmother would sell toothpaste. But then, as my father pointed out, you wouldn't think Rufus's way of advertising the toothpaste would sell toothpaste, either.

Joe Smiley is the kind of guy who is always saying things are the "greatest" thing he ever heard of. Or the most "fantastic." If a girl comes on his show in a pink coat that Joe thinks is attractive, he'll say, "That's the most fantastic coat!"

There's nothing that special about the coat. He just means it's nice.

What I mean is, he exaggerates. And everybody Joe has on his show is one of the greatest people he ever met or has done the most fantastic thing.

So when Joe does get to Rufus's toothpaste, he naturally gives it this big build–up. Which is what I was counting on. And what does Rufus do?

The conversation went something like this:

JOE: Now, Rufus, this fantastic toothpaste you make — I suppose it has a special, secret formula.

RUFUS: No. It's made out of stuff anybody can buy for a few cents and mix up at home in a few minutes.

JOE: Fantastic! And, of course, it's much better than the kind you buy at the store.

RUFUS: I don't know about that. But it tastes pretty good. And for about 2¢ you can make as much as you get in a 79¢ tube.

JOE: Fantastic! And where can people get some of this great toothpaste?

RUFUS: If they live in East Cleveland, I'll deliver it to them on my bike. Three ounces costs 3¢—it costs me 2¢ to make and I make 1¢ profit. If anyone outside East Cleveland wants some, I'll have to charge 3¢ plus postage.

JOE: Fantastic! And what do you call this marvelous new product?

RUFUS: TOOTHPASTE.

JOE: Just toothpaste? It doesn't have a name like SPARKLE or SHINE or SENSATION or WHITE LIGHTNING or PERSONALITY PLUS?

RUFUS: No, it's just plain TOOTHPASTE. It doesn't do anything sensational such as improve your smile or your personality. It just keeps your teeth clean.

Who would have thought that telling people toothpaste wouldn't do one thing for their personality would sell toothpaste?

But three days after Rufus was on "The Joe Smiley Show," he got 689 orders for TOOTHPASTE. One came all the way from Venice, California, from a man who happened to be telephoning his daughter while she was watching the show in Cleveland. The daughter said, "There's a kid here who's selling toothpaste for 3¢ a jar." And her father ordered three dozen jars.

Fantastic!

Reader's Response ∽ What qualities led Rufus to become a millionaire? Which one do you most admire?

Chester's Ears Were Cold...

Rufus Mayflower wasn't the first young person to create a business from an inventive idea. Inventions often start with questions like "If I only had a..." or "Why doesn't someone invent a...."

Chester Greenwood probably said something like that every time he went skating on the pond near his home in Farmington, Maine. Fifteen-year-old Chester loved to skate, but his ears could not take the cold—they hurt!

One day it got to be just too much for Chester. He ran home, got a piece of wire, twisted the ends into circles and asked his mother to cover them with cloth. Would his "earmuffs" keep his ears warm? Yes, but they kept slipping off his head. Chester fixed that easily by connecting the muffs with a piece of spring instead of wire.

Before long everyone in town wanted a pair of Greenwood's Champion Ear Protectors. By the time he was eighteen, in 1877, Chester had received a patent for his invention and opened a factory to manufacture his earmuffs.

Now, if you go to Farmington, Maine, on the first Saturday of December, you can help the citizens there celebrate Chester Greenwood Day!

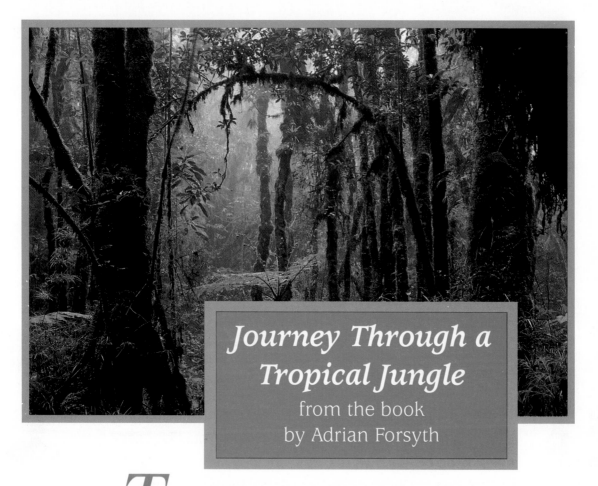

Journey Through a Tropical Jungle

from the book
by Adrian Forsyth

Tropical forests are the richest places on our planet. But the riches they contain are not gold or silver or diamonds: they are rich in life. Although tropical forests cover only 6 percent of the Earth's surface, they are home to two-thirds of all the species of plants and animals on our planet.

These plants and animals are now threatened with rapid extinction. In just the past 100 years half of the world's tropical rain forests have been razed to the ground for the lumber they contain, and to make way for farmland. The birds, the orchids, the butterflies, the monkeys—all the animals and plants that depend on these jungles are being destroyed by logging, burning and bulldozing.

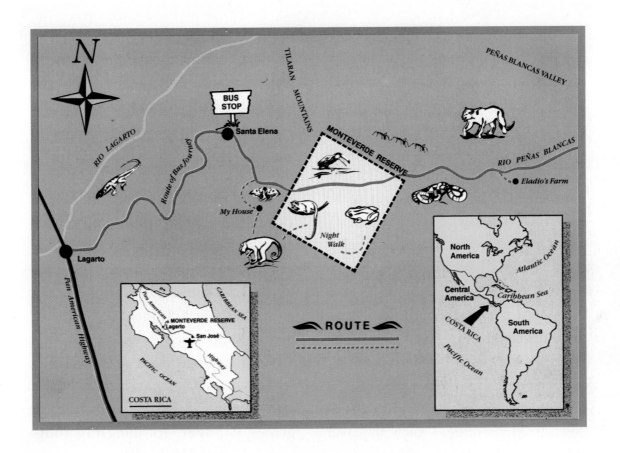

The remaining half of the world's tropical forests are under growing pressure. About 20 hectares (50 acres) a minute are being destroyed—that's an area of tropical forest almost as large as England every year.

As a biologist I wanted to see these fantastic forests and the wildlife they contain before they disappear. I set out to visit Costa Rica, a tiny Central American country that is working hard to protect as much of its jungles as it can.

My trip could only last a few short weeks, but I knew those weeks would be filled with wonder.

I had come a long way in one day, and it was time to think about finding a place to spend the night. I continued along the ridge and down to a shack maintained as a shelter by the Cloud Forest Reserve. Supper was crackers and canned tuna, which tasted unexpectedly delicious. Hunger is the best sauce, they say.

I slipped into my sleeping bag. For a few minutes I lay awake listening to the wind rattle the tin roofing. I could hear forest mice scuttling up and down the walls hunting for insects. But soon I fell into a heavy and sound sleep.

The next morning I decided to get off the trail and follow a riverbed back down to Monteverde. I knew the river passed right below my cabin. It was a rough route back. The riverbed was a jumble of slick round boulders, waterfalls and fallen trees. Once, as I jumped from a rock to a log, the rotten wood gave way and I pitched face first into the water.

When I reached the stretch of river just below my cabin, I took a breather under a towering twisted tree standing weirdly on a row of great legs. It was a giant strangler fig, the largest tree in the forest.

A strangler starts life as a tiny seed that a fig-eating parrot or monkey drops in the top of a tree. The seed lodges in the crease where a limb joins the trunk. Rotten leaves collect there, and the seedling begins to grow in the mulch. As soon as it has turned into a small bush, the strangler begins to dangle long roots down to the ground. It was on one of these aerial roots that I had been swinging earlier. When the roots touch the earth they grow rapidly, anchoring and feeding the strangler tree high at the top of the host tree. The fig now puts on a spurt of growth. It shoots up, growing higher than the host on which it is growing, and puts out a dense umbrella of leaves. As the host tree grows weaker, starving in the shade, the fig grows stronger. Its dangling roots become woody, and as they touch one another they fuse together, wrapping the host tree inside a solid curtain of fig.

Shaded and perhaps squeezed, the host tree eventually dies, giving up its space in the forest to the strangler fig.

I saw that the roots of this strangler had grown and fused, but not completely. There were cracks and crannies everywhere. These protected spaces had become homes for many animals. Using a pencil I poked around in one of these holes. I jumped back when a big mother scorpion came scuttling out with her stinger tail held up in the air.

I knew it was a mother because her back was covered with baby scorpions. The mother scorpion carries her young around so that she can keep them out of harm's reach. She is better at catching food than her youngsters, so they stay with her until they are large enough to catch supper by themselves. Until then the mother grabs large insects such as cockroaches with her strong pincers, then prepares a meal by chewing open the skin of the roach and adding her saliva, which is full of digestive enzymes. These enzymes begin to pre-digest the food. The young scorpions can then climb down and drink their dinner of liquid cockroach.

I wondered what was living in the space left when the dead tree rotted away. When I stuck my head inside, the

hollow rang with high-pitched squeaks. Mice? I shone my flashlight up. Squeaking bats were hanging upside down with their wings wrapped around their bodies like cloaks. At night the bats would fly out and catch insects such as moths. It seemed that insects were sometimes brought back to the bat roost, because I saw moth wings piled beneath the tree. Ants were busily scavenging, cleaning up these crumbs beneath the bats' dining area and carrying them down into their nests under the forest floor.

The fig had killed another tree and I could see that now it was being eaten, in its turn, by caterpillars. These caterpillars would turn into moths. The fig also provided a haven for bats. The bats caught the moths and left food for the ants. The ants loosened the earth, and when they died their bodies would enrich the soil. Finally, the roots of the fig and other trees would absorb the nutrients in the soil.

Each animal and plant was working, providing something useful for some other organism. When a plant or animal died, its body was quickly converted into a new form of life. All around the strangler fig this recycling was going on right before my eyes.

There is something about a huge old tree that makes you stop and wonder about the meaning of things. I sat on a rock in the river. Alone in the forest I found peace and quiet and the time to think. What did the name "killer tree" mean? Is a strangler fig good, or is it bad because it lives by killing other trees? All the life around the fig made the answer clear to me. The death of one tree had meant life for other creatures. Because everything is connected in the forest, life and death are never wasted.

High Life

"Aaaaarrrrrooooooo — oooo — oooo — gaaaahhhh!" I almost jumped out of my rubber boots. It sounded as if there was a huge and fierce creature right above me. Branches were rattling, sticks and leaves rained down, along with an avalanche of noise.

I had startled a large male howler monkey feeding at the end of a branch not far above my head. And he had startled *me*! The howler glared down, shaking the shaggy mane and beard around his face. He thrust out his strong lower jaw and began bellowing out more threats at me.

I wasn't worried. Howlers are big monkeys, but they are harmless in spite of their fearsome calls. In fact the animal's annoyance was my good luck. I had hoped to get a good look at the special equipment the male howler has for producing his deep roars. I could see clearly that his throat was massive, with a giant voice box. He was using this sound system for producing deep gravelly bass notes.

The howler's roaring is an important social behavior directed at other howler monkeys. A troop normally roars together, led by the largest dominant male. These howling sessions begin each morning as the monkeys wake up. Often they repeat the chorus just before bedding down in the treetops for the night. You can hear the calls echoing down the vast valleys. The clamor advertises their location and probably discourages other troops from using the same area of forest and fighting over the same feeding trees.

Soon I came upon the rest of the howler troop, quietly feeding on leaf buds. Small babies were riding on their mothers' backs or clinging to their bellies as the females wandered slowly from one branch to another, looking for fresh new growth. They seemed slow and sleepy. Sometimes they would stop feeding to scratch, groom each other or do a little sunbathing, dozing peacefully with their legs draped over the tree limbs. One of their common gestures was to stick their tongues out at one another. It was just like watching a family on a picnic.

I was glad I had my binoculars because most of the monkeys were high above my head. It was the binoculars that helped me spot an animal so slow it made the howler monkeys look like racecars.

Grasping tightly onto a branch by a set of long arms and legs with huge claws was a two-toed sloth. It was a female, carrying her baby. They remained completely motionless, and their coats of long greenish-gray hair kept them well camouflaged. Because tiny green algae grow all through their hair, sloths at rest look like big chunks of moss.

The reason why the English name for this animal is "sloth" and its Spanish name means "lazy" is that it moves slowly to save energy. The sloth uses energy at half the rate of other mammals its size. Its body temperature is also lower than that of most mammals, which helps the sloth get by on its low-energy diet of leaves. At night the body temperature of a sloth may drop close to the air temperature, and it becomes even more sluggish. It's as though the sloth

goes into hibernation every time the sun goes down. When the sun comes up in the morning, a sloth often heads for a basking spot on an exposed limb where it sprawls out just like a lizard, letting the sun's energy gently bring its body temperature up again. After a sunbath, the sloth is ready for a new day.

On this hike I hadn't set out with anything particular in mind. I had just started heading downhill into the forest, hoping to get more sunshine. But it was turning out to be a great day. Seeing monkeys and sloths was what this trip was all about.

As I worked my way along a sharp cliff edge, I saw what I thought was a very familiar animal, a porcupine. It had been eating flat velvety-brown seed pods in an inga tree. The porcupine didn't seem interested in running away, and I got a good look at it. It was smaller than our North American porcupine and less spiny, and its tail

was naked, like a giant rat tail. The North American porcupine has a club-like tail covered with a bristling coat of spines. But this porcupine's tail is more like the tail of a monkey or possum. It can be used as another holding limb, a clear sign that the porcupine is well equipped for life in the treetops.

By hoisting myself a short way up the trunk, I found the cavity the porcupine used as a retreat. I could probably have found it just by using my nose—it was giving off a powerful stench. Like many of the mammals who live spread out in the treetops, porcupines communicate their presence and position by marking the trees with urine or other smelly glandular secretions.

The cliff edge looked like a good place for a rest and a water stop. I stretched out in the sun and watched the vultures gliding overhead. They spiraled round and round in huge circuits. Riding on the hot air currents, they never had to move a muscle. I felt just as relaxed and was on the verge of a siesta when I heard a thrashing and whooping on the slope below. I suspected the commotion was being caused by spider monkeys.

I jumped up and began working my way down through the trees along

49

the steep slope, trying to get a glimpse of these agile skinny monkeys. They are called spider monkeys because of their long skinny limbs and tails. Their hands and feet are also long so that their fingers can wrap firmly around branches. The agile tail can grab at branches, just like an arm, and it is strong enough to allow the tiny monkey to dangle without any other support. These features enable spider monkeys to swing wildly arm over arm at high speed through the treetops. They seem to be fearless leapers, running down to the end of a branch and springing out into space with their arms spread, then landing in the next tree crown. They are exciting and uncommon, and I was eager to get a good look at them.

It was almost my last look at anything! I was trying so hard to get a better look at the monkeys that I found

myself slipping in a slurry of loose earth and dry leaves down a steep slope. At the bottom of the slope was a bone-breaking drop. It was sheer luck that I grabbed a mass of dangling tree roots and stopped my slide before I reached the edge. Slowly I pulled myself hand over hand to the base of a large tree, then up to the next tree, until I was on secure footing.

That was enough monkey-watching for the day.

Or so I thought.

Later that afternoon I was back sitting in the loft of my cabin, writing up my field notes, when I got the funny feeling that someone was watching me. I looked out the window. In the trees beside the house was a troop of white-faced monkeys; *they* were doing the watching this time. They stared at me seriously with the most intelligent faces for a few seconds, and then continued on their travels.

Wings of the Jungle

One of the things I was enjoying most about being in Costa Rica was all the tropical fruits I could buy. There were orange-fleshed papayas, tangy star fruits, rich red sapotes, slippery white lichees, juicy golden mangoes, creamy custard apples and rich oily avocadoes for sale.

All these fruits, now cultivated in many parts of the world, were first discovered growing wild in jungles. So I knew I could find wild fruits in the Monteverde jungle, and I planned to look for the birds that feed upon them on my next hike.

It didn't take long for me to find fruit-eating birds. As I stepped out of a woodlot and into a sheltered pasture, a pair of the gaudiest birds I had ever seen flew by me. Their ruby-red chests and streaming long emerald tails flashed brilliantly as they climbed steeply up into the air and plunged down across the clearing. I had stumbled on quetzals (pronounced *ket-sals*), some of the most beautiful birds in the world.

The quetzals were feeding mostly on a kind of wild avocado, a fat glossy black fruit that looked like a giant olive. A quetzal would fly to the tip of an avocado branch to pluck a fruit off. Then it would fly off to another tree to perch with the avocado held in its bill. It opens its mouth fantastically wide and almost magically swallows the avocado whole. A short while later it spits out the large hard seed, but without its coat of oily black flesh.

I picked up some of the avocado seeds. They were big and hard as cherry pits—too large and solid for the quetzal to pass through its digestive system. Like most fruit-eating birds the quetzal has a soft stomach. When it eats, it removes the fleshy coating around the pit and then coughs the seed up and out. Under one perch where I had seen quetzals eating avocadoes were hundreds of seeds; some had even sprouted. This made it clear to me why fleshy rich fruits developed in the tropical forest. Their bright tasty flesh feeds the birds, and the birds disperse the seeds to places where the young tree seedlings can get started.

As I walked on through the forest, I began to take more notice of the colors and arrangements of the fruits. In the midst of all the greenery, the clusters of bright orange, bold red and black, and pink and yellow berries and fruits were really eye-catching. I tried sampling some, but few of them were sweet enough for my taste.

I found a fig tree along the road that was loaded with emerald toucanets. There were at least six of these birds feeding so busily that I was sure the little pink figs must be delicious. They were using their long colorful bills like tweezers to pluck the pink figs, toss them back in the air and swallow, all with one quick flick of the head.

As I watched, a larger keel-billed toucan flew in and all the toucanets scattered. The toucan was even more fantastically colored. But it was a bit nervous at my presence and soon left, giving me an opportunity to try the figs myself. To my disappointment they tasted totally bland. Evidently the birds could appreciate something that I couldn't.

In fact, along the same stretch of road I saw brilliant yellow, green and blue chlorophonias eating mistletoe berries. I knew that mistletoe berries are poisonous for people. But the chlorophonias are able to digest the fruit covering without damaging or digesting any of the poisonous seeds. As a result the mistletoe has its seeds spread all through the jungle by the chlorophonias.

This relationship is good for the mistletoe but bad for the trees. When a bird deposits a mistletoe seed on a tree branch, the seed sprouts and its roots burrow into the tree. The mistletoe roots then absorb water and nutrients from the tree's circulatory system. It was clear that the chlorophonias were doing an effective job of seed dispersal because there was mistletoe all over the trees. But evidently the relationship was a tolerable one because the trees were

green and healthy-looking in spite of their unwanted guests.

Heading back across a pasture near my cabin, I watched a bird damaging a tree more directly. A red-headed woodpecker was pounding a nest hole in the side of the tree. Each chiseling stroke of the head made a powerful

thunk as the bill dug in. To me it seemed incredible that a bird could pound away like that without damaging its brain or at least getting a severe headache. Nearby were a pair of masked tityras, delightful white birds with black face masks and metallic twangy voices, watching the woodpecker at work.

Tityras can't make their own nest holes, so they often steal those of woodpeckers or even those of large birds like toucans. The big woodpeckers and toucans are strong enough to throw the tityras out, so the tityras don't confront them directly; they just pester the bigger birds into leaving. Every time the owners go away to forage, the tityras bring leaves and trash and stuff them in the nest hole. When they return the owners remove it, but the tityras keep stuffing it back in. Eventually the bigger birds give up and the tityras take over the space.

It was late in the day and the woodpecker was still working while the tityras were just watching. So I headed on, hoping to watch this relationship develop on another day.

Reader's Response ∼ If Adrian Forsyth invited you to go with him on a return visit to the rain forest, would you accept? Why or why not?

56

Tropical Rain Forest Features

Seasons

There are just two seasons in most tropical rain forests: wet and dry.

Temperature

The temperature in a tropical rain forest ranges between 68 and 93 degrees Fahrenheit, depending on the season.

Rain Fall

It rains at least 80 inches and up to 400 inches of rain each year depending on the location of a tropical rain forest. An inch of rain in one day is not unusual. How does this compare to the average rainfall where you live?

Location

Tropical rain forests are located near the equator where the weather is hot and steamy. These areas are: South and Central America, Africa and Madagascar, South and Southeast Asia, Australia and New Guinea.

57

AWARD
WINNING
ILLUSTRATOR

The Librarian and the Robbers

written by Margaret Mahy
illustrated by Quentin Blake

One day Serena Laburnum, the beautiful librarian, was carried off by wicked robbers. She had just gone for a walk in the woods at the edge of the town, when the robbers came charging at her and carried her off.

"Why are you kidnapping me?" she asked coldly. "I have no wealthy friends or relatives. Indeed I am an orphan with no real home but the library."

"That's just it," said the Robber Chief. "The City Council will pay richly to have you restored. After all, everyone knows that the library does not work properly without you."

This was especially true because Miss Laburnum had the library keys.

"I think I ought to warn you," she said, "that I spent the weekend with a friend of mine who has four little boys. Everyone in the house had the dread disease of Raging Measles."

"That's all right!" said the Robber Chief, sneering a bit. "I've had them."

"But I haven't!" said the robber at his elbow, and the other robbers looked at Miss Laburnum uneasily. None of them had had the dread disease of Raging Measles.

As soon as the robbers' ransom note was received by the City Council there was a lot of discussion. Everyone was anxious that things should be done in the right way.

"What is it when our librarian is kidnapped?" asked a councillor. "Is it staff expenditure or does it come out of the cultural fund?"

"The Cultural Committee meets in a fortnight," said the Mayor. "I propose we let them make a decision on this."

But long before that, all the robbers (except the Robber Chief) had Raging Measles.

First of all they became very irritable and had red sniffy noses.

"I *think* a hot bath brings out the rash," said Miss Laburnum doubtfully. "Oh, if only I were in my library I would be able to look up measles in my *Dictionary of Efficient and Efficacious Home Nursing.*"

The Robber Chief looked gloomily at his gang.

"Are you sure it's measles?" he said. "That's a very undignified complaint for a robber to suffer from. There are few people who are improved by spots, but for robbers they are disastrous. Would you take a spotty robber seriously?"

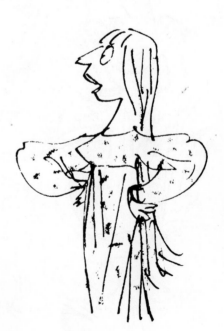

"It is no part of a librarian's duty to take any robber seriously, spotty or otherwise," said Miss Laburnum haughtily. "And, anyhow, there must be no robbing until they have got over the Raging Measles. They are in quarantine. After all you don't want to be blamed for spreading measles everywhere, do you?"

The Robber Chief groaned.

"If you will allow me," said Miss Laburnum, "I will go back to my library and borrow *The Dictionary of Efficient and Efficacious Home Nursing*. With the help of that invaluable book I shall try to alleviate the sufferings of your fellows. Of course I shall only be able to take it out for a week. It is a special reference book, you see."

The groaning of his fellows suffering from Raging Measles was more than the Robber Chief could stand.

"All right," he said. "You can go and get that book, and we'll call off the kidnapping for the present. Just a temporary measure."

In a short time Miss Laburnum was back with several books.

"A hot bath to bring out the rash!" she announced reading clearly and carefully. "Then you must have the cave darkened, and you mustn't read or play cards. You have to be careful of your eyes when you have measles."

The robbers found it very dull, lying in a darkened cave. Miss Laburnum took their temperatures and asked them if their ears hurt.

"It's very important that you keep warm," she told them, pulling blankets up to their robberish beards, and tucking them in so tightly that they could not toss or turn. "But to make the time go quickly I will read to you. Now, what have you read already?"

These robbers had not read a thing. They were almost illiterate. "Very well," said Miss Laburnum, "we shall start with

Peter Rabbit and work our way up from there."

Never in all their lives had those robbers been read to. In spite of the fever induced by Raging Measles they listened intently and asked for more. The Robber Chief listened too, though Miss Laburnum had given him the task of making nourishing broth for the invalids.

"Tell us more about that Br'er Rabbit!" was the fretful cry of the infectious villains. "Read to us about *Alice in Wonderland*."

Robin Hood made them uneasy. He was a robber, as they were, but full of noble thoughts such as giving to the poor. These robbers had not planned on giving to the poor, but only on keeping for themselves.

After a few days the spots began to disappear, and the robbers began to get hungry. Miss Laburnum dipped into her *Dictionary of Efficient and Efficacious Home Nursing*, and found some tempting recipes for the convalescent. She wrote them out for the Robber Chief. Having given up the idea of

kidnapping Miss Laburnum, the Robber Chief now had the idea of kidnapping the book, but Miss Laburnum wouldn't let him have it.

"It is used by a lot of people who belong to the library," she said. "But, of course, if you want to check up on anything later you may always come to the library and consult it."

Shortly after this the robbers were quite recovered and Miss Laburnum, with her keys, went back to town. It seemed that robbers were a thing of the past. *The Dictionary of Efficient and Efficacious Home Nursing* was restored to the library shelves. The library was open once more to the hoards who had been starved for literature during the days of Miss Laburnum's kidnapping.

Yet, about three weeks after all these dramatic events, there was more robber trouble!

Into the library, in broad daylight, burst none other than the Robber Chief.

"Save me!" he cried. "A policeman is after me."

Miss Laburnum gave him a cool look.

"You had better give me your full name," she said. "Quickly!"

The Robber Chief sprang back, an expression of horror showing through his black tangled beard.

"No, no!" he cried, "anything but that!"

"Quickly," repeated Miss Laburnum, "or I won't have time to help you."

The Robber Chief leaned across the desk and whispered his name to her... "Salvation Loveday."

Miss Laburnum could not help smiling a little bit. It certainly went very strangely with those wiry whiskers.

"They used to call me Sally at school," cried the unhappy robber. "It's that name that has driven me to a life of crime. But hide me, dear Miss Laburnum, or I shall be caught."

Miss Laburnum stamped him with a number, as if he was a library book, and put him into a bookshelf with a lot of books whose authors had surnames beginning with 'L'. He was in strict alphabetical order. Alphabetical order is a habit with librarians.

The policeman who had been chasing the Robber Chief burst into the library. He was a good runner, but he had fallen over a little boy on a tricycle, and this had slowed him down.

"Miss Laburnum," said the policeman, "I have just had occasion to pursue a notable Robber Chief into your library. I can see him there in the bookshelves among the 'L's. May I take him out please?"

"Certainly!" said Miss Laburnum pleasantly. "Do you have your library membership card?"

The policeman's face fell.

"Oh dear," he said. "No...I'm afraid it's at home marking the place in my *Policeman's Robber-Catching Compendium*."

Miss Laburnum gave a polite smile.

"I'm afraid you can't withdraw anything without your membership card," she said. "That Robber Chief is Library Property."

The policeman nodded slowly. He knew it was true: you weren't allowed to take anything out of the library without your library card. This was a strict library rule. "I'll just tear home and get it," he said. "I don't live very far away."

"Do that," said Miss Laburnum pleasantly. The policeman's strong police boots rang out as he hurried from the library.

Miss Laburnum went to the 'L' shelf and took down the Robber Chief. "Now, what are you doing *here*," she said severely. However, the Robber Chief was not fooled—she was really very pleased to see him.

"Well," he replied, "the fact is, Miss Laburnum, my men are restless. Ever since you read them those stories they've been discontented in the evening. We used to sit around our campfire singing rumbustical songs and indulging in rough humour, but they've lost their taste for it. They're wanting more *Br'er Rabbit*, more *Treasure Island*, and more stories of kings and clowns. Today I was coming to join the library and take some books out for them. What shall I do? I daren't go back without books, and yet that policeman may return. And won't he be very angry with you when he finds I'm gone?"

"That will be taken care of," said Miss Laburnum, smiling to herself. "What is your number? Ah yes. Well, when the policeman returns I will tell him someone else has taken you out, and it will be true, for you are now issued to me."

The Robber Chief gave Miss Laburnum a very speaking look.

"And now," said Miss Laburnum cheerfully, "you must join the library yourself and take out some books for your poor robbers."

"If I am a member of the library myself, perhaps I could take you out," said the Robber Chief with robberish boldness. Miss Laburnum quickly changed the subject, but she blushed as she did so.

She sent the Robber Chief off with some splendid story books.

He had only just gone when the policeman came back.

"Now," said the policeman, producing his membership card, "I'd like to take out that Robber Chief, if I may."

He looked so expectant it seemed a pity to disappoint him. Miss Laburnum glanced towards the 'L's.

"Oh," she said, "I'm afraid he has already been taken out by someone else. You should have reserved him."

The policeman stared at the shelf very hard. Then he stared at Miss Laburnum.

"May I put my name down for him?" he asked after a moment.

"Certainly," said Miss Laburnum, "though I ought to warn you that you may have a long wait ahead of you. There could be a long waiting list."

After this the Robber Chief came sneaking into town regularly to change books. It was dangerous, but he thought it was worth it.

As the robbers read more and more, their culture and philosophy deepened, until they were the most cultural and philosophic band of robbers one could wish to encounter.

As for Miss Laburnum, there is no doubt that she was aiding and abetting robbers; not very good behaviour in a librarian, but she had her reasons.

Then came the day of the terrible earthquake. Chimneys fell down all over town. Every building creaked and rattled. Out in the forest the robbers felt it and stood aghast as trees swayed and pinecones came tumbling around them like hailstones. At last the ground was still again. The Robber Chief went pale.

"The library!" he called. "What will have happened to Miss Laburnum and the books?"

Every other robber turned pale too. You never saw such a lot of pale-faced robbers at one and the same time.

"Quickly!" they shouted. "To the rescue! Rescue! Rescue Miss Laburnum. Save the books."

Shouting such words as these they all ran down the road out of the forest and into town.

The policeman saw them, but when he heard their heroic cry he decided to help them first and arrest them afterwards.

"Save Miss Laburnum!" he shouted. "Rescue the books."

What a terrible scene in the library! Pictures had fallen from the walls and the flowers were upset. Boxes of stamps were overturned and mixed up all over the floor. Books had fallen from their shelves like autumn leaves from their trees, and lay all over the floor in helpless confusion.

There was no sign of Miss Laburnum that anyone could see.

Actually Miss Laburnum had been shelving books in the old store—the shelves where they put all the battered old books—when the earthquake came. Ancient, musty encyclopaedias showered down upon her. When the earthquake was over she was still alive, but so covered in books that she could not move.

"Pulverized by literature," thought Miss Laburnum. "The ideal way for a librarian to die."

She did not feel very pleased about it, but there was nothing she could do to save herself. Then she heard a heroic cry!

"Serena, Serena Laburnum!" a voice was shouting. Someone was pulling books off her. It was the Robber Chief.

"Salvation is a very good name for you," said Miss Laburnum faintly.

Tenderly he lifted her to her feet and dusted her down.

"I came as soon as I could," he said. "Oh, Miss Laburnum, this may not be the best time to ask you but as I am giving up a life of crime and becoming respectable, will you marry me? You need someone to lift the books off you, and generally rescue you from time to time. It would make things so much simpler if you would marry me."

"Of course I will," said Miss Laburnum simply. "After all, I did take you out with my library membership card. I must have secretly admired you for a long time."

Out in the main room of the library there was great activity. Robbers and councillors, working together like brothers, were sorting the mixed-up stamps, filing the spilled cards, reshelving the fallen books. The policeman was hanging up some of the pictures. They all cheered when the Robber Chief appeared with Miss Laburnum, bruised but still beautiful.

"Ahem," said the Robber Chief. "I am the happiest man alive. Miss Laburnum had promised to marry me."

A great cheer went up from everyone.

"On one condition," said Miss Laburnum. "That all you robbers give up being robbers and become librarians instead. You weren't very good at being robbers, but I think as librarians you might be excellent. I have come to feel very proud of you all."

The robbers were struck to breathless silence. Never when they were mere inefficient robbers in the forest had they dreamed of such praise. Greatly moved by these sentiments, they then and there swore that they would cease to be villains and become librarians instead.

It was all very exciting. Even the policeman wept with joy.

So, ever after, that particular library was remarkably well run. With all the extra librarians they suddenly had, the council was able to open a children's library with story readings and adventure plays every day. The robber librarians had become very good at such things practising around their campfires in the forest.

Miss Laburnum, or Mrs. Loveday as she soon became, sometimes suspected that the children's library in their town was—well—a little wilder, a little more humorous, than many other fine libraries she had seen, but she did not care. She did not mind that the robber librarians all wore wiry black whiskers still, nor that they took down all the notices saying "Silence" and "No talking in the library".

Perhaps she herself was more of a robber at heart than anyone ever suspected...except, of course, Robber Chief-and-First-Library-Assistant Salvation Loveday, and he did not tell anyone.

Reader's Response ⌁ What did you find most amusing about this story?

Library Link ⌁ *If you want to read another silly story by Margaret Mahy, check out* The Great Piratical Rumbustification *at your local library.*

Language Gap

You probably noticed some unusual spellings in "The Librarian and the Robbers." Even though we speak the same language, Americans and British sometimes spell words a little differently. The British also use different words than Americans do to describe the same object or event.

For example, if you asked an Englishwoman if she lived in an apartment, she might not know what you meant. An apartment in England is called a *flat*.

Some common words that Americans and British spell differently.

American	British
center	centre
curb	kerb
jail	gaol
labor	labour
pajamas	pyjamas
realize	realise
theater	theatre

Here are other common words and their British equivalents.

American	British
candy	sweets
cracker	biscuit
drugstore	chemist's
elevator	lift
line	queue
oven	cooker
truck	lorry

The No-Guitar Blues

by Gary Soto

The moment Fausto saw the group Los Lobos on "American Bandstand," he knew exactly what he wanted to do with his life— play guitar. His eyes grew large with excitement as Los Lobos ground out a song while teenagers bounced off each other on the crowded dance floor.

He had watched "American Bandstand" for years and had heard Ray Camacho and the Teardrops at Romain Playground, but it had never occurred to him that he too might become a musician. That afternoon Fausto knew his mission in life: to play guitar in his own band; to sweat out his songs and prance around the stage; to make money and dress weird.

Fausto turned off the television set and walked outside, wondering how he could get enough money to buy a guitar. He couldn't ask his parents because they would just say, "Money doesn't grow on trees" or "What do you think we are, bankers?" And besides, they hated rock music. They were into the *conjunto*[1] music of Lydia Mendoza, Flaco Jimenez,[2] and Little Joe and La Familia. And, as Fausto recalled, the last album they bought was *The Chipmunks Sing Christmas Favorites*.

But what the heck, he'd give it a try. He returned inside and watched his mother make tortillas. He leaned against the kitchen counter, trying to work up the nerve to ask her for a guitar. Finally, he couldn't hold back any longer.

"Mom," he said, "I want a guitar for Christmas."

She looked up from rolling tortillas. "Honey, a guitar costs a lot of money."

¹conjunto (con hoon′ to): band
²Jimenez (Hē men′ ez)

"How 'bout for my birthday next year," he tried again.

"I can't promise," she said, turning back to her tortillas, "but we'll see."

Fausto walked back outside with a buttered tortilla. He knew his mother was right. His father was a warehouseman at Berven Rugs, where he made good money but not enough to buy everything his children wanted. Fausto decided to mow lawns to earn money, and was pushing the mower down the street before he realized it was winter and no one would hire him. He returned the mower and picked up a rake. He hopped onto his sister's bike (his had two flat tires) and rode north to the nicer section of Fresno in search of work. He went door-to-door, but after three hours he managed to get only one job, and not to rake leaves. He was asked to hurry down to the store to buy a loaf of bread, for which he received a grimy, dirt-caked quarter.

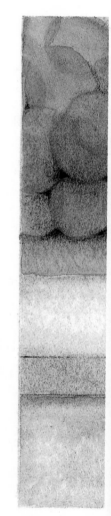

He also got an orange, which he ate sitting at the curb. While he was eating, a dog walked up and sniffed his leg. Fausto pushed him away and threw an orange peel skyward. The dog caught it and ate it in one gulp. The dog looked at Fausto and wagged his tail for more. Fausto tossed him a slice of orange, and the dog snapped it up and licked his lips.

"How come you like oranges, dog?"

The dog blinked a pair of sad eyes and whined.

"What's the matter? Cat got your tongue?" Fausto laughed at his joke and offered the dog another slice.

At that moment a dim light came on inside Fausto's head. He saw that it was sort of a fancy dog, a terrier or something, with dog tags and a shiny collar. And it looked well fed and healthy. In his neighborhood, the dogs were never licensed, and if they got sick they were placed near the water heater until they got well.

This dog looked like he belonged to rich people. Fausto cleaned his juice-sticky hands on his pants and got to his feet. The light in his head grew brighter. It just might work. He called the dog, patted its muscular back, and bent down to check the license.

"Great," he said. "There's an address."

The dog's name was Roger, which struck Fausto as weird because he'd never heard of a dog with a human name. Dogs should have names like Bomber, Freckles, Queenie, Killer, and Zero.

Fausto planned to take the dog home and collect a reward. He would say he had found Roger near the freeway. That would scare the daylights out of the owners, who would be so happy that they would probably give him a reward. He felt bad about lying, but

the dog *was* loose. And it might even really be lost, because the address was six blocks away.

Fausto stashed the rake and his sister's bike behind a bush, and, tossing an orange peel every time Roger became distracted, walked the dog to his house. He hesitated on the porch until Roger began to scratch the door with a muddy paw. Fausto had come this far, so he figured he might as well go through with it. He knocked softly. When no one answered, he rang the doorbell. A man in a silky bathrobe and slippers opened the door and seemed confused by the sight of his dog and the boy.

"Sir," Fausto said, gripping Roger by the collar. "I found your dog by the freeway. His dog license says he lives here." Fausto looked down at the dog, then up to the man. "He does, doesn't he?"

The man stared at Fausto a long time before saying in a pleasant voice, "That's right." He pulled his robe tighter around him because of the cold and asked Fausto to come in. "So he was by the freeway?"

"Uh-huh."

"You bad, snoopy dog," said the man, wagging his finger. "You probably knocked over some trash cans, too, didn't you?"

Fausto didn't say anything. He looked around, amazed by this house with its shiny furniture and a television as large as the front window at home. Warm bread smells filled the air and music full of soft tinkling floated in from another room.

"Helen," the man called to the kitchen. "We have a visitor." His wife came into the living room wiping her hands on a dish towel and smiling. "And who have we here?" she asked in one of the softest voices Fausto had ever heard.

"This young man said he found Roger near the freeway."

Fausto repeated his story to her while staring at a perpetual clock with a bell-shaped glass, the kind his aunt got when she celebrated her twenty-fifth anniversary. The lady frowned and said, wagging a finger at Roger, "Oh, you're a bad boy."

"It was very nice of you to bring Roger home," the man said. "Where do you live?"

"By that vacant lot on Olive," he said. "You know, by Brownie's Flower Place."

The wife looked at her husband, then Fausto. Her eyes twinkled triangles of light as she said, "Well, young man, you're probably hungry. How about a turnover?"

"What do I have to turn over?" Fausto asked, thinking she was talking about yard work or something like turning trays of dried raisins.

"No, no, dear, it's a pastry." She took him by the elbow and guided him to a kitchen that sparkled with copper pans and bright yellow wallpaper. She guided him to the kitchen table and gave him a tall glass of milk and something that looked like an *empanada.*[3] Steamy waves of heat escaped when he tore it in two. He ate with both eyes on the man and woman who stood arm-in-arm smiling at him. They were strange, he thought. But nice.

"That was good," he said after he finished the turnover. "Did you make it, ma'am?"

"Yes, I did. Would you like another?"

"No, thank you. I have to go home now."

As Fausto walked to the door, the man opened his wallet and took out a bill. "This is for you," he said. "Roger is special to us, almost like a son."

Fausto looked at the bill and knew he was in trouble. Not with these nice folks or with his parents but with himself. How could he have been so deceitful? The dog wasn't lost. It was just having a fun Saturday walking around.

[3]empanada (em pä nä′ dä)

"I can't take that."

"You have to. You deserve it, believe me," the man said.

"No, I don't."

"Now don't be silly," said the lady. She took the bill from her husband and stuffed it into Fausto's shirt pocket. "You're a lovely child. Your parents are lucky to have you. Be good. And come see us again, please."

Fausto went out, and the lady closed the door. Fausto clutched the bill through his shirt pocket. He felt like ringing the doorbell and begging them to please take the money back, but he knew they would refuse. He hurried away, and at the end of the block, pulled the bill from his shirt pocket: it was a crisp twenty-dollar bill.

"Oh, man, I shouldn't have lied," he said under his breath as he started up the street like a zombie. He wanted to run to church for Saturday confession, but it was past four-thirty, when confession stopped.

He returned to the bush where he had hidden the rake and his sister's bike and rode home slowly, not daring to touch the money in his pocket. At home, in the privacy of his room, he examined the twenty-dollar bill. He had never had so much money. It was probably enough to buy a secondhand guitar. But he felt bad, like the time he stole a dollar from the secret fold inside his older brother's wallet.

Fausto went outside and sat on the fence. "Yeah," he said. "I can probably get a guitar for twenty. Maybe at a yard sale—things are cheaper."

His mother called him to dinner.

The next day he dressed for church without anyone telling him. He was going to go to eight o'clock mass.

"I'm going to church, Mom," he said. His mother was in the kitchen cooking *papas*[4] and *chorizo con huevos*[5]. A pile of tortillas lay warm under a dishtowel.

---

[4]papas (pä´ päs): potatoes
[5]chorizo con huevos (chô rē´ zo côn weh´ vôs): sausage with eggs

"Oh, I'm so proud of you, Son." She beamed, turning over the crackling *papas*.

His older brother, Lawrence, who was at the table reading the funnies, mimicked, "Oh, I'm so proud of you, my son," under his breath.

At Saint Theresa's he sat near the front. When Father Jerry began by saying that we are all sinners, Fausto thought he looked right at him. Could he know? Fausto fidgeted with guilt. No, he thought. I only did it yesterday.

Fausto knelt, prayed, and sang. But he couldn't forget the man and the lady, whose names he didn't even know, and the *empanada* they had given him. It had a strange name but tasted really good. He wondered how they got rich. And how that dome clock worked. He had asked his mother once how his aunt's clock worked. She said it just worked, the way the refrigerator works. It just did.

Fausto caught his mind wandering and tried to concentrate on his sins. He said a Hail Mary and sang, and when the wicker basket came his way, he stuck a hand reluctantly in his pocket and pulled out the twenty-dollar bill. He ironed it between his palms, and dropped it into the basket. The grown-ups stared. Here was a kid dropping twenty dollars in the basket while they gave just three or four dollars.

There would be a second collection for Saint Vincent de Paul, the lector announced. The wicker baskets again floated in the pews, and this time the adults around him, given a second chance to show their charity, dug deep into their wallets and purses and dropped in fives and tens. This time Fausto tossed in the grimy quarter.

Fausto felt better after church. He went home and played football in the front yard with his brother and some neighbor kids.

He felt cleared of wrongdoing and was so happy that he played one of his best games of football ever. On one play, he tore his good pants, which he knew he shouldn't have been wearing. For a second, while he examined the hole, he wished he hadn't given the twenty dollars away.

Man, I coulda bought me some Levi's, he thought. He pictured his twenty dollars being spent to buy church candles. He pictured a priest buying an armful of flowers with *his* money.

Fausto had to forget about getting a guitar. He spent the next day playing soccer in his good pants, which were now his old pants. But that night during dinner, his mother said she remembered seeing an old bass guitarrón[6] the last time she cleaned out her father's garage.

"It's a little dusty," his Mom said, serving his favorite enchiladas, "But I think it works. Grandpa says it works."

Fausto's ears perked up. That was the same kind the guy in Los Lobos played. Instead of asking for the guitar, he waited for his mother to offer it to him. And she did, while gathering the dishes from the table.

"No, Mom, I'll do it," he said, hugging her. "I'll do the dishes forever if you want."

It was the happiest day of his life. No, it was the second-happiest day of his life. The happiest was when his grandfather Lupe placed the guitarrón, which was nearly as huge as a washtub, in his arms. Fausto ran a thumb down the strings, which vibrated in his throat and chest. It sounded beautiful, deep and eerie. A pumpkin smile widened on his face.

[6]guitarrón (gē tär rone′): large guitar

"OK, *hijo,*[7] now you put your fingers like this," said his grandfather, smelling of tobacco and aftershave. He took Fausto's fingers and placed them on the strings. Fausto strummed a chord on the guitarrón, and the bass resounded in their chests.

The guitarrón was more complicated than Fausto imagined. But he was confident that after a few more lessons he could start a band that would someday play on "American Bandstand" for the dancing crowds.

Reader's Response ~ If Fausto were your friend and told you how he felt about the twenty-dollar bill after he got it, what would you have said to him?

[7]hijo (ē′ ho): son

GARY SOTO

Have you ever written a story about something that made you feel sad or unhappy? Gary Soto did. As a Mexican-American boy growing up in southern California, he often felt like an outsider. Many years later, he still remembered how painful those days were, and decided to write stories, poems, and essays about them. Writing helped him understand the painful times in his life and begin to feel better about them.

Soto's writings are about people he knew in his childhood, including his friends and relatives. He works very hard on his stories and poems because he feels strongly that the people he writes about are important. He tries to paint pictures with his words that make them come alive for his readers. Each time he writes he tries to do better than ever before.

A Time to Talk

When a friend calls to me from the road
And slows his horse to a meaning walk,
I don't stand still and look around
On all the hills I haven't hoed,
And shout from where I am, "What is it?"
No, not as there is a time to talk.
I thrust my hoe in the mellow ground,
Blade-end up and five feet tall,
And plod: I go up to the stone wall
For a friendly visit.

Robert Frost

I Hear America Singing

I hear America singing, the varied carols I hear,
Those of mechanics, each one singing his as it should
        be blithe and strong,
The carpenter singing his as he measures his plank or
        beam,
The mason singing his as he makes ready for work, or
        leaves off work,
The boatman singing what belongs to him in his boat,
        the deckhand singing on the steamboat deck,
The shoemaker singing as he sits on his bench, the
        hatter singing as he stands,
The wood-cutter's song, the ploughboy's on his way in
        the morning, or at noon intermission or at
        sundown,
The delicious singing of the mother, or of the young
        wife at work, or of the girl sewing or washing,
Each singing what belongs to him or her and to none
        else,
The day what belongs to the day—at night the party of
        young fellows, robust, friendly,
Singing with open mouths their strong melodious songs.

Walt Whitman

Business Is
Looking Up

from the book

written by Barbara Aiello and Jeffrey Shulman

illustrated by Loel Barr

"Renaldo. Hey, Renaldo!"

I was sitting in class trying to pay attention to Mr. Beame, my fifth-grade teacher. He was describing the four basic food groups. I heard him turn towards the blackboard and start to write. The chalk made a squeaky sound as he began to draw. It sent a shiver down my spine. (Ouch!)

"Hey, Renaldo!" My friend Jeremy Kendall was trying to whisper my name, but it was coming out kind of loud.

"Renaldo, over here!"

I was thinking about *my* four favorite food groups—pizza, ice cream, hamburgers, and french fries—when I heard Jeremy calling my name again.

"Pssst, Renaldo! I have a big problem," Jeremy said.

He had looked all over the Woodburn Shopping Center for a birthday card for his stepmother. Not a real corny one, and not a real mushy one, not even a funny one—just a nice card to tell his stepmother that he liked having her around.

Sure, there were plenty of cards for "Mom" or "Mother," cards for "Mommy," and even "Mother Darling." But none of them said "Stepmom" or "Stepmother" or step-anything!

"You know what I found?" he whispered. "Not a one. Nothing." He stopped for a moment. "Nada," he said with a smile in his voice.

"So make your own card," I whispered back.

When I heard the box of markers clatter out of Jeremy's desk, I knew that's exactly what he was doing. In seconds I smelled magic marker drifting through the air. The smell must have drifted to Mr. Beame's nose, too, because he put on his best "I mean business" voice and called Jeremy to the front of the room.

That was when it hit me—the idea, I mean. The business idea! I started thinking about all the kids I knew who had stepparents or stepbrothers or stepsisters and—well, believe me, it can get pretty complicated. Especially when it comes to birthdays and holidays. And what about Father's Day and Mother's Day? It's hard enough on a kid without spending half the day looking for . . . looking for . . . for a STEPCARD!

I was still thinking about stepcards at dinner. I was thinking so hard that I even forgot where the broccoli was on my plate—and I actually ate some!

You see, since I'm blind, Mom helps me find my food by pretending my plate is like a clock. My meatloaf was at nine o'clock, my salad was at three o'clock, and the broccoli was at six. I was so busy thinking about stepcards that I got my times mixed up!

"Renaldo Rodriguez eating broccoli! Now that's a sight for sore eyes," my Mom said and laughed to herself. She thought that was very funny. "Something on your mind?" she said.

I knew great business ideas need time to grow, and this one had just been planted in my head. So I didn't say a word. I just aimed my fork for six o'clock and choked down another piece of broccoli.

"Hey, Mom, this is great!" I said. That threw her off the track.

My younger brother is Josue. That's Spanish for Joshua. (It's pronounced "Ho-sway.") If you really want to know about Josue, though, I think you should try looking up the Spanish word for "pest."

We like to play Scrabble after dinner. That night Josue had the game out before I even had a chance to clear the table. But I just wasn't paying attention. I wasn't taking the time to feel the Braille dots on the Scrabble letters.

"Josue," I said. "Do you remember that calculator I told you about? The one made special for blind people? I have an idea how I might get the money to buy one."

"Oh, you've told me about that calculator a hundred times already," Josue complained. I heard the Scrabble letters swishing off the board and clattering back into the box. I guess Josue had heard enough. "You've got that calculator on the brain," he complained. "Tell it to somebody else!"

And that's just what I did. "Dial B for Braxton," I said to myself, and I headed for the telephone. "Now, this is an idea that Jinx Braxton will love."

"Jinx!" I shouted when she answered the phone. I sure was excited about my business idea. "It's me! Renaldo. Renaldo Rodriguez!"

"Renaldo, you're the only Renaldo I know," Jinx said. "And you don't have to holler! I can hear you."

I explained the whole idea to her—"R.R. Stepcards" I called it. That was a pretty clever name, even I have to admit. I told her how I would make and sell cards for people who had

stepfamilies: birthday cards, get well cards, Valentine cards—the list was endless!

"What do you think, Jinx? Am I going to be Woodburn's first millionaire?"

There was silence on the other end. I could tell Jinx was thinking about it. She always thinks about things before she gives her opinion. And she always thinks about what other people might think. "Opposing viewpoints," she calls them. Jinx does a lot of thinking.

"Well," she finally asked, "have you done any marketing research?"

"Marketing research?"

"Have you thought about your investment?"

"Investment?"

Jinx was on a roll. I felt doomed.

"Oh, how will you advertise?"

I felt it coming, but I couldn't stop it. "Advertise?" I said.

"Just listen to me," I thought to myself, "Renaldo Rodriguez, the human echo!"

Research? Investment? Advertising? "Jinx," I said, "this is starting to sound like work! Explain this stuff to me."

I knew Jinx was excited. I could hear the excitement in her voice. "Look," she began, "marketing research is the first thing you do. You find out if someone else has already thought of your idea. You find out if there's such a thing as a stepcard. If there's not, then you can figure out your investment. That's how much money you want to spend to get the business started."

"Spend?" I said. "But I want to *make* money, Jinx."

"I know," Jinx said in her most patient voice. "But you can't get something for nothing. We will have to buy markers and paper, maybe even paints and stencils, too. That's our investment."

"*Our* investment? When did it become *our* investment?"

"Renaldo, this is an excellent idea," Jinx continued. "But there's a lot to do. You're going to need a partner." And I didn't even have the time to say "A partner?" before Jinx jumped in again. "Hmmmm . . . I do like the sound of it," she said. "Yes, 'R.R. and J.B. Stepcards.' I like the sound of it very much."

And you know what? So did I. With J.B. as my partner, I was more excited than ever—so excited that I couldn't get to sleep that night. I turned my pillow to the cold side a hundred times until I gave up trying to sleep. I got out my stylus and slate and started to write: "R.R. and J.B. Stepcards. For Your Favorite Stepfriend." There were stepfathers, stepmothers, stepbrothers, stepsisters, stepgrandmothers—the list went on and on. "For All Occasions." There were birthdays, anniversaries, graduations, holidays—and so many more. I started counting our profits. I couldn't help it.

"Excuse me, Mr. Businessman," Josue said, hiding a big yawn. "Mom already came in here. She made me stop reading.

We're supposed to be asleep, you know."

Josue was right. Mom doesn't let us read or write after lights out. But, you see, I don't have to sneak under the covers with a flashlight the way Josue does.

"I'm not reading," I told Josue. "This, my little brother, is marketing research—I think."

"It looks like reading to me. It's not fair. I ought to tell on you!" Josue climbed out of bed to get a better look. "Just what kind of business is this anyway?"

"None of *your* business," I said firmly. And I closed my slate. I wasn't taking any chances on someone stealing the business idea of the century, certainly not a nosy little brother. I turned my pillow over for the last time.

"Let's go to sleep."

The next day was Saturday, and with lots of kids from Woodburn, Jinx and I headed for the mall. We take turns delivering the "Woodburn Flyer" to the stores at the Woodburn Shopping Center. The "Flyer" is the free newspaper that tells about all the things happening at Woodburn. Then it's time for fun.

But this Saturday was different. Today, there were no video games, no french fries, no window-shopping. Today, we were all business.

I knew we were near Calloway's Cards and Gifts when I smelled the tempting aroma of cheese, tomato sauce, and special toppings. Polotti's Pizza Palace was just next door to the card store.

"I don't think I can do the marketing research on an empty stomach. How about a business lunch?" I was tapping my cane toward the sweet smell of Polotti's.

"Renaldo," Jinx said sternly, "we don't have much time."

"Okay. Okay," I said. "Give me your arm." Jinx was right.

We really didn't have much time. "It will be faster for me to walk alongside you—and less temptation, too."

There must have been a thousand different kinds of cards in Calloway's, and each one was cornier or mushier than the last. One thing about those cards, though—they really cracked us up!

"Look at this one, Renaldo," Jinx said.

"*To My Daughter and Her Husband on This Special Day*," Jinx read. She described the card to me. "It's big," she said, passing it to me.

"It's almost the size of our spelling notebook," I said, feeling around the edges of the card.

"It has two pink hearts with bows on them. Two white doves are holding the ends of the ribbons in their mouths. It looks like the words *Happy Anniversary* are coming right out of their beaks," Jinx giggled.

I could feel the raised lines of the hearts, the bows, and the birds. "Yuk," I said, "it sounds pretty corny to me."

"Listen to this, Renaldo."

To My Daughter and Her Husband on This Special Day:

'Like two white doves are lovers true,
Like two pink hearts forever new.
I hope this day will always view
A ribbon of happiness just for you.'

"Double yuk," I said. "Who buys this mush?"

"Here's another one, Renaldo," Jinx said. "*Congratulations on Your New Baby!* It has a picture of a stork with a baby in a diaper hanging in its mouth."

"It must look so silly," I said, trying hard not to giggle too loudly.

"It gets worse." Jinx was cracking up. "When you open up the card, the stork drops the baby—plop!—right on somebody's doorstep!"

"It sounds like a wet diaper to me!" I squealed. Jinx was laughing, too. But then she suddenly stopped. I could tell she was really thinking.

"But, Renaldo," she said in a serious voice," somebody buys these cards, and"—she was getting very excited—"there are no stepcards!"

Now I was getting excited, too. We did a high-five right there in Calloway's. "We're going to be rich!" we both shouted.

"C'mon, Renaldo," Jinx urged, "let's go home and get to work."

"Be sure to save an extra large pepperoni and sausage for Woodburn's youngest millionaires!" I shouted when we passed Polotti's.

Getting to work was not as easy as it sounded. Jinx and I had to buy the paper for the cards. We put our money together for an investment of twelve dollars and thirty-two cents. ("That's a lot of french fries," I thought.) We had to decide what kind of cards to make. We had to think of designs for the front of the cards and messages to go inside. We had to find a way to let people know about "R.R. and J.B. Stepcards."

Let's face it: We had a lot to learn about starting a business.

When I have more questions than answers, I always turn to the expert—my Mom. "Mom," I said when she got home from work, "Jinx and I need to speak to an old hand in the business world."

"Good luck finding one," she replied as she started to take off the running shoes she wears to work.

"No, Mom," I explained, "I meant you."

"Oh," she said, looking up. "What can this 'old hand' do for you?"

My Mom knows about business, especially bad businesses. She works in an office helping people who bought things that don't work or aren't safe. I figured if she knew all about bad businesses, she could tell us how to start a good one.

Jinx and I explained our business idea. "How do we get started?" Jinx asked.

"How do you make lots of money?" (I guess you can figure out who asked that one!)

Mom thought for a while. Then she spoke slowly. "Jinx, Renaldo, starting and running a business is not so easy. It's more than just making money. A successful business needs a good product to sell or a useful service to offer. And a successful businessman—or businesswoman—thinks about the customer all the time. Ask yourself: 'What do they want?' 'How can my product or my service help them?'"

Jinx and I were trying to listen to all of this, but it wasn't easy. We *did* have a lot to learn.

"Now, you two have a good product," Mom continued. "I'm proud of you for coming up with this idea. But a good idea is not enough. You need to plan carefully."

"What do we do, Mrs. Rodriguez?" Jinx asked.

"Well," Mom said, "you need to figure out how much money you'll need to get started and where the money will come from. You need to decide who will do the work and, believe me, a business *is* work. Now, if you're still interested in 'R.R. and J.B. Stepcards,' let's make a plan!"

"Always ask the expert," I shouted. I could hear the rubber soles of Mom's shoes make that familiar squeegy sound. Mom wears business suits and running shoes every day to work. Dad says she's dressed for success from her head to her knees—but her feet are dressed for failure! That always makes me laugh.

With Mom's help we really got started. Jinx and I used our "investment" to buy paper, paints, markers, and stencils. We worked every day after school. We took turns with the stencils to make the designs. We'd take a small roller and dip it into a bright color of paint. When we'd smooth the roller over the stencil, there was a butterfly or flower or other designs. Jinx said they looked great!

I liked making up the words for our stepcards. I thought of some pretty good ones, if I must say so myself.

To My Stepfather:

'Getting to know you hasn't been half bad.
I'm glad Mom picked you to be my Stepdad!'

Well, I didn't say they were great cards.

To My Stepsister:

'You have two families, I know that's true.
But I want you to know that I love you, too!'

All right, so Renaldo Rodriguez has a mushy side. Don't rub
it in!

❖

At the end of just one week, Jinx and I had 34 cards ready
to go.

"To go where?" I asked.

"Where else?" Jinx said. "Why, the Woodburn School and
Community Center!" It was time to advertise, and Woodburn
was the place to start.

The Woodburn School was the oldest school building in
the city. It almost closed the year before. There just weren't
enough kids to fill it up, I guess. That's why the school board
decided to add a Community Center. Now there was a day-care
room for little kids and an activity center for older people, too.
Woodburn is like a little city all its own.

The first thing on Monday morning Jinx and I marched
down to Woodburn and showed our cards to Mr. Mohammadi,
the assistant principal. Boy, was he excited!

"A sound idea," he said. "A very sound business idea. And
you'll get a real education in the bargain. A real education.
How can I help?"

We explained that advertising "R.R. and J.B. Stepcards"
was the next part of our business plan.

"Let's see now." Mr. Mohammadi was thinking out loud.
"You can put advertisements in the school newspaper, posters
in the Senior Center, flyers to go home. . . ." Mr. Mohammadi
was pacing the floor and spouting new ideas faster than . . . faster
than . . . well, faster than Jinx and I could write them down.

"This is going to be a snap," I predicted. "I should have started a business years ago. Think of all the time I've wasted in school!"

That stopped Mr. Mohammadi in his tracks. "Just a little business joke," I gulped.

If you want to start a business, take it from me: advertise! With Mr. Mohammadi's help, Jinx and I spread the word about "R.R. and J.B. Stepcards." Believe it or not, within one week, we sold 17 of our cards and had orders for 20 more. That's 37 cards! We'd make back all the money we spent on supplies. We'd even have some left over.

"Now that we'll have a little extra money, why not buy some stickers and glitter?" Jinx suggested. "Let's make the cards even prettier."

I was thinking about my calculator. I wanted to buy it as soon as I could. "But, Renaldo," Jinx said, "if we make our cards prettier, we'll sell more and make more money."

That made sense. Then I could buy the calculator and a new pair of soccer shoes.

"Don't forget," Jinx reminded me, "we have to pay to use the copying machine." We had to make copies of the advertisement Mr. Mohammadi was going to send home with the kids.

"And we need copies to take to the Senior Center, too," I told Jinx. I remember Mom saying, "You have to spend some money to make money." We thought that advertising was the best way to get more sales.

We thought right! Every day more orders came in the mail.

This was going to be a snap.

Jinx and I had to work every afternoon that week to fill the orders. And every day more orders came in.

Jeremy Kendall's stepsisters had their birthdays coming up, so he ordered two cards from "R.R. and J.B. Stepcards." Mrs. Rothman (from the Senior Center) told us her son had just married a woman with twin boys, and she needed birthday cards for her stepgrandchildren. Roger Neville's stepfather was in the hospital, so he wanted a special get well card. And Joanne Spinoza's mother, Lena, wanted a stepcousin Valentine.

Phew! Jinx and I could hardly believe how well our business was going. We just didn't expect how happy people would be with our cards.

"You know, Jinx," I said, as I lined up the paint jars, "it's nice to give people something special."

Jinx agreed. "Jeremy told me that our card really helped him tell his stepmother how much he liked her."

"No kidding?"

"You know what else? He said she cried a little when she read it, and then she said she really liked him, too."

"Hey," I said, "making people happy is a pretty good way to make a living."

We talked so long that it was soon time for Jinx to go home. We planned to get together again on Tuesday night.

Then came Tuesday morning.

"That's right," Mr. Beame was saying, "there will be a test tomorrow on the four food groups. Be sure you have food on the brain."

"Well, there goes our business for tonight," Jinx whispered. "We'll have to start again on Wednesday."

"But Wednesday we have Computer Club," I pointed out.

"And Thursday is gymnastics," Jinx said. "We have to work sometime. We have orders to fill."

Jinx was only partly right. We had *lots* of orders to fill. Whether we worked or not, the orders still kept coming in. Somewhere, from far away, I heard a little voice telling me to "plan carefully," and that voice sounded much too much like my Mom's.

"Okay," I whispered back, "we'll work all day Saturday to make up for the days we lost this week."

"That's okay with me," said Jinx. I could tell it wasn't completely okay. But what could we do?

"Saturday it is!"

❖

Saturday. Mall Day. But not for us. We were up to our eyeballs in "R.R. and J.B. Stepcards."

"What do you mean we're out of paint?" Jinx shouted. Jinx didn't shout much, but, boy, she was making up for lost time now. "Who was in charge of supplies, Renaldo Rodriguez?"

"Who took so many orders?" I asked.

"I was supposed to take orders!"

Jinx has a point there, but that just made me angrier.

"So what do we do now?"

What we did was work. Saturday. Mall Day. The whole day. I didn't think it was possible to do so much work in one day, and I wasn't exactly thrilled finding out you could. But at last the cards were done and ready to be delivered.

"I'm bushed," Jinx said.

"Bushed! Is that all? I'm ready to pass out!" We were still a little angry with one another, but too tired to fight. We were also too tired to sort and deliver all of the stepcards. But the work had to be done.

The question was, "How?"

"I have a good idea," I said mysteriously.

"Josue! Josue!" I called. "Oh, Josue, would you mind coming here for a minute?"

You've probably guessed it by now. I hired Josue to sort and deliver the cards. What made it great was that he worked for next to nothing. Two dollars was just fine with him.

Jinx wasn't too impressed with my new plan, but she was too beat to argue. "Jinx, you worry too much," I said. "Let's go celebrate! Pizza all around. My treat!"

Jinx was still worried. "Hey," I shouted. "This was a snap."

❖

To make the whole world seem brighter, there's nothing like a Polotti's pepperoni and sausage pizza. Jinx and I were friends again, our business was booming, and I could even get my little brother to work for peanuts! Jinx and I made new business plans as we walked back home.

"Renaldo Rodriguez!" I heard as soon as I opened the door. I knew something was very wrong. That little voice in my head that was warning me to "plan carefully" was now a great big voice, and it was coming from a very real, and a very angry, mother—my mother!

"Renaldo, just what did you do with the cards?"

"What do you mean, Mom?" I asked in my most innocent voice.

"What I mean is that the phone has been ringing off the hook with people complaining that they received the wrong stepcards."

"Well, Mom," I began to explain. It didn't matter. Mom hardly stopped to take a breath. She was going strong.

"The last call was from Mrs. Rothman. She has twin stepgrandsons. They're having a birthday. Know what she got?"

"The wrong card?" I thought that was a safe bet.

"I'll tell you what she got!"

'So sorry you're sick,
So sorry you're blue.
An R.R. and J.B. Stepcard
Is just the thing for you!'

"Ouch!" I thought. That was one of my favorite cards. I was especially proud of how we worked in our initials.

"Then there's the card Roger Neville's stepfather got in the hospital."

'You're a cute little angel,
We know that's true.
Here's a cute little card,
On the day you turn two.'

Double ouch. I began to wonder how much a lawyer would cost.

"Do you want me to go on?" my mother asked us in a way only mothers can ask things.

"No," I said and explained the whole thing to her and how Josue must have gotten the cards mixed up. I knew it would do no good to blame Josue. "You get what you pay for," I sighed.

"What should we do, Mrs. Rodriguez?" Jinx asked.

Back to the expert, I thought.

"We? We! We!" she kept saying. I was going to tell her that she sounded like the one little pig that cried all the way home, but I thought I would save that observation for another time.

"Well, Renaldo," she said as she calmed down, "perhaps your friends could help you out of this mess. Perhaps they could collect the cards and deliver them—to the correct addresses this time."

"Right, Mom," I exclaimed. "I mean, what are friends for, after all? A friend in need is a friend indeed! Right, Mom?" My spirits rose. Always go to the expert—that was the lesson of this business venture.

"And what are you going to pay those friends?" the expert asked.

"Pay?"

"Pay."

One thing about spirits: no sooner do they head up, than they're right on their way down again. "But, Mom, if I pay my friends, there won't be any money left for me or for Jinx."

"And if you don't pay them?"

I knew what she meant. That's the trouble with the expert: you don't always get the answer that you're looking for.

Yes, Jinx and I paid our friends to collect all the cards and deliver them again.

No, we did not make any money from "R.R. and J.B. Stepcards."

Yes, we were pretty upset about the way things worked out. "Business!" I grumbled. "Who needs it?"

One night several weeks later, I was out in the backyard playing soccer with my Dad. Dad thinks he's a champion goalie, but I hold back a lot. After all, he tries so hard.

When we stopped for a break, Dad said, "Renaldo, do you remember that stepcard business you started?"

"Dad, I could hardly forget it."

"Well, I was thinking," Dad went on in his quiet way. "What if . . ." And my very own Dad told me about the greatest business idea I had ever heard! I can't tell you about it here. I'm not taking any chances, you know.

"Renaldo, where are you going?" Dad shouted as I ran toward the house.

"Where am I going?" I shouted back. "Dial B for Braxton!" And I ran inside to get Jinx on the phone.

Reader's Response ∽ What were the qualities Renaldo showed in the story that will make you most remember him?

Questions for Renaldo

Lots of kids have questions for me about what it's like to be blind. I bet you do, too. Here are some questions other kids have asked me before. Take a look. Your question might be here.

Q. If you're blind, how do you eat?

A. I have a special way to find the food on my plate. I just pretend my plate is like a clock. Then my Mom or Dad or whoever is around tells me where the different foods are. Like, my sandwich is at twelve o'clock, or my chips at three o'clock, or (ugh!) the broccoli is at seven o'clock. If I want my sandwich, my hand goes right to old twelve o'clock. This way I can always find exactly what I want to eat.

If I'm with someone who doesn't know my clock system, I teach it to them. Or I just ask them to tell me what there is to eat. I can usually tell what I'm eating by the way it feels with my fork or fingers.

Q. When you ate your broccoli, your Mom said that you were "a sight for sore eyes." How do you feel about people making jokes like that or when they say words like "look" or "see"?

A. Everybody likes to laugh and joke around, and I'm just like everyone else. Sometimes I make jokes about being blind, too. Once my friend Brenda said to me, "Are you really blind?" And I held my hand up to my face and said, "Since the last time I checked!" But I don't like jokes that hurt my feelings or make fun of me, just like everyone else.

I don't mind when people use words like "look" and "see." I use them myself. That's because those words are used all the time. Lots of times kids say, "Look!" when they're trying to get someone's attention. Or they say, "See what I mean!" Those words are just part of the usual way of talking.

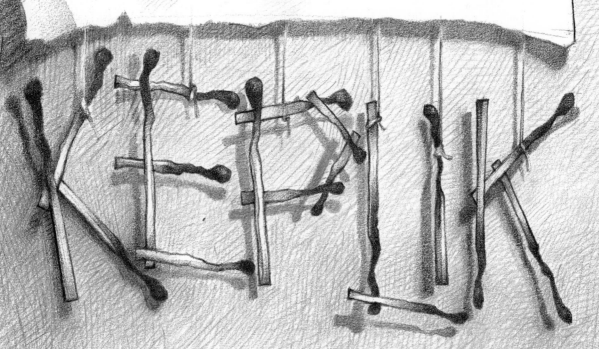

If you have a matchstick,
sell it to Keplik.

the
Match Man

by Myron Levoy

READERS'
CHOICE
AWARD

There once was a little old man who lived in a big old tenement on Second Avenue. His name was Mr. Keplik and he had once been a watchmaker. In the window of his tiny watch-repair shop he had put up a sign that read: WHEN YOUR WRIST WATCH WON'T TICK, IT'S TIME FOR KEPLIK. Keplik loved watches and clocks and had loved repairing them. If a clock he was repairing stopped ticking he would say to himself, "Eh, eh, eh, it's dying." And when it started ticking again he would say, "I am *gebentsht.*[1] I am blessed. It's alive."

Whenever an elevated train[2] rumbled by overhead, Keplik would have to put down his delicate work, for his workbench and the entire shop would shake and vibrate. But Keplik would close his eyes and say, "Never mind. There are worse things. How many people back in Lithuania wouldn't give their right eye to have a watch-repair shop under an el train in America."

While he worked Keplik never felt lonely, for there were always customers coming in with clocks and watches and complaints.

[1]gebentsht (gə bensht′): blessed
[2]elevated train: a train that runs above street level, also called "the el"

across the living room from the kitchen to the bedroom, and the two towers would stand as high as his head. "For this I need matches!" Keplik said aloud. "Matches! I must have matches."

And he posted a new sign: MATCH FOR MATCH, YOU CANNOT MATCH KEPLIK'S PRICE FOR USED MATCHES. ONE CENT FOR FIFTY. HURRY! HURRY! HURRY!

Vincent DeMarco, who lived around the corner, brought fifty matches that very afternoon, and Cathy Dunn and Noreen Callahan brought a hundred matches each the next morning. Day after day, the matches kept coming, and day after day, Keplik the Match Man glued and fixed and bent and pressed the matches into place.

The bridge was so complicated that Keplik had decided to build it in separate sections, and then join all the sections afterward. The bridge's support towers, the end spans, and the center span slowly took shape in different parts of the room. The room seemed to grow smaller as the bridge grew larger. A masterpiece, thought Keplik. There is no longer room for me to sit in my favorite chair. But I must have more matches! It's time to build the cables!

Even the long support cables were made from matchsticks, split and glued and twisted together. Keplik would twist the sticks until his fingers grew numb. Then he would go into the kitchen to make a cup of coffee for himself, not so much for the coffee, but for the fact that lighting the stove would provide him with yet another matchstick. And sometimes, as he was drinking his coffee, he would get up and take a quick look at his bridge, because it always looked different when he was away from it for a while. "It's beginning to be alive," he would say.

And then one night, it was time for the great final step. The towers and spans and cables all had to be joined together to give the finished structure. A most difficult job. For everything was supported from the cables above, as in a real bridge, and all the final connections had to be glued and tied almost at the same moment. Nothing must shift or slip for a full half hour, until the glue dried thoroughly.

Keplik worked carefully, his watchmaker's hands steadily gluing and pressing strut after strut, cable after cable. The end spans were in place. The center span was ready. Glue, press, glue, press. Then suddenly, an el train rumbled by outside. The ground trembled, the old tenement shivered as it always did, the windows rattled slightly, and the center span slid from its glued moorings. Then one of the end cables vibrated loose, then another, and the bridge slipped slowly apart into separate spans and towers. "Eh, eh, eh," said Keplik. "It's dying."

Keplik tried again, but another train hurtled past from the other direction. And again the bridge slowly slipped apart. I am too tired, thought Keplik. I'll try again tomorrow.

Keplik decided to wait until late the next night, when there would be fewer trains. But again, as the bridge was almost completed, a train roared past, the house shook, and everything slipped apart. Again and again, Keplik tried, using extra supports and tying parts together. But the bridge seemed to enjoy waiting for the next train to shake it apart again.

Ah me, thought Keplik. All my life those el trains shook the watches in my hands, down below in my shop. All my life I said things could be worse; how many people back in Lithuania wouldn't give their left foot to have a watch-repair shop under an el train in America.

But why do the el trains have to follow me three flights up? Why can't they leave me alone in my old age? When I die, will there be an el train over my grave? Will I be shaken and rattled around while I'm trying to take a little well-deserved snooze? And when I reach heaven, will there be an el train there, too, so I can't even play a nice, soothing tune on a harp without all this *tummel*, this noise? It's much too much for me. This is it. The end. The bridge will be a masterpiece in parts. The Brooklyn Bridge after an earthquake.

At that moment, another el train roared by and Keplik the Match Man called toward the train, "One thing I'll *never* do! I'll never make an el train out of matches! Never! How do you like *that*!"

When the children came the next afternoon, to see if the bridge was finished at last, Keplik told them of his troubles with the el trains. "The bridge, my children, is *farpotshket*.[3] You know what that means? A mess!"

The children made all sorts of suggestions: hold it this way, fix it that way, glue it here, tie it there. But to all of them, Keplik the Match Man shook his head. "Impossible. I've tried that. Nothing works."

Then Vincent DeMarco said, "My father works on an el station uptown. He knows all the motormen, he says. Maybe he can get them to stop the trains."

[3]farpotshket (far puch′kət)

Keplik laughed. "Ah, such a nice idea. But not even God can stop the Second Avenue el."

"I'll bet my father can," said Vincent.

"Bet he can't," said Joey Basuto. And just then, a train sped by: raketa, raketa, raketa, raketa, raketa. "The trains never stop for nothing," said Joey.

And the children went home for dinner, disappointed that the bridge made from all their matchsticks was farpoot . . . farbot . . . *whatever* that word was. A mess.

Vincent told his father, but Mr. DeMarco shrugged. "No. Impossible. Impossible," he said. "I'm not important enough."

"But couldn't you *try*?" pleaded Vincent.

"I know *one* motorman. So what good's that, huh? One motorman. All I do is make change in the booth."

"Maybe he'll tell everybody else."

"*Assurdità*. Nonsense. They have more to worry about than Mr. Keplik's bridge. Eat your soup!"

But Mr. DeMarco thought to himself that if he did happen to see his friend, the motorman, maybe, just for a laugh, he'd mention it. . . .

Two days later, Vincent ran upstairs to Keplik's door and knocked. *Tonight* his father had said! Tonight at one A.M.! Keplik couldn't believe his ears. The trains would stop for his bridge? It couldn't be. Someone was playing a joke on Vincent's father.

But that night, Keplik prepared, just in case it was true. Everything was ready: glue, thread, supports, towers, spans, cables.

A train clattered by at five minutes to one. Then silence. Rapidly, rapidly, Keplik worked. Press, glue, press, glue. One cable connected. Two cables. Three. Four. First tower finished. Fifth cable connected. Sixth. Seventh. Eighth.

Other tower in place. Now gently, gently. Center span in position. Glue, press, glue, press. Tie threads. Tie more threads. Easy. Easy. Everything balanced. Everything supported. Now please. No trains till it dries.

The minutes ticked by. Keplik was sweating. Still no train. The bridge was holding. The bridge was finished. And then, outside the window, he saw an el train creeping along, slowly, carefully: cla . . . keta . . . cla . . . keta . . . cla . . . keta . . . cla . . . keta . . . Then another, moving slowly from the other direction: cla . . . keta . . . cla . . . keta . . . .

And Keplik shouted toward the trains, "Thank you, Mister Motorman! Tomorrow, I am going to start a great new masterpiece! The Second Avenue el from Fourteenth Street to Delancey Street! Thank you for slowing up your trains!"

And first one motorman, then the other, blew his train whistle as the trains moved on, into the night beyond. "Ah, how I am gebentsht," said Keplik to himself. "In America there are kind people everywhere. All my life, the el train has shaken my hands. But tonight, it has shaken my heart."

Keplik worked for the rest of the night on a little project. And the next morning, Keplik hung this sign made from matches outside his window, where every passing el train motorman could see it:

Reader's Response ～ How would you feel about having Keplik as a friend? Explain your answer.

Library Link ～ *The story of Keplik is from* The Witch of Fourth Street and Other Stories *by Myron Levoy. Look for it at the library.*

MATCH MAKING

Keplik needed matches to create his sculpture. But did you ever wonder how matches were invented?

Would you believe—

❖ The wooden matches we use today weren't perfected until 1911.

❖ One of the earliest versions of a "match" was called the phosphoric candle and was created in 1780 by a group of French chemists.

❖ The first friction matches similar to today's were not invented until 1827. These matches were lit by drawing the match head through a folded piece of sandpaper. The match burst into flame in a series of little explosions, showering sparks all over the person using it. This problem was solved by using phosphorus. Unfortunately, phosphorus presented a new and even more serious problem. It gave off fumes that caused people who worked in match factories to become ill and even die.

❖ A young engineer named William Fairburn adapted a safe form of phosphorus, developed in France, to the climate of America. The year was 1911—eighty-four years after the first modern friction match!

PHILBERT PHLURK

written by *Jack Prelutsky*
illustrated by *Victoria Chess*

The major quirk of Philbert Phlurk
was tinkering all day,
inventing things that didn't work,
a scale that wouldn't weigh,
a pointless pen that couldn't write,
a score of silent whistles,
a bulbless lamp that wouldn't light,
a toothbrush with no bristles.

He built a chair without a seat,
a door that wouldn't shut,
a cooking stove that didn't heat,
a knife that couldn't cut.
He proudly crafted in his shop
a wheel that wouldn't spin,
a sweepless broom, a mopless mop,
a stringless violin.

He made a million useless things
like clocks with missing hands,
like toothless combs and springless springs
and stretchless rubber bands.
When Phlurk was through with something new,
he'd grin and say with glee,
''I know this does not work for you,
but ah! it works for me.''

The Brooklyn Bridge:

EMILY'S TRIUMPH

by Charnan Simon

Emily Warren Roebling was a person to be reckoned with. As a girl growing up in Cold Spring, New York, she would lean out her bedroom window, see the busy, hurrying Hudson River, and think about all the places that it visited.

Emily could only yearn to visit these places herself. It wasn't easy for girls to go places in America in the middle of the nineteenth century, not by themselves, at any rate.

Emily first found this out when it came to her education. Emily was good in math, languages, and history. When she finished the convent school in Georgetown, D.C., she wanted to study further.

Her older brother Gouverneur said it was out of the question. Gouverneur had been head of the family since Emily's father died in 1859. He always decided family matters. He said she had gone to school long enough.

Emily thought that was nonsense. But Gouverneur was thirty and she was sixteen, and in the 1850s sixteen-year-old girls didn't argue with their thirty-year-old brothers. Instead, Emily kept on studying by herself—even going so far as to borrow some of Gouverneur's own army engineering books!

During the Civil War, Gouverneur was a major general in the Union Army. Emily wanted to help her country, too. In the spring of 1864 she visited her brother's Army Corps' camp on the banks of the Potomac River.

She firmly told Gouverneur that she wanted to be a nurse. She reminded him that Clara Barton and her Red Cross workers needed all the help they could get. She appealed to him on the grounds that she was another Warren who wanted to fight for the Union cause.

But her brother wouldn't listen. He thought a field hospital was no place for a respectable young woman. Emily fumed on the train ride home. She couldn't go against her brother's decision, though she thought it was unfair.

Emily learns about bridge building

During her short stay at the Army Camp, Emily had met a young lieutenant named Washington Roebling. Gouverneur had described him as one of his best engineers, a young man with a good head on his shoulders. Emily thought so, too. She had enjoyed talking to Lieutenant Roebling more than anyone she'd ever met. He seemed to enjoy talking with her, too. In fact, six weeks

Rensselaer Polytechnic Institute Archive

Emily Warren, twenty years old at the time of this photograph, was determined to learn all she could about bridge building.

after they had met, he asked Emily to marry him. They were married on January 18, 1865.

After Washington was discharged from the Army, the young couple headed for Cincinnati to join Washington's father, John Roebling. He was a brilliant engineer who was now building the world's longest single-span bridge over the Ohio River.

Emily had heard a lot about Washington's father, and how he had carefully raised Washington to be his partner. Now she was glad of the hours she'd stolen to read Gouverneur's engineering books. It helped her understand what Washington was talking about—and sometimes it seemed that all he *did* talk about was bridges!

The Brooklyn Bridge begins

For two years Washington and his father worked on the Ohio River Bridge. Then, in the spring of 1867 came the big news the Roeblings had been waiting for. After years of debate, the New York legislature had authorized the building of a bridge over the East River from New York to Brooklyn. The Chief Engineer of this bridge was to be John Roebling.

It was the beginning of a hectic time for Emily and Washington. First they made a year-long trip to Europe, so Washington could study how bridges were built there. Washington especially wanted to learn more about the new method of digging bridge foundations in *pneumatic caissons.* A pneumatic caisson was a huge, waterproof box that opened on the bottom. After a caisson was placed in a river, air was pumped in to drive the water out. The caisson was weighted down so it rested on the river bottom, and men worked inside it to dig out the foundation for the bridge towers.

Emily shared Washington's excitement over the bridge he was going to build. There would be two towers for the bridge, one on the Brooklyn side, and one on the New York side. Each tower would have to be dug deeply enough to rest on solid bedrock. Only then would the towers be secure enough to hold up the weight, 6,620 tons, that would be suspended between them.

Most bridges were supported by piers, but this would be a suspension bridge. Cables strung between the towers would have to support the full weight of the roadway.

The roadway had to be stiff enough not to shake. For this, girders and trusses were necessary, as well as stays above and below the floor of the road. To further strengthen the bridge, Washington decided to use steel instead of iron wire. Only a few wire companies could be counted on to produce the high quality steel wire needed.

Emily and Washington came home from Europe with much new information about building bridges—and with a newborn son, named John Augustus Roebling II after his grandfather. The next few months were busy ones. Washington and his father still had to convince doubters that a suspension bridge this size could be built. Emily listened and offered suggestions, but mainly she took care of her family.

Everything seemed to be going smoothly. The doubters had been silenced, and money—over five million dollars—had been raised to start construction. The engineers had begun surveying locations for the Brooklyn tower. Then disaster struck. A ferry boat hit the pier where John Roebling was standing and badly crushed his foot. Four weeks later, on July 22, 1869, the Chief Engineer was dead.

There wasn't time to mourn. Washington knew that it was up to him to realize his father's dream. Several weeks later came the official word— Washington Roebling would succeed his father as Chief Engineer.

Now Washington and Emily committed themselves completely to the bridge. Final plans had to be made, machines and materials purchased, and workmen and assistant engineers hired.

The New York Public Library

1.—ENTRANCE TO THE SUPPLY-SHAFT OF THE CAISSON.

The New York Public Library

2.—MOUTH OF SUPPLY-SHAFT OF THE CAISSON.

Newspaper illustrations from 1870 show the caisson in detail. *Left*, men wait for pressure within the caisson to be equalized. *Right*, workers enter the bottom hatchway leading to the caisson.

Finally, on Jaunary 3, 1870, the construction began on the Brooklyn tower.

First, the giant caisson had to be built and placed in the river. The caissons depended on air pressure inside the box being great enough to keep water from rushing in around the bottom. Sometimes workers could suffer a bad reaction to the pressure—a painful and sometimes fatal reaction known as the "bends," or "caisson disease."

Washington made sure everyone was careful when working in the caisson. Slowly, slowly, the work proceeded despite many setbacks. Several times fire threatened to destroy the caisson. Once it nearly flooded. Emily watched proudly as the Brooklyn tower gradually rose about 275 feet above the river.

By the fall of 1871, work could start on the New York tower. The Brooklyn caisson rested on bedrock at forty-four feet. The New York caisson would have to go down to seventy-eight feet. This called for greater air pressure inside the caisson—and the first cases of the bends occurred. Three men died that spring—and one early summer afternoon Washington Roebling was carried out of the New York caisson unconscious.

The New York Public Library

—DRILLING THE ROCK AT THE SHOE OF THE CAISSON.

The New York Public Library

—FILLING THE BUCKET OF THE WATERSHAFT IN THE CAISSON.

Left, men in the caissons broke up rocks and boulders found on the river bottom. *Right,* fragments were then hauled to a water shaft where they were lifted to the surface by a clam-shell scoop.

Emily oversees the construction of the bridge

For weeks Washington drifted in and out of consciousness, while Emily did all she could to nurse him to health. When it became obvious that Washington would remain an invalid, he began feverishly writing exact directions for finishing the bridge. If he couldn't supervise the work himself, at least he could spell out precisely what was to be done! All winter he worked, but when spring came he despaired. He told Emily he would have to resign as Chief Engineer, because he was unable to work on the site of the bridge.

Immediately Emily asked to become his assistant. She told him she could visit the bridge site for him and do what was needed to finish the bridge. Washington wearily reminded her she was not an engineer. He felt that, in any case, women didn't belong at construction sites. But Emily had lived with the bridge for five years and wasn't ready to give it up. She finally convinced her husband, and they both continued work on the Brooklyn Bridge.

For weeks Emily pored over Washington's engineering books, just as she'd pored over Gouverneur's so many years before. She studied Washington's plans for building the anchorages, for stringing the cables, and for suspending the spans. She learned how to determine the stress various materials could stand and how to read and understand bridge specifications. Then she set out.

At first she acted as Washington's messenger. She carried his instructions to the workers and relayed their messages back to him. But soon that wasn't enough. Emily had to start making judgments about men and materials on the spot. She smoothed the way between city officials and rival engineers. She dealt with dishonest contractors and corrupt politicians who saw the bridge as a means of making personal fortunes.

Every day she made critical decisions about the specifications and stability of the bridge—and more than once stopped substandard materials from being built into it. She visited the construction site two or three times each day. At home she worried about so many visitors coming to see Washington. Emily spoke with each caller herself, so carefully and skillfully that they felt honored to speak with her instead. An editorial of the day called Emily the "chief engineer of the work,"

admired and respected by everyone connected with the bridge.

Perhaps Emily's most triumphant moment was on December 11, 1881, when she led the way across the newly completed floor system of the bridge. It was a glorious feeling to walk from Brooklyn to New York on a bridge that *she* had helped construct!

Or perhaps her greatest triumph took place in 1882, when Emily became the first woman to speak before the American Society of Civil Engineers. There she defended her invalid husband's ability to continue as Chief Engineer. In an age when the idea of a woman engineer was laughed at as unthinkable, Emily won a standing ovation!

Finally, on the sun-washed morning of May 24, 1883, the opening of the Brooklyn Bridge was officially celebrated. On the Brooklyn side, Emily Roebling and many officials started toward the bridge. On the Manhattan side, the President of the United States, Chester A. Arthur, led the ceremonial march to Brooklyn. Then the President officially opened the span to traffic. Thousands of well-wishers cheered the bridge as the Eighth Wonder of the World. Later, Abram S. Hewitt, the

Observers such as the man shown above often watched the construction of the Brooklyn Bridge from a temporary slat-floored footbridge. Also shown in this photograph are the steel deck beams that formed the base for the bridge roadway.

main speaker, hailed both John and Washington Roebling as the geniuses behind the bridge.

Hewitt concluded his remarks by saying, "... One name, which may find no place in the official records, cannot be passed over here in silence ... The name of Mrs. Emily Warren Roebling will thus be inseparably associated with all that is admirable in human nature, and with all that is wonderful in the constructive world of art."

Yes, Emily Warren Roebling was a person to be reckoned with!

Reader's Response ⁓ At what point in the story did you most admire Emily? Why did you choose that event?

Library Link ⁓ *For enjoyable stories about nineteenth-century girls and women as adventurous as Emily, read* Little Women *by Louisa May Alcott and* Lucy Makes a Match *by Patricia Beatty.*

Ancient Wonders

When it opened in 1883, the Brooklyn Bridge was hailed by people as "The Eighth Wonder of the World." Do you know what the other seven wonders of the world are? The Seven Wonders of the World were buildings and statues created in ancient times that were so vast or beautiful that people could not believe humans were capable of creating them. The list on this page was originally compiled by an ancient Greek scholar. Today, people call these the Seven Wonders of the Ancient World.

The Brooklyn Bridge marked the first time in hundreds of years that human beings had completed anything as challenging as the ancient wonders. In the years since 1883, men and women have made achievements considered even more remarkable than the Brooklyn Bridge. Do you have your own candidate for the eighth wonder of the world?

shown above right,
The Colossus of Rhodes

The Lighthouse of Alexandria

The Hanging Gardens of Babylon

The Pyramids of Egypt

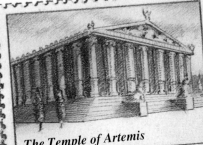

The Temple of Artemis

The Mausoleum at Halicarnassus

The Statue of Zeus

131

WORKING WITH

from *Shoeshine Girl*
by Clyde Robert Bulla

Sarah Ida Becker is spending the summer with her Aunt Claudia because Sarah Ida's mother is ill. Sarah Ida feels lonely, unhappy, and bored so she decides to find a summer job. Al is the only person in town who will hire a ten-and-a-half-year-old girl. He agrees to give Sarah Ida a job helping him at his shoeshine stand.

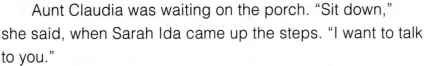

Aunt Claudia was waiting on the porch. "Sit down," she said, when Sarah Ida came up the steps. "I want to talk to you."

Sarah Ida sat in the porch swing.

"You must never do this again," said Aunt Claudia. "You must always let me know where you're going. Do you understand?"

"Yes," said Sarah Ida.

"Where have you been?"

"On the avenue."

"What were you doing?"

"Looking for a job. And I found one."

"You found one?"

"Yes, I did."

"Where?"

"On Grand Avenue. Working for the shoeshine man."

"Who?"

"Al Winkler, the shoeshine man."

Aunt Claudia looked dazed. "How did you know him?"

"I didn't know him. He had a 'Help Wanted' sign and I stopped."

"Al Winkler," said Aunt Claudia, as if she were talking to herself. "I remember him so well. He came to the library when I worked there. He hadn't gone to school much, and he wanted to learn more. I helped him choose books." She asked, "Does he want you to work at his stand?"

"He said to talk to you about it."

"Do you want to work for him?" asked Aunt Claudia.

"I told you, I want some money of my own."

"This might be a good way to earn some," said Aunt Claudia.

"You *want* me to shine shoes on Grand Avenue?"

"If that's what you want to do."

Sarah Ida was quiet for a while. Things weren't working out the way she'd planned. She'd never thought Aunt Claudia would let her work in the shoeshine stand, and Aunt Claudia didn't seem to care!

Unless—Sarah Ida had another thought. Maybe Aunt Claudia didn't believe she'd go through with it. Maybe she was thinking, *That child is playing another game.*

Sarah Ida said, "You really want me to go tell Al Winkler I'll work for him?"

"If it's what you want to do," said Aunt Claudia.

Sarah Ida started down the steps. Aunt Claudia didn't call her back. There was nothing for her to do but go.

She found Al sitting in one of his chairs.

"What did she say?" he asked.

"She said yes."

"You want to start now?"

"I don't care," she said.

He opened a drawer under the platform and took out an old piece of cloth. "Use this for an apron. Tie it around you."

She tied it around her waist.

A man stopped at the stand. He was a big man with a round face and a black beard. He climbed into a chair and put his feet on the shoe rests.

"How are you, Mr. Naylor?" said Al.

"Not bad," said the man. "Who's the young lady?"

"She's helping me," said Al. "She needs practice. You mind if she practices on you?"

"I don't mind," said Mr. Naylor.

Al said to Sarah Ida, "I'm going to shine one shoe. You watch what I do. Then you shine the other one."

He took two soft brushes and brushed the man's shoe.

"That takes off the dust," he said. "Always start with a clean shoe."

He picked up a jar of water with an old toothbrush in it. With the toothbrush he sprinkled a few drops of water on the shoe.

"That makes a better shine." He opened a round can of brown polish. With his fingers he spread polish on the shoe.

"Now you lay your cloth over the shoe," he said. "Stretch it tight—like this. Pull it back and forth—like this. Rub it hard and fast. First the toe—then the sides—then the back."

When he put down the cloth, the shoe shone like glass. He untied the man's shoelace. He drew it a little tighter and tied it again.

He asked Sarah Ida, "Did you see everything I did?"

"Yes," she said.

"All right. Let's see you do it."

She picked up the brushes. She dropped one. When she bent to pick it up, she dropped the other one. Her face grew hot.

She brushed the shoe. She sprinkled the water.

"Not so much," Al told her. "You don't need much."

She looked at the brown polish. "Do I have to get this on my fingers?"

"You can put it on with a rag, but it's not the best way. You can rub it in better with your fingers."

"I don't want to get it on my hands."

"Your hands will wash."

She put the polish on with her fingers. She shined Mr. Naylor's shoe. She untied his shoelace, pulled it tight, and tried to tie it again.

Al tied it for her. "It's hard to tie someone else's shoe when you never did it before."

Mr. Naylor looked at his shoes. "Best shine I've had all year," he said. He paid Al. He gave Sarah Ida a dollar bill.

After he had gone, she asked Al, "Why did he give me this?"

"That's your tip," said Al. "You didn't earn it. He gave it to you because you're just getting started."

"Will everybody give me a dollar?" she asked.

"No," he said, "and don't be looking for it."

Others stopped at the stand. Sometimes two or three were there at once. Part of the time Sarah Ida put polish on shoes. Part of the time she used the polishing cloth.

Toward the end of the day she grew tired. She tried to hurry. That was when she put black polish on a man's brown shoe.

The man began to shout. "Look what you did!"

"It's not hurt," said Al. "I can take the black polish off. Sarah Ida, hand me the jar of water."

She reached for the jar and knocked it over. All the water ran out.

"Go around the corner to the filling station," Al told her. "There's a drinking fountain outside. Fill the jar and bring it back."

Sarah Ida brought the water. Al washed the man's shoe. All the black polish came off.

"See?" he said. "It's as good as new."

"Well, maybe," said the man, "but I don't want *her* giving me any more shines."

He went away.

Sarah Ida made a face. "He was mean."

"No, he wasn't," said Al. "He just didn't want black polish on his brown shoes."

"Anyone can make a mistake," she said.

"That's right. Just don't make too many." He said, "You can go now." He gave her a dollar. "This is to go with your other dollar."

"Is that all the pay I get?"

"You'll get more when you're worth more," he said. "You can come back tomorrow afternoon. That's my busy time. Come about one."

She didn't answer. She turned her back on him and walked away.

In the morning she told Aunt Claudia, "I'm going to the drugstore."

"Aren't you working for Al?" asked Aunt Claudia.

"Maybe I am, and maybe I'm not," said Sarah Ida.

In the drugstore she looked at magazines. She looked at chewing gum and candy bars. None of them seemed to matter much. Her money was the first she had ever worked for. Somehow she wanted to spend it for something important.

She went home with the two dollars still in her pocket.

She and Aunt Claudia had lunch.

"If you aren't working for Al," said Aunt Claudia, "you can help me."

"I'm going to work," said Sarah Ida. Working for Al was certainly better than helping Aunt Claudia.

She went down to the shoeshine stand.

"So you came back," said Al.

"Yes," she said.

"I didn't know if you would or not."

Customers were coming. Al told Sarah Ida what to do. Once she shined a pair of shoes all by herself.

They were busy most of the afternoon. Her hair fell down into her eyes. Her back hurt from bending over.

Late in the day Al told her, "You've had enough for now. You can go. You got some tips, didn't you?"

"Yes," she said. "Do you want me to count them?"

"No. You can keep them. And here's your pay." He gave her two dollars. "And I want to tell you something. When you get through with a customer, you say 'thank you.'"

"All right," she said.

"One more thing. You didn't say yesterday if you were coming back or not. This time I want to know. Are you coming back tomorrow?"

"Yes," she said.

"Come about the same time," he said. "I'm going to bring you something."

What he brought her was a white canvas apron. It had two pockets. It had straps that went over her shoulders and tied in the back. There were black letters across the front.

"Why does it say 'Lane's Lumber Company'?" she asked. "Why doesn't it say 'Al's Shoeshine Corner'?"

"Because it came from Lane's Lumber Company," he said. "Fred Lane is a friend of mine, and he gave it to me."

It was nothing but a canvas apron. She didn't know why she should be so pleased with it. But it was a long time since anything had pleased her as much. She liked the stiff, new feel of the cloth. The pockets were deep. She liked to put her hands into them.

That night she thought about the apron. She had left it locked up at the stand. She almost told her mother and father about it in the letter she wrote them. She had promised to write twice a week—to make Aunt Claudia happy. But she didn't think they would care about her apron. All she wrote was:

Dear Mother and Father,
    I am all right. Everything is all right here. It was hot today.

Good-by,
SARAH IDA

She didn't tell Aunt Claudia about her apron. She didn't feel too friendly toward Aunt Claudia.

There were times when she didn't even feel too friendly toward Al.

There was the time when she shined an old man's shoes. He paid her and went away.

Al said, "I didn't hear you say 'thank you.'"

"He didn't give me any tip," she said. "The old stingy-guts."

They were alone at the stand. Al said, "What did you call him?"

"Old stingy-guts," she said. "That's what he is."

"Don't you ever say a thing like that again," said Al in a cold, hard voice. "He didn't have to give you a tip. Nobody has to. If he wants to give you something extra, that's his business. But if he doesn't, that's his business, too. I want to hear you say 'thank you' whether you get any tip or not."

It scared her a little to see him so angry. She didn't speak to him for quite a while.

140

But that evening he said, as if nothing had happened, "I could use some help in the morning, too. You want to work here all day?"

"I don't know," she said.

"You can if you want to. Ask your aunt."

She started home. On the way, a boy caught up with her. His arms and legs were long, and he took long steps. He looked ugly, with his lower lip pushed out. He asked, "What are you doing working for Al?"

She walked faster. He kept up with her. "How much is he paying you?"

"I don't see why I should tell you," she said.

"You've got my job, that's why."

The light turned green, and she crossed the street. He didn't follow her.

All evening she thought about what the boy had said. In the morning she asked Al about it.

"Was he a skinny boy?" asked Al. "Did he have light hair?"

"Yes," she said.

"That was Kicker."

"His name is *Kicker?*"

"That's what he called himself when he was little. Now we all call him that. He's my neighbor."

"What did he mean when he said I had his job?"

"I don't know. Once I asked him if he wanted to work for me. He said he did. Then he never came to work. He didn't want the job, but I guess he doesn't want you to have it, either."

"Maybe he changed his mind," she said. "Maybe he wants to work for you now."

"Maybe," said Al. "I'll have a talk with him. I don't think you'll see him any more."

But later in the week she did see him. He was across the street, watching her.

Every evening, after work, Sarah Ida was tired. But every morning she was ready to go back to Shoeshine Corner. It wasn't that she liked shining shoes, but things *happened* at the shoeshine stand. Every customer was different. Every day she found out something new.

Some things she learned by herself. Like how much polish to use on a shoe. A thin coat gave a better and quicker shine. Some things Al told her. "When a customer comes here, he gets more than a shine," he said. "He gets to rest in a chair. When you rub with the cloth, it feels good on his feet. When you tie his shoelaces a little tighter, it makes his shoes fit better. My customers go away feeling a little better. Anyway, I *hope* they do."

One warm, cloudy afternoon, he said, "We might as well close up."

"Why?" she asked. "It's only three o'clock."

"It's going to rain. Nobody gets a shine on a rainy day."

He began to put away the brushes and shoe polish. She helped him.

"Maybe you can run home before the rain," he said. A few big drops splashed on the sidewalk. "No. Too late now."

They sat under the little roof, out of the rain.

"Hear that sound?" he said. "Every time I hear rain on a tin roof, I get to thinking about when I was a boy. We lived in an old truck with a tin roof over the back."

"You *lived* in a truck?"

"Most of the time. We slept under the tin roof, and when it rained, the sound put me to sleep. We went all over the South in that truck."

"You and your mother and father?"

"My dad and I."

"What were you doing, driving all over the South?"

"My dad sold medicine."

"What kind?"

"Something to make you strong and keep you from getting sick."

"Did you take it?"

"No. I guess it wasn't any good."

She had never heard him talk much about himself before. She wanted him to go on.

"Was it fun living in a truck?"

"Fun? I wouldn't say so. Riding along was all right. Sometimes my dad and I stopped close to the woods, and that was all right, too. But I never liked it when we were in town selling medicine. Dad would play the mouth harp, and he made me sing. He wanted me to dance a jig, too, but I never could."

She tried to imagine Al as a little boy. She couldn't at all. "Why did he want you to sing and dance?" she asked.

"To draw a crowd. When there was a crowd, he sold medicine. We didn't stay anywhere very long. Except once. We stayed in one place six months. My dad did farm work, and I went to school."

He told her about the school. It was just outside a town. The teacher was Miss Miller. The schoolhouse had only one room.

"There was this big stove," he said, "and that winter I kept the fire going. Miss Miller never had to carry coal when I was there."

"Did you like her?" asked Sarah Ida. "Was she a good teacher?"

"Best teacher I ever had. Of course, she was just about the *only* one. I hadn't been to school much, but she took time to show me things. Do teachers still give medals in school?"

"Sometimes. Not very often."

"Miss Miller gave medals. They were all alike. Every one had a star on it. At the end of school you got one if you were the best in reading or spelling or writing or whatever it was. Everybody wanted a medal, but I knew I'd never get one because I wasn't the best in anything. And at the end of school, you know what happened?"

"What?"

"She called my name. The others all thought it was a joke. But she wasn't laughing. She said, 'Al wins a medal for building the best fires.'"

"And it *wasn't* a joke?" asked Sarah Ida.

"No. She gave me the medal. One of the big boys said, 'You better keep that, Al, because it's the only one you'll ever get.'"

"And did you keep it?"

He held up his watch chain. Something was hanging from it—something that looked like a worn, old coin.

"That's what you won?" asked Sarah Ida.

He nodded.

"That's a medal?" she said. "That little old piece of tin?"

She shouldn't have said it. As soon as the words were out, she was sorry.

Al sat very still. He looked into the street. A moment before, he had been a friend. Now he was a stranger.

He said, "Rain's stopped. For a while, anyway."

He slid out of his chair. She got up, too. "I—" she began.

He dragged the folding door across the stand and locked up.

"Go on. Run," he said. "Maybe you can get home before the rain starts again."

She stood there. "I didn't mean what you think I did," she said. "That medal—it doesn't matter if it's tin or silver or gold. It doesn't matter *what* it's made of, if it's something you like. I said the wrong thing, but it wasn't what I *meant*. I—" He had his back to her. She didn't think he was listening. She said, *"Listen* to me!"

He turned around. "You like ice cream?"

"Yes," she said.

"Come on. I'll buy you a cone."

She went with him, around the corner to Pearl's Ice Cream Shack.

"What kind?" he asked.

"Chocolate," she said.

They sat on a bench inside the Shack and ate their chocolate cones.

"It's raining again," he said.

"Yes," she said.

Then they were quiet, while they listened to the rain. And she was happy because the stranger was gone and Al was back.

Reader's Response ~ During the summer, Sarah Ida gets to know Al by working with him. How would you feel about having a boss like Al?

Library Link ~ *If you want to find out what happens to Sarah Ida when the summer is over, read the rest of the book* Shoeshine Girl *by Clyde Robert Bulla.*

The Land of the Free

Some writers capture the dynamic spirit of America in words.

What are some elements of that lively spirit?

JOHNS, Jasper. FLAG (1954–55; dated on reverse 1955). Encaustic, oil and collage on fabric mounted on plywood, 42 1/4 x 60 5/8". Collection, The Museum of Modern Art, New York. Gift of Phillip Johnson in honor of Alfred H. Barr, Jr. Photograph © 1989 The Museum of Modern Art, New York.

Theme Books for

The Land of the Free

*H*ow has our courage, determination, hard work, and standing up for what we believe in made America what it is today?

❖ What is it like to immigrate to America from China? For Shirley Temple Wong, it's fascinating! But can she fit in *and* keep her Chinese heritage? Experience Shirley's new life in Bette Bao Lord's *In the Year of the Boar and Jackie Robinson.*

❖ Little Wolf has heard a legend about buffaloes that rise up from the middle of a great lake. In *Where the Buffaloes Begin* by Olaf Baker, Little Wolf's curiosity about the legend gets the best of him. He must discover for himself if the ancient story is true or not.

❖ In *George Washington Wasn't Always Old* by Alice Fleming, George acts like any other boy—riding horses, going to school, teasing his sister. But how did he grow up to become our nation's first president?

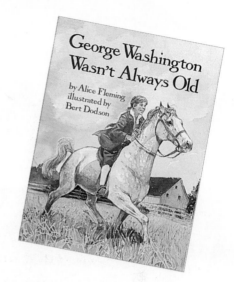

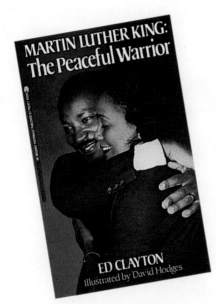

❖ Through courage and determination, Martin Luther King, Jr., became one of America's greatest leaders. Read *Martin Luther King: The Peaceful Warrior* by Ed Clayton to learn how this great man inspired not only our nation, but the entire world.

More Books to Enjoy

Ben and Me by Robert Lawson
The Pilgrims of Plimoth by Marcia Sewall
The Double Life of Pocahontas by Jean Fritz
Ida Early Comes over the Mountain by Robert Burch

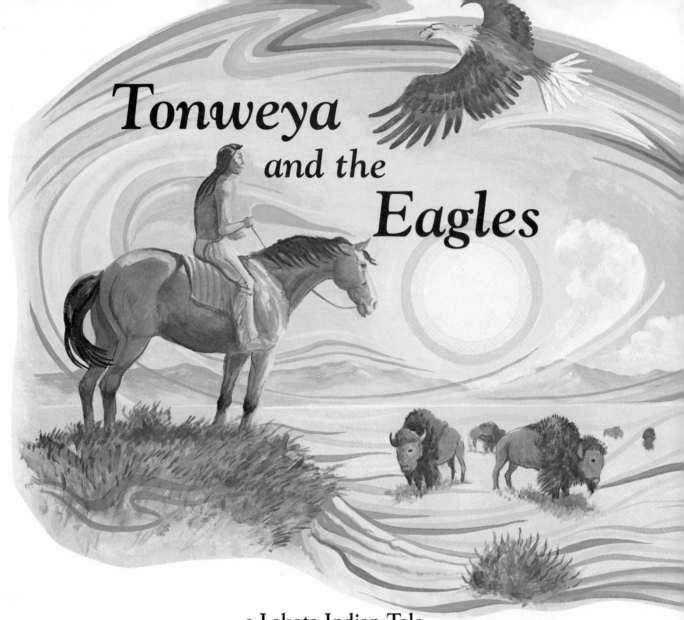

Tonweya
and the
Eagles

a Lakota Indian Tale
retold by Rosebud Yellow Robe

The red-winged eagle represents bravery to the Lakota. One day when Chano, a Lakota boy, and his father, Tasinagi, were out riding, Chano caught sight of a pair of these eagles, the sacred birds of Tonweya. In the following legend, Tasinagi relates to his son how the eagles became sacred to the great chief and medicine man, Tonweya.

AMERICAN

LIBRARY

ASSOCIATION

1979

It was the summer when the big ball of fire fell from the sky. A band of Lakotas were camping just about where we are now. Among them was a young man whose name was Tonweya.[1] He was not only good to look upon, but he was a great runner and hunter. He was very brave in the face of danger. Everyone said that someday he would be a chief. Brave and good chiefs are always needed in every tribe.

One day Tonweya went out hunting. He found a small herd of buffalo grazing near the hills and picking out a young fat cow sent an arrow straight into her heart. While he was skinning the buffalo, he noticed a large eagle circling above him. Watching her flight he saw that she settled on a ledge of rock projecting from a high, steep cliff about a quarter mile away. Tonweya knew there must be a nest there.

[1]Tonweya (tōn wā´ yə)

153

He was determined to find it. If there were young eaglets, he could capture them and raise them for their feathers.

He looked carefully at the ledge. He saw it would be impossible to climb up to it from the plain below. The only way was from above and getting down would be very dangerous. After skinning the buffalo, Tonweya cut the green hide into one long narrow strip. Then he stretched and twisted the strip through the dust until he had a long strong rope of hide.

Coiling this about him, he made his way to the tip of the cliff right above the eagle's nest on the ledge. Fastening one end of this rawhide rope to a jack pine, he let the other fall over the ledge. Looking down he saw that it hung within a few feet of the nest.

His plan was to slide down the rope and tie the eaglets to the end. Then after he had pulled himself up again, he could draw them up after him. Great honor would come to him. A pair of captive eagles would supply feathers for many warriors.

Tonweya carefully lowered himself over the edge of the cliff and soon stood on the ledge. There were two beautiful young eaglets in the nest, full feathered, though not yet able to fly. He tied them to his rope and prepared to climb up. But just as he placed his weight on the rope, to his great surprise it fell down beside him. The green hide had been slipping at the knot where he had tied it to the tree; when he pulled on it to go up again, the knot came loose and down came the rope.

Tonweya realized immediately that he was trapped. Only Wakan-tanka,[2] the Great Mystery, could save him from a slow death by starvation and thirst. He looked below him. There was a sheer drop of many hundreds of feet with not even the slightest projection by which he might climb down. When he tried to climb up, he could find neither handhold nor foothold. Waŋbli[3] had chosen well the place for a nest.

Despite his brave heart terror gripped Tonweya. He stood looking off in the direction he knew his people to be. He cried out, 'Ma hiyopo! Ma hiyopo![4] Help me!' but only the echo of his own voice answered.

[2]Wakan-tanka (wa´ kän täng´ kä)
[3]Waŋbli (wän´ blē)
[4]Ma hiyopo (mä´ hē yō´ pō)

As the sun was setting, the mother eagle returned to her nest. She screamed in rage when she saw a man with her eaglets. Round and round she flew. Now and then she would charge with lightning speed toward Tonweya and the young birds. The two eaglets flapped their wings wildly and called out to her. Finally in despair the mother eagle made one more swoop toward her nest, and then screaming defiantly, flew off and disappeared. Night fell and the stars came out. Tonweya was alone on the ledge with the two little birds.

When the sun came up, Tonweya was very tired. He had not slept during the night. The ledge was so narrow, he was afraid he might roll off if he fell asleep. The sun rose high in the heavens and then started its descent into the west. Soon it would be night. Tonweya looked forward with dread to the lonely vigil he must again keep. He was very hungry and so terribly thirsty.

The second day Tonweya noticed a small spruce growing in a cleft of the rocks some four feet above him. He tied a piece of his rope to this tree and he fastened the other end around his waist. That way even if he stumbled, he would not fall off the ledge. More important still, he could chance some sleep, which he needed badly.

The third day passed as the others had; heat, hunger, unquenchable thirst. The hope that some of his people might come in search of him was gone. Even if they came, they would never think of looking for him on the cliffs. The mother of the eaglets did not return. Tonweya's presence had frightened her away.

By this time the two eaglets, seeing that Tonweya had no intention of hurting them, had made friends with him. They allowed Tonweya to touch them at will. Tonweya could see that they were as hungry as he was, so taking out his knife he cut small pieces from the rawhide rope and fed them. This act of kindness removed the last vestige of fear they might have had. They played all about him. They allowed him to hold them aloft. They flapped their wings bravely as he lifted them toward the sun. As he felt the upward pull of their wings, there came to him an idea. Since he had no wings of his own, why could he not make use of the wings of his eagle brothers? He raised his arms toward the sky and called upon Wakan-tanka for wisdom.

The night of the third day, the one on which he had fed the eaglets for the first time, was raw and chill. When Tonweya stretched out for what little sleep he could get, he shivered with the cold. As if understanding his need, the two little eaglets left their nest and coming over to where he lay nestled their warm, fluffy bodies close beside him. In a few moments Tonweya was asleep.

While he was asleep, he dreamed. In his dream Wakan-tanka spoke to him. He told him to be brave, the two eaglets would save him. Tonweya awoke suddenly. The eagles were still beside him. As they felt him move, they nestled even closer to him. He placed his arms around them. He knew that his time to die had not yet come. He would once more see his people. He was no longer afraid.

For days thereafter Tonweya fed the rawhide rope to his eagle friends. Luckily it was a long rope, for it was, of course, almost a whole buffalo hide. But while the eaglets thrived on it and grew larger and stronger each day, Tonweya grew thinner and weaker. It rained one day and water gathered in the hollows of the rocks on the ledge. Still he was very hungry and thirsty. He tried to think only of caring for the eaglets.

Each day Tonweya would hold them up by their legs and let them try their wings. Each day the pull on his arms grew stonger. Soon it was so powerful it almost lifted him from his feet. He knew the time was coming for him to put his idea into action. He decided he must do it quickly, for weak as he was he would be unable to do it after a few more days.

The last of the rawhide was gone, the last bit of water on the ledge was drunk. Tonweya was so weak, he could hardly stand. With an effort he dragged himself upright and called his eagle brothers to him. Standing on the edge of the ledge he called to Wakan-tanka for help. He grasped the eaglets' legs in each hand and closing his eyes he jumped.

For a moment he felt himself falling, falling. Then he felt the pull on his arms. Opening his eyes he saw that the two eagles were flying easily. They seemed to be supporting his weight with little effort. In a moment they had reached the ground. Tonweya lay there too exhausted, too weak to move. The eagles remained by his side guarding him.

After resting awhile Tonweya slowly made his way to a little stream nearby. He drank deeply of its cool water. A few berries were growing on the bushes there. He ate them ravenously. Strengthened by even this little food and water, he started off in the direction of the camp. His progress was slow, for he was compelled to rest many times. Always the eaglets remained by his side guarding him.

On the way he passed the spot where he had killed the buffalo. The coyotes and vultures had left nothing but bones. However his bow and arrows were just where he had left them. He managed to kill a rabbit upon which he and his eagle friends feasted. Late in the afternoon he reached the camp, only to find that his people had moved on. It was late. He was very tired so he decided to stay there that night.

He soon fell asleep, the two eagles pressing close beside him all night.

The sun was high in the sky when Tonweya awoke. The long sleep had given him back much strength. After once more giving thanks to Wakan-tanka for his safety he set out after his people. For two days he followed their trail. He lived on the roots and berries he found along the way and what little game he could shoot. He shared everything with his eagle brothers, who followed him. Sometimes they flew overhead, sometimes they walked behind him, and now and then they rested on his shoulders.

Well along in the afternoon of the second day he caught up with the band. At first they were frightened when they saw him. Then they welcomed him with joy.

They were astonished at his story. The two eagles who never left Tonweya amazed them. They were glad that they had always been kind to Waŋbli and had never killed them.

The time came when the eagles were able to hunt food for themselves and though everyone expected them to fly away, they did not. True, they would leave with the dawn on hunting forays, but when the evening drew near, they would fly back fearlessly and enter Tonweya's tipi, where they passed the night. Everyone marveled at the sight.

But eagles, like men, should be free. Tonweya, who by now understood their language, told them they could go. They

were to enjoy the life the Great Mystery, Wakan-tanka, had planned for them. At first they refused. But when Tonweya said if he ever needed their help he would call for them, they consented.

The tribe gave a great feast in their honor. In gratitude for all they had done Tonweya painted the tips of their wings a bright red to denote courage and bravery. He took them up on a high mountain. He held them once more toward the sky and bidding them good-bye released them. Spreading their wings they soared away. Tonweya watched them until they disappeared in the eye of the sun.

Many snows have passed and Tonweya has long been dead. But now and then the eagles with the red-tipped wings are still seen. There are always two of them and they never show any fear of people. Some say they are the original sacred eagles of Tonweya, for the Waŋbli lives for many snows. Some think they are the children of the sacred ones. It is said whoever sees the red-tipped wings of the eagles is sure of their protection as long as he is fearless and brave. And only the fearless and brave may wear the eagle feather tipped with red.

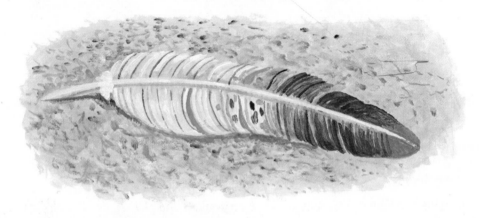

Reader's Response ∾ What words best describe Tonweya in this story? Which one makes him seem most heroic to you?

Library Link ∾ *If you found Tonweya's adventure fascinating, read more in the book* Tonweya and the Eagles and Other Lakota Indian Tales *retold by Rosebud Yellow Robe.*

Robert Freeman

"Art is an ingrained gift that always stirred inside of me."

The spirit of the drawings in "Tonweya and the Eagles" speaks of the illustrator's Native American roots as well as his wish to communicate through his art.

Robert Freeman was born and raised on an Indian Reservation in the western United States where he lived with his mother and sister. During his youth, he always made his own toys, including trains, boats, swords, and whatever else he wanted to play with. The desire to create has never left him.

Despite a lack of encouragement, he pursued his interest in art. Mr. Freeman began to paint using the abstract style of the painter Jackson Pollock as his model. When a friend told him that painting realistically was the sign of a true artist, Mr. Freeman decided to teach himself to draw that way.

In addition to his work as an illustrator, Mr. Freeman is a muralist, sculptor, cartoonist, and printmaker. His work has been exhibited all over the United States and has earned many top awards in fine arts, including several gold medals.

Mr. Freeman urges all children to pursue their natural artistic instincts because "art is sometimes the only clear way to express life and make statements."

You can learn about the American spirit by reading Robert Frost's poems, which celebrate nature, or by listening to the effortless grace of Ella Fitzgerald (inset) singing.

What Is An
American?

by Loren Gary

What is an American? That is a question almost too big to answer.

What is an American? Whom do we mean when we speak of Americans? There are the Native Americans whose ancestors inhabited the land before the European explorers. An American is the descendant of the early colonists who settled the East and Southwest. An American is the great-great-great grandchild of the rugged western pioneers. An American is the grandchild of immigrants from anywhere on the globe. An American is a brand-new citizen from another land.

What is an American? There are so many millions of Americans—the question has as many answers as there are people in this great land.

What is an American? Who can answer the question best? A young person? An old person? A factory worker? A traveling salesman? A dreamer? A speaker of English or Spanish or Yiddish or Khmer or Polish or Swahili or Swedish or Arabic or Creole or Japanese? A housewife? A teacher? An inventor? A basketball player? A farmer? A legislator? An artist? . . .

An artist! Perhaps an artist can answer the question. After all, a work of art can often mirror the artist's society. A work of art can help people see who they are.

What is an American? Here are some American artists: architects, writers, and musicians. Think of each artist's work as holding up a little mirror to America, each mirror reflecting a part of the answer.

Architects

Frank Lloyd Wright was born in the 1860s in Richland Center, Wisconsin. He was the son of Welsh parents who had immigrated to the United States in the 1840s. Even as a boy, Wright knew that he wanted to become an architect. At the age of nineteen, he went to work in an architectural firm in Chicago, Illinois. Six years later, he decided to design buildings on his own.

Wright believed that American architecture needed to break free from traditional designs. At the time, most American architects were building homes that looked like massive Greek or Roman temples, or like the towering cathedrals of the Middle Ages. Wright thought that houses should be built on a smaller, more human scale. He also believed that a building should be as close to nature as possible. It should have plenty of open spaces. It should blend in with its natural surroundings and should even be built out of materials taken from those surroundings.

Frank Lloyd Wright (inset) gave the Robie House a low, horizontal design to make it seem closer to its surroundings.

In 1909, Wright had a chance to put his ideas into practice when he designed a house in Chicago for Frederic Carleton Robie. Wright made the Robie House long and horizontal, rather than tall and vertical. He eliminated interior walls and ran rooms together, so that it was possible to look through from front to back with nothing blocking the view. Such a design, Wright reasoned, would be more in keeping with the openness of the Midwestern prairies which stretched out to the south of the house when it was built.

Frank Lloyd Wright worked as an architect for over fifty years. By the time of his death in 1959, he had permanently changed American architecture with his fresh visions and his bold designs.

I. M. Pei is another bold designer. In fact, he is one of the most acclaimed architects in America. But Pei's style is very different from Wright's. Pei is a promoter of modernist architecture, which can be recognized by its simplicity of design and by the use of such building materials as steel and glass.

Pei was born in 1917, in Canton, China. He came to America in 1935 to attend college. When he graduated in 1939, he was unable to return to China because of the outbreak of World War II. So he stayed and worked as an architect. Later he became a professor at the Graduate School of Design at Harvard University in Cambridge, Massachusetts. In 1955, he formed his own architectural firm.

Pei's firm designed the John Hancock Building in Boston. This striking tower, which was completed in 1976,

The Hancock Building, by I. M. Pei (inset) and Partners.

rises some sixty stories high. No two sides have the same length, so the building looks noticeably different depending on the angle from which a person views it. The building's exterior is made of pale blue glass. On a clear day, the surrounding buildings can be seen brilliantly reflected in the Hancock's glass sides.

Laurinda Spear and Bernardo Fort-Brescia, like I. M. Pei, consider themselves modernists. Spear was born in Miami. Fort-Brescia was born in Peru. He came to America to attend school and stayed here to work after he had finished. The two are married and make their home in Miami. Their firm, Arquitectonica—the Spanish word for "architectural"—is known for buildings that imaginatively use color and design.

In 1980, Spear and Fort-Brescia designed Atlantis, a condominium development in Miami. One side of the building is curved. A prism-shaped structure, painted bright red, sits on top of the roof. In the middle of the building and twelve stories up is a hole known as the "skycourt." With a whirl-pool, a spiral staircase, and a palm tree, it is a place where the residents of the building can relax.

Atlantis, designed by Spear and Fort-Brescia, has a red prism on top and a skycourt (inset) in the middle.

Writers

Laura Ingalls Wilder was born in Pepin, Wisconsin, in 1867. She and her family lived in a log cabin at the edge of a large wood. In later years, they moved to Kansas, Minnesota, and eventually to the Dakota Territory.

Wilder wrote eight books that tell the story of her life and travels. At least one of the books, *Little House on the Prairie*, is probably familiar to most Americans. The books tell of the hard work that was required to build a new life out on the frontier. They bring alive the hard times that the pioneers

Laura Ingalls Wilder's Kansas home has been rebuilt on its original site.

endured, but they also record the simple joys of farm life and celebrate the courage and independence of the pioneer spirit. Laura Ingalls Wilder died in 1957, in Ohio.

Robert Frost was not a pioneer, but he knew about the self-reliance that goes with rural life. He was born in San Francisco but spent most of his life in New England.

For Frost, something as ordinary as watching woods fill up with snow was an occasion for poetry.

Frost's poetry captures the simple beauty of New England.

He started writing poetry early on. One of his most famous volumes is entitled *North of Boston*. Frost's poems show a deep love of nature. Their earthy wisdom and simple language reflect the lean and hardy New England spirit. Frost was awarded the Pulitzer Prize for poetry four times. He died in 1963.

August Wilson, Pulitzer Prize-winning playwright

August Wilson says he got his start as a writer in 1965, when he wrote an essay on Robert Frost. Today, people are writing about Wilson. He is one of the most respected playwrights in America. He was born in 1945 in Pittsburgh. Later he moved to St. Paul, Minnesota, where he has written some of his best plays.

Wilson's best-known plays include: *Joe Turner's Come and Gone, The Piano Lesson,* and *Fences.* For *Fences* he was awarded the 1987 Pulitzer Prize for drama. *Fences* belongs to a series of ten plays that Wilson plans to write. His goal is to portray the history of black life in the twentieth century. In his view, "black Americans have the most dramatic story of all mankind to tell." For Wilson's characters, the struggle to maintain dignity continues even when dreams have been shattered.

Musicians

Jazz is perhaps America's greatest gift to the world of music. Jazz is not so much a kind of music as it is a way of playing music. Improvisation is an important part of jazz. Jazz musicians often improvise, or make up notes, while they are playing or singing. And when it comes to improvisation, few people can match Ella Fitzgerald.

Ella Fitzgerald has been a jazz singer for over fifty years.

Ella Fitzgerald has been singing for over fifty years. No other jazz singer has been able to sing so well for so long. Fitzgerald is a master at "scat" singing—improvising with the voice. Scatting is done by making up and singing nonsense syllables to go with the music. For instance, instead of humming a few notes, a scat singer might sing, "De zat zoo zat, de zat zoo zat." Hearing Ella Fitzgerald scat is a very special musical experience. Her voice is so smooth, it's almost like honey.

When Fitzgerald was just a teenager growing up in New York City's Harlem in 1934, a drummer and bandleader named Chick Webb heard her at an amateur singing contest. He invited her to join his jazz band. Five years later Ella Fitzgerald was a star, and she has been shining ever since.

Modern composer Aaron Copland, who died in 1990, was no stranger to jazz. Works such as his "Jazz Concerto" for piano show very clearly that he understood what jazz is all about. At the time Copland composed the concerto, jazz was considered to be merely a popular art form—not the kind of material to be used by serious composers. But Copland's musical genius enabled him to use that popular art form in a more formal composition.

Copland's parents were Russian Jews who immigrated to New York City at the beginning of the twentieth century. Copland himself was born in Brooklyn in 1900. He studied music for several years in France, where he learned to compose according to the latest theories. At the same time, he experimented with adding bits of popular songs and folk music to his compositions. The results were a fresh and powerful blend of the traditional and the modern.

What is an American? That is a question with about 245,000,000 answers! Like the artists we've read about, Americans come from many different backgrounds and have many different interests. Despite such diversity, these artists' work points to characteristics that we all may share.

An American may love our natural world as did Robert Frost and Frank Lloyd Wright. An American may share with Laura Ingalls Wilder an adventurous and pioneering spirit. An American may have the courage to break with tradition and explore new ideas as I. M. Pei, Laurinda Spear, and Bernardo Fort-Brescia have done with their buildings. An American may have the lively creativity of Ella Fitzgerald scat singing, or may combine the old and the new as Aaron Copland did. An American can be one who cherishes the dignity of the individual as August Wilson does.

What is an American? American artists can suggest some answers. Fresh, proud, independent, and bold—their work is a mirror of the American spirit.

Reader's Response ∾ You have read about several architects, writers, and musicians. Which one of these individuals would you most like to meet? Why?

As American As...

In the United States, we are fortunate to enjoy the contributions of many different cultures. One of the many ways we share in each other's culture is through food. On the menu below are some of the foods people from many lands have brought to the U.S. How many of these have you tried?

MENU

APPETIZERS

antipasto
Italy

egg rolls
China

empanadas
South America

BREADS

soda bread
Ireland

pita
Middle East

injera
Ethiopia

MAIN COURSE

tandoori chicken
India

borscht
Eastern Europe

sushi
Japan

paella
Spain

DESSERT

baklava
Greece

leechee nuts
Southeast Asia

torte
France

173

THE WHITE HOUSE

by June Swanson

This engraving shows the White House partially repaired after the 1814 British attack.

On June 18, 1812, President James Madison approved an act of Congress declaring war on Great Britain. The British had been stopping American ships on the high seas and illegally searching them. They often carried off American sailors who they claimed were deserters from the British navy. The United States felt it had to put a stop to this, so Congress declared war.

In the summer of 1814, a British fleet sailed into the Chesapeake Bay. A large party of soldiers went ashore. The American forces were not strong enough to hold them back, and the British were soon marching on Washington, D.C. They burned much of the city, including the Capitol building, the Library of Congress, and the president's house.

President Madison was away at the time on an inspection tour of American troops, but through the bravery and quick thinking of his wife, Dolley, many of America's historical documents and other items were saved. Into an old wagon she loaded her husband's official papers, the original Declaration of Independence (which had been framed and placed under glass), silver from the dining room, and a famous portrait of George Washington painted by Gilbert Stuart.

Dolley Madison then dressed herself and her maid in clothes that a farmer's wife and her servant might have worn. She took along a friend and a soldier who also dressed as farmers. In this way they were able to leave the burning city in safety.

After the burning of Washington, D.C., the British moved on to Baltimore, but that city was defended by Fort McHenry. Both the British army and the British naval fleet were driven back, and Baltimore was saved.

As soon as it was safe, members of the U.S. Government returned to Washington, and President Madison ordered the rebuilding of the city. The president's house had been badly burned. Only the blackened shell of its walls remained standing. The house probably would have been completely destroyed if the fire hadn't been put out by a summer thunderstorm during the night of the burning.

As it was, the president's house had to be rebuilt practically from the bottom up. The inside had been totally destroyed, and all of the furnishings were gone. The rebuilding took almost four years.

For a few months the Madisons lived in a private house just west of the old president's house. Then in 1815 they moved to a house on the corner of Pennsylvania Avenue and 19th Street, where they lived until the end of Madison's term of office.

The White House is shown here, in the background, as it appeared immediately after the British attack.

176

National Portrait Gallery, Smithsonian Institution

The Pennsylvania Academy of Fine Arts

Above, **this famous portrait of George Washington was among the items saved from burning by Dolley Madison,** *right.*

When James Monroe became president in 1817, the house still was not ready. The Monroes lived in their own house in Washington for nine months. Finally the president's house was finished, and on New Year's Day in 1818, President and Mrs. Monroe held a reception to reopen it. At that time its name was officially declared to be the Executive Mansion.

Because workmen had applied numerous coats of white paint to hide the smoke-blackened walls, the outside of the Executive Mansion was now a dazzling white. For this reason, in spite of its new official name, it was often called simply the white house.

Its official name changed several times throughout the next 80 years, to the President's Mansion, the President's Home, and even the President's Palace. To most people, though, it was still the white house.

Then in 1902 President Theodore Roosevelt authorized this popular name as the official title of the president's home, and it has been the White House ever since.

An 1801 painting shows part of Washington, D.C., and surroundings.

Designing Washington, D.C.

from Benjamin Banneker,
Genius of Early America
by Lillie Patterson

On a blustery afternoon, Benjamin Banneker rode down the hill to Ellicott's Lower Mills. He tied his horse to a hitching post in front of the store and hurried inside.

George Ellicott rushed to meet him, waving a letter in welcome. "Here it is," Ellicott called out, his eyes reflecting the excitement in his voice. "Major Ellicott writes that he will come in a few days to take you with him."

"It seems beyond belief," Banneker said in a voice equally animated. "This will be the greatest adventure of my life."

The two men moved to a small room that served as an office. Sitting near a stove that glowed because of the icy chill, they talked about the letter that had come from Major Andrew Ellicott. This was the same Andrew who as a boy had helped his father, Joseph Ellicott, design the four-faced clock. Andrew Ellicott had now become the most notable surveyor in the nation. Just the year before, he had surveyed the western boundary of the state of New York. The letter told of a far more dramatic assignment.

"Major Ellicott's experience will serve him well," Banneker mused. "President Washington chose wisely in giving him the commission."

"George Washington made another wise choice in making you Andrew's assistant." George Ellicott rubbed his chin in a reflective mood. "This will be the first time in our nation's history that a man of your race has received a presidential appointment."

"I know." Banneker nodded in agreement. "I will try to do justice to this high honor."

"You will," George reassured him. "Remember, it was none other than Thomas Jefferson who urged the President to appoint you."

The voices of Banneker and George Ellicott quickened as they talked over the events that had led to the receipt of the letter. The surveying task was part of a new undertaking by the young United States. Until this time the Congress had temporarily been sitting in first one city, then another—eight cities in all. Now Congress decided that the nation should have a permanent capital city.

But where? Congress left the choice to the President. In 1790 George Washington selected a centrally located spot near the majestic Potomac River, between the states of Maryland and Virginia. Each state donated a parcel of land for the project.

This ten-mile-square federal district had to be surveyed before the city could be built. In January, 1791, President Washington decreed that this survey should be made, and Andrew Ellicott was the logical choice.

Ellicott, in turn, needed an assistant with skills in both astronomy and mathematics. The President and Thomas Jefferson, who was then secretary of state, readily agreed that Benjamin Banneker should be appointed for this position.

The recalling of these events that February day ended with Banneker and George Ellicott shaking hands gravely. They knew that the task ahead was a difficult challenge. The results could affect the development and the destiny of the country. A dynamic capital city, Americans hoped, would unite the various sections of the country, resulting in a strong union.

Suddenly, a look of consternation crossed Banneker's face. "My almanac! I must complete calculations for my almanac."

"Your country comes first," George Ellicott said firmly. "Besides, I know that nothing is going to keep you from taking on this challenge."

So it was that Benjamin Banneker rode home and began preparing for his new adventure. Minta and Molly shared his pride in the assignment. Their oldest sister was now dead, but her son, John Henden, kept in touch with Banneker. John Henden promised to keep an eye on the place while his uncle was away. Molly's son, Greenbury Morton, agreed to care for the animals and the orchard.

What should he take with him? Banneker pondered this problem as he packed. His sisters came to wash and iron his best linen shirts and handkerchiefs to perfection.

Elizabeth Brooke Ellicott, George's young bride, came to Banneker's cottage and helped him pick out the coats and trousers she felt would be suitable. "You will be meeting some of the most distinguished leaders in the nation," she told him. "We want you to be as handsome as any man among them."

Benjamin did look handsome when he joined Andrew Ellicott at the Mills a few days later. The two men made a stunning pair as they rode away on horseback. Ellicott, at thirty-eight, was dressed in heavy woolen clothes, a close-fitting vest, and a tricorn hat. Banneker, a few months from sixty, was dressed in a neat, plain suit of heavy broadcloth. A broad-brimmed hat covered his curly hair, now turning gray.

Surveying instruments and luggage were strapped behind their saddles.

They took the turnpike for the forty-mile trip, making a stop along the way for food and a brief rest. By the time they reached Alexandria, Virginia, they were soaked from the icy rain that had been falling steadily. They found lodging at a popular inn looking out on the busiest part of the town. Alexandria was then a thriving tobacco-shipping port.

Illustration of compass used during the initial survey of Washington, D.C.

The next morning, Banneker went out to explore the site of the new city. He rode through wooded areas, broken here and there by cleared spaces of cornfields and tobacco farms and a few isolated farmhouses and fruit orchards. Deep in thought, Banneker tramped up and down the hills. His imagination saw far beyond the bogs and rough hills, the woodland and wild marshes. "The spot is perfect for a magnificent city," he told Major Ellicott.

Losing no time, Banneker and Ellicott set to work in the rain and fog. They hired workmen to chop down trees and bushes. They bought packhorses, equipment, and supplies. They set up a temporary camp. The President wanted the survey completed in a hurry so that plans for building the city could be approved.

Banneker and Ellicott made a good team. Ellicott decided to supervise the workmen in the field, while Banneker made the astronomical observations and mathematical calculations they needed. Their measurements must be precise. Jefferson said in a letter to Ellicott that the lines "must run with all the accuracy of which your art is susceptible."

Since the measurement of angles plays an important part in surveying, the two men needed a knowledge of geometry, trigonometry, and practical astronomy. They had to make difficult computations in order to determine such things as latitude, time, longitude, and azimuths (angles measured in a clockwise direction from any meridian).

And these computations were based upon observations made of the sun, stars, and other celestial objects. In making these observations, the heavenly bodies are assumed to be situated on the surface of a huge imaginary "celestial sphere" whose center is at the center of the earth. So, the measurement of horizontal and vertical angles could be done in relation to celestial objects.

This required an observatory tent. Ellicott and Banneker placed the tent upon the highest

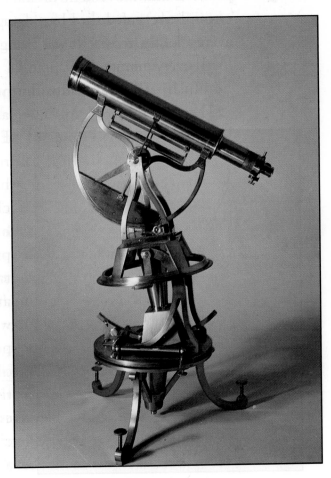

Equatorial Telescope ca. 1775

America the Beautiful

by Katharine Lee Bates

O beautiful for spacious skies,
For amber waves of grain,
For purple mountain majesties
Above the fruited plain!
America! America!
God shed His grace on thee,
And crown thy good with brotherhood
From sea to shining sea!

O beautiful for pilgrim feet,
Whose stern, impassioned stress
A thoroughfare for freedom beat
Across the wilderness!
America! America!
God mend thine every flaw,
Confirm thy soul in self-control,
Thy liberty in law!

O beautiful for heroes proved
In liberating strife,
Who more than self their country loved,
And mercy more than life!
America! America!
May God thy gold refine,
Till all success be nobleness,
And every gain divine!

O beautiful for patriot dream
That sees beyond the years
Thine alabaster cities gleam
Undimmed by human tears!
America! America!
God shed His grace on thee,
And crown thy good with brotherhood
From sea to shining sea!

The Thanksgiving Play

from *Felita*
by Nicholasa Mohr

*Felita was glad when her family decided
to move back to the old neighborhood. She
would be near her friends again, especially
her best friend, Gigi. Felita's grandmother,
who always seemed to understand her,
would also be close by.*

A wonderful thing happened this new school year. Gigi, Consuela,[1] Paquito,[2] and I were all going into the fourth grade, and we were put in the same class. It had never happened before. Once I was in the same class with Consuela, and last year Gigi and Paquito were together. But this—it was too good to be true! Of course knowing Gigi and I were in the same class made me the happiest.

Our teacher, Miss Lovett, was friendly and laughed easily. In early October, after we had all settled into our class and gotten used to the routine of school once more, Miss Lovett told us that this year our class was going to put on a play for Thanksgiving. The play we were going to perform was based on a poem by Henry Wadsworth Longfellow, called "The Courtship of Miles Standish." It was about the Pilgrims and how they lived when they first landed in America.

We were all so excited about the play. Miss Lovett called for volunteers to help with the sets and costumes.

[1]Consuela (kōn swe´ lə)

[2]Paquito (pä kē´ tō)

Paquito and I agreed to help with the sets. Consuela was going to work on makeup. Gigi had not volunteered for anything. When we asked her what she was going to do, she shrugged and didn't answer.

Miss Lovett said we could all audition for the different parts in the play. I was really interested in being Priscilla. She is the heroine. Both Captain Miles Standish and the handsome, young John Alden are in love with her. She is the most beautiful maiden in Plymouth, Massachusetts.

That's where the Pilgrims used to live. I told my friends how much I would like to play that part. Everyone said I would be perfect... except Gigi. She said that it was a hard part to do, and maybe I wouldn't be able to play it. I really got annoyed and asked her what she meant.

"I just don't think you are right to play Priscilla. That's all," she said.

"What do you mean by right?" I asked. But Gigi only shrugged and didn't say another word. She was beginning to get on my nerves.

Auditions for the parts were going to start Tuesday. Lots of kids had volunteered to audition. Paquito said he would try out for the brave Captain Miles Standish. Consuela said she was too afraid to get up in front of everybody and make a fool of herself. Gigi didn't show any interest in the play and refused to even talk to us about it. Finally the day came for the girls to read for the part of Priscilla. I was so excited I could hardly wait. Miss Lovett had given us some lines to study. I had practiced real hard. She called out all the names of those who were going to read. I was surprised when I heard her call out "Georgina Mercado." I didn't even know Gigi wanted to try out for Priscilla. I looked at Gigi, but she ignored me. We began reading. It was my turn. I was very nervous and kept forgetting my lines. I had to look down at the script a whole lot. Several other girls were almost as nervous as I was. Then it was Gigi's turn. She recited the part almost by heart. She hardly looked at the script. I noticed that she was wearing one of her best dresses. She had never looked that good in school before. When she finished, everybody clapped. It was obvious that she was the best one.

Miss Lovett made a fuss.

"You were just wonderful, Georgina," she said, "made for the part!" Boy, would I have liked another chance. I bet I could have done better than Gigi.

Why hadn't she told me she wanted the part? It's a free country,

John Alden asked you to marry Captain Miles Standish and you said, 'Why don't you speak for yourself, John?' You turned your head like this." Paquito imitated Gigi and closed his eyes. "That was really neat!" Consuela and the others laughed and agreed.

I decided I wasn't walking home with them.

"I have to meet my brothers down by the next street," I said. "I'm splitting. See you." They hardly noticed. Only Consuela said goodbye. The rest just kept on hanging all over Gigi. Big deal, I thought.

Of course walking by myself and watching out for the tough kids was not something I looked forward to. Just last Friday Hilda Gonzales had gotten beat up and had her entire allowance stolen. And at the beginning of the term Paquito had been walking home by himself and gotten mugged. A bunch of big bullies had taken his new schoolbag complete with pencil and pen case, then left him with a swollen lip. No, sir, none of us ever walked home from school alone if we could help it. We knew it wasn't a safe thing to do. Those mean kids never bothered us as long as we stuck together. Carefully I looked

after all. She could read for the same part as me. I wasn't going to stop her! I was really angry at Gigi.

After school everyone was still making a fuss over her. Even Paquito had to open his stupid mouth.

"Oh, man, Gigi!" he said. "You were really good. I liked the part when around to make sure none of the bullies were in sight. Then I put some speed under my feet, took my chances, and headed for home.

Just before all the casting was completed, Miss Lovett offered me a part as one of the Pilgrim women. All I had to do was stand in the background like a zombie. It wasn't even a speaking part.

"I don't get to say one word," I protested.

"Felicidad Maldonado, you are designing the stage sets and you're assistant stage manager. I think that's quite a bit. Besides, all the speaking parts are taken."

"I'm not interested, thank you," I answered.

"You know"—Miss Lovett shook her head—"you can't be the best in everything."

I turned and left. I didn't need to play any part at all. Who cared?

Gigi came over to me the next day with a great big smile all over her face. I just turned away and made believe she wasn't there.

"Felita,³ are you taking the part of the Pilgrim woman?" she asked me in her sweetest voice, just like noth-

ing had happened.

"No," I said, still not looking at her. If she thought I was going to fall all over her like those dummies, she was wasting her time.

"Oh," was all she said, and walked away. Good, I thought. I don't need her one bit!

At home Mami⁴ noticed that something was wrong.

"Felita, what's the matter? You aren't going out at all. And I haven't seen Gigi for quite a while. In fact I haven't seen any of your friends."

"Nothing is the matter, Mami. I just got lots of things to do."

"You're not upset because we couldn't give you a birthday party this year, are you?" Mami asked. "You know how hard the money situation has been for us."

My birthday had been at the beginning of November. We had celebrated with a small cake after dinner, but there had been no party.

"No. It's not that," I said and meant it. Even though I had been a little disappointed, I also knew Mami and Papi⁵ had done the best they could.

"We'll make it up to you next year, Felita, you'll see."

³Felita (fe lē′ tə)

⁴Mami (mä′ mē): mother
⁵Papi (pä′ pē): father

198

"I don't care, Mami. It's not important now."

"You didn't go having a fight with Gigi or something? Did you?"

"Now why would I have a fight with anybody!"

"Don't raise your voice, miss," Mami said. "Sorry I asked. But you just calm down."

The play was going to be performed on the day before Thanksgiving. I made the drawings for most of the scenery. I made a barn, a church, trees and grass, cows, and a horse. I helped the others make a real scarecrow. We used a broom and old clothes. Paquito didn't get the part of Captain Miles Standish, but he made a wonderful fence out of cardboard. It looked just like a real wooden fence. Consuela brought in her mother's old leftover makeup. She did a good job of making up everybody.

By the time we set up the stage, everything looked beautiful. Gigi had tried to talk to me a few times. But I just couldn't be nice back to her. She acted like nothing had happened, like I was supposed to forget she hadn't told me she was going to read for the part! I wasn't going to forget that just because she was now Miss Popularity.

She could go and stay with all her new-found friends for all I cared!

The morning of the play, at breakfast, everybody noticed how excited I was.

"Felita," Papi exclaimed, "stop jumping around like a monkey and eat your breakfast."

"She's all excited about the school play today," Mami said.

"That's right. Are you playing a part in the play?" Papi asked.

"No," I replied.

"But she's done most of the sets. Drawing and designing. Isn't that right, Felita?"

"Mami, it was no big deal."

"That's nice," said Papi. "Tell us about it."

"What kind of sets did you do?" Johnny asked.

"I don't know. Look, I don't want to talk about it."

"Boy, are you touchy today," Tito said with a laugh.

"Leave me alone!" I snapped.

"Okay." Mami stood up. "Enough. Felita, are you finished?" I nodded. "Good. Go to school. When you come back, bring home a better mood. Whatever is bothering you, no need to take it out on us." Quickly I left the table.

"Rosa," I heard Papi say, "sometimes you are too hard on her."

"And sometimes you spoil her, Alberto!" Mami snapped. "I'm not raising fresh kids."

I was glad to get out of there. Who needs them, I thought.

The play was a tremendous hit. Everybody looked wonderful and played their parts really well. The stage was brilliant with the color I had used on my drawings. The background of the countryside, the barn, and just about everything stood out clearly. Ernesto Bratter, the stage manager, said I was a good assistant. I was glad to hear that, because a couple of times I'd had to control my temper on account of his ordering me around. But it had all worked out great.

No doubt about it. Gigi was perfect as Priscilla. Even though the kids clapped and cheered for the entire cast, Gigi got more applause than anybody else. She just kept on taking a whole lot of bows.

Afterward Miss Lovett had a party for our class. We had lots of treats. There was even a record player and we all danced. We had a really good time.

Of course Priscilla, alias Gigi, was the big star. She just couldn't get enough attention. But not from me, that was for sure. After the party Gigi spoke to me.

"Your sets were really great. Everyone said the stage looked wonderful."

"Thanks." I looked away.

"Felita, are you mad at me?"

"Why should I be mad at you?"

"Well, I did get the leading part, but..."

"Big deal," I said "I really don't care."

"You don't? But...I..."

"Look," I said, interrupting her, "I gotta go. I promised my mother I'd get home early. We have to go someplace."

I rushed all the way home. I didn't know why, but I was still furious at Gigi. What was worse was that I was unhappy about having those feelings. Gigi and I had been real close for as far back as I could remember. Not being able to share things with her really bothered me.

We had a great Thanksgiving. The dinner was just delicious. Abuelita[6] brought her flan.[7] Tío Jorge[8] brought lots of ice cream. He always brings us kids a treat when he visits. Sometimes he even brings each one of us a small

[6]Abuelita (ä bwe lē´ tə): grandmother

[7]flan (flän): a special dessert made with custard

[8]Tío Jorge (tē´ ō hōr´ hā): Uncle Jorge

202

gift—a nature book or crayons for me and puzzles or sports magazines for my brothers. He's really very nice to us. One thing about him is that he's sort of quiet and doesn't talk much. Papi says that Tío Jorge has been like that as far back as he can remember.

Abuelita asked me if I wanted to go home with her that evening. Boy, was I happy to get away from Mami. I just couldn't face another day of her asking me questions about Gigi, my friends, and my whole life. It was getting to be too much!

It felt good to be with Abuelita in her apartment. Abuelita never questioned me about anything really personal unless I wanted to talk about it. She just waited, and when she sensed that I was worried or something, then she would ask me. Not like Mami. I love Mami, but she's always trying to find out every little thing that happens to me. With my abuelita sometimes we just sit and stay quiet, not talk at all. That was nice too. We fixed the daybed for me. And then Tío Jorge, Abuelita, and I had more flan as usual.

"Would you like to go to the park with me this Sunday?" Tío Jorge asked me.

"Yes."

"We can go to the zoo and later we can visit the ducks and swans by the lake."

"Great!" I said.

Whenever Tío Jorge took me to the zoo, he would tell me stories about how he, Abuelita, and their brothers and sisters had lived and worked as youngsters taking care of farm animals. These were the only times I ever heard him talk a whole lot.

"It's not just playing, you know," he would say. "Taking care of animals is hard work. Back on our farm in Puerto Rico we worked hard, but we had fun too. Every one of us children had our very own favorite pets. I had a pet goat by the name of Pepe. He used to follow me everywhere." No matter how many times he told me the same stories, I always enjoyed hearing them again.

"Well." Tío Jorge got up. "It's a date then on Sunday, yes?"

"Yes, thank you, Tío Jorge."

"Good night," he said and went off to bed.

Abuelita and I sat quietly for a while, then Abuelita spoke.

"You are getting to be a big girl now, Felita. You just turned nine years old. My goodness! But I still hope you will come to bed with your abuelita for a little while, eh?"

I got into bed and snuggled close to Abuelita. I loved her the best, more than anybody. I hadn't been to stay with her since the summer, and somehow this time things felt different. I noticed how tired Abuelita looked. She wasn't moving as fast as she used to. Also I didn't feel so little next to her anymore.

"Tell me, Felita, how have you been? It seems like a long time since we were together like this." She smiled her wonderful smile at me. Her dark, bright eyes looked deeply into mine. I felt her warmth and happiness.

"I'm okay, Abuelita."

"Tell me about your play at school. Rosa tells me you worked on the stage sets. Was the play a success?"

"It was. It was great. The stage looked beautiful. My drawings stood out really well. I never made such big drawings in my life. There was a farm in the country, a barn, and animals. I made it the way it used to be in the olden days of the Pilgrims. You know, how it was when they first came to America."

"I'm so proud of you. Tell me about the play. Did you act in it?"

"No." I paused. "I didn't want to."

"I see. Tell me a little about the story."

I told Abuelita all about it.

"Who played the parts? Any of your friends?"

"Some."

"Who?"

"Well, this boy Charlie Martinez played John Alden. Louie Collins played Captain Miles Standish. You don't know them. Mary Jackson played the part of the narrator. That's the person who tells the story. You really don't know any of them."

I was hoping she wouldn't ask, but she did.

"Who played the part of the girl both men love?"

"Oh, her? Gigi."

"Gigi Mercado, your best friend?" I nodded. "Was she good?"

"Yes, she was. Very good."

"You don't sound too happy about that."

"I don't care." I shrugged.

"But if she is your best friend, I should think you would care."

"I...I don't know if she is my friend anymore, Abuelita."

"Why do you say that?"

I couldn't answer. I just felt awful.

"Did she do something? Did you two argue?" I nodded. "Can I ask what happened?"

"Well, it's hard to explain. But what she did wasn't fair."

"Fair about what, Felita?"

I hadn't spoken about it before. Now with Abuelita it was easy to talk about it.

"Well, we all tried out for the different parts. Everybody knew what everybody was trying out for. But Gigi never told anybody she was going to try out for Priscilla. She kept it a great big secret. Even after I told her that I wanted to try for the part, she kept quiet about it. Do you know what she did say? She said I wasn't right for it...it was a hard part and all that bunch of baloney. She just wanted the part for herself, so she was mysterious about the whole thing. Like...it was...I don't know." I stopped for a moment, trying to figure this whole thing out. "After all, I am supposed to be her best friend...her very best friend. Why shouldn't she let me know that she wanted to be Priscilla? I wouldn't care. I let her know my plans. I didn't go sneaking around."

"Are you angry because Gigi got the part?"

It was hard for me to answer. I thought about it for a little while. "Abuelita, I don't think so. She was really good in the part."

"Were you as good when you tried out for Priscilla?"

"No." I looked at Abuelita. "I stunk." We both laughed.

"Then maybe you are not angry at Gigi at all."

"What do you mean?"

"Well, maybe you are a little bit...hurt?"

"Hurt?" I felt confused.

"Do you know what I think? I think you are hurt because your best friend didn't trust you. From what you tell me, you trusted her, but she didn't have faith in you. What do you think?"

"Yes." I nodded. "Abuelita, yes. I don't know why. Gigi and I always tell each other everything. Why did she act like that to me?"

"Have you asked her?"

"No."

"Why not? Aren't you two speaking to each other?"

"We're speaking. Gigi tried to be friendly a few times."

"Don't you want to stay her friend?"

"I do. Only she came over to me acting like...like nothing ever happened.

And something did happen! What does she think? That she can go around being sneaky and I'm going to fall all over her? Just because she got the best part, she thinks she's special."

"And you think that's why she came over. Because she wants to be special?"

"I don't know."

"You should give her a chance. Perhaps Gigi acted in a strange way for a reason."

"She wasn't nice to me, Abuelita. She wasn't."

"I'm not saying she was. Or even that she was right. Mira,[9] Felita, friendship is one of the best things in this whole world. It's one of the few things you can't go out and buy. It's like love. You can buy clothes, food, even luxuries, but there's no place I know of where you can buy a real friend. Do you?"

I shook my head. Abuelita smiled at me and waited. We were both silent for a long moment. I wondered if maybe I shouldn't have a talk with Gigi. After all, she had tried to talk to me first.

"Abuelita, do you think it's a good idea for me to...maybe talk to Gigi?"

"You know, that's a very good idea." Abuelita nodded.

[9]Mira (mē´ rə): look

206

"Well, she did try to talk to me a few times. Only there's just one thing. I won't know what to say to her. I mean, after what's happened and all."

"After so many years of being close, I am sure you could say 'Hello, Gigi. How are you?' That should be easy enough."

"I feel better already, Abuelita."

"Good," Abuelita said. "Now let's you and I get to sleep. Abuelita is tired."

"You don't have to tuck me in. I'll tuck you in instead." I got out of bed and folded the covers carefully over my side. Then I leaned over her and gave her a kiss. Abuelita hugged me real tight.

"My Felita has become a young lady," she whispered.

I kept thinking of what Abuelita had said, and on Monday I waited for Gigi after school. It was as if she knew I wanted to talk. She came over to me.

"Hello, Gigi," I said. "How are you?"

"Fine," Gigi smiled. "Wanna walk home together?"

"Let's take the long way so we can be by ourselves," I said.

We walked without saying anything for a couple of blocks. Finally I spoke.

"I wanted to tell you, Gigi, you were really great as Priscilla."

"Did you really like me? Oh, Felita, I'm so glad. I wanted you to like me, more than anybody else. Of course it was nothing compared to the sets you did. They were something special. Everybody liked them so much."

"You were right too," I said. "I wasn't very good for the part of Priscilla."

"Look." Gigi stopped walking and looked at me. "I'm sorry about…

about the way I acted. Like, I didn't say anything to you or the others. But, well, I was scared you all would think I was silly or something. I mean, you wanted the part too. So, I figured, better not say nothing."

"I wouldn't have cared, Gigi. Honest."

"Felita… it's just that you are so good at a lot of things. Like, you draw just fantastic. You beat everybody at hopscotch and kick-the-can. You know about nature and animals, much more than the rest of us. Everything you do is always better than... what I do! I just wanted this part for me. I wanted to be better than you this time. For once I didn't wanna worry about you. Felita, I'm sorry."

I was shocked. I didn't know Gigi felt that way. I didn't feel better than anybody about anything I did. She looked so upset, like she was about to cry any minute. I could see she was miserable and I wanted to comfort her. I had never had this kind of feeling before in my whole life.

"Well, you didn't have to worry. 'Cause I stunk!" We both laughed with relief. "I think I was the worst one!"

"Oh, no, you weren't." Gigi laughed. "Jenny Fuentes was the most awful."

"Worse than me?"

"Much worse. Do you know what she sounded like? She sounded like this. 'Wha... wha... why don't you... speeek for your... yourself Johnnnn?'" Gigi and I burst into laughter.

"And how about that dummy, Louie Collins? I didn't think he read better than Paquito."

"Right," Gigi agreed. "I don't know how he got through the play. He was shaking so much that I was scared the sets would fall right on his head."

It was so much fun, Gigi and I talking about the play and how we felt about everybody and everything. It was just like before, only better.

Reader's Response ～ Did your feelings about Felita change during the story? When did they change and why?

Library Link ～ If you are interested in reading about friendship, try Soup or Soup for President by Robert Newton Peck, and Me and the Terrible Two by Ellen Conford.

Nicholasa Mohr

Have you ever wondered what writing is like for a professional writer? Nicholasa Mohr talks about the hard work and the joy of making her living as a writer. Her story has important lessons for young writers.

Q What is the hardest part of your work?

A I think the hardest part of my work is the nitty-gritty. Most writers have to rewrite and rewrite and rewrite. We have to look up words, make sure words are used correctly, and check spelling and grammar so that another person can read our work and understand what we want to say.

Q What is the easiest part of your work?

A The easiest part of my work is wanting so much to do it and loving to do it, despite all the complaining. I love what I do.

Q How much revising do you do? Do you get feedback from a friend or an editor?

A Lots of revising. For example, the book that I am working on now needs revising because there was too much dialogue and not enough prose in it. That's because I finished a screenplay recently. It's very good to read your work aloud to a friend. I have two people whose opinions I really trust, and I read to them.

© Phil Cantor

Nicholasa Mohr

READERS'
CHOICE
AWARD

The Liberty Bell

**from *Fireworks, Picnics, and Flags*
by James Cross Giblin**

To many people, nothing symbolizes American independence as much as the Liberty Bell. Fourth of July fireworks often trace the outline of the Liberty Bell against the night sky. And almost every Independence Day parade includes a replica of the Bell on one of the floats.

The Liberty Bell wasn't known by that name when it arrived from England in September 1752. It was called the State House Bell, since it had been ordered for the new State House in Philadelphia.

Before the bell was raised to the top of the State House tower, it was hung from a temporary stand in the yard. People wanted to hear it ring, so one morning the bell was tested. While a crowd looked on, a smiling bellringer stepped up to the bell and swung its heavy clapper. A loud *bong* resounded through the air, but almost at once the bellringer's smile changed to a worried frown. For a crack had split the rim and raced up the side of the bell.

Everyone was horrified. Some wanted to send the ruined bell back to England and order a replacement. Others thought that would take too long. At last it was decided to recast the bell in Philadelphia. John Stow, who owned a brass foundry that made everything from candlesticks to kettles, was hired to do the job. He took on John Pass as his assistant.

Pass and Stow broke the original bell into small pieces with sledgehammers so they could melt down the metal. Then they made new molds, poured in the metal, and recast the bell in Stow's foundry.

However, this first recasting wasn't a success. When the new bell was hung in the State House tower in April 1753, it made only a dull *bonk* when struck. Someone said it sounded like two coal scuttles[1] being banged together.

So Pass and Stow took down the bell and started all over again. They worked quickly, and the third bell was ready by June. It was hung in the State House tower, and everyone in the yard below waited breathlessly as it was struck. They smiled when the bell gave out a loud, echoing *bong-g-g*.

On the side of the bell there is an inscription from the Bible: "Proclaim Liberty throughout the land to all the Inhabitants Thereof" (Leviticus 25:10). Many people think this refers to the Declaration of Independence. But of course it couldn't, since it was carved on the bell twenty-three years before the Declaration was written. It refers instead to the freedom of religion that all citizens of Pennsylvania enjoyed.

Also on the bell is a statement that it was ordered for the State House of Pennsylvania, the names of Pass and Stow, and the year the bell was made. Someone made a mistake, though, and misspelled the word *Pennsylvania*. To this day it appears as "Pensylvania" on the side of the Liberty Bell.

From 1753 until 1776, the bell summoned public officials to meetings at the State House. It was rung often during sessions of the Second Continental Congress. But there is no record that it was rung on July 4, 1776, the day the Declaration of Independence was adopted.

---

[1]coal scuttle: a metal pail for carrying coal

Many people mistakenly believe that the Liberty Bell did ring loud and long on that day because of a story that was published in 1846. According to the story, an old, white-haired bell-ringer waited all afternoon in the steeple of the State House for word that the Declaration had been adopted. As he waited, he kept muttering to himself, "They'll never do it, they'll never do it!"

Suddenly a boy came racing up the tower steps. "They've signed!" he shouted. "Ring, Grandfather! Ring for Liberty!"

The old man's face broke into a huge smile. He grasped the bell ropes and gave them a mighty tug. The sound of the State House Bell rang out, carrying the glad news to everyone in Philadelphia.

It makes a good story, but there is no evidence that it really happened on July 4, 1776. We do know, however, that the State House Bell rang on July 8 to announce the first public reading of the Declaration. And that night it rang in celebration with all the other bells of Philadelphia.

When the British army approached Philadelphia in September 1777, the State House Bell was hastily removed from the building. People

were afraid the British would melt down the bell for ammunition. Its 2,080 pounds of metal would have given them nearly 33,000 rounds at one ounce per shot.

The State House Bell and ten other large city bells were loaded onto sturdy farmers' wagons and covered with straw. Then they were smuggled out of Philadelphia in the middle of the night so that British spies wouldn't know what was going on.

The wagons carrying the bells joined a convoy of 700 wagons loaded with refugees and goods. All of them headed northwest, away from the British army. Just as the convoy reached Bethlehem, Pennsylvania, on September 24, the wagon with the State House Bell broke down under its great weight.

The bell was transferred to another wagon and taken on to Allentown. There it was hidden in the basement of the Zion High German Reformed Church. The church itself was used as a military hospital for wounded soldiers from George Washington's army.

The State House Bell stayed in Allentown until the British left Philadelphia in June 1778. Then it was shipped back to Philadelphia along with the other city bells, and was rehung in the State House steeple. It rang when General Cornwallis of Great Britain surrendered to George Washington at Yorktown in 1781. It rang when the United States signed a peace treaty with Britain in 1783. And it rang over and over again when the U.S. Constitution was adopted in 1788.

The State House Bell kept on ringing on important occasions until July 8, 1835. On that morning it was tolling for the funeral procession of John Marshall, chief justice of the U.S. Supreme Court, when suddenly it cracked for the second time. Strangely enough, it was fifty-nine years to the day since the bell had rung out to celebrate the first reading of the Declaration of Independence.

The bell remained silent until 1846. Then the edges of the crack were filed down so that they wouldn't vibrate against each other, and the

bell was rung on George Washington's birthday. At first it gave out loud, clear notes, but then the crack spread. After that, the bell could never be rung again.

But even though it was now silent for good, the bell lived on as a national symbol. It was first called "the Liberty Bell" in an antislavery booklet published in 1839. The new name quickly took hold. In 1852, on the 100th anniversary of its arrival in Philadelphia, the Liberty Bell was put on display in the State House, which was now known as Independence Hall. The bell was placed on a pedestal with thirteen sides to represent the thirteen original states.

Why did the Liberty Bell become such a strong symbol of American freedom and independence? Perhaps because, unlike the Declaration of Independence, it was a three-dimensional object that could be seen and touched. Thousands of Americans and people from other

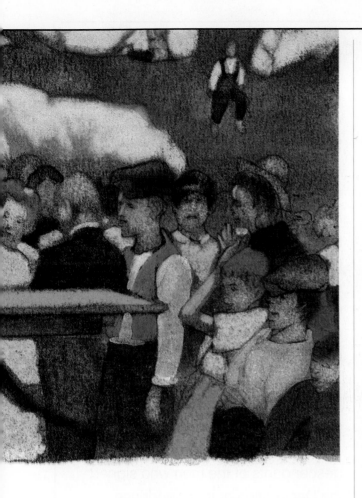

bell was suspended from a wooden yoke with the words "1776—Proclaim Liberty" lettered on it. Flowers, ribbons, and evergreen wreaths decorated the yoke and the flatcar.

As the Liberty Bell traveled on, people back in Philadelphia became more and more concerned about its safety. They feared that the bumping and jolting of the railroad would lengthen the crack in its side.

In 1915 the bell made one final trip to an exposition in San Francisco after 200,000 schoolchildren signed a petition asking that it be sent. Upon its return to Philadelphia, the bell was examined carefully. When it was discovered that the crack had widened, word went out: the Liberty Bell will travel no more. It has stayed in Philadelphia ever since.

Meanwhile, other bells rang in the Liberty Bell's place. As part of the Centennial celebrations of 1876, a wealthy merchant, Henry Seybert, gave money for a new bell to be installed in the tower of Independence Hall. The bell weighed 13,000 pounds—a thousand for each of the thirteen colonies—and was made from four Civil War cannons, melted down. It chimed for the first time at 12:01 A.M. on July 4, 1876.

countries came to view the bell when it was displayed at the great Centennial Exhibition in Philadelphia in 1876.

After that exhibition closed, the Liberty Bell traveled to many other cities. It was shown in New Orleans in 1885, in Chicago in 1893, in Boston in 1903, and in St. Louis in 1904.

Millions of people saw the bell on its tours around the country. It rode on a flat, open railroad car surrounded by a protective railing. The

To honor the 200th anniversary of the Declaration of Independence, Queen Elizabeth II of England presented a Bicentennial Bell to the people of the United States in July 1976. It was made in the Whitechapel Foundry in London, the same foundry that cast the original Liberty Bell. On its side are inscribed the words "Let Freedom Ring!"

At the presentation, Queen Elizabeth said: "It seems to me that Independence Day, the Fourth of July, should be celebrated as much in Britain as in America. Not in rejoicing at the separation of the American colonies from the British crown, but in sincere gratitude to the Founding Fathers of this great Republic for having taught Britain a very valuable lesson. . . . We learned to respect the right of others to govern themselves in their own ways."

The Bicentennial Bell now hangs in a simple brick belfry that is part of the Independence Park Visitors Center in Philadelphia. It is rung every day at 11:00 A.M. and 3:00 P.M., and on special occasions.

But it is the silent Liberty Bell to which hundreds of thousands of visitors still flock every year. Since New Year's Eve 1976, it has been displayed in a modern pavilion on the grassy mall below Independence Hall. Guides in the pavilion encourage people to touch the smooth surface of the bell and feel a part of it.

In 1962, author Eric Sloane started a campaign to have the nation celebrate the Fourth of July by ringing bells all across the country at 2:00 P.M. The Liberty Bell soon became the focal point of this campaign, which gained many supporters.

Now, on the Fourth of July, descendants of the men who signed the Declaration of Independence gather at the Liberty Bell pavilion. Often they are children. Promptly at two o'clock they tap the Liberty Bell gently with rubber-tipped hammers. At the same time the Centennial Bell atop Independence Hall chimes thirteen times, once for each of the thirteen colonies.

Reader's Response ∾ The Liberty Bell rang out to celebrate many important moments in history. In which event would you have wanted to participate? Explain your answer.

Our National Parks

The Liberty Bell is part of Independence National Historical Park in Philadelphia. But did you know that the park is just one of 355 sites maintained by the National Park Service? These sites cover 80,005,211 acres in the United States and its territories, an area larger than the state of New Mexico! Over 255 million people visit our national parks every year.

The idea of national parks began in the United States after the Civil War. The idea was to preserve wilderness for the enjoyment of all people in the United States. It is part of our heritage as Americans.

The first national park in the United States was Yellowstone, established in 1872. The National Park Service was created in 1916 to run the National Park System and is part of the Department of the Interior. The park system includes:

50 National Parks

14 National Preserves

10 National Seashores

69 Historical Sites

23 National Memorials

11 National Battlefields

29 National Historical Parks

18 National Recreation Areas

John Henry

A Ballad from Southern United States

1. When John Hen - ry ___ was just a lit - tle ba - by,
2. Well, the cap - tain ___ said to John ___ Hen - ry,

Sit - tin' on his dad - dy's knee,
"Gon - na bring that steam drill round,

He ___ gave one long and ___ lone - some cry,
Gon - na take that steam drill ___ out on the job,

Said, "A ham - mer be the death of me." me."
Gon - na whop that steel ___ on ___ down." down."

3. John Henry told his captain,
   "Well, a man ain't nothin' but a man,
   But before I let your steam drill beat me down,
   I'll die with a hammer in my hand.
   I'll die with a hammer in my hand."

4. Oh, the man that invented the steam drill,
   He thought that he was mighty fine,
   But John Henry drove his steel fifteen feet,
   And the steam drill drove only nine.
   And the steam drill drove only nine.

5. John Henry kept hammerin' on the mountain,
   There was lightnin' in his eye.
   He drove so hard that he broke his heart,
   And he laid down his hammer and he died.
   And he laid down his hammer and he died.

6. They carried him off to the graveyard,
   They buried him in the sand.
   And people came from near and far
   To praise that steel-drivin' man.
   To praise that steel-drivin' man.

The POPCORN Blizzard

from Paul Bunyan Swings His Axe
by Dell J. McCormick

When Paul Bunyan had cut down all the trees in North Dakota, he decided to go west. It was summertime, and the forest was sweet with the smell of green trees. The spreading branches cast their cool shadows on the ground.

"We must cross vast plains," said Paul to his men, "where it is so hot that not even a blade of grass can grow. You must not become too thirsty as there will be very little water to drink."

Paul knew it would be a long, hard journey, so he decided to send all the heavy camp equipment by boat down the Mississippi River and around the Horn to the Pacific Ocean. Paul told Billy Whiskers, a little bald-headed logger with a bushy beard, to take a crew of men and build a boat. Billy had once been a sailor. In a short time the boat was finished and loaded with all the heavy camp tools.

Everyone cheered as Billy Whiskers and his men started down the Mississippi River on their long trip. Billy wore an admiral's hat and looked every inch the sailor, although he hadn't been on board a ship for thirty-five years.

With Paul and Babe the Blue Ox leading the way, the rest of the camp then started across the plains on their long journey west. In a few days they had left the woods and were knee deep in sand that stretched out before them for miles and miles. The sun became hotter and hotter!

"I made some vanilla ice-cream," said Hot Biscuit Slim one day as he gave the men their lunch, "but the ice became so hot under this boiling sun that I couldn't touch it!"

Tiny Tim, the water boy, was so hot and tired that Paul had to put him up on Babe's back where he rode the rest of the trip. Every time Babe took a step forward, he moved ahead two miles, and Tiny Tim had to hold on with all his might. Even Ole the Big Swede, who was so strong he could carry a full-grown horse under each arm, began to tire.

There was not a tree in sight. Paul Bunyan's men had never before been away from the forest. They missed the cool shade of the trees. Whenever Paul stopped to rest, thirty or forty men would stand in his shadow to escape the boiling sun.

"I won't be able to last another day," cried Brimstone Bill, "if it doesn't begin to cool off soon!"

Even Paul Bunyan became tired finally and took his heavy double-bitted axe from his shoulder and dragged it behind him as he walked. The huge axe cut a ragged ditch through the sand that can be seen to this day. It is now called the Grand Canyon, and the Colorado River runs through it.

It became so hot that the men were exhausted and refused to go another step. Hot Biscuit Slim had complained that there was very little food left in camp. That night Paul took Babe the Blue Ox and went on alone into the mountains to the north. In the mountains Paul found a farmer with a barnful of corn.

"I will buy your corn," said Paul to the farmer. So he loaded all the corn on Babe's back and started for camp. By the time he arrived there, the sun was shining again and the day grew hotter as the sun arose overhead. Soon it became so hot that the corn started popping. It shot up into the air in vast clouds of white puffy popcorn.

It kept popping and popping and soon the air was filled with wonderful white popcorn. It came down all over the camp and almost covered the kitchen. The ground became white with popcorn as far as the eye could see. It fell like a snowstorm until everything was covered two feet deep with fluffy popcorn.

"A snowstorm! A snowstorm!" cried the men as they saw it falling. Never had they seen anything like it before. Some ran into the bunkhouses and put on their mittens and others put on heavy overcoats and woolen caps. They clapped each other on the back and laughed and shouted for joy.

"Let's make snowshoes!" cried Ole the Big Swede. So they all made snowshoes and waded around in the white popcorn and threw popcorn snowballs at each other, and everybody forgot how hot it had been the day before.

Even the horses thought it was real snow, and some of them almost froze to death before the men could put woolen blankets on them and lead them to shelter.

Babe the Blue Ox knew it was only popcorn and winked at Paul.

Paul Bunyan chuckled to himself at the popcorn blizzard and decided to start west again while the men were feeling so happy. He found them all huddled around the kitchen fire.

"Now is the time to move on west," said Paul, "before it begins to get hot again." So they packed up and started. The men waded through the popcorn and blew on their hands to keep them warm. Some claimed their feet were frostbitten, and others rubbed their ears to keep them from freezing.

After traveling for a few weeks more, they saw ahead of them the great forest they had set out to reach. They cheered Paul Bunyan who had led them safely over the hot desert plains. Babe the Blue Ox laughed and winked at Paul whenever anyone mentioned the great blizzard.

Reader's Response ∼ Of all the humorous exaggerations in this story, which one do you most remember?

Library Link ∼ *More adventures of Paul Bunyan and other American tall-tale heroes can be found in* American Tall Tales *by Adrien Stoutenburg.*

Legendary FEATS

"The Popcorn Blizzard" is just one of many legends about Paul Bunyan. For instance, there's a legend that Paul Bunyan was born somewhere in Maine. From there he chopped his way right to the Pacific Ocean, clearing the trees and making way for pioneers heading west. The American landscape would not be the same without Paul Bunyan!

Legend has it that...

- The Green Mountains of Vermont are really the mounds of dirt created when Paul Bunyan was digging the St. Lawrence River.

- The Great Lakes are holes in the ground scooped out by Paul Bunyan so that Babe, the Blue Ox, would have water to drink.

- The Mississippi River started as a leak from Paul Bunyan's water tank. (He dug the rest of the river so that he would have a good route for his log drive!)

- The Red River got its color when one of the ketchup drivers for Paul's camp spilled his load into the water.

- Puget Sound is Paul's gift of a harbor for the city of Seattle, and a place to float his logs to the mill.

Is there a natural wonder where you live that Paul might have created?

Star Fever

by Claire Boiko

CHARACTERS

LT. JOSEPH JENKINS

CAPTAIN JASON RIFKIN

LT. CARLA TORRES

LT. KAREN PRANG

ASTRONAUT MIKE STONE

ASTRONAUT ROSA MADRAS

ASTRONAUT JOEY JENKINS (*Lt. Jenkins as a boy of 12*)

JOHN KRAMER

BEFORE RISE: LT. JOSEPH JENKINS *enters in front of the curtain. He carries a log book.*

LT. JENKINS: (*Reading from book*) "Today, June 1, 2182, I returned to Earth after a ten-year voyage to another star. At the Moon base where all deep-space ships touch down, my family greeted me uncertainly; they weren't sure who I was. For as Joey Jenkins, I had left Earth as a child astronaut, and now return as an officer, and a space hero. The official captain's log of the voyage is short, but triumphant." (CAPTAIN JASON RIFKIN *enters, speaking into tape recorder.*)

CAPTAIN: Voice log…Spaceship *Goddard*…final entry. Our mission has been accomplished; all hands are safe. We pioneered a flight to Alpha Centauri, nearest star to Earth. We have discovered and claimed an uninhabited planet now named Terra Two. Special scout John Kramer remains on Terra Two awaiting the first colonists from Earth. (*He exits.*)

LT. JENKINS: Those are the facts, but they don't tell the real story. For instance, you won't find John Kramer's name anywhere on the roster of officers and crew. But Earth should know about him. That's why I am writing an *un*official log of the Spaceship *Goddard*. (*Electronic music is heard behind the narration.*) We left ten years ago . . . it seems more like a million years ago. I was barely twelve years old, just graduated from the Space Academy, and making my first trip into deep space. Many of us at the Academy had been chosen to become astronauts at an early age. Seems strange, doesn't it? At a time when most twelve-year-olds are out on a sandlot with nothing more on their minds than the next pop fly, I was computing the food supplies needed for a ten-year mission.

Destiny had put my name on the roster of the World Confederation Deep-Space Probe, *Goddard.* Captain Jason Rifkin, 15-year veteran of a grand tour of the solar system, was my commanding officer . . . . (*Music stops.* LT. JENKINS *sits down right. Curtains open.*)

SETTING: *Interior of the Spaceship* Goddard. *A console with computer, oval viewplate with flashing lights, navigational charts, gyroscope, and communications instruments runs across rear. Silver stools are left, right, and center, in front of console. At right, hatch door leads to ship's other compartments. At left is another hatch opening, leading outside. Beside it is a bulkhead closet with a working sliding door, marked* SPACE SUIT STORAGE.

AT RISE: LT. CARLA TORRES *sits left, working with instruments on star chart.* CAPTAIN RIFKIN *stands center, opens large manila envelope, takes out documents and frowns as he reads it over silently.* LT. KAREN PRANG *is seated right. She adjusts her headset and adjusts dials.* JOHN KRAMER *is hidden inside bulkhead closet.* LT. JENKINS *remains seated right to watch action on stage.*

TORRES: (*Turning to* CAPTAIN RIFKIN) Are those the orders, sir? Can you tell us anything new?

PRANG: All that Space Command would tell us was—"Stock up for a ten-year voyage—destination unknown."

TORRES: (*With sweeping gesture*) An awful lot of "unknowns" are out there.

CAPTAIN: Not quite "unknown." These are the orders from Space Command, all right. Our destination is Alpha Centauri!

TORRES and PRANG: (*Incredulously*) Alpha Centauri?

TORRES: Space Command has to be kidding.

CAPTAIN: It's no joke, Carla. The situation down on Earth is critical. The planet's resources are depleted. Half of North America is a desert.

PRANG: (*Indignantly*) How could the people in the twentieth century have been so stupid? Wasting, spoiling, using up the Earth as if there were no end to pure water, clean air, and cheap energy. Now *we're* paying for it.

CAPTAIN: At least those old timers gave us a springboard to space.

TORRES: But, Alpha Centauri! That's a million light years away. We don't have infinite speed, Captain.

CAPTAIN: We don't need it. Space Command has mapped out a route with a shortcut—through the Light Barrier.

PRANG: The Light Barrier! Captain, don't they remember what happens to ships in the Light Barrier? It was only a year ago that they sent our sister ship, the *Goldstone*, into the Light Barrier.

TORRES: It's a suicide mission! The *Goldstone* flew into the Barrier like a moth into a candle. I remember her last message: "Star Fever." That was all. (*Shakes head*) That was enough.

PRANG: Not one ship has ever come out of the Light Barrier. Not one astronaut has lived through Star Fever.

CAPTAIN: (*In clipped tones*) You know they wouldn't send us if the situation weren't desperate. We have our orders. Prepare for lift-off. (*He turns and places tape reel on computer. Computer sounds are heard.* TORRES *consults chart.*)

PRANG: (*On microphone*) *Goddard* to Earth. *Goddard* to Earth. Final phase of lift-off from Moon Base Tranquillity now commencing. Heading, Centaurus six-zero-zero-eight, toward the Light Barrier. We're getting help for you, Earth. Hang on for just a little while…So long… (*Lights dim. Blackout. Spotlight goes up on* LT. JENKINS, *right.*)

LT. JENKINS: It's funny…. Back in the twentieth century, scientists dreamed of fuels so powerful, a spaceship would be able to fly almost at the speed of light. But strangely enough, it was not fuel but the shape of the universe that gave us the answer. For in the twenty-first century, explorers beyond Jupiter discovered a kind of tunnel, something called "anti-space," a void that made the vacuum of space seem crowded. Scientists called it the Light Barrier. By going through this anti-space tunnel, a spaceship could skip years in its travels to the stars—theoretically. Actually, there were two terrifying dangers: The first spaceships to explore anti-space moved too slowly and dissolved like lumps of sugar. The next ships moved faster and could travel through the Barrier, but a malady called Star Fever, unknown to the space medics, struck their crews. We knew it was up to us aboard the *Goddard* to conquer Star Fever. We didn't know that still another problem would shortly burst upon us. Little things began to go wrong as we started to close in on the Light Barrier. (JENKINS *returns to seat, right.*

Electronic music is heard as lights go up onstage. TORRES *stands beside her stool, marking star chart with grease pencil.* PRANG *is watching viewplate intently.* CAPTAIN *is checking list on clipboard, center. A comet streaks by the viewplate.*)

PRANG: Hey, look! A comet!

TORRES: She's a beaut! Let me check. (*She consults chart.*) Congratulations! You had a preview as well as a grandstand seat, Prang. That's old Halley's Comet. Your friends on Earth won't see her for another seventy-five years.

PRANG: They'll be too old to enjoy it by then! (*Pause*) Look at that sky. Look at those stars out there, Carla! Red

ones and white ones and yellow ones. You never get a close look at stars when you're smothered in an atmosphere. But out here, you can almost reach for a handful.

CAPTAIN: Enjoy the stars, Karen. Once we hit the Light Barrier you won't see anything but the inside of the ship for a solar month.

TORRES: If we ever see anything again. (*Softly*) Star Fever. What is it? We know what it's not…

PRANG: Not a virus, not bacteria, not even a fever. It's a phantom. A deadly phantom.

CAPTAIN: Reminds me of another phantom disease I read about in ancient marine history. Remember the old sailing ships? They almost went out of business for good because of a terrible disease. Scurvy, they called it. The sailors died by the thousands. Then along came an explorer—Captain Cook, I think his name was—who noticed that if you took aboard one simple little item, the sailors never developed scurvy. (*To the officers*) You know—he probably set exploration ahead a hundred years.

PRANG: What was his cure, Captain?

CAPTAIN: Just—limes, Karen. Fresh limes.

PRANG: Limes, sir? Why limes? (*Suddenly, an insistent buzzer is heard.* PRANG *picks up intercom.*) Prang here. This is the bridge. (*After a moment, she speaks to* CAPTAIN.) Some minor problems, sir. The crew requests permission to speak to you.

CAPTAIN: Permission granted. Open the hatch. (*Hatch at right slides open.* ASTRONAUTS JOEY JENKINS, ROSA MADRAS *and* MIKE STONE *enter, saluting.*)

CAPTAIN: (*To* STONE) What's the trouble, Mike?

STONE: Speed check reveals the ship is a hundred pounds heavier than she should be, sir.

MADRAS: There's oxygen leakage, too, sir. Nothing serious, but we're using slightly more than we should. Almost as if another person were breathing.

JENKINS: Some food is unaccounted for, too, sir. It may be just a miscount but I thought you should know, Captain.

CAPTAIN: Thanks. We'll run a check. Could be a computer malfunction. (*Loud siren is heard and lights on viewplate flash.*)

TORRES: We've picked up a signal from the outer limits of the Light Barrier, sir. The siren is warning us—five minutes until we hit anti-space.

CAPTAIN: Right. Prang, notify Earth we've hit the point of no return.

MADRAS: Captain—we're really going into that...that anti-space? Once we're in it, we can't turn back, can we? I mean, it's like an irreversible arrow—we can only go one way.

CAPTAIN: That's right, Madras. No U-turns in the tunnel. (*He pats* MADRAS's *shoulder.*) We're going to make it. Don't worry.

PRANG: *Goddard* to Earth. *Goddard* to Earth. Approaching the Light Barrier. This will be our final communication until we re-enter normal space. Over…and…out.

TORRES: That's that. I can just file my star charts under unfinished business, too. Alpha Centauri—we're on our way!

CAPTAIN: There will be a strong vibration as we hit the rim of anti-space. Crew—you remain on the bridge with us until the phase change is complete. In a minute, the electrical systems will go off. I will switch us onto anti-space override, the lights will go on again, and the ship will continue on course through the Light Barrier.

TORRES: We hope. (MADRAS *begins to whistle.*)

PRANG: What's the matter, Rosa? You're whistling.

MADRAS: I am? Sorry, Lieutenant. I always seem to start whistling when I'm scared.

TORRES: Scared? There's nothing to be scared of. Just think of this as a long subway ride.

MADRAS: (*Nervously*) I never did like subways. (*Lights blink on and off.*)

CAPTAIN: Override. (*High whining sound begins.*)

PRANG: No matter how many times you go through this in a simulator, the real thing still makes your scalp prickle. (*Stage lights go off.*)

JOEY: Is this—it, sir?

CAPTAIN: Yes, Jenkins. This is it. Anti-space.

JOEY: It's…spooky. Like having an inside—with no outside. I never saw such darkness.

TORRES: It's like the old riddle at the Space Academy—what is the color of absolute zero? Well, now I've seen the color of absolute zero. It's absolute black.

PRANG: I hear something. It sounds as if the hatch is opening. If the lights go on—I mean, when the lights go on—we should secure that hatch.

TORRES: You know, Prang, you sound worried. I never worry. I just figure as far as anti-space is concerned, if anything happens, we'll never know what didn't hit us. (*Stage lights come on. All sigh, relieved. Closet door is open.*)

CAPTAIN: We are now in the Light Barrier. Stand by to begin Special Discipline.

ALL: (*Together*) Yes, sir.

PRANG: (*Pointing to the open closet door*) The phase change must have jarred the door open.

MADRAS: I'll close it, sir. That door was my responsibility. The bolt must have worked loose. (*She crosses to door left, then flings herself against door, facing others.*) Something moved in there!

TORRES: (*Crossing to door*) You're just shook up from phase change, Madras. (*Peers into closet; then intensely*) Don't move. Someone—or something—*is* in there. (*Whispers*) Move aside. (MADRAS *fearfully moves away.*)

CAPTAIN: Come out of there, on the double! (*Door opens, and Kramer steps out, facing them defiantly.*)

TORRES: A stowaway!

CAPTAIN: Impossible!

PRANG: That would account for the extra weight and the oxygen loss.

JOEY: It's Joker Kramer! He was at the Academy with us.

CAPTAIN: (*To KRAMER; angrily*) What do you mean, jeopardizing the mission?

KRAMER: I'm John Kramer, Captain Rifkin. I was at the Academy with Joey, but I never finished. (TORRES *crosses to computer console, makes calculations.*) If I had, I would have been aboard this mission. The Academy said I lack something called "high seriousness." That hurt, Captain. So I made a vow that I'd get aboard the best ship going, and I'd stick it out until I hit deep space. I won't jeopardize your mission, Captain, I promise you that.

CAPTAIN: You already have, Kramer. You're using up our air, our time and our patience. We'll have to use time to figure out how to save you—time that we should use against Star Fever. (*Sarcastically*) They call you Joker, eh? Well, you're a bad joke.

TORRES: (*Crossing to* CAPTAIN) May I speak to you, Captain? (*She and* CAPTAIN *cross down left.*) I've been doing a rapid check of the odds. We'll never get to Alpha

	Centauri and back to Earth with him aboard. It's either him—or us.
CAPTAIN:	Do you mean put him out of the ship? That's harsh, Carla. Very harsh. Well, we have to hold a court-martial, anyway. There are no written regulations covering a stowaway. (*Turning toward the others*) I want all officers and crew in the chart room immediately. I'm convening a court-martial. Kramer, you will remain on the bridge to await the verdict. (KRAMER *stands alone, center stage, as* TORRES *and* PRANG, *led by* CAPTAIN, *and followed by* JOEY, MADRAS *and* STONE, *exit through hatch right.*)
KRAMER:	I made it, and it was worth every minute. I'd rather be in a closet aboard the *Goddard* than anyplace on Earth. At least I've been on a real spaceship, even for a little while. But I meant what I said, Captain. I won't take any more of your precious food, or air, or time. (*He crosses to locker and takes out space suit. He opens outside hatch, left.*) So long, Spaceship *Goddard.* Exit, one joker. (*He exits through hatch. Right hatch opens.* CAPTAIN *enters, followed by officers and crew. They do not notice that* KRAMER *is gone.*)
CAPTAIN:	Kramer, we're going to power down and keep you aboard. You'd better pray that there's a breathable planet where we're going. (*Looking around*) Kramer? Where are you? (PRANG *crosses to viewplate.*)
PRANG:	(*Upset*) Captain, he's taken a suit, and he's floating out in space! (*Frantically pressing buttons*) Maybe I can get him back. I'll try the intergalactic space channel. (*Puts on headset*) *Goddard* to Kramer. *Goddard* to Kramer. Come back immediately. (*Shouts*) Kramer— reply! (*Turns to* CAPTAIN) There's no response, Captain. (CAPTAIN *crosses to look at viewplate.*)

CAPTAIN: (*Shaking head*) He has three minutes left before he dissolves. Switch on the magnabeam so we can see through that black. (PRANG *flips switch.*) His outline has begun to blur. He's losing space....

TORRES: (*Looking at viewplate*) What's that, dead ahead? Why, it's a ship!

CAPTAIN: It's the *Goldstone*! Holding space on a pre-set course. (*To* PRANG) Karen, get Kramer aboard the *Goldstone*—and quickly!

PRANG: But, sir—that's a ghost ship. The crew all died of Star Fever.

CAPTAIN: Kramer's better off with ghosts than anti-space. Carla, switch on the magnetic grapples and put the *Goldstone* in tow.

TORRES: Yes, sir. (*Flips switch*) Grapples in place, sir. (*Pause*) The *Goldstone* is in tow.

CAPTAIN: Now—get that idiot Kramer aboard her, Karen.

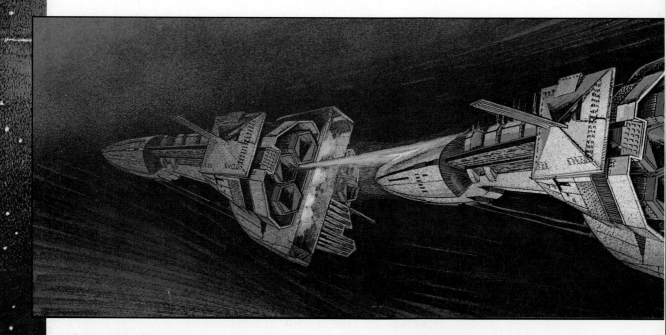

PRANG: Yes, sir. (*Into headset*) *Goddard* to Kramer. Starship *Goldstone* following. Board the *Goldstone*. Repeat. Board the *Goldstone*. Reply, Kramer.... (*There is a moment of tense silence.*) Yes, Kramer, I hear you loud and clear. (*To* CAPTAIN) He's aboard, sir. He's safe aboard the *Goldstone!* (*All cheer.*)

CAPTAIN: (*Crossing slowly and thoughtfully down center, as all turn toward him*) One problem down. One to go. Star Fever. From this moment on, you are all under Special Discipline. You know what that means. This is the zone of the unknown. This is the zone of Star Fever! (*Blackout. Spotlight goes up on* LT. JENKINS, *down right.*)

LT. JENKINS: Oh, yes, we knew what Special Discipline meant. Special Discipline—a schedule of duties taking care of every minute of every day of our time in anti-space. We were to perform those duties with complete concentration, like robots. No conversation. No recreation. Nothing but an endless checking and re-checking of the ship. Why? You had only to look out the viewplate to understand it. We were surrounded by anti-space—no glittering stars, no comets, no meteors. We would not have known we were moving, except for the clicking of numbers on the distance dial. Special Discipline was designed to keep us from going mad. But after two weeks, something began to go wrong. (*Spotlight goes out. Lights go up onstage.* PRANG *wears headset, presses various knobs and instruments, listening intently.* TORRES *stares at viewplate.*)

CAPTAIN: (*Reading from clipboard*) Read-out on the fuel consumption gauges. Third check. Gamma emissions point seven-four-nine-nine. (*Turns to* TORRES) Read that back to me, Carla.

TORRES: (*Dreamily*) Look out there! It's a cloud. A big, fluffy, white cloud. It's going to be a nice day, Captain.

CAPTAIN: (*Crossing to her and shaking her vigorously*) Come on. Come on, Torres. Snap out of it.

PRANG: (*Handing headset to* CAPTAIN) Captain—it's Kramer calling in. He wants to speak to you. (CAPTAIN *crosses to* PRANG, *puts on headset.*)

CAPTAIN: (*Irritably*) What is it now, Kramer?...What?...No, you cannot come aboard for any reason. You know you're under quarantine.... A theory about Star Fever? We've heard all the theories—and none of them solved our problem. Over. (*Hands headset to* PRANG) Here, Prang. Remind Kramer to follow his check list. (PRANG *nods, dully. Hatch right opens.* STONE *and* JOEY *enter, carrying* MADRAS *between them. She stares blankly, ties and unties a piece of rope.*)

CAPTAIN: (*Snapping his fingers in front of* MADRAS's *eyes*) Madras! Madras! Come out of it! (*To others*) How long has she been like this, Stone?

STONE: Too long, sir. We've done everything we could think of. Nothing works. She acts as if she's in a trance.

CAPTAIN: Take her to sick bay. I'll be there directly.

STONE: Yes, sir. (*Exits with* MADRAS. JOEY *remains at rigid attention, saluting automatically.*)

CAPTAIN: Stop that, Jenkins. (*He shakes him.* JOEY *stops, but remains at rigid attention.*) Prang, take Jenkins to sick bay.

PRANG: (*Like a broken record*) We-have-to-follow-the-checklist-sir. We-have-to-follow-the-checklist-sir. We-have-to-follow-the-checklist-sir. (*She stops, staring blankly.* CAPTAIN *crosses to* TORRES.)

CAPTAIN: (*Urgently*) We're in bad trouble, Torres. Help me get them to sick bay. Carla…. (TORRES *turns with vacant smile, glides from stool toward outside hatch, left.*)

TORRES: Let's go for a walk, Captain. (*Stretches her hand*) Did you ever feel such a warm sun? Come on, Captain. (*She beckons, opening hatch at left.*) It's so warm out there you don't even have to wear a suit. (*She exits through hatch, as* CAPTAIN, *horrified, dashes left. Hatch shuts before he reaches it.*)

CAPTAIN: Torres, come back here! That's an order! Torres don't go out there! (*Left hatch slowly opens.* KRAMER, *in space suit, drags* TORRES *in.*)

KRAMER: (*Removing his helmet*) A funny thing happened on the way to the *Goddard*. I had to sock the chief navigator. She wanted to go for a stroll in anti-space. (*He drops* TORRES *onto floor.*)

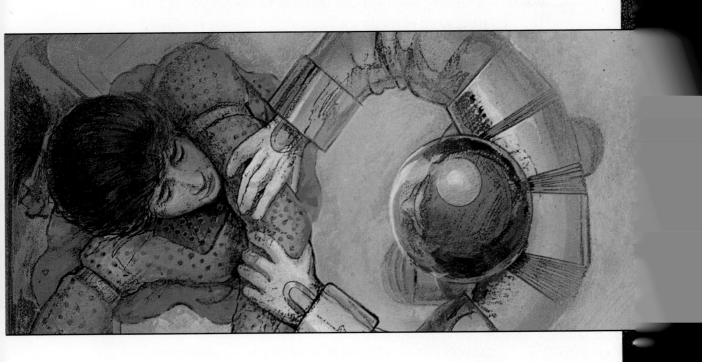

CAPTAIN: Thanks, Kramer. How did you know we were in trouble?

KRAMER: Prang left a communicator open. (TORRES *sits up, rubbing her jaw groggily.*) Now, let's wake up the other sleeping beauties. Let's get them good and mad. (*He dances around* PRANG, *cuffing her lightly, then does the same to* JOEY. *He keeps trying to provoke them.*) Come on. Put 'em up. How about getting into the fight, Captain? (CAPTAIN *nods with sudden understanding, and pantomimes "punching"* PRANG.)

CAPTAIN: Come on, Prang. You always wanted to spar with your superior officer. Now's your chance. Let's go. (PRANG *begins to spar weakly.*) You call that a punch? You couldn't fight your way out of a lace doily.

PRANG: (*Angrily*) Have you gone stark raving mad, Captain? (CAPTAIN *cuffs her*) Ow!

JOEY: Get away, Kramer! Get away or I'll knock you flat! (*He strikes out at* KRAMER.)

KRAMER: Awake now? Had enough?

PRANG: (*Angrily*) Didn't you hear Jenkins? Yes, we've had enough! Now, let us alone! (PRANG, TORRES *and* JOEY *return to seats, glare at* KRAMER *and* CAPTAIN.)

KRAMER: (*To* CAPTAIN) O.K., Captain. They're out of it. They're alive and kicking.

CAPTAIN: They're alive, all right, and mad as hornets. I'm not sure what we did—but we did it!

KRAMER: Am I entitled to a theory, sir? Just a small one?

CAPTAIN: Kramer, you're entitled to fifty theories. You've made the only dent in curing Star Fever so far.

KRAMER: Face it, sir, Star Fever isn't a disease at all. Crews don't die of it—they die of neglect or accidents. The crew of the *Goldstone* died of oxygen malfunction.

I've checked the ship. If they had been alert, they could have saved themselves easily.

JOEY: (*Turning*) If Star Fever isn't a disease, what is it? (PRANG *and* TORRES *turn to listen.*)

KRAMER: It's a kind of hypnosis brought on by Special Discipline. Special Discipline has the effect of making men into robots. But we can't be robots—not even for thirty days. We have to be laughing, crying, angry, worried human beings, or we'll be—(*Shrugs*) nothing.

PRANG: Whew! When I think how close I came to being nothing!

JOEY: But, Captain, what brought us out of it? I vaguely remember a fight. I wanted to flatten Kramer, I was so mad.

CAPTAIN: That was it, Jenkins. Kramer gave you a lime. A fresh lime.

PRANG: (*Confused*) A lime, sir? I don't get it.

CAPTAIN: Don't you remember, Prang? I was telling you about those ancient sea voyagers. Their sickness was cured by limes. The limes contained one substance absolutely necessary to human life: Vitamin C.

PRANG: And what about Star Fever? What vitamin cures that?

CAPTAIN: I'll have to coin a name for it. I'll call it Vitamin J for Joker. Laughing Joker was our fresh lime. He made us angry. He brought back our absolute necessity: human emotion. (*A siren is heard. Viewplate lights up.*)

TORRES: (*Crossing to viewplate and looking out*) Look, everybody. You're seeing something no one has ever passed before. The halfway beacon! We're going to make it!

KRAMER: And I'll be with you, seeing a new sun with you…making landfall on a new planet with you. I'll be there! (*Blackout. Spotlight goes up on* LT. JENKINS.)

LT. JENKINS: And so, a brave speck of Earth called Spaceship *Goddard* bridged the span from sun to sun. We were the first to reach another star. Like the *Santa Maria*, the *Spirit of St. Louis*, and the *Eagle*, we found a new world, uninhabited and unspoiled, with clear air and silver rivers. Kramer stayed on that world, a lonely sentry waiting for the first colonists. Somehow, he belonged there: a dauntless pioneer who'd face shame and exile rather than miss the curtain going up on Act One of mankind among...the stars. (*Blackout; curtain*)

The End

Reader's Response ∼ Kramer took a great risk to be on the *Goddard* for "just a little while." Is that a chance you would take? Explain.

Star Gazing

The crew of the Spaceship *Goddard* saw white, yellow, and red stars during their voyage. But do you know why stars have different colors?

The color of a star depends on the temperature of its surface.

Stars that are blue in the color of their light have the highest surface temperature, up to 50,000 degrees Fahrenheit.

Yellow stars, like our sun, have surface temperatures of approximately 10,000 degrees Fahrenheit.

Eventually a star runs out of hydrogen fuel, and the core contracts and becomes very hot. The star's outer layers expand greatly. This expansion cools off the star so that its surface temperature drops to about 5,500 degrees Fahrenheit. These stars glow with a red light and are called red giants.

To give you an idea of how hot even a red giant is, the average oven has a maximum temperature of about 575 degrees Fahrenheit. Even the coolest star is many times hotter than your oven at home!

"It's here because it's also the home of Abner Doubleday. Some people say that he invented baseball," Ezra explained to his father.

They parked their car between one with a license plate from Michigan and another with plates from Florida.

"Imagine! People seem to travel here from all over the country," Mr. Feldman marveled aloud. This observation didn't surprise Ezra at all.

Inside, the museum was like a treasure chest full of wonderful things for Ezra to see. There were huge enlarged photographs of all the record-making events in baseball history. And enclosed in glass cases were the very balls and gloves and uniforms that had taken part in the major events of the game.

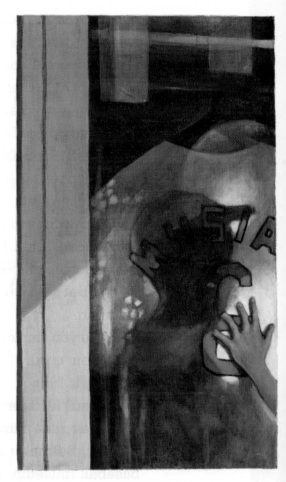

Ezra didn't know which way to look first, whether to start upstairs and work his way down or downstairs and work his way up. He wanted to be everywhere at once, seeing everything at the same time.

Ezra and Mr. Feldman waited while a family of six people read an inscription, and when they moved on, they were able to see the locker in which Stan Musial of the Cardinals had stored his uniform. There was a glass door on the locker so Ezra could look inside and see Musial's old uniform with the number six on it. Musial's old playing shoes were there too, worn and dirty. They looked as if any moment the baseball player would return and put them on.

"Look! There's the bat Musial used when he became the first major-league player to hit five home runs in a doubleheader," Ezra read aloud. "It was on May 2, 1954."

"May 2, 1954," said Mr. Feldman. "That was the day Prime Minister Jawaharlal Nehru of India concluded his first Asian conference with the rulers from Ceylon, Pakistan, Burma, and Indonesia."

Ezra looked at his father with amazement. How could somebody say so many words in English and not make a single bit of sense? He didn't know what his father was talking about. Then he remembered how often his father had said the very same thing to him when he tried to explain a baseball game to him.

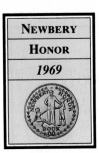

NEWBERY
HONOR
1969

When Shlemiel Went to Warsaw

by Isaac Bashevis Singer

CHEL

Though Shlemiel[1] was a lazybones and a sleepyhead and hated to move, he always daydreamed of taking a trip. He had heard many stories about faraway countries, huge deserts, deep oceans, and high mountains, and often discussed with Mrs. Shlemiel his great wish to go on a long journey. Mrs. Shlemiel would reply: "Long journeys are not for a Shlemiel. You better stay home and mind the children while I go to market to sell my vegetables." Yet Shlemiel could not bring himself to give up his dream of seeing the world and its wonders.

A recent visitor to Chelm had told Shlemiel marvelous things about the city of Warsaw.[2] How beautiful the streets were, how high the buildings and luxurious the stores. Shlemiel decided once and for all that he must see this great city for himself. He knew that one had to prepare for a journey. But what was there for him to take? He had nothing but the old clothes he wore. One morning, after Mrs. Shlemiel left for the market, he told the older boys to stay home from cheder[3] and mind the younger children. Then he took a few slices of bread, an onion, and a clove of garlic, put them in a kerchief, tied it into a bundle, and started for Warsaw on foot.

There was a street in Chelm called Warsaw Street and Shlemiel believed that it led directly to Warsaw. While still in the village, he was stopped by several neighbors who asked him where he was going. Shlemiel told them that he was on his way to Warsaw.

"What will you do in Warsaw?" they asked him.

Shlemiel replied: "What do I do in Chelm? Nothing."

He soon reached the outskirts of town. He walked

[1]Shlemiel (shlə mēl')
[2]Chelm (khelm), Warsaw: cities in Poland
[3]cheder (khā′ dər): a Jewish religious school for young children

263

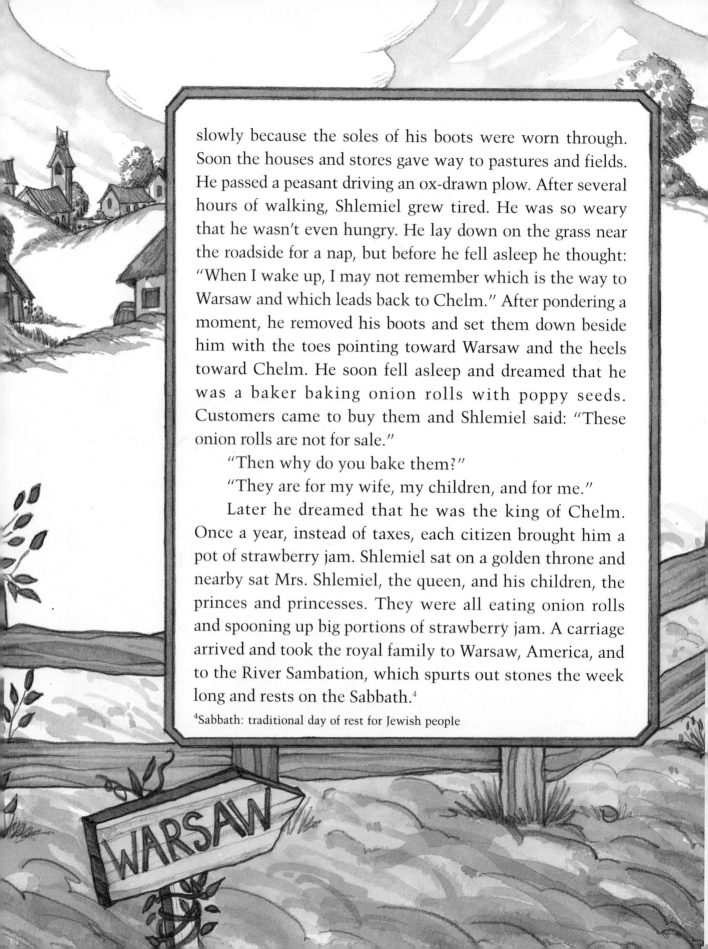

slowly because the soles of his boots were worn through. Soon the houses and stores gave way to pastures and fields. He passed a peasant driving an ox-drawn plow. After several hours of walking, Shlemiel grew tired. He was so weary that he wasn't even hungry. He lay down on the grass near the roadside for a nap, but before he fell asleep he thought: "When I wake up, I may not remember which is the way to Warsaw and which leads back to Chelm." After pondering a moment, he removed his boots and set them down beside him with the toes pointing toward Warsaw and the heels toward Chelm. He soon fell asleep and dreamed that he was a baker baking onion rolls with poppy seeds. Customers came to buy them and Shlemiel said: "These onion rolls are not for sale."

"Then why do you bake them?"

"They are for my wife, my children, and for me."

Later he dreamed that he was the king of Chelm. Once a year, instead of taxes, each citizen brought him a pot of strawberry jam. Shlemiel sat on a golden throne and nearby sat Mrs. Shlemiel, the queen, and his children, the princes and princesses. They were all eating onion rolls and spooning up big portions of strawberry jam. A carriage arrived and took the royal family to Warsaw, America, and to the River Sambation, which spurts out stones the week long and rests on the Sabbath.[4]

[4]Sabbath: traditional day of rest for Jewish people

WARSAW

Near the road, a short distance from where Shlemiel slept, was a smithy. The blacksmith happened to come out just in time to see Shlemiel carefully placing his boots at his side with the toes facing in the direction of Warsaw. The blacksmith was a prankster and as soon as Shlemiel was sound asleep he tiptoed over and turned the boots around. When Shlemiel awoke, he felt rested but hungry. He got out a slice of bread, rubbed it with garlic, and took a bite of onion. Then he pulled his boots on and continued on his way.

He walked along and everything looked strangely familiar. He recognized houses that he had seen before. It seemed to him that he knew the people he met. Could it be that he had already reached another town, Shlemiel wondered. And why was it so similar to Chelm? He stopped a passer-by and asked the name of the town. "Chelm," the man replied.

Shlemiel was astonished. How was this possible? He had walked away from Chelm. How could he have arrived back there? He began to rub his forehead and soon found the answer to the riddle. There were two Chelms and he had reached the second one.

Still it seemed very odd that the streets, the houses, the people were so similar to those in the Chelm he had left behind. Shlemiel puzzled over this fact until he suddenly remembered something he had learned in cheder: "The earth is the same everywhere." And so why shouldn't the second Chelm be exactly like the first one? This discovery gave Shlemiel great satisfaction. He wondered if there was a street here like his street and a house on it like the one he lived in. And indeed he soon arrived at an identical street and house. Evening had fallen. He opened the door and to his amazement saw a second Mrs. Shlemiel with children just like his. Everything was exactly the same as in his own household. Even the cat seemed the same. Mrs. Shlemiel at once began to scold him.

"Shlemiel, where did you go? You left the house alone. And what have you there in that bundle?" The children all ran to him and cried: "Papa, where have you been?"

Shlemiel paused a moment and then he said: "Mrs. Shlemiel, I'm not your husband. Children, I'm not your papa."

"Have you lost your mind?" Mrs. Shlemiel screamed.

"I am Shlemiel of Chelm One and this is Chelm Two."

Mrs. Shlemiel clapped her hands so hard that the chickens sleeping under the stove awoke in fright and flew out all over the room.

"Children, your father has gone crazy," she wailed. She immediately sent one of the boys for Gimpel, the healer. All the neighbors came crowding in. Shlemiel stood in the middle of the room and proclaimed: "It's true, you all look like the people in my town, but you are not the same. I come from Chelm One and you live in Chelm Two."

"Shlemiel, what's the matter with you?" someone cried. "You're in your own house, with your own wife and children, your own neighbors and friends."

"No, you don't understand. I come from Chelm One. I was on my way to Warsaw, and between Chelm One and Warsaw there is a Chelm Two. And that is where I am."

"What are you talking about? We all know you and you know all of us. Don't you recognize your chickens?"

"No, I'm not in my town," Shlemiel insisted. "But," he continued, "Chelm Two does have the same people and the same houses as Chelm One, and that is why you are mistaken. Tomorrow I will continue on to Warsaw."

"In that case, where is my husband?" Mrs. Shlemiel inquired in a rage, and she proceeded to berate Shlemiel with all the curses she could think of.

"How should I know where your husband is?" Shlemiel replied.

Some of the neighbors could not help laughing; others pitied the family. Gimpel, the healer, announced that he knew of no remedy for such an illness. After some time, everybody went home.

Mrs. Shlemiel had cooked noodles and beans that evening, a dish that Shlemiel liked especially. She said to him: "You may be mad, but even a madman has to eat."

"Why should you feed a stranger?" Shlemiel asked.

"As a matter of fact, an ox like you should eat straw, not noodles and beans. Sit down and be quiet. Maybe some food and rest will bring you back to your senses."

"Mrs. Shlemiel, you're a good woman. My wife wouldn't feed a stranger. It would seem that there is some small difference between the two Chelms."

The noodles and beans smelled so good that Shlemiel needed no further coaxing. He sat down and as he ate he spoke to the children.

"My dear children, I live in a house that looks exactly like this one. I have a wife and she is as like your mother as two peas are like each other. My children resemble you as drops of water resemble one another."

The younger children laughed; the older ones began to cry. Mrs. Shlemiel said: "As if being a Shlemiel wasn't enough, he had to go crazy in addition. What am I going to do now? I won't be able to leave the children with him when I go to market. Who knows what a madman may do?" She clasped her head in her hands and cried out: "God in heaven, what have I done to deserve this?"

Nevertheless, she made up a fresh bed for Shlemiel; and even though he had napped during the day, near the

smithy, the moment his head touched the pillow he fell
fast asleep and was soon snoring loudly. He again
dreamed that he was the king of Chelm and that his wife,
the queen, had fried for him a huge panful of blintzes.
Some were filled with cheese, others with blueberries or
cherries, and all were sprinkled with sugar and cinnamon
and were drowning in sour cream. Shlemiel ate twenty
blintzes all at once and hid the remainder in his crown
for later.

In the morning, when Shlemiel awoke, the house
was filled with townspeople. Mrs. Shlemiel stood in their
midst, her eyes red with weeping. Shlemiel was about to
scold his wife for letting so many strangers into the
house, but then he remembered that he himself was a
stranger here. At home he would have gotten up, washed,
and dressed. Now in front of all these people he was at a

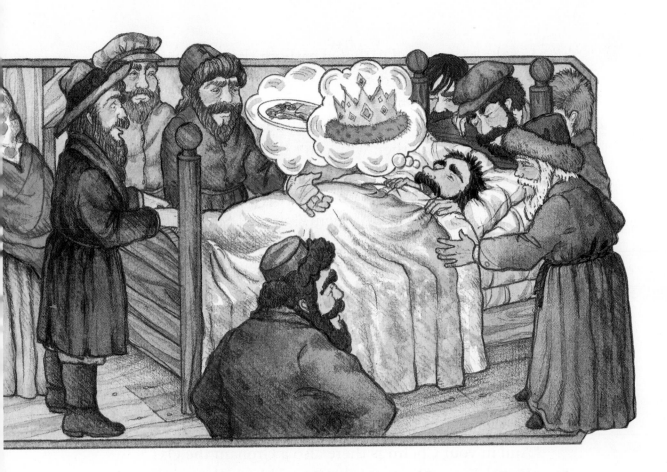

loss as to what to do. As always when he was embarrassed, he began to scratch his head and pull at his beard. Finally, overcoming his bashfulness, he decided to get up. He threw off the covers and put his bare feet on the floor. "Don't let him run away," Mrs. Shlemiel screamed. "He'll disappear and I'll be a deserted wife, without a Shlemiel."

At this point Baruch, the baker, interrupted. "Let's take him to the Elders. They'll know what to do."

"That's right! Let's take him to the Elders," everybody agreed.

Although Shlemiel insisted that since he lived in Chelm One, the local Elders had no power over him, several of the strong young men helped him into his pants, his boots, his coat and cap and escorted him to the house of Gronam the Ox. The Elders, who had already heard of the matter, had gathered early in the morning to consider what was to be done.

As the crowd came in, one of the Elders, Dopey Lekisch, was saying, "Maybe there really are two Chelms."

"If there are two, then why can't there be three, four, or even a hundred Chelms?" Sender Donkey interrupted.

"And even if there are a hundred Chelms, must there be a Shlemiel in each one of them?" argued Shmendrick Numskull.

Gronam the Ox, the head Elder, listened to all the arguments but was not yet prepared to express an opinion. However, his wrinkled, bulging forehead indicated that he was deep in thought. It was Gronam the Ox who questioned Shlemiel. Shlemiel related everything that had happened to him, and when he finished, Gronam asked: "Do you recognize me?"

"Surely. You are wise Gronam the Ox."

"And in your Chelm is there also a Gronam the Ox?"

"Yes, there is a Gronam the Ox and he looks exactly like you."

"Isn't it possible that you turned around and came back to Chelm?" Gronam inquired.

"Why should I turn around? I'm not a windmill," Shlemiel replied.

"In that case, you are not this Mrs. Shlemiel's husband."

"No, I'm not."

"Then Mrs. Shlemiel's husband, the real Shlemiel, must have left the day you came."

"It would seem so."

"Then he'll probably come back."

"Probably."

"In that case, you must wait until he returns. Then we'll know who is who."

"Dear Elders, my Shlemiel has come back," screamed Mrs. Shlemiel. "I don't need two Shlemiels. One is more than enough."

"Whoever he is, he may not live in your house until everything is made clear," Gronam insisted.

"Where shall I live?" Shlemiel asked.

"In the poorhouse."

"What will I do in the poorhouse?"

"What do you do at home?"

"Good God, who will take care of my children when I go to market?" moaned Mrs. Shlemiel. "Besides, I want a husband. Even a Shlemiel is better than no husband at all."

"Are we to blame that your husband left you and went to Warsaw?" Gronam asked. "Wait until he comes home."

Mrs. Shlemiel wept bitterly and the children cried too. Shlemiel said: "How strange. My own wife always scolded me. My children talked back to me. And here a strange woman and strange children want me to live with them. It looks to me as if Chelm Two is actually better than Chelm One."

"Just a moment. I think I have an idea," interrupted Gronam.

"What is your idea?" Zeinvel Ninny inquired.

"Since we decided to send Shlemiel to the poorhouse, the town will have to hire someone to take care of Mrs. Shlemiel's children so she can go to market. Why not hire Shlemiel for that? It's true, he is not Mrs. Shlemiel's husband or the children's father. But he is so much like the real Shlemiel that the children will feel at home with him."

"What a wonderful idea!" cried Feyvel Thickwit.

"Only King Solomon could have thought of such a wise solution," agreed Treitel the Fool.

"Such a clever way out of this dilemma could only have been thought of in our Chelm," chimed in Shmendrick Numskull.

"How much do you want to be paid to take care of Mrs. Shlemiel's children?" asked Gronam.

For a moment Shlemiel stood there completely bewildered. Then he said, "Three groschen[5] a day."

"Idiot, moron, ass!" screamed Mrs. Shlemiel. "What are three groschen nowadays? You shouldn't do it for less than six a day." She ran over to Shlemiel and pinched him on the arm. Shlemiel winced and cried out, "She pinches just like my wife."

The Elders held a consultation among themselves. The town budget was very limited. Finally Gronam announced: "Three groschen may be too little, but six groschen a day is definitely too much, especially for a stranger. We will compromise and pay you five groschen a day. Shlemiel, do you accept?"

[5]groschen (gru′ shən): a German coin no longer in use

"Yes, but how long am I to keep this job?"

"Until the real Shlemiel comes home."

Gronam's decision was soon known throughout Chelm and the town admired his great wisdom and that of all the Elders of Chelm.

At first, Shlemiel tried to keep for himself the five groschen that the town paid him. "If I'm not your husband, I don't have to support you," he told Mrs. Shlemiel.

"In that case, since I'm not your wife, I don't have to cook for you, darn your socks, or patch your clothes."

And so, of course, Shlemiel turned over his pay to her. It was the first time that Mrs. Shlemiel had ever gotten any money for the household from Shlemiel. Now when she was in a good mood, she would say to him: "What a pity you didn't decide to go to Warsaw ten years ago."

"Don't you ever miss your husband?" Shlemiel would ask.

"And what about you? Don't you miss your wife?" Mrs. Shlemiel would ask.

And both would admit that they were quite happy with matters as they stood.

Years passed and no Shlemiel returned to Chelm. The Elders had many explanations for this. Zeinvel Ninny believed that Shlemiel had crossed the black mountains and had been eaten alive by the cannibals who live there. Dopey Lekisch thought that Shlemiel most probably had come to the Castle of Asmodeus, where he had been forced to marry a demon princess. Shmendrick Numskull came to the conclusion that Shlemiel had reached the edge of the world and had fallen off. There were many other theories. For example, that the real

Shlemiel had lost his memory and had simply forgotten that he was Shlemiel. Such things do happen.

Gronam did not like to impose his theories on other people; however, he was convinced that Shlemiel had gone to the other Chelm, where he had had exactly the same experience as the Shlemiel in this Chelm. He had been hired by the local community and was taking care of the other Mrs. Shlemiel's children for a wage of five groschen a day.

As for Shlemiel himself, he no longer knew what to think. The children were growing up and soon would be able to take care of themselves. Sometimes Shlemiel would sit and ponder. Where is the other Shlemiel? When will he come home? What is my real wife doing? Is she waiting for me, or has she got herself another Shlemiel? These were questions that he could not answer.

Every now and then Shlemiel would still get the desire to go traveling, but he could not bring himself to start out. What was the point of going on a trip if it led nowhere? Often, as he sat alone puzzling over the strange ways of the world, he would become more and more confused and begin humming to himself:

> "Those who leave Chelm
> End up in Chelm.
> Those who remain in Chelm
> Are certainly in Chelm.
> All roads lead to Chelm.
> All the world is one big Chelm."

Reader's Response ∾ What tickled your funny bone about this story?

Looks Are Deceiving

Shlemiel never made it to Warsaw, but if you get there, you will find not one but two very different cities. One is the modern city of concrete, glass, and steel buildings. The other is the old city of narrow twisting streets and beautiful houses, churches, and shops made of brick and stone.

There is really nothing unusual about that. Many modern cities in Europe have old parts that look much the same as they did when they were built between 800 and 1,000 years ago. What makes Warsaw unusual is that both parts of the city were built at the same time— about forty years ago. How did that happen?

During World War II, Warsaw was severely damaged. After the war, the citizens wanted to rebuild their city. Putting up modern buildings was the easy part. But the people of Warsaw knew that they would not be happy if they could not stroll through the streets of their beautiful old city again. Fortunately, many photographs and sketches of the old city survived the war. Architects and historians used them to recreate the old part of their city as it had been before the war.

The citizens of Warsaw now point to "Old Town" with great pride.

Lee Bennett Hopkins
INTERVIEWS

Isaac Bashevis Singer

"I was born in Radzymin,[1] Poland, on July 14, 1904, and grew up in Warsaw. My father was an orthodox rabbi; my mother was the daughter of the Rabbi of Bilgoray. I studied in cheder, a religious school, and only studied one subject, religion," stated Isaac Bashevis Singer.

[1]Radzymin (răd zē′ min)

His family included a younger brother, Moshe, and an older brother and sister, Israel Joshua and Hinde Esther.

One can read about Mr. Singer's childhood years in the author's own words in *A Day of Pleasure: Stories of a Boy Growing up in Warsaw*, a book that won the 1970 National Book Award for children's literature.

Although Singer was a student at the Rabbinical Seminary in Warsaw, he chose not to become a rabbi. "I do not deserve to be a rabbi. In our Orthodox household every second word was 'forbidden.' In my later years, I'm practicing many of the things that were forbidden!"

Instead he went to work as a journalist for the Yiddish[2] press in Poland after completion of his studies. In 1935 Mr. Singer came to the United States and worked as a journalist and book reviewer for New York's *Jewish Daily Forward*.

"In 1935, when I came here, I got a job on the *Forward*. I said to my editor, 'What I want is a steady job.' He replied, 'A steady job? In a language that will die in ten years?' Yet, you see, Yiddish is still with us."

And indeed it is. Mr. Singer has done much to make the culture, customs, and idiomatic language of the Jewish people familiar the world over. Although he originally wrote in Hebrew,[3] he long ago adopted Yiddish as his medium of expression; he personally supervises the translation of his works into the English language.

His first book for children was *Zlateh the Goat and Other Stories*. I asked Mr. Singer why he turned to writing for children. "Because I felt I could do it," he answered. "I still believe there is no basic difference in writing for grown-ups or for children."

[2]Yiddish: a language developed from German, and written in Hebrew characters with words borrowed from Hebrew, Russian, Polish, and English

[3]Hebrew: the official language of Israel

Zlateh the Goat is a collection of seven tales set in Chelm, a village of fools where the seven elders are the most foolish of all the inhabitants. The book's illustrations, done by the Caldecott Award-winning artist Maurice Sendak, beautifully capture the bittersweetness of Jewish folklore and perfectly depict what Mr. Singer's text is all about. In 1967 *Zlateh the Goat* was designated a Newbery Honor Book.

The same year *The Fearsome Inn* appeared, as well as *Mazel and Shlimazel or the Milk of a Lioness*, a handsome picture book illustrated by Margot Zemach. This tale was inspired by Singer's memory of a story his mother told when he was a boy.

His fourth book for children, *When Shlemiel Went to Warsaw and Other Stories*, also illustrated by Margot Zemach, was a 1969 Newbery Honor Book. Mr. Singer relates eight stories, some inspired by traditional Jewish tales, ranging from hilarious trickery in "Shrewd Todie and Lyzer the Miser" to the tender "Menaseh's Dreams."

In 1970 the author received the National Book Award for his unforgettable *A Day of Pleasure*. The stories in this volume actually took place during the first fourteen years of his life. The last story, "Shosha," deals with a later time.

In a brief foreword to the text, the author wrote: "I have a good deal more to tell about myself, my family, and the Poland of days gone by. I hope to continue these memoirs and reveal a world that is little known to you, but which is rich in comedy and tragedy, rich in its individuality, wisdom, foolishness, wildness, and goodness."

In preparing his books, Mr. Singer told me, "I write the stories, translate them, and edit them together with another translator. If they are bad, the critics let me know."

The author is not worried about the Yiddish language slowly disappearing. "I should worry? I put all my capital, you might say, in Yiddish. But I'm not at all worried. Declining it is. But you know that in our history there is a long way between declining and dying."

In addition to his writing, he does a great deal of lecturing. "I also steal chickens," he jested. He lives with his wife in an apartment house on New York's Upper West Side. His favorite possessions are his books. In his spare time he enjoys "working and walking and visits with his son and three grandchildren."

The Search for the MAGIC

a tale told by the Inca Indians of Ecuador
by Genevieve Barlow

Long ago there was a ruler of the vast Inca[1] Empire who had an only son. This youth brought great joy to his father's heart but also a sadness, for the prince had been born in ill health.

As the years passed the prince's health did not improve, and none of the court doctors could find a cure for his illness.

One night the aged emperor went down on his knees and prayed at the altar.

"Oh Great Ones," he said, "I am getting older and will soon leave my people and join you in the heavens. There is no one to look after them but my son, the prince. I pray you make him well and strong so he can be a fit ruler for my people. Tell me how his malady can be cured."

[1] Inca (iŋg′ kə): an ancient people of South America

The emperor put his head in his hands and waited for an
answer. Soon he heard a voice coming from the fire that
burned constantly in front of the altar.

"Let the prince drink water from the magic lake at the
end of the world," the voice said, "and he will be well."

At that moment the fire sputtered and died. Among the
cold ashes lay a golden flask.

But the emperor was much too old to make the long
journey to the end of the world, and the young prince was
too ill to travel. So the emperor proclaimed that whosoever
should fill the golden flask with the magic water would be
greatly rewarded.

Many brave men set out to search for the magic lake,
but none could find it. Days and weeks passed and still the
flask remained empty.

In a valley, some distance from the emperor's palace, lived a poor farmer who had a wife, two grown sons, and a young daughter.

One day the older son said to his father, "Let my brother and me join in the search for the magic lake. Before the moon is new again, we shall return and help you harvest the corn and potatoes."

The father remained silent. He was not thinking of the harvest, but feared for his sons' safety.

When the father did not answer, the second son added, "Think of the rich reward, Father!"

"It is their duty to go," said his wife, "for we must all try to help our emperor and the young prince."

After his wife had spoken, the father yielded.

"Go if you must, but beware of the wild beasts and evil spirits," he cautioned.

With their parents' blessing, and an affectionate farewell from their young sister, the sons set out on their journey.

They found many lakes, but none where the sky touched the water.

Finally the younger brother said, "Before another day has passed we must return to help father with the harvest."

"Yes," agreed the other, "but I have thought of a plan. Let us each carry a jar of water from any lake along the way. We can say it will cure the prince. Even if it doesn't, surely the emperor will give us a small reward for our trouble."

"Agreed," said the younger brother.

On arriving at the palace, the deceitful youths told the emperor and his court that they brought water from the magic lake. At once the prince was given a sip from each of the brothers' jars, but of course he remained as ill as before.

"Perhaps the water must be sipped from the golden flask," one of the high priests said.

But the golden flask would not hold the water. In some mysterious way the water from the jars disappeared as soon as it was poured into the flask.

In despair the emperor called for his magician and said to him, "Can you break the spell of the flask so the water will remain for my son to drink?"

"I cannot do that, your majesty," replied the magician. "But I believe," he added wisely, "that the flask is telling us that we have been deceived by the two brothers. The flask can be filled only with water from the magic lake."

When the brothers heard this, they trembled with fright, for they knew their falsehood was discovered.

So angry was the emperor that he ordered the brothers thrown into chains. Each day they were forced to drink water from their jars as a reminder of their false deed. News of their disgrace spread far and wide.

Again the emperor sent messengers throughout the land pleading for someone to bring the magic water before death claimed him and the young prince.

Súmac,[2] the little sister of the deceitful youths, was tending her flock of llamas when she heard the sound of the royal trumpet. Then came the voice of the emperor's servant with his urgent message from the court.

Quickly the child led her llamas home and begged her parents to let her go in search of the magic water.

"You are too young," her father said. "Besides, look at what has already befallen your brothers. Some evil spirit must have taken hold of them to make them tell such a lie."

And her mother said, "We could not bear to be without our precious Súmac!"

"But think how sad our emperor will be if the young prince dies," replied the innocent child. "And if I can find the magic lake, perhaps the emperor will forgive my brothers and send them home."

"Dear husband," said Súmac's mother, "maybe it is the will of the gods that we let her go."

Once again the father gave his permission.

"It is true," he murmured, "I must think of our emperor."

---

[2]Súmac (soo′ mäk)

288

Súmac was overjoyed, and went skipping out to the cor-
ral to harness one of her pet llamas. It would carry her
provisions and keep her company.

Meanwhile her mother filled a little woven bag with food
and drink for Súmac—toasted golden kernels of corn and a
little earthen jar of *chicha,*[3] a beverage made from crushed
corn.

The three embraced each other tearfully before Súmac
set out bravely on her mission, leading her pet llama along
the trail.

The first night she slept, snug and warm against her
llama, in the shelter of a few rocks. But when she heard
the hungry cry of the puma, she feared for her pet animal
and bade it return safely home.

The next night she spent in the top branches of a tall
tree, far out of reach of the dreadful puma. She hid her
provisions in a hole in the tree trunk.

At sunrise she was aroused by the voices of gentle sparrows resting on a nearby limb.

"Poor child," said the oldest sparrow, "she can never find
her way to the lake."

"Let us help her," chorused the others.

"Oh please do!" implored the child, "and forgive me for
intruding in your tree."

"We welcome you," chirped another sparrow, "for you
are the same little girl who yesterday shared your golden
corn with us."

"We shall help you," continued the first sparrow, who
was the leader, "for you are a good child. Each of us will
give you a wing feather, and you must hold them all together in one hand as a fan. The feathers have magic powers that will carry you wherever you wish to go. They will

[3]chicha (chē chä)

289

also protect you from harm." Each sparrow then lifted a wing, sought out a special feather hidden underneath, and gave it to Súmac. She fashioned them into the shape of a little fan, taking the ribbon from her hair to bind the feathers together so none would be lost.

"I must warn you," said the oldest sparrow, "that the lake is guarded by three terrible creatures. But have no fear. Hold the magic fan up to your face and you will be unharmed."

Súmac thanked the birds over and over again. Then, holding up the fan in her chubby hands, she said politely, "Please, magic fan, take me to the lake at the end of the world."

A soft breeze swept her out of the top branches of the tree and through the valley. Then up she was carried, higher and higher into the sky, until she could look down and see the great mountain peaks covered with snow.

At last the wind put her down on the shore of a beautiful lake. It was, indeed, the lake at the end of the world, for, on the opposite side from where she stood, the sky came down so low it touched the water.

Súmac tucked the magic fan into her waistband and ran to the edge of the water. Suddenly her face fell. She had

left everything back in the forest. What could she use for carrying the precious water back to the prince?

"Oh, I do wish I had remembered the jar!" she said, weeping.

Suddenly she heard a soft thud in the sand at her feet. She looked down and discovered a beautiful golden flask— the same one the emperor had found in the ashes.

Súmac took the flask and kneeled at the water's edge. Just then a hissing voice behind her said, "Get away from my lake or I shall wrap my long, hairy legs around your neck."

Súmac turned around. There stood a giant crab as large as a pig and as black as night.

With trembling hands the child took the magic fan from her waistband and spread it open in front of her face. As soon as the crab looked at it, he closed his eyes and fell down on the sand in a deep sleep.

Once more Súmac started to fill the flask. This time she was startled by a fierce voice bubbling up from the water.

"Get away from my lake or I shall eat you," gurgled a giant green alligator. His long tail beat the water angrily.

Súmac waited until the creature swam closer. Then she held up the fan. The alligator blinked. He drew back.

Slowly, quietly, he sank to the bottom of the lake in a sound sleep.

Before Súmac could recover from her fright, she heard a shrill whistle in the air. She looked up and saw a flying serpent. His skin was red as blood. Sparks flew from his eyes.

"Get away from my lake or I shall bite you," hissed the serpent as it batted its wings around her head.

Again Súmac's fan saved her from harm. The serpent closed his eyes and drifted to the ground. He folded his wings and coiled up on the sand. Then he began to snore.

Súmac sat for a moment to quiet herself. Then, realizing that the danger was past, she sighed with great relief.

"Now I can fill the golden flask and be on my way," she said to herself.

When this was done, she held the flask tightly in one hand and clutched the fan in the other.

"Please take me to the palace," she said.

Hardly were the words spoken, when she found herself safely in front of the palace gates. She looked at the tall guard.

"I wish to see the emperor," Súmac uttered in trembling tones.

"Why, little girl?" the guard asked kindly.

"I bring water from the magic lake to cure the prince."

The guard looked down at her in astonishment.

"Come!" he commanded in a voice loud and deep as thunder.

In just a few moments Súmac was led into a room full of sadness. The emperor was pacing up and down in despair. The prince lay motionless on a huge bed. His eyes were closed and his face was without color. Beside him knelt his mother, weeping.

Without wasting words, Súmac went to the prince and gave him a few drops of magic water. Soon he opened his eyes. His cheeks became flushed. It was not long before he sat up in bed. He drank some more.

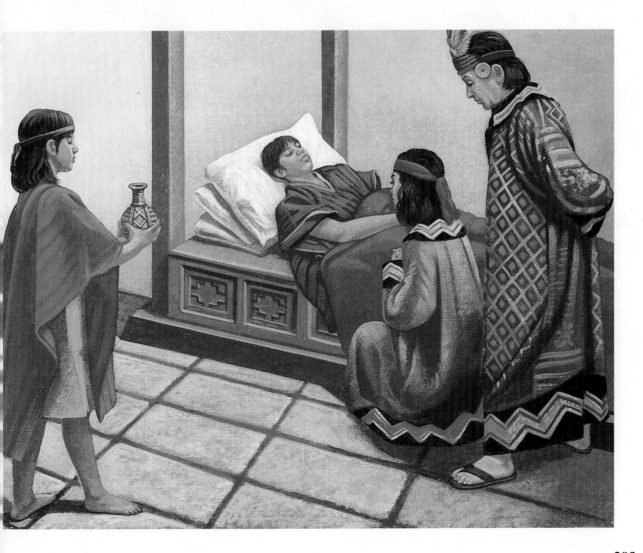

"How strong I feel!" the prince cried joyfully.

The emperor and his wife embraced Súmac. Then Súmac told them of her adventurous trip to the lake. They praised her courage. They marveled at the reappearance of the golden flask and at the powers of the magic fan.

"Dear child," said the emperor, "all the riches of my empire are not enough to repay you for saving my son's life. Ask what you will and it shall be yours."

"Oh, generous emperor," said Súmac timidly, "I have but three wishes."

"Name them and they shall be yours," urged the emperor.

"First, I wish my brothers to be free to return to my parents. They have learned their lesson and will never be false again. I know they were only thinking of a reward for my parents. Please forgive them."

"Guards, free them at once!" ordered the emperor.

"Secondly, I wish the magic fan returned to the forest so the sparrows may have their feathers again."

This time the emperor had no time to speak. Before anyone in the room could utter a sound, the magic fan lifted itself up, spread itself wide open, and floated out the window toward the woods. Everyone watched in amazement. When the fan was out of sight, they applauded.

"What is your last wish, dear Súmac?" asked the queen mother.

"I wish that my parents be given a large farm and great flocks of llamas, vicuñas, and alpacas, so they will not be poor any longer."

"It will be so," said the emperor, "but I am sure your parents never considered themselves poor with so wonderful a daughter."

"Won't you stay with us in the palace?" ventured the prince.

"Yes, stay with us!" urged the emperor and his wife. "We

will do everything to make you happy."

"Oh thank you," said Súmac blushing happily, "but I must return to my parents and to my brothers. I miss them as I know they have missed me. They do not even know I am safe, for I came directly to your palace."

The royal family did not try to detain Súmac any longer.

"My own guard will see that you get home safely," said the emperor.

When she reached home, she found that all she had wished for had come to pass: her brothers were waiting for her with their parents; a beautiful house and huge barn were being constructed; her father had received a deed granting him many acres of new, rich farm land.

Súmac ran into the arms of her happy family.

At the palace, the golden flask was never empty. Each time it was used, it was refilled. Thus the prince's royal descendants never suffered ill health and the kingdom remained strong.

But it is said that when the Spanish conqueror of the ancient Incas demanded a room filled with golden gifts, the precious flask was among them. Whatever happened to this golden treasure is unknown, for the conqueror was killed and the Indians wandered over the mainland in search of a new leader. Some say the precious gifts—including the golden flask—are buried at the bottom of the lake at the end of the world, but no one besides Súmac has ever ventured to go there.

Reader's Response ∿ How did you feel about the wishes that Súmac made? Explain your answer.

Architectural MARVELS

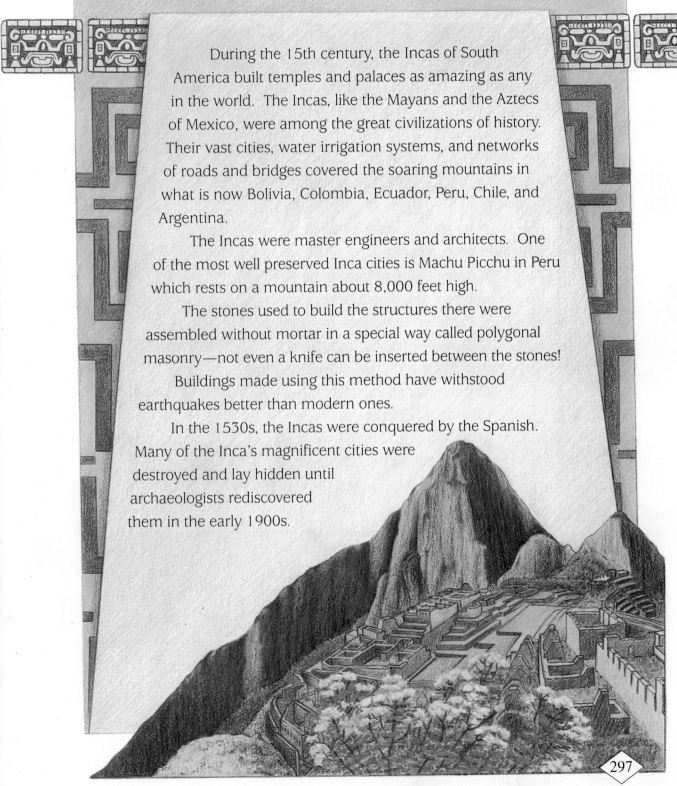

During the 15th century, the Incas of South America built temples and palaces as amazing as any in the world. The Incas, like the Mayans and the Aztecs of Mexico, were among the great civilizations of history. Their vast cities, water irrigation systems, and networks of roads and bridges covered the soaring mountains in what is now Bolivia, Colombia, Ecuador, Peru, Chile, and Argentina.

The Incas were master engineers and architects. One of the most well preserved Inca cities is Machu Picchu in Peru which rests on a mountain about 8,000 feet high.

The stones used to build the structures there were assembled without mortar in a special way called polygonal masonry—not even a knife can be inserted between the stones!

Buildings made using this method have withstood earthquakes better than modern ones.

In the 1530s, the Incas were conquered by the Spanish. Many of the Inca's magnificent cities were destroyed and lay hidden until archaeologists rediscovered them in the early 1900s.

The Way Through The Woods

by Rudyard Kipling

They shut the road through the woods
Seventy years ago.
Weather and rain have undone it again,
And now you would never know
There was once a road through the woods
Before they planted the trees.
It is underneath the coppice and heath,
And the thin anemones.
Only the keeper sees
That, where the ring-dove broods,
And the badgers roll at ease,
There was once a road through the woods.

Yet, if you enter the woods
Of a summer evening late,
When the night-air cools on the trout-ringed pools
Where the otter whistles his mate
(They fear not men in the woods,
Because they see so few),
You will hear the beat of a horse's feet,
And the swish of a skirt in the dew,
Steadily cantering through
The misty solitudes,
As though they perfectly knew
The old lost road through the woods . . .
But there is no road through the woods!

AWARD
WINNING
AUTHOR

Snowshoe Trek to Otter River

by David Budbill

Early in the morning after Daniel finished breakfast, he took his backpack off the wall and unpacked it. He had packed everything carefully last night, but now that it was time to go, he had to be sure everything was there, ready, in case he needed it. Daniel could see his mother moving about the kitchen, watching him out of the corner of her eye. He knew she was laughing to herself about the way he fussed over his equipment. But the gear was important. If he got caught out there in a blizzard, or if _____ hing happened to him and he

couldn't get back, his life might depend on the few things he carried on his back.

He spread the backpack's contents on the kitchen floor. Nested cookpots: one 8-inch skillet with folding handle, one 6-inch plate, one quart pail with lid, a metal cup, a fork and spoon. His pocketknife would do the cutting. A bunch of waterproof matches wrapped in tinfoil. Two fire starters he had made by rolling paper tightly, tying it with string, and soaking it in hot paraffin. A compass, a hatchet, and a sleeping bag. Daniel

READERS'
CHOICE
AWARD

cut three thick slices of his mother's homemade bread, buttered them, then took two chunks of bacon and three eggs from the refrigerator. He wrapped everything carefully and put it in the backpack with a bag of nuts and raisins, a little salt, a small jar of sugar, and a handful of tea in a small bag. As far as Daniel was concerned, bacon and eggs, bread, and tea was the perfect campfire lunch for a winter's day of snowshoeing.

Daniel was only twelve, but he knew a lot about getting along in the woods. His parents were dairy farmers. Although they lived surrounded by the wilderness, they never really were a part of it. But down the road from Daniel's house there was an old man, a Frenchman by the name of Mr. Bateau, who had come down from Canada years ago. Mr. Bateau was Daniel's favorite person. He was a man of the woods—a logger, a hunter, a fisherman, and a trapper. Mr. Bateau had taught Daniel all he knew about the wild world. He had shown him how to fish, build wilderness camps, identify wild flowers and animal tracks, how to talk to birds, call foxes, make coyotes howl. But most of all Mr. Bateau had given Daniel a love of the wilderness that drew Daniel out now into the white, cold world beyond his house.

Daniel's plan was to strike out across the high swamp behind his farm and continue down the mountain to Otter River in the valley below. Last summer he and his best friend, Seth, had built a lean-to on the far side of Otter River. Daniel planned to have his lunch at the camp, check the supplies they had stashed there, and return home before dark.

When the backpack was packed again, Daniel put on two pairs of heavy wool socks and pulled his rubber-bottom, leather-top winter boots over them. He wore long underwear and wool pants. Over a long-sleeved undershirt he wore a cotton shirt and over that a wool shirt and over that another, heavier wool shirt. If he got hot, he could peel off a layer or two, but he doubted he'd get hot. He looked out the window at the thermometer. It said ten degrees below zero. By noon it might be ten above.

He was ready. He slipped his backpack on, kissed his mother good-bye, and went onto the porch. He pulled his wool cap down over his ears, put on his mittens, picked up his snowshoes, and stepped out into the snow. He slipped his boots into the snowshoe harnesses and adjusted the bindings carefully.

It was a clear, bright, still day. The spruce and fir trees on the horizon made a deep green band that separated the bright blue sky from the white, pure white earth. As Daniel struck out across the pasture behind the house, the cold air stung his face. It felt good. It was the perfect day for a hike.

Last night's snow had added six inches to the three feet already on the ground. Daniel knew the new snow meant animal tracks would be fresh. He'd do some tracking along the way.

Soon he was beyond the open fields and deep into the swamp. It was a different world, darker, quieter. The big spruce and fir trees covered up the sky. There was no sound. It was as if this swamp were a noiseless chamber. All Daniel could hear were his snowshoes, whispering, hissing as he moved along. He stopped. Listened. Now there was no sound at all. None. It was as if everything in the world were dead except for one boy who stood silent and alone, deep in a snowy evergreen swamp.

Suddenly, out of nowhere, the sound of galloping broke the silence. Daniel's heart jumped. He crouched down and waited. Then, in a crash of twigs, a shower of snow, three deer burst into a clearing right in front of him—a buck, a doe, and last year's fawn. The three deer stopped. They stood silent in their tracks. Slowly the buck raised his head and sniffed the wind. He caught Daniel's scent. The buck gave a terrible snorting roar, stomped his foot, and away the three went in a muffled thunder of hooves, their sleek, brown bodies plowing through the snow. Daniel stood up and watched the three deer disappear into the dark trees. His heart was still pounding.

He came to a broad open place in the middle of the swamp. Beavers had dammed the swamp brook and made a pond. Daniel could see a large hump in the level snow near the dam. It was a beaver house. As Daniel crossed the pond, he thought about the beavers under all that snow and ice, lazing away the winter, safe in their underwater home. At this very moment there could be a beaver swimming only a few feet below his snowshoes.

When he reached the other side of the beaver pond, Daniel found some rabbit tracks. They weren't really made by a rabbit, even though everybody called them rabbits. They were made by a snowshoe hare, the kind that turns white in the winter and has big, webbed feet for getting around in deep snow. Daniel could tell from the size of the tracks that it was a young rabbit. He followed the tracks up the hill to a place where they stopped abruptly. Here there was a pool of frozen blood and beside the blood on either side, printed neatly in the snow, the marks of two large wings. Daniel knew what had happened.

The hare had been hopping along, when, out of the sky, swiftly, silently, a large hawk had dropped down, his wings set back, his large claws thrust out and down. Thud! Daniel could see the hawk's sharp claws sink into the rabbit's back. He could hear the rabbit scream as it died. Then the hawk beat his wings, leaving the prints there in the snow, and was away, up into the air with his breakfast.

Daniel felt sorry for the rabbit, but he knew this was the way the hawk ate, the way he stayed alive. Last fall Daniel had helped his father slaughter a pig so they could eat meat all winter. The hawk had slaughtered a rabbit so he could eat meat too. But Daniel couldn't help feeling sorry for the rabbit, just as he had felt sorry for the pig. He stood for a long time staring at the rabbit tracks that went nowhere, the frozen blood, the imprint of the hawk's wings. Then he pushed on.

He was out of the evergreen swamp now and starting down the mountain toward the river. Here the trees were all hardwoods, and the sun shone brightly through the bare branches. A chickadee scolded Daniel from a nearby tree.

Daniel saw tiny ruffed grouse tracks everywhere. The grouse had come to the hardwoods to eat the buds off birch trees. Suddenly there was a thundering rush, a wild flutter of wings. Daniel stopped. Grouse were flying everywhere, weaving crazily between the trees. One bird flew right at him. He threw his hands up in front of his face. Then the bird was gone.

Soon Daniel was down the mountain. Otter River was before him. He could see the snow-covered camp on the other side. He walked up and down the riverbank looking for a place to cross. Daniel knew that where the river ran still and deep the ice would

be the thickest. There was a place like that about a hundred yards upstream, but the river looked safe here too and it wasn't quite so wide. Daniel took off his snowshoes. If he fell through with them on, his feet would be trapped under the ice. He stepped out onto the river and jumped up and down a couple of times. The ice was solid. He started across.

When he was almost to the far shore, he heard a loud, thundering crack begin near him and shoot up the river. Slowly, he began to sink. Then more and louder cracks. Then a deep, rumbling roar. He was going down! The whole river was opening up!

Daniel heaved his snowshoes onto the shore and grabbed for solid ice. His boots were full of water, his legs numbed by the cold. Again and again he reached for the edge of solid ice. Each time the ice broke away and bobbed uselessly in front of him. Then his feet struck bottom. He stood waist deep in icy water. He could wade to shore. But there were great slabs of loose ice floating between him and the bank. When he tried to climb on top of them, they sank. When he tried to push them out of his way, they bumped into each other and blocked the way. He was trapped.

Daniel's mind raced. He had to think of something fast. In only a few minutes he would be so cold he'd faint. That would be the end. Quickly he took his pack off his back, undid the top, and grabbed his hatchet. He threw the pack up on the bank. Then, slowly, painfully, Daniel began chopping a channel through the slabs of ice toward the shore.

He reached the bank and pulled himself cold and numb out of the water. He was soaked. The instant his wet clothes met the cold air, they froze. His troubles had only begun.

By now his pants had frozen so hard he could barely bend his knees. He gathered up his snowshoes and pack and limped, stiff-legged, to his camp. Daniel was freezing, not just freezing cold, but actually freezing, freezing to death.

He took the small shovel he and Seth had stashed in the lean-to and cleaned the snow away from the fire pit. He broke an armful of dead branches off a hemlock tree for kindling, took one of the fire starters out of his pack, and lit a fire. He was glad now that last summer he and Seth had stacked dry wood next to the camp.

Soon the fire was burning. Daniel was sleepy and cold, so cold. All he wanted to do was lie down, but he knew he couldn't. Not yet.

He stuck two forked sticks in the snow, one on each side of the fire. Then he laid a long pole between the two sticks above the fire. He propped his snowshoes near the fire, crawled inside the lean-to, and spread his sleeping bag on the bare, dry ground inside the shelter. Then he put more wood on the fire.

When all this was done, he was ready to do the only thing left to do. He couldn't go home. It was too far away. He'd freeze before he got there. He couldn't call for help. There was no one for miles. He'd have to thaw and dry out before he could go any farther.

Although it was below zero, Daniel took off his clothes. He draped his pants and long underwear, socks, and mittens over the long pole. He hung a wool shirt on each snowshoe. He put his boots on a rock near the fire. The snow was so cold on his bare feet that it felt hot. When all his clothes were hung over the fire, he limped into the lean-to and climbed inside his sleeping bag. He shivered violently. He wanted to cry, but he was too cold. Slowly, very slowly, his body heat began to fill the sleeping bag. He began to warm up. He took the bag of nuts and raisins from his pack and ate. He could see his clothes dripping and steaming over the fire. Daniel was relaxed now. His eyes grew heavy. He fell asleep.

When Daniel woke up, the fire was down to coals. It was warm inside the bag. He had no idea how long he had slept. It may have been an hour or two. He got up and put more wood on the fire. He felt his clothes. They were dry, except for his boots. He got dressed. His clothes smelled like wood smoke. He hung his boots from the pole by their laces and began to fix lunch. He set the bacon to frying in the skillet and put some snow to melt in the quart pail for tea. Since snow water always tasted flat, he added a little salt to the melting snow.

When the water boiled, he added tea and put the pail on a rock at the edge of the fire. He reached into his backpack for the eggs. They were smashed. They must have broken when he threw the pack up on the bank. He dumped the slimy mixture into his metal plate and separated shell from egg as best he could. He took the cooked bacon out of the skillet and put the eggs in, scrambling them with his fork. They cooked quickly. Then he ate. It seemed to Daniel like the best meal he had ever eaten. Crisp bacon, eggs scrambled in bacon grease, good bread with lots of butter, and hot, sweet tea. It was good.

Daniel laughed to himself. Here he was, in the middle of winter, sitting by a fire, by a river he had just fallen into, eating lunch, thinking how good the tea was! It was hard to believe. A couple of hours ago he was almost dead. Now he sat comfortably, his feet warmed by the fire, almost as if nothing had happened.

When the last of the tea was gone, he put his boots on, cleaned and packed his gear, shoveled snow on the fire, rolled the sleeping bag, and started home. This time he headed upstream to where the river moved slowly and the ice was thick. Nobody ever crossed a frozen river more carefully than Daniel did that afternoon.

When he reached the other side, he noticed that the sun was low in the southern sky. It got dark early this time of year, and home was a long way off. He'd have to travel to get there before dark.

He followed his own trail up through the hardwoods, over the brow of the mountain, and down into the swamp.

308

By the time he reached the other side of the beaver pond, the sun was almost down. It was dark in the thick trees of the swamp. Daniel had trouble finding his trail. It got darker and darker. He was hurrying now, and, although it was growing colder, he was sweating. Then out of the darkening sky fear dropped down and seized him. He had gotten off the trail. He was lost.

Daniel was running. He had to find his old trail and fast. But the faster he moved, the more confused he got. Then he stopped. He found a log sticking up above the snow, brushed the snow off its top, and sat down. He knew that to get panicky when lost was the worst thing that could happen. He took the bag of nuts and raisins from his pack and ate a handful. He would sit here until he quieted down and decided what to do. But it was hard. He had to force himself to sit on that log. Something inside urged him to get up and run. It didn't matter where, just run! He fought the urge with all the strength he had.

Then he heard the soft rustle of wings. A large white bird floated silently into a tree above him. It was a snowy owl. It seemed to Daniel like a ghost. Its fierce yellow eyes shot through him like needles. Why did that bird sit there, staring? What did it want? Daniel couldn't stand it. He jumped up, made a snowball, and threw it at the owl. The snowball almost hit the owl, but the owl didn't move. He sat there, staring, as if to say, "I'm not the one who is afraid." Then, as if nothing had happened, the snowy owl rolled backward off the branch and disappeared without a sound into the dark trees.

The owl, the noiseless chamber of a forest, the darkness, frightened Daniel more than falling in the river. When he had gone down in the river, he knew what he had to do to save himself. The only question was whether he could do it. But here, in this wild place, there was something unknown, something strange. He felt out of place, alone, deserted. It seemed as if even the trees around him were about to grab him, take him off somewhere, deeper into the swamp, where he would be lost forever.

He decided what to do. He would get up, calmly, and follow his tracks back to where he lost the trail. He'd get back on the trail and go home. It was hard to go back, but he had to do it.

When he found the trail again, he moved along it slowly. It was so dark

now he couldn't afford to get lost again. At last, after what seemed like hours, he found himself standing at the edge of a broad, open field. At the far end of the field he could see his house. The kitchen window glowed warm and orange in the dusky evening light. He struck off across the meadow toward the lighted window.

Daniel took off his snowshoes and stuck them in the snow in front of the house. He dumped his backpack on the porch and stepped into the bright,

warm kitchen. His parents were fixing supper.

"Well, where have you been? We were beginning to worry," his father said.

"The hike took longer than I thought."

"How was it?" his mother asked.

"It was okay."

"Didn't you have any fantastic adventures?"

Daniel looked at his mother and smiled. He said, "No, not today."

Reader's Response ⁓ Did you feel Daniel's danger as you read? Explain your answer.

Snow Trek

Daniel used snowshoes on his trek because they are a practical way to walk through deep snow. In North America, snowshoes were first used by northern Native American tribes several thousand years ago. Snowshoes are traditionally made from white ash, a particularly durable wood, and rawhide lacings.

Different styles of snowshoes were developed for different kinds of terrain. The Bearpaw, for example, is used in dense woods because it is short and easy to maneuver. The Ojibwa, on the other hand, has a narrower body and a distinct nose and tail. These features provide greater stability in the deep powder of open areas.

Four traditional styles of snowshoes are illustrated on this page. In what kind of terrain do you think the Maine and Beavertail styles of snowshoes are used?

Bearpaw

Beavertail

Maine

Ojibwa

311

Odysseus and the Sea Kings

retold by James Reeves

"Odysseus and the Sea Kings" retells part of the poet Homer's
Odyssey, a three-thousand-year-old tale that is one of the most fa-
mous epics in all of literature. The Greek king Odysseus, a hero in
the ten-year war with Troy, is returning home to Ithaca. But when
he blinds the Cyclops Polyphemus, a one-eyed giant, the angry gods
make his journey home long and dangerous.

When Odysseus[1] had finished eating and drinking, Nausicaa[2]
spoke to him.

"Let us go to the city, stranger," she said.

"I will take you to my father's palace. As we go through the
fields, follow close behind me. But when we come to the city,
you must be careful. You will see the walls and the harbour[3] and
the market square, through which you must pass. Among our
people, I fear, are some rude men who will look with curiosity at
a handsome stranger. They will know you are not of this country,
and would wonder what I was doing in your presence, when it is
thought that I must choose a husband from among our own people.

[1]Odysseus (ō dis′ ē əs)

[2]Nausicaa (nô sik′ ā ə)

[3]Some words in this selection are spelled in the British style.

313

"This is what you must do. On the way you will find a grove sacred to Athene.[4] There, there are poplar trees and a clear-running spring. Stay there until you think that I and my maidens have had time to reach home. Then go into the city and ask for the house of Alcinous.[5] You will have no trouble in finding it. When you reach it, go straight in to where my mother spins her sea-blue yarn at the fireside; my father sits there beside her, drinking his wine. Greet my mother courteously, for, if you win her favour, you will the sooner reach your home."

Nausicaa climbed into the wagon, touched the mules with her whip, and they began to move through the fields towards the city. At sundown they came to the grove of Athene. Here Odysseus bade the Princess farewell; and when the wagon was out of sight, he prayed to the goddess Athene and begged her to help him win favour in the eyes of the Sea Kings, so that they might help him to get home. Athene heard the prayer of Odysseus.

Nausicaa reached home, and her brother unyoked the mules and carried in the clean linen. The Princess was greeted by her old nurse. Meanwhile Odysseus began his journey to the city on foot. In order to protect him from prying eyes, Athene covered him with a mist. Soon he saw the houses and the towers of the Sea Kings. Reaching a little square, he was greeted by Athene in the guise of a maiden carrying a pitcher to fetch water. He asked her where he could find the palace of Alcinous. She said she would show him the way and added:

"Don't talk to anyone, because my people, the proud Sea Kings, are very suspicious towards strangers."

When they got to the palace, Athene told Odysseus to walk boldly in and go straight up to the Queen, whose name was Arete.[6]

"She is held in high honour by her husband and her children," Athene said, "and by all other men. She is wise, and if you can gain her goodwill she will help you as no one else can."

---

[4]Athene (ə thē′ nē): ancient Greek goddess of wisdom (also spelled *Athena*)
[5]Alcinous (al sin′ ə wəs)
314 [6]Arete (ar ē tā′)

Then Athene, still in the form of the maiden with the pitcher,
made her departure, and Odysseus entered the palace. The sight
caused him to marvel, for the walls shone like the full moon; they
were of bronze and the doors plated with gold. The great hall was
lined with seats covered with fine cloths which the women of the
house had woven. There were fifty maidservants in the palace of
Alcinous, to do the cooking, the spinning and the weaving. They
were as skilled at their weaving as the Sea Kings were at managing their swift ships. Outside the palace was a rich and beautiful
garden, where grew all manner of fruit—pomegranates, grapes,
apples and figs—so that they gave a sweet harvest all the year

round. There were beds full of bright flowers, and two fountains, one to water the garden and the other for passers-by to drink at.

Dazzled by the beauty of the garden and the splendour of the palace, Odysseus went through the hall to where the King and Queen were seated at one end. The Sea Kings and the princess were sitting round the table with wine cups before them; none saw him because of the cloud of invisibility which Athene had wrapped about him. But when he reached Queen Arete, the cloud dispersed, and everyone marvelled to see the stranger in their midst. Odysseus knelt before the Queen and said:

"Great Queen, take pity on me and help a poor, travel-worn

317

stranger to return to his home and his people. I will pray the gods to send happiness and prosperity to you and all your house."

All were silent, until an old, wise lord said:

"Alcinous, let this stranger be given an honourable place at your table, and let us all drink to his health."

Alcinous led Odysseus by the hand to a place at his side. Servants were commanded to bring water to wash his hands, and food and wine were set before him. When the feast was over, Alcinous told his guests to come to the palace next morning, when they would sit in council and hear the stranger's tale.

"Noble Alcinous," said Odysseus, "I could make a long history of all my griefs and misfortunes, but now all I wish is to return safely to my own country. In the morning, I will beg you to help me on my way."

When the nobles had departed for their houses, Odysseus was left alone with the King and Queen. Now the Queen had been looking closely at the doublet and cloak worn by Odysseus, and she knew that they had been made by herself and her servants.

"Stranger," said Arete, looking into Odysseus' weather-beaten face, "Where do you come from? Who gave you the clothes you are wearing?"

Then Odysseus told the Queen how he had stayed for years on the island of Calypso and how he had made himself a raft and put to sea, for the only thought in his mind was somehow to return to his own country. He told her, how after seventeen days he had been wrecked by the anger of Poseidon[7] and cast up on the coast of the Sea Kings' land. He told how he had passed the night under the bushes, and how next day he had seen Nausicaa and her maidens who had given him food and clothing.

"These are the clothes I am wearing now," he said. "Your daughter told me how to reach your palace, after she herself departed with the wagon and the mules."

[7]Poseidon (pō sīd' ən): ancient Greek god of the sea

318

"My daughter did well," said Alcinous, "except in one matter. She should have brought you to the palace herself."

"Noble sir," replied Odysseus, "your daughter did right. I had feared that if I had come to your palace in her presence, you might have been offended to see her with a stranger."

"I would not have taken offence," said Alcinous. "If you should choose to stay here and marry my daughter, it would give me the keenest pleasure. You are the sort of man I look to have for a son-in-law. But we will not try to keep you here if you are set on returning to your own country. Stay with us tonight, and tomorrow one of our fastest ships shall be made ready to carry you wherever you desire to go."

So Odysseus went gladly to rest, for he was weary; and in the morning the King roused him and took him to the public square near the harbour. Here they sat down on the stone seats while a herald went round the town bidding the people come and see the lordly stranger. When the square was thronged with townspeople, Alcinous stood up and said:

"My people, I do not know this stranger's name. But yesterday he came to my house and asked for help to sail back to his own country. Let us treat him as is our custom with strangers in our midst. Let us give him the help he asks. Prepare a swift ship and choose fifty of your most skilful sailors. Then come to the palace where we will hold a feast in honour of our visitor."

After a ship was made ready, the princes crowded into the hall. A minstrel came in, led by a herald, for he was blind. He had lost his eyesight, but he had the voice of a great singer. He sang of the siege of Troy and of the heroes who had died there. The minstrel's singing brought bitter tears to Odysseus' eyes. He hid his face in his cloak; only Alcinous knew that he was weeping.

So he ended the feast and told his guests that they ought to give the stranger an exhibition of their skill at games. They threw

quoits, wrestled, boxed and ran races. Then one of the Sea Kings said to the others:

"Let us ask the stranger if he has a particular skill in one or other game. He looks strong and well built."

But when they challenged Odysseus, he shook his head sadly and said:

"I am not in the mood for games. I would rather be left to my sorrow. All I can think of is the wife and the home I left so long ago. All I want from your King and his people is to be helped on my way."

Then one of the young men, whose name was Euryalus,[8] scoffed at Odysseus and said:

"I can well understand why you have no skill in games. I should think you have spent your life as a trader, buying, selling and making bargains. No wonder you will not join in our sports."

Odysseus frowned angrily at the young man and said:

"The gods have given you grace and strength, young man, but they have not given you courtesy. Your rude words have stung me, and I will show you what I can do, stiff and weary though I am with the toils and hardships of my wandering."

So saying, he did not even stop to remove his cloak but stooped and picked up a huge stone quoit. He swung it round and hurled it through the air so that all the onlookers shrank back in fear and amazement. The quoit came to rest far beyond all the others. He smiled as he turned to Euryalus and said:

"There! Make as good a throw as that, young man. Or would you rather I wrestled with you, or boxed, or ran races? I can shoot an arrow too, if that is what you want."

At this there was silence until Alcinous said:

"There is no doubt of your strength and skill, my friend. We have fast ships but, to tell you the truth, games and sports are not our strong point. We like dancing best, so now let two of my sons give you an exhibition of their ability."

[8]Euryalus (yoo rē′ ə los)

321

A space was cleared, a minstrel struck up a lively tune on his pipes, and two princes danced with agility and grace, throwing a crimson ball back and forth between them, catching it in the air and dancing all the while, until Odysseus marvelled at their nimbleness. When the dance was finished, Alcinous told all the Kings to go and fetch gifts for Odysseus to take with him on his journey home.

"Euryalus," he said, "shall make a special gift, to pay for his rudeness."

The young man readily agreed and presented Odysseus with a handsome bronze sword with a cunningly-wrought scabbard of carved ivory. He smiled at Odysseus in a frank and friendly way and said:

"Pardon me, sir, for my rough words. I beg you, let them be forgotten; and may I wish you a safe and speedy return to your home from which you have been so long away."

Slinging the sword over his shoulder, Odysseus said:

"I thank you for your kindness, friend. May good fortune go with you always, and may you never stand in need of this fine blade!"

Then Alcinous led Odysseus back into the palace where the princes were already drinking wine. Before entering the hall, Odysseus went to the room that had been set aside for him and bathed. As he entered the hall, he saw that the Princess Nausicaa was standing at the door in all her beauty.

"I have come to say farewell, stranger," she said in a low voice. "When you are home again, think of me, for I was the first to help you when you were cast up on this shore."

"I will never forget you, Princess," answered Odysseus. "You will always be to me like one of the gods, for it was you who brought me back to life after my desperate journey."

Odysseus went and took his seat beside Alcinous, and the minstrel played and sang a song of Troy. Once more Odysseus wept, so that the King told the minstrel to cease singing. He turned to his guest.

"Now, stranger, surely your secret is out. If the tale of Troy causes you such grief, tell us whether you lost a friend or a kinsman in that war. Or what is it that makes you weep?"

So Odysseus told the King and his guests that he was Odysseus. That, from the time of the burning of Troy, he had been away from his home and his people for a full ten years, and that he longed to return. The Princes listened with close attention and wonder as their guest kept them from their beds, telling of all his adventures on the storm-tossed seas—how he had blinded the Cyclops Polyphemus and passed the island of the Sirens, how he had come safely through the straits between Scylla[9] and Charybdis,[10] and how he had lost his ship and all his men and been wrecked on the island of Calypso. He told of his visit to the enchantress Circe; and finally he described his escape from Calypso's island on his raft, and how it was broken to pieces, and of his being thrown up on the Sea Kings' shore when he was almost drowned beneath the waves.

When Odysseus' tale was done, the guests all departed for their homes. In the morning they returned with their gifts, and Alcinous sacrificed an ox to Zeus[11] to ensure a safe journey for Odysseus. All day they feasted and drank, and all the time Odysseus looked towards the sun, longing for it to go down beyond the western wave. That was to be the time for his departure. At last Odysseus turned to King Alcinous and Queen Arete and bade them farewell. He thanked them for all their kindness and their entertainment, and wished them good fortune, happiness and long life.

The heralds led the way to the ship moored in the harbour. The Queen sent her servants with warm clothing for the voyage; the rowers took their places on the benches, while Odysseus lay

[9]Scylla (sil' ə): a six-headed monster
[10]Charybdis (kə rib' dis): a monster who created a mighty whirlpool
[11]Zeus (zoos): ancient Greek god who ruled the other Greek gods and goddesses

323

Voyage by Canoe

from Island of the Blue Dolphins
by Scott O'Dell

An island shaped like a blue dolphin lies off the coast of
California. Most of the Indians who lived on the island were
killed in a fierce battle with Aleut hunters—including twelve-
year-old Karana's father, the chief.

A few months later, Kimki, the new chief, left the island in
a canoe to find a new place for his people to live. When Kimki
did not return, Matasaip, who had taken Kimki's place, and the
others left with sailors who offered them safe passage. Karana,
however, jumped off the ship and swam back to the island to join
her brother, Ramo, who had missed the ship. Soon Ramo was
killed by wild dogs, and Karana was left completely alone.

While Karana waited and hoped for the ship to return for
her, she survived by building a shelter, hunting food, and making
weapons to defend herself against the wild dogs.

NEWBERY
MEDAL
1961

Summer is the best time on the Island of the Blue Dolphins. The sun is warm then and the winds blow milder out of the west, sometimes out of the south.

It was during these days that the ship might return and now I spent most of my time on the rock, looking out from the high headland into the east, toward the country where my people had gone, across the sea that was never-ending.

Once while I watched I saw a small object which I took to be the ship, but a stream of water rose from it and I knew that it was a whale spouting. During those summer days I saw nothing else.

The first storm of winter ended my hopes. If the white men's ship were coming for me it would have come during the time of good weather. Now I would have to wait until winter was gone, maybe longer.

The thought of being alone on the island while so many suns rose from the sea and went slowly back into the sea filled my heart with loneliness. I had not felt so lonely before because I was sure that the ship would return as Matasaip had said it would. Now my hopes were dead. Now I was really alone.

327

I could not eat much, nor could I sleep without dreaming terrible dreams.

The storm blew out of the north, sending big waves against the island and winds so strong that I was unable to stay on the rock. I moved my bed to the foot of the rock and for protection kept a fire going throughout the night. I slept there five times. The first night the dogs came and stood outside the ring made by the fire. I killed three of them with arrows, but not the leader, and they did not come again.

On the sixth day, when the storm had ended, I went to the place where the canoes had been hidden, and let myself down over the cliff. This part of the shore was sheltered from the wind and I found the canoes just as they had been left. The dried food was still good, but the water was stale, so I went back to the spring and filled a fresh basket.

I had decided during the days of the storm, when I had given up hope of seeing the ship, that I would take one of the canoes and go to the country that lay toward the east. I remembered how Kimki, before he had gone, had asked the advice of his ancestors who had lived many ages in the past, who had come to the island from that country, and likewise the advice of Zuma, the medicine man who held power over the wind and the seas. But these things I could not do, for Zuma had been killed by the Aleuts, and in all my life I had never been able to speak with the dead, though many times I had tried.

Yet I cannot say that I was really afraid as I stood there on the shore. I knew that my ancestors had crossed the sea in their canoes, coming from that place which lay beyond. Kimki, too had crossed the sea. I was not nearly so skilled with a canoe as these men, but I must say that whatever might befall me on the endless waters did not trouble me. It meant far less than the thought of staying on the island alone, without a home or companions, pursued by wild dogs, where everything reminded me of those who were dead and those who had gone away.

Of the four canoes stored there against the cliff, I chose the smallest, which was still very heavy because it could carry six people. The task that faced me was to push it down the rocky shore and into the water, a distance four or five times its length.

This I did by first removing all the large rocks in front of the canoe. I then filled in all these holes with pebbles and along this path laid down long strips of kelp, making a slippery bed. The shore was steep and once I got the canoe to move with its own weight, it slid down the path and into the water.

The sun was in the west when I left the shore. The sea was calm behind the high cliffs. Using the two-bladed paddle I quickly skirted the south part of the island. As I reached the sandspit the wind struck. I was paddling from the back of the canoe because you can go faster kneeling there, but I could not handle it in the wind.

Kneeling in the middle of the canoe, I paddled hard and did not pause until I had gone through the tides that run fast around the sandspit. There were many small waves and I was soon wet, but as I came out from behind the spit the spray lessened and the waves grew long and rolling. Though it would have been easier to go the way they slanted, this would have taken me in the wrong direction. I therefore kept them

on my left hand, as well as the island, which grew smaller and smaller, behind me.

At dusk I looked back. The Island of the Blue Dolphins had disappeared. This was the first time that I felt afraid.

There were only hills and valleys of water around me now. When I was in a valley I could see nothing and when the canoe rose out of it, only the ocean stretching away and away.

Night fell and I drank from the basket. The water cooled my throat.

The sea was black and there was no difference between it and the sky. The waves made no sound among themselves, only faint noises as they went under the canoe or struck against it. Sometimes the noises seemed angry and at other times like people laughing. I was not hungry because of my fear.

The first star made me feel less afraid. It came out low in the sky and it was in front of me, toward the east. Other stars began to appear all around, but it was this one I kept my gaze upon. It was in the figure that we call a serpent, a star which shone green and which I knew. Now and then it was hidden by mist, yet it always came out brightly again.

Without this star I would have been lost, for the waves never changed. They came always from the same direction and in a manner that kept pushing me away from the place I wanted to reach. For this reason the canoe made a path in the black water like a snake. But somehow I kept moving toward the star which shone in the east.

This star rose high and then I kept the North Star on my left hand, the one we call "the star that does not move." The wind grew quiet. Since it always died down when the night was half over, I knew how long I had been traveling and how far away the dawn was.

About this time I found that the canoe was leaking. Before dark I had emptied one of the baskets in which food was stored and used it to dip out the water that came over the sides. The water that now moved around my knees was not from the waves.

I stopped paddling and worked with the basket until the bottom of the canoe was almost dry. Then I searched around, feeling in the dark along the smooth planks, and found the place near the bow where the water was seeping through a crack as long as my hand and the width of a finger. Most of the time it was out of the sea, but it leaked whenever the canoe dipped forward in the waves.

The places between the planks were filled with black pitch which we gather along the shore. Lacking this, I tore a piece of fiber from my skirt and pressed it into the crack, which held back the water.

Dawn broke in a clear sky and as the sun came out of the waves I saw that it was far off on my left. During the night I had drifted south of the place I wished to go, so I changed my direction and paddled along the path made by the rising sun.

There was no wind on this morning and the long waves went quietly under the canoe. I therefore moved faster than during the night.

I was very tired, but more hopeful than I had been since I left the island. If the good weather did not change I would cover many leagues before dark. Another night and another day might bring me within sight of the shore toward which I was going.

Not long after dawn, while I was thinking of this strange place and what it would look like, the canoe began to leak again. This crack was between the same planks, but was a larger one and close to where I was kneeling.

The fiber I tore from my skirt and pushed into the crack held back most of the water which seeped in whenever the canoe rose and fell with the waves. Yet I could see that the planks were weak from one end to the other, probably from the canoe being stored so long in the sun, and that they might open along their whole length if the waves grew rougher.

It was suddenly clear to me that it was dangerous to go on. The voyage would take two more days, perhaps longer. By turning back to the island I would not have nearly so far to travel.

Still I could not make up my mind to do so. The sea was calm and I had come far. The thought of turning back after all this labor was more than I could bear. Even greater was the thought of the deserted island I would return to, of living there alone and forgotten. For how many suns and how many moons?

The canoe drifted idly on the calm sea while these thoughts went over and over in my mind, but when I saw the water seeping through the crack again, I picked up the paddle. There was no choice except to turn back toward the island.

I knew that only by the best of fortune would I ever reach it.

The wind did not blow until the sun was overhead. Before that time I covered a good distance, pausing only when it was necessary to dip water from the canoe. With the wind I went more slowly and had to stop more often because of the water spilling over the sides, but the leak did not grow worse.

This was my first good fortune. The next was when a swarm of dolphins appeared. They came swimming out of the west, but as they saw the canoe they turned around in a great circle and began to follow me. They swam up slowly and so close that I could see their eyes, which are large and the color of the ocean. Then they swam on ahead of the canoe, crossing back and forth in front of it, diving in and out, as if they were weaving a piece of cloth with their broad snouts.

Dolphins are animals of good omen. It made me happy to have them swimming around the canoe, and though my

hands had begun to bleed from the chafing of the paddle, just watching them made me forget the pain. I was very lonely before they appeared, but now I felt that I had friends with me and did not feel the same.

The blue dolphins left me shortly before dusk. They left as quickly as they had come, going on into the west, but for a long time I could see the last of the sun shining on them. After night fell I could still see them in my thoughts and it was because of this that I kept on paddling when I wanted to lie down and sleep.

More than anything, it was the blue dolphins that took me back home.

Fog came with the night, yet from time to time I could see the star that stands high in the west, the red star called Magat which is part of the figure that looks like a crawfish and is known by that name. The crack in the planks grew wider so I had to stop often to fill it with fiber and to dip out the water.

The night was very long, longer than the night before. Twice I dozed kneeling there in the canoe, though I was more afraid than I had ever been. But the morning broke clear and in front of me lay the dim line of the island like a great fish sunning itself on the sea.

I reached it before the sun was high, the sandspit and its tides that bore me into the shore. My legs were stiff from kneeling and as the canoe struck the sand I fell when I rose to climb out. I crawled through the shallow water and up the beach. There I lay for a long time, hugging the sand in happiness.

I was too tired to think of the wild dogs. Soon I fell asleep.

Reader's Response ～ If you had been Karana, what would have been the most difficult part of this experience? What would have made it so difficult?

Dolphins

It is not surprising that dolphins helped Karana to navigate her way back to the island. Throughout history, dolphins have been praised as nature's friendliest creatures. They have been known to swim into beaches and let children ride on their backs. They love to be petted and scratched.

They may be the smartest animals as well. Scientists have long believed that one of the main differences between humans and animals is that while both can learn to DO things, humans can learn the REASONS for things.

A dolphin at a marineland in Florida, however, showed us that this difference may not be true. This dolphin had been trained to jump out of the water with two others at the same time. Each one got a piece of fish as a reward. During one show, one of the three did not jump properly and there were no rewards. Instead, the trainer signaled for the three to try the trick again. Again the same dolphin missed and there was no reward. This time one of the dolphins who had done the trick correctly swam over to the one who had missed and bit it on the head. It seemed clearly to have "figured out" that one's goofing off had cost everyone the reward. The biting worked, incidentally, because on the next try the third dolphin finally got it right.

THROUGH THE TOLLBOOTH

from **The Phantom Tollbooth**
written by Norton Juster
illustrations by Jules Feiffer

There was once a boy named Milo who didn't know what to do with himself—not just sometimes, but always.

When he was in school he longed to be out, and when he was out he longed to be in. On the way he thought about coming home, and coming home he thought about going. Wherever he was he wished he were somewhere else, and when he got there he wondered why he'd bothered. Nothing really interested him—least of all the things that should have.

"It seems to me that almost everything is a waste of time," he remarked one day as he walked dejectedly home from school. "I can't see the point in learning to solve useless problems, or subtracting turnips from turnips, or knowing where Ethiopia is or how to spell February." And, since no one bothered to explain otherwise, he regarded the process of seeking knowledge as the greatest waste of time of all.

As he and his unhappy thoughts hurried along (for while he was never anxious to be where he was going, he liked to get there as quickly as possible) it seemed a great wonder that the world, which was so large, could sometimes feel so small and empty.

"And worst of all," he continued sadly, "there's nothing for me to do, nowhere I'd care to go, and hardly anything worth seeing." He punctuated this last thought with such a deep sigh that a house sparrow singing nearby stopped and rushed home to be with his family.

Without stopping or looking up, he rushed past the buildings and busy shops that lined the street and in a few minutes reached home—dashed through the lobby—hopped onto the elevator—two, three, four, five, six, seven, eight, and off again—opened the apartment door—rushed into his room—flopped dejectedly into a chair, and grumbled softly, "Another long afternoon."

He looked glumly at all the things he owned. The books that were too much trouble to read, the tools he'd never learned to use, the small electric automobile he hadn't driven in months—or was it years?—and the hundreds of other games and toys, and bats and balls, and bits and pieces scattered around him. And then, to one side of the room, just next to the phonograph, he noticed something he had certainly never seen before.

Who could possibly have left such an enormous package and such a strange one? For, while it was not quite square, it was definitely not round, and for its size it was larger than almost any other big package of smaller dimension that he'd ever seen.

Attached to one side was a bright-blue envelope which said simply: "FOR MILO, WHO HAS PLENTY OF TIME."

Of course, if you've ever gotten a surprise package, you can imagine how puzzled and excited Milo was; and if you've never gotten one, pay close attention, because someday you might.

"I don't think it's my birthday," he puzzled, "and Christmas must be months away, and I haven't been out-standingly good, or even good at all." (He had to admit this even to himself.) "Most probably I won't like it anyway, but since I don't know where it came from, I can't possibly send it back." He thought about it for quite a while and then opened the envelope, but just to be polite.

"ONE GENUINE TURNPIKE TOLLBOOTH," it stated—and then it went on:

"EASILY ASSEMBLED AT HOME, AND FOR USE BY THOSE WHO HAVE NEVER TRAVELED IN LANDS BEYOND."

"Beyond what?" thought Milo as he continued to read.

"THIS PACKAGE CONTAINS THE FOLLOWING ITEMS:

"One (1) genuine turnpike toll-booth to be erected according to directions.

"Three (3) precautionary signs to be used in a precautionary fashion.

"Assorted coins for use in paying tolls.

"One (1) map, up to date and carefully drawn by master cartographers, depicting natural and man-made features.

"One (1) book of rules and traffic regulations, which may not be bent or broken."

And in smaller letters at the bottom it concluded:

"Results are not guaranteed, but if not perfectly satisfied, your wasted time will be refunded."

Following the instructions, which told him to cut here, lift there, and fold back all around, he soon had the toll-booth unpacked and set up on its stand. He fitted the windows in place and attached the roof, which extended out on both sides and fastened on the coin box. It was very much like the toll-booths he'd seen many times on family trips, except of course it was much smaller and purple.

"What a strange present," he thought to himself. "The least they

could have done was to send a highway with it, for it's terribly impractical without one." But since, at the time, there was nothing else he wanted to play with, he set up the three signs,

SLOW DOWN APPROACHING TOLLBOOTH

PLEASE HAVE YOUR FARE READY

HAVE YOUR DESTINATION IN MIND

and slowly unfolded the map.

As the announcement stated, it was a beautiful map, in many colors, showing principal roads, rivers and seas, towns and cities, mountains and valleys, intersections and detours, and sites of outstanding interest both beautiful and historic.

The only trouble was that Milo had never heard of any of the places it indicated, and even the names sounded most peculiar.

"I don't think there really is such a

country," he concluded after studying it carefully. "Well, it doesn't matter anyway." And he closed his eyes and poked a finger at the map.

"Dictionopolis," read Milo slowly when he saw what his finger had chosen. "Oh, well, I might as well go there as anywhere."

He walked across the room and dusted the car off carefully. Then, taking the map and rule book with him, he hopped in and, for lack of anything better to do, drove slowly up to the tollbooth. As he deposited his coin and rolled past he remarked wistfully, "I do hope this is an interesting game, otherwise the afternoon will be so terribly dull."

Suddenly he found himself speeding along an unfamiliar country high-

way, and as he looked back over his shoulder neither the tollbooth nor his room nor even the house was anywhere in sight. What had started as make-believe was now very real.

"What a strange thing to have happen," he thought (just as you must be thinking right now). "This game is much more serious than I thought, for here I am riding on a road I've never seen, going to a place I've never heard of, and all because of a tollbooth which came from nowhere. I'm certainly glad that it's a nice day for a trip," he concluded hopefully, for, at the moment, this was the one thing he definitely knew.

The sun sparkled, the sky was clear, and all the colors he saw seemed to be richer and brighter than he could ever remember. The flowers shone as if they'd been cleaned and polished, and the tall trees that lined the road shimmered in silvery green.

"WELCOME TO EXPECTATIONS," said a carefully lettered sign on a small house at the side of the road.

"INFORMATION, PREDICTIONS, AND ADVICE CHEERFULLY OFFERED. PARK HERE AND BLOW HORN."

With the first sound from the horn a little man in a long coat came rushing

many travelers these days. Now what can I do for you? I'm the Whether Man."

"Is this the right road for Dictionopolis?" asked Milo, a little bowled over by the effusive greeting.

"Well now, well now, well now," he began again, "I don't know of any wrong road to Dictionopolis, so if this road goes to Dictionopolis at all it must be the right road, and if it doesn't it must be the right road to somewhere

from the house, speaking as fast as he could and repeating everything several times:

"My, my, my, my, my, welcome, welcome, welcome to the land of Expectations, to the land of Expectations, to the land of Expectations. We don't get many travelers these days; we certainly don't get

else, because there are no wrong roads to anywhere. Do you think it will rain?"

"I thought you were the Weather Man," said Milo, very confused.

"Oh no," said the little man, "I'm the Whether Man, not the Weather Man, for after all it's more important to know whether there will be weather than what the weather will be." And with that he released a dozen balloons that sailed off into the sky. "Must see which way the wind is blowing," he said, chuckling over his little joke and watching them disappear in all directions.

"What kind of a place is Expectations?" inquired Milo, unable to see the humor and feeling very doubtful of the little man's sanity.

"Good question, good question," he exclaimed. "Expectations is the place you must always go to before you get to where you're going. Of course, some people never go beyond Expectations, but my job is to hurry them along whether they like it or not. Now what else can I do for you?" And before Milo could reply he rushed into the house and reappeared a moment later with a new coat and an umbrella.

"I think I can find my own way," said Milo, not at all sure that he could. But, since he didn't understand the little man at all, he decided that he might as well move on—at least until he met someone whose sentences didn't always sound as if they would make as much sense backwards as forwards.

"Splendid, splendid, splendid," exclaimed the Whether Man. "Whether or not you find your own way, you're bound to find some way. If you happen to find my way, please return it, as it was lost years ago. I imagine by now it's quite rusty. You did say it was going to rain, didn't you?" And with that he opened the umbrella and walked with Milo to the car.

"I'm glad you made your own decision. I do so hate to make up my mind about anything, whether it's good or bad, up or down, in or out, rain or shine. Expect everything, I always say, and the unexpected never happens. Now please drive carefully; good-by, good-by, good-by, good . . ." His last good-by was drowned out by an enormous clap of thunder, and as Milo drove down the road in the bright sunshine he could see the Whether Man standing in the middle of a fierce cloudburst that seemed to be raining only on him.

The road dipped now into a broad green valley and stretched toward the horizon. The little car bounced along with very little effort, and Milo had hardly to touch the accelerator to go as fast as he wanted. He was glad to be on his way again.

"It's all very well to spend time in Expectations," he thought, "but talking to that strange man all day would certainly get me nowhere. He's the most peculiar person I've ever met," continued Milo—unaware of how many peculiar people he would shortly encounter.

As he drove along the peaceful highway he soon fell to daydreaming and paid less and less attention to where he was going. In a short time he wasn't paying any attention at all, and that is why, at a fork in the road, when a sign pointed to the left, Milo went to the right, along a route which looked suspiciously like the wrong way.

Things began to change as soon as he left the main highway. The sky became quite gray and, along with it, the whole countryside seemed to lose its color and assume the same monotonous tone. Everything was quiet, and even the air hung heavily. The birds sang only gray songs and the road wound back and forth in an endless series of climbing curves.

Mile after

mile after

mile after

mile he drove, and now, gradually the car went slower and slower, until it was hardly moving at all.

"It looks as though I'm getting nowhere," yawned Milo, becoming very drowsy and dull. "I hope I haven't taken a wrong turn."

Mile after

mile after

mile after

mile, and everything became grayer and more monotonous. Finally the car just stopped altogether, and, hard as he tried, it wouldn't budge another inch.

"I wonder where I am," said Milo in a very worried tone.

343

"You're . . . in . . . the . . . Dol . . . drums," wailed a voice that sounded far away.

He looked around quickly to see who had spoken. No one was there, and it was as quiet and still as one could imagine.

"Yes . . . the . . . Dol . . . drums," yawned another voice, but still he saw no one.

"WHAT ARE THE DOL-DRUMS?" he cried loudly, and tried very hard to see who would answer this time.

"The Doldrums, my young friend, are where nothing ever happens and nothing ever changes."

This time the voice came from so close that Milo jumped with surprise, for, sitting on his right shoulder, so lightly that he hardly noticed, was a small creature exactly the color of his shirt.

"Allow me to introduce all of us," the creature went on. "We are the Lethargarians, at your service."

Milo looked around and, for the first time, noticed dozens of them—sitting on the car, standing in the road, and lying all over the trees and bushes. They were very difficult to see, because whatever they happened to be sitting on or near was exactly the color they happened to be. Each one looked very much like the other (except for the color, of course) and some looked even more like each other than they did like themselves.

"I'm very pleased to meet you," said Milo, not sure whether or not he was pleased at all. "I think I'm lost. Can you help me please?"

"Don't say 'think,' " said one sitting on his shoe, for the one on his shoulder had fallen asleep. "It's against the law." And he yawned and fell off to sleep, too.

"No one's allowed to think in the Doldrums," continued a third, beginning to doze off. And as each one spoke, he fell off to sleep and another picked up the conversation with hardly any interruption.

"Don't you have a rule book? It's local ordinance 175389-J."

Milo quickly pulled the rule book from his pocket, opened to the page, and read, "Ordinance 175389-J: It shall be unlawful, illegal, and unethical to think, think of thinking, surmise, presume, reason, meditate, or speculate while in the Doldrums. Anyone breaking this law shall be severely punished!"

"That's a ridiculous law," said Milo, quite indignantly. "Everybody thinks."

"We don't," shouted the Lethargarians all at once.

"And most of the time you don't," said a yellow one sitting on a daffodil. "That's why you're here. You weren't thinking, and you weren't paying attention either. People who don't pay attention often get stuck in the Doldrums." And with that he toppled out of the flower and fell snoring into the grass.

Milo couldn't help laughing at the little creature's strange behavior, even though he knew it might be rude.

"Stop that at once," ordered the plaid one clinging to his stocking. "Laughing is against the law. Don't you have a rule book? It's local ordinance 574381-W."

Opening the book again, Milo found Ordinance 574381-W: "In the Doldrums, laughter is frowned upon and smiling is permitted only on alternate Thursdays. Violators shall be dealt with most harshly."

"Well, if you can't laugh or think, what can you do?" asked Milo.

"Anything as long as it's nothing, and everything as long as it isn't anything," explained another. "There's lots to do; we have a very busy schedule——

"At 8 o'clock we get up, and then we spend

"From 8 to 9 daydreaming.

"From 9 to 9:30 we take our early midmorning nap.

"From 9:30 to 10:30 we dawdle and delay.

"From 10:30 to 11:30 we take our late early morning nap.

"From 11:00 to 12:00 we bide our time and then eat lunch.

"From 1:00 to 2:00 we linger and loiter.

"From 2:00 to 2:30 we take our early afternoon nap.

"From 2:30 to 3:30 we put off for tomorrow what we could have done today.

"From 3:30 to 4:00 we take our early late afternoon nap.

"From 4:00 to 5:00 we loaf and lounge until dinner.

"From 6:00 to 7:00 we dillydally.

"From 7:00 to 8:00 we take our early evening nap, and then for an hour before we go to bed at 9:00 we waste time.

"As you can see, that leaves almost no time for brooding, lagging, plodding, or procrastinating, and if we stopped to think or laugh, we'd never get nothing done."

"You mean you'd never get anything done," corrected Milo.

"We don't want to get anything done," snapped another angrily; "we want to get nothing done, and we can do that without your help."

"You see," continued another in a

more conciliatory tone, "it's really quite strenuous doing nothing all day, so once a week we take a holiday and go nowhere, which was just where we were going when you came along. Would you care to join us?"

"I might as well," thought Milo; "that's where I seem to be going anyway."

"Tell me," he yawned, for he felt ready for a nap now himself, "does everyone here do nothing?"

"Everyone but the terrible watchdog," said two of them, shuddering in chorus. "He's always sniffing around to see that nobody wastes time. A most unpleasant character."

"The watchdog?" said Milo quizzically.

"THE WATCHDOG," shouted another, fainting from fright, for racing down the road barking furiously and kicking up a great cloud of dust was the very dog of whom they had been speaking.

"RUN!"

"WAKE UP!"

"RUN!"

"HERE HE COMES!"

"THE WATCHDOG!"

Great shouts filled the air as the Lethargarians scattered in all directions and soon disappeared entirely.

"R-R-R-G-H-R-O-R-R-H-F-F," exclaimed the watchdog as he dashed up to the car, loudly puffing and panting.

Milo's eyes opened wide, for there in front of him was a large dog with a perfectly normal head, four feet, and a tail—and the body of a loudly ticking alarm clock.

"What are you doing here?" growled the watchdog.

"Just killing time," replied Milo apologetically. "You see——"

"KILLING TIME!" roared the dog—so furiously that his alarm went off. "It's bad enough wasting time without killing it." And he shuddered at the thought. "Why are you in the Doldrums anyway—don't you have anywhere to go?"

"I was on my way to Dictionopolis when I got stuck here," explained Milo. "Can you help me?"

"Help you! You must help yourself," the dog replied, carefully winding himself with his left hind leg. "I suppose you know why you got stuck."

"I guess I just wasn't thinking," said Milo.

"PRECISELY," shouted the dog as his alarm went off again. "Now you know what you must do."

"I'm afraid I don't," admitted Milo, feeling quite stupid.

"Well," continued the watchdog impatiently, "since you got here by not thinking, it seems reasonable to expect that, in order to get out, you must start thinking." And with that he hopped into the car.

"Do you mind if I get in? I love automobile rides."

Milo began to think as hard as he could (which was very difficult, since he wasn't used to it). He thought of birds that swim and fish that fly. He thought of yesterday's lunch and tomorrow's dinner. He thought of words that begin with J and numbers that end in 3. And, as he thought, the wheels began to turn.

"We're moving, we're moving," he shouted happily.

"Keep thinking," scolded the watchdog.

The little car started to go faster and faster as Milo's brain whirled with activity, and down the road they went. In a few moments they were out of the Doldrums and back on the main highway. All the colors had returned to their original brightness, and as they raced along the road Milo continued to think of all sorts of things; of the many detours and wrong turns that were so easy to take, of how fine it was to be moving along, and, most of all, of how much could be accomplished with just a little thought. And the dog, his nose in the wind, just sat back, watchfully ticking.

Reader's Response ∾ If Milo were your best friend, what questions would you ask him about his unusual adventure?

Library Link ∾ *Milo's adventures in the Lands Beyond have just begun. If you are curious to find out what happens to Milo and the watchdog, read the rest of the book* The Phantom Tollbooth *by Norton Juster.*

JULES FEIFFER

Have you thought about what you want to be when you grow up? Jules Feiffer says that when he was a child, the only thing he wanted to be was "grown up." He felt like a failure when he was young because he couldn't throw or catch a ball as well as his friends. It was a feeling he never forgot.

One thing he could do was draw. He used to spend his time sketching his fantasies about movies, radio programs, and newspaper comics. Being a cartoonist was the only real occupation he can remember wanting to have.

He went to college to study art, but he dropped out because his teachers did not think being a cartoonist was a serious job for an artist. He did not give up. One day he got a job helping create a comic book called *The Spirit*. His first project was a children's series called "Clifford." It had always bothered him that children in comics were pictured the way adults saw them. He believed comics about children should picture the way children themselves thought and felt.

Now he writes plays, movie scripts, and novels in addition to drawing cartoons. But whenever he draws children, he always tries to show the way they really think and feel. Can you see how he has done that in the illustrations for "Through the Tollbooth"?

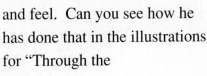

Photo by Fred McDarrah

AWARD
WINNING
AUTHOR

Night Journey

Now as the train bears west,
Its rhythm rocks the earth,
And from my Pullman berth
I stare into the night
While others take their rest.
Bridges of iron lace,
A suddenness of trees,
A lap of mountain mist
All cross my line of sight,
Then a bleak wasted place,
And a lake below my knees.
Full on my neck I feel
The straining at a curve;
My muscles move with steel,
I wake in every nerve.
I watch a beacon swing
From dark to blazing bright;
We thunder through ravines
And gullies washed with light.
Beyond the mountain pass
Mist deepens on the pane;
We rush into a rain
That rattles double glass.
Wheels shake the roadbed stone,
The pistons jerk and shove,
I stay up half the night
To see the land I love.

Theodore Roethke

353

Mars
A Close-up Picture

from *Journey to the Planets*
by Patricia Lauber

Is there life on Mars? Was there ever life on Mars? The possibility catches the imagination. In many ways Mars seems a likely place to look for life, past or present.

Is Mars Like Earth?

Fourth planet from the sun, Mars is like Earth in many ways. It is smaller than the earth and reddish, because of some kind of rusted iron in its soil. But it has an atmosphere in which white clouds appear, and it has polar ice caps. Since its axis is tilted at the same angle as Earth's, Mars has seasons in its northern and southern hemispheres. They last nearly twice as long as Earth's, because Mars is farther from the sun. It travels a bigger orbit at slower speeds, taking 687 Earth days to make one trip around the sun. Its day, however, is just a little longer than ours.

Mars, like Earth, is a planet on which changes take place with the seasons.

Each ice cap grows in winter and shrinks in summer. Colors change. Seen even blurrily through a telescope, the dark markings of spring and summer turn pale as winter approaches.

Mars is like the earth in another way. Among the inner planets, only Mars and Earth have moons. Mars has two tiny, potato-shaped moons, named Phobos and Deimos.

About a hundred years ago, some astronomers began seeing straight lines on Mars. The more they studied Mars, the more lines they saw crisscrossing the planet in a network. Since straight lines were obviously the work of intelligent beings, imaginations leaped ahead. The lines must be canals, dug to move water from melting polar ice caps to croplands near the equator. What had forced the Martians to dig these canals? There was

Phobos appears heavily cratered in this photograph taken by the Viking Orbiter.

355

only one answer. Mars was slowly drying up. It was a dying planet whose desperate inhabitants had tried to buy time.

Today no one knows what those earlier astronomers were seeing. Modern astronomers have never seen straight lines on Mars—but they have seen changing colors that hinted of plant life.

Part of the *Viking Lander 2* appears in front of the rocky Martian landscape.

Is Mars Like Our Moon?

The first flybys[1] put an end to hopes of finding widespread plant life on Mars. Photographs showed a cratered landscape that looked more like the moon than like Earth. But on Mars the craters were flat-bottomed and appeared to be filled with dust. Instruments reported on the carbon dioxide atmosphere. It was very thin; air pressure was less than one one-hundredth the air pressure on Earth at sea level. Because the atmosphere was thin, the carbon dioxide did not create a greenhouse effect.[2] Temperatures on most of Mars were well below the freezing point of water. During a polar winter, temperatures fell below minus 200 degrees. At such levels, carbon dioxide freezes into ice, the kind called dry ice on Earth. A polar ice cap grew on Mars when carbon dioxide froze out of the atmosphere as dry ice. It shrank when temperatures rose, and the ice turned into gas.

Was Mars then, just like the moon, only with ice caps? The answer turned out to be no, not at all. It came from the photographs taken by *Mariner 9*, which went into orbit around Mars, and from those taken by two *Viking* orbiters and the landers that sent back the first pictures from the surface of Mars.

[1]flybys: the first exploratory spacecraft

[2]greenhouse effect: warming of the earth caused by too much carbon dioxide in the atmosphere

Turquoise areas indicate surface frosts and fogs at the polar ice cap of Mars.

Surprises on Mars

Mariner 9 arrived in the middle of a planet-wide dust storm. When the dust finally settled, *Mariner 9* began sending back pictures that took scientists by complete surprise. No one had ever imagined that Mars might look as it did.

The first thing to come into sight was the top of a gigantic volcano, the biggest anyone had ever seen. Named Olympus Mons, this giant is the biggest mountain so far known in the solar system. It towers three times as high as Mount Everest. Its broad, cliff-edged base would barely fit between San Francisco and Los Angeles.

Olympus Mons is one of four huge volcanoes that rise from the Tharsis Plateau at the equator of Mars. Tharsis itself would more than cover the United States from Los Angeles to New York. It is a huge dome-shaped bulge in the crust.

Some 3,000 miles away is another group of big volcanoes. For unknown reasons, most of the volcanoes on Mars are in the northern hemisphere, while most of the craters are in the southern hemisphere. By chance, the flybys photographed only parts of the southern hemisphere.

This photo taken as *Viking* came within 348,000 miles of Mars shows volcanoes rising from the Tharsis Plateau.

To the east of Tharsis is an enormous rift valley, called Valles Marineris. It starts as jumbled land and becomes a canyon that is three times as deep as Arizona's Grand Canyon and so long that it would span the United States from coast to coast.

How did the valley form? One idea is that it marks a place where two huge plates of crust began to move apart. Since Mars is a small planet, it may have lost heat so quickly that nothing more happened. Another idea is that heat inside Mars made it expand, tearing the crust apart. Whatever happened, it is clear that Mars has been—and perhaps still is—hot inside. At times, molten rock has poured out, building giant volcanoes.

Below, Viking **approaches the dawn side of Mars.** *Right,* **the great canyon of Mars, Valles Marineris, appears.**

Large parts of Mars are covered with fine dust. In some places the dust forms dunes, like the sand dunes in Earth's deserts. The dust moves with the winds. It has filled in crater bottoms. It erodes and carves rock. And it accounts for the color changes seen on Mars.

Dust storms occur seasonally on Mars. When a storm ends, surface colors have changed. Light-colored dust covers areas that were dark. In other areas, winds have stripped away the dust, revealing darker material.

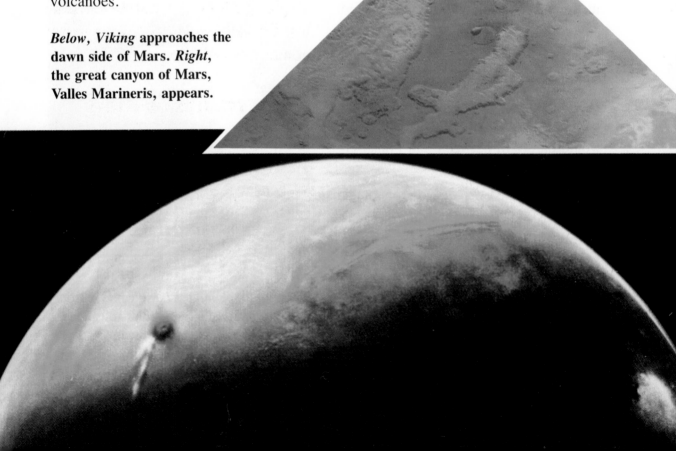

Water on Mars

Because the surface of Mars is bone dry, no one expected to see signs of ancient floods. Yet parts of the surface appear to have been shaped by streams and flash floods. There are places that look as if they had once been a sea of mud. This discovery was perhaps the biggest surprise of all.

Where could water have come from? The answer has to be, from Mars itself. There are traces of water vapor in the planet's atmosphere. But even if it could all condense and fall as rain, there's not enough to cause a flood.

There is water ice in the polar ice caps. Each pole has a year-round ice cap to which frozen carbon dioxide is added in winter. The north polar cap is made entirely of water ice, mixed with dust. The south polar cap seems to be made mostly of water ice and perhaps some frozen carbon dioxide.

Much more water is frozen in the ground, near the surface. It is like the permafrost[3] of Earth's arctic regions.

And recent radar studies seem to show that a few parts of Mars have underground supplies of liquid water.

In one form or another, water does exist on Mars. But at present liquid

This photo from *Viking Lander 2* reveals late-winter frost on the rocky ground around the lander.

water cannot exist on the surface. The air pressure is too low and the temperature too cold. Any liquid water would turn to vapor or to ice.

Temperatures on Mars

Suppose, though, there was a time when Mars was warmer. Less carbon dioxide would be locked up as ice. More would be in the atmosphere, and air pressure would increase. The carbon dioxide in the air would trap most of the sun's heat. The heat would melt water ice and permafrost. Floods of water

---

[3]permafrost: permanently frozen subsoil

might then occur. Water could stay liquid with warmer temperatures and greater air pressure.

Two things could make Mars warmer, some scientists suggest. One is an increase in heat from the sun itself; our star is a steady producer of light and heat, but changes do take place in its output. The other is a change in the tilt of Mars's axis; such changes do occur, caused by the pull of Jupiter and other planets. Perhaps in the past some parts of Mars received more heat than they do today. If these scientists are right, then Mars has had periods of being warmer and wetter than it now is.

If Mars has water, has it also had life? We don't know. The *Viking* landers carried out experiments to look for life in the soil. None was found. But that does not prove there has never been life on Mars. It does not prove there is no life on Mars. The landers looked for it in only two places. Besides, the experiments may have asked the wrong questions. They may have looked for the wrong kind of life.

Understanding Mars is important for us. Earth has had warm periods and cold periods. There have been times when, in the cold parts of the earth, more snow fell than the summer sun could melt. The snow packed down into ice that built up into glaciers. And the glaciers advanced over large parts of the earth. No one knows for sure why this happened. But we do know that the tilt of Earth's axis is slightly affected by Jupiter and other planets. We also know that Mars and Earth share the same sun. Our histories are twined together. Clues to our own past and future may lie in the ice caps of Mars, for thick ice holds a record of past climates.

Reader's Response ∼ If you were offered a chance to go on a scientific exploration to Mars, would you go? Why or why not?

Library Link ∼ *If you enjoyed this article about Mars and want to find out more about other planets, read the whole book* Journey to the Planets *by Patricia Lauber.*

A Martian Landing?

Is NASA (the National Aeronautics and Space Administration) planning to send astronauts to Mars? Yes! Most scientists see the Mars Mission as the most important and exciting challenge of the future. Before a Mars Mission can happen, though, there are important steps to take along the way.

First a space station must be built. This will be a large orbiting laboratory where scientists can study the many problems future astronauts will face, like living for a long time with weightlessness and producing food and fuel for long voyages.

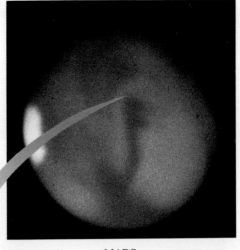

MARS

MOON

SPACE STATION

EARTH

Next are more unmanned landings on Mars to gather information about its soil, atmosphere, and the conditions on its surface. Then an operating spaceport will be needed to transfer people and materials to spacecraft headed for a base station on the Moon. Space "busses" and space "tugs" will have to carry astronauts and equipment from Earth to orbiting space stations and the lunar base.

The lunar base will be the most important step of all. Living and working on the Moon will be much easier than in space stations because the Moon, like Earth, has at least some gravity.

With those important preparations made, we will be able to take the last giant step toward Mars.

EARTHLINGS

by Eve Bunting

When Cort was six or seven, he realized that he was not like the other Martians.

"Why am I so much bigger than all my friends?" he asked his father.

"Because you are an Earthling, my son. We Martians are small so that we are well adapted to our wind and our cold and our life underground."

"Is it because I am an Earthling that my eyes are such a strange shape?"

"Yes," his father said.

"Tell me about Earth and how I got here," Cort asked, and his father told him.

"We on Mars are a very advanced people. We took our spaceships to Earth and to Moon and to Saturn before other worlds dreamed of such things. One of our space travellers brought you back once, a long time ago. It was wrong. He should not have done such a thing; but it was done, and we made the best of it."

"Were the people angry with him?"

"They were. Such a terrible thing has never happened again." He reached to touch Cort's hair. "Your mother and I had no children. We took you, and we have loved you always."

"I know," Cort said.

Slowly, delicately the Lander eased down. One foot pad touched Martian ground. The wind gusted, and the metal trembled. Then the other two feet took hold, and the craft swayed and settled. Cort held his breath. His heart-sound was loud in his ears. Soon he would have his first glimpse of Earthlings—his own kind, his very own. Soon now.

Inside the Lander, Ellis and Jonty Johnson carried out their first tasks. Ellis relayed their safe touchdown to the orbiting mother ship. Jonty used the remote scoop to pick up soil samples and store them in the thermal vault. The Lander's camera moved down below the ship to photograph the foot pads and the ground around them. The high television camera on top of the craft activated and began rolling. It was time to leave the Lander. But whatever happened now, this much had been accomplished. Whatever happened now!

Jonty swung the side hatch up and let down the runway. His wave to Ellis said, "You first."

Ellis stood by the side of one of the small mobile Rovers and looked through the dust at the Red Planet. It wasn't red. He felt awe and a sense of something of tremendous importance. His eyes were seeing what no human eyes had seen before.

Ahead of him lay desert, more lifeless than anything on Earth. No shrub grew—no plant. There was only a broad, barren plain, the wind whipping its rocky sand knee high, flinging it against the Lander as if sensing an alien object. In the distance he could see a rim of sharp-edged craters. Ellis drew a deep breath. They'd been lucky. Suppose they'd tried to land there?

Mars! He said the word under his breath. For this second he was Columbus on the deck of the *Santa Maria,* seeing the New World for the first time.

Jonty tapped his shoulder, and Ellis nodded. He checked his air tanks and tubes. Then he climbed behind the Rover's wheel, his body awkward in his heat-controlled suit. The sound of the Rover's engines was lost in the whine of the wind. His headlights gilded the dust that snapped through the air. Slowly the Rover rolled on its tractor treads down the runway.

He would travel due North; Jonty due South. Tonight they'd re-charge their air tanks and refuel the Rovers. Tomorrow they'd head East and West. The Rover's control panel would buzz at the return point. When the buzzer sounded, half the air and half the fuel was gone. There was a half-volume reserve tank.

Ellis sat in the Rover at the foot of the Lander and looked up at it. It was like a great silver beetle on a rock, a dragonfly maybe. Its searchlight shone reassuringly from above, giving light for the television camera—light for them too, a hope in the dark to look back to. Ellis took a shivery breath. Air wasting. Time to start.

The strange stone desert stretched ahead and to either side. From time to time he stopped to gather and store a strange, glittering rock, a blackened, burned-out lump of stone. From time to time he checked his space compass. There was no sign of life, but Ellis felt no disappointment. He knew now that he had not expected to find any. "Why do we climb mountains?" he asked himself.

"Because they are there."

"Why do we look for other worlds?"

"Because we must always reach for new knowledge." He looked back at the Lander, and it was a beacon that would guide him home.

The Rover rolled slowly up to one of the craters. Ellis stopped it. What had caused this round, black hole? A meteor, crashing into Mars billions of years ago? An ancient volcano? He should have a soil sample. He got out of the Rover and stepped close to the crater's rim. Then suddenly, unbelievably he wasn't standing on rock; he was standing on sand. Then he was standing on nothing, and he was falling, tumbling into what looked like a grey snowdrift below.

Cort saw the Earth man fall. His periscope brought everything close enough to touch, and Cort had been watching hungrily. He wanted to press his face close to the window on that space helmet. He wanted to see Earth eyes, to touch Earth skin; and then the Earth man fell.

Cort heard the gasps, the faint hissing of breath as the Martians realized what had happened. His father raised his periscope to get a down-view into the crater.

"He can't get up," he said sadly.

Cort wound his periscope high. The Earthling lay face down on top of the powder sand. Somehow he had sense not to struggle. With the weight of his tanks and thermal suit, to struggle would be to sink and suffocate.

Cort wet his lips and looked at his father.

"What will we do?"

His father's eyes held the same sadness as his voice. "There is nothing we can do. To help him we would have to reveal ourselves. Perhaps the other Earth man will come to his rescue." He spoke so softly that Cort could scarcely hear him. "Perhaps he'll be in time."

Cort swallowed. "How much air does he have?"

"I see the red light on his Rover. The warning buzzer is on. One Earth hour left. Perhaps a half-hour emergency oxygen, no more."

Cort looked at the stranded Earthling one more time and could bear to look no longer. "You taught me that life is precious," he told his father. His anger burned inside him. "Is an Earth life not precious?"

"It is," his father said. "But we must count the cost."

Cort sat by himself and tried to understand his feelings. The pull was back, drawing him strongly, surely toward the Earth man. Leave him to die? How could they do that? And yet . . . and yet . . . Cort chewed at his underlip till he felt the sting of blood.

The other Martians watched intently through their periscopes. No one saw Cort take the coil of woven rope and slip away.

Ellis listened to the Rover's buzzer and made his time calculations. Then he accepted the fact that he was going to die.

The shock of the rope dropping over his shoulders made him flounder and sink several inches.

"Don't move," a voice said.

Ellis' heart fluttered wildly. Jonty . . . it must be Jonty! Cautiously he raised his head.

What? Who?

A boy stood at the crater's rim holding the end of the rope. "Slowly. Put it under your arms," the boy said in halting English.

Ellis got his arms through the loop and held on to the rope with all his strength. He felt dazed, in some sort of shock where he knew this was happening and knew too that it couldn't be.

"Good." The boy wore Eskimo clothes of some glowing fabric, but that was a human face under the hood and that was a human voice. There was a drop of dried blood on the boy's lower lip.

The boy stepped back out of sight, and Ellis panicked and moved. He felt himself sink. "Hey," he called; but his word was hollow inside his helmet. Then he heard the Rover's motor start, and the rope under his arms tightened. He was dragged like a big fish through the sand drift and up the edge of the crater. On level ground he lay gasping, too stunned to move as the boy wrapped the rope round and around him, trussing him like a chicken.

"I will let you go," the boy said. "But first you must give me your word. No one is to know that you saw me. No one is to know what happened. Do you give me your word as an Earth man?"

Ellis looked at the face so close to his own. A human, breathing Martian air, living here. It couldn't be. It couldn't.

"Promise!" The boy tugged savagely at the binding ropes. "Promise, or I will throw you back in."

Ellis managed to move his head in a nod. He mouthed, "I promise." Reacts well under stress, the report had said. Reacts well.

"You saw nothing. You got yourself out." The voice was fierce. The human face was pressed close against his helmet window. Their eyes met and held.

"Who are you?" Ellis begged silently. "How are you here?"

Shadows like clouds moved behind the boy's eyes. To Ellis it seemed as though he stared at him forever. The boy raised his hand and gently touched the side of Ellis' helmet. Then he unwound the rope, bunched it loosely, and edged back.

Ellis struggled to his knees. He held on to the side of the Rover and pulled himself up. The boy had disappeared. Should he try to follow him through the speckled dark? Which way had he gone? Had there been a boy at all? There must have been. Someone, something had dragged him from death.

Ellis shook his head. For a few seconds he stared into the emptiness; then he climbed behind the Rover's wheel and turned it toward the light of the Lander.

His mind was a jumble of unanswered questions. He'd promised. . . . What had he promised? But this was the cosmic discovery of all time, and he was a scientist. Nothing should stand in the way of this truth.

It could be that they wouldn't believe him. It sure wasn't easy to believe. And he'd promised the boy. Ellis thought of the boy's eyes, the way he'd touched his helmet as if saying goodbye.

Now he was under the Lander. He looked up at it and remembered what he'd forgotten, and he knew that the decision wasn't his to make.

Cort leaned against the outside wall of the dugout. He had disobeyed his father and gone against the will of his people. The race across the rocky ground was like a dream now, the running so fast that there had been no time to think. The Earth man's face, so like his own and yet so different! For a second, as he'd looked down at that face, his mind had been filled with impossible thoughts. He could ask the Earthling to take him back with him. The operations could be reversed. He'd be with his own people. He'd leave Mars forever. He'd looked down, and there had been a moment of choice, and for the first time he'd known what that choice was. *These* were his people. He belonged here with the known things, with the acceptance, with the love. There was a sadness in finally knowing who he was, and a relief too.

Now his hands trembled as he pushed open the door. His father and the others must have seen him through their periscopes as he ran to help the Earth man. They hadn't tried to stop him. There was some hope in realizing that.

They faced him as he stood against the door, and he saw at once that there was no anger. But there was something else.

"He won't tell," Cort said shakily. "He gave me his word as an Earth man."

The room held silence, and something else.

Cort spoke to his father, "I had to go."

"I know," his father said. "But there was one thing you didn't know, my son, or didn't remember." He spread out his hands. "We saw you running; and we could have brought you back, but it was already too late. The Lander has a television camera with a dark-view eye. You are there, my son, on film. The pictures must already be on their way back to Earth."

Someone pulled down his periscope, and the click of it was the only sound in the room.

"It will take them many years to build another spaceship," his father said, "but nothing will stop them now. We will leave here, move to the opposite side of our planet, but they will find us."

"What have I done?" Cort heard his voice rising out of control.

"Not you alone," his father said. "What happened to-night was started many years ago when you were brought here. The fault is also ours."

There was the crackle of static. Cosmos 21.

They froze, listening.

The words that came from the box were slurred with excitement, but no one in the room failed to understand.

"*Patriot 1* reports life found on Mars," the space voice said. "Repeat. *Patriot 1* reports life found on Mars."

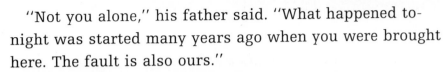

Reader's Response ～ If you had been Cort, would you have behaved the same or differently? Explain what you might have done.

The
HOME
of the
BRAVE

There are all kinds of houses in all
kinds of places.

What is the special something that
makes a house a home?

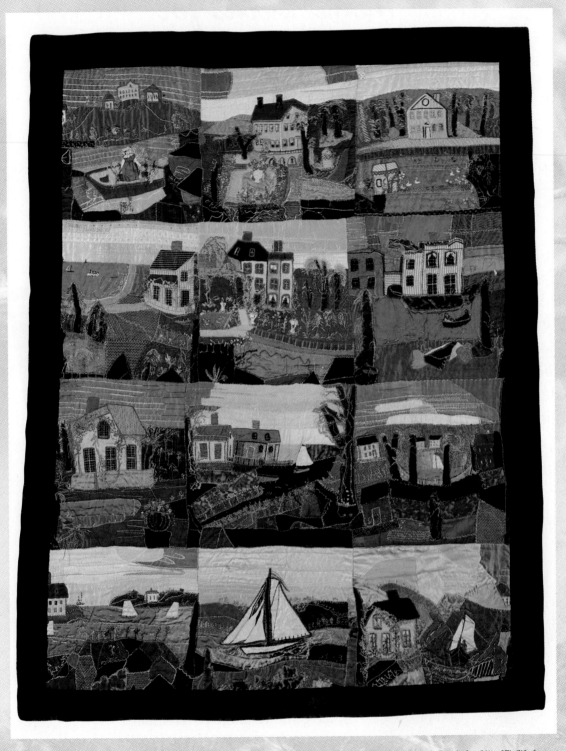

CRAZY QUILT BEDCOVER, *quilt c. 1850–1900 by Celestine Bacheller. American. Quilt made of pieced, appliquéd, and embroidered silk and velvet. 74¼ x 57". Gift of Mr. & Mrs. Edward J. Healy in Memory of Mrs. Charles O'Malley. Courtesy, Museum of Fine Arts, Boston. 63.655.*

Theme Books for
The Home of the Brave

Where do you feel most at home? Home can be any special place that makes you braver than you ever thought you could be.

❖ What is it like to live in the woods with only animals for companions? In ***My Side of the Mountain***, Jean Craighead George describes exactly how Sam survives a year alone in the wild. But he does more than just survive: he makes himself a home.

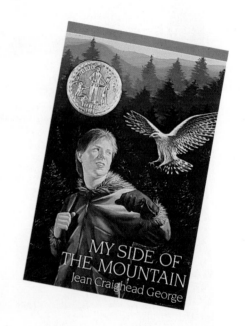

❖ In ***The Midnight Fox*** by Betsy Byars, Tom is miserable at his uncle's farm until he glimpses a rare black fox. Watching the fox makes the farm a fascinating place for Tom. When the fox's life is in danger, will Tom have the courage to save her?

❖ Would you brave frigid weather and danger just so you could be in your favorite place? Read **Woodsong** by Gary Paulsen to discover how the author and his dogs survive a wintry wilderness. Then race with them in an exciting sled dog race—the Iditarod.

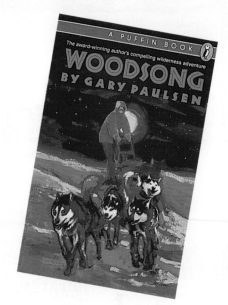

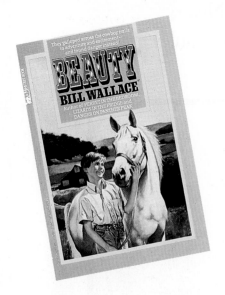

❖ Luke feels out of place in his new home until he befriends a beautiful horse. But when his love for Beauty is tested, he must do the hardest and bravest thing he has ever done. Read about Luke's challenge in **Beauty** by Bill Wallace.

More Books to Enjoy

The Borrowers by Mary Norton
The House of Dies Drear by Virginia Hamilton
Look Through My Window by Jean Little
Owls in the Family by Farley Mowat

IF YOU SAY SO, CLAUDE

written by Joan Lowery Nixon
illustrated by Lorinda Bryan Cauley

READING

TEACHER:

CHILDREN'S

CHOICE

1981

In the spring, after the last of the big snows, Shirley and Claude drove down from the silver-mining towns of the Rocky Mountains. They headed for that great state called Texas.

Claude was as short as he was broad, with a curly gray beard that waggled when he talked. Shirley was as tall as a doorpost, and almost as thin, with hair and skin the color of prairie dust with the sun on it. They drove in a covered wagon pulled by two sway-backed, but good-natured, horses.

"I can't abide those minin' towns any longer, Shirley," Claude said. "All that shootin' and yellin' is too rough a life for me. I've heard there's plenty of peace and quiet to be found in that great state called Texas."

"If you say so, Claude," Shirley said. But she missed the mountains and the forests and the plumb good looks of the Colorado Territory.

They followed a trail that cut south and turned east into upper West Texas, where long canyons dug deep into the hard rock.

"Will you look at that!" Claude cried. He eased the horses and wagon down a trail to the bottom of a narrow, rocky canyon. The purple shadows lay over them, and the silence lay around them.

"Shirley, I do believe this is the peaceful place we've been lookin' for," Claude said.

"I hope not," Shirley said. "I don't really take to this place, Claude. I feel like I'm in a four-sided box."

"Never mind. This land will grow on you, Shirley," Claude said. "For now, why don't you take the rifle and see if you can hunt up some meat for the table. I'll get our sleepin' pallets out of the wagon and tend to the horses."

So Shirley unfolded her long legs, stuck her feet in her boots, hiked up her skirts, and climbed down from the

383

wagon. She took the rifle and edged past the back of the wagon. Right off she spied a fat, lop-eared rabbit sitting on a rock ledge just across the narrow canyon; so she raised the rifle and fired.

Shirley's aim never was very good, so she missed the rabbit; and that old bullet bounced off the rock and back and forth across the canyon, whanging and banging, zinging and zanging, making a terrible racket. Shirley and the rabbit just froze, staring wide-eyed at each other.

Well, Claude took that moment to stick his head out the back of the wagon to see what that awful noise was, and the bullet tore right through the top of his hat, dropping it in the dust at Shirley's feet.

Claude looked across the canyon just in time to see the rabbit hightail it behind the ledge. He thought on it for

a moment. Then he said, "Shirley, get back in the wagon. I
don't think we want to live in a place where we can't go
out to get meat for the table without the rabbits shootin'
back. We're gonna have to move on."

Shirley picked up Claude's hat, climbed back into the
wagon, and gave a happy sigh of relief.

"If you say so, Claude," she said.

For two days Shirley and Claude headed south, farther
down into that great state called Texas. The sun was mean
enough to sizzle lizards and curl up the cracks in the
dried-out earth, when Claude pulled the sweating, but
good-natured, horses to a stop.

He said, "Shirley, I do believe this is the peaceful place
we've been lookin' for."

Shirley gazed at the flat landscape that stretched before
her gray and bleak, broken only by clumps of scrubby mesquite. And she said, "I hope not, Claude. This land has got
the worst case of the uglies I've ever seen."

"Never mind. It'll grow on you, Shirley," Claude said.
"For now, why don't you go see what you can find in the
way of firewood. I'll get our sleepin' pallets out of the
wagon and tend to the horses."

So Shirley unfolded her long legs, stuck her feet in her
boots, hiked up her skirts, and climbed down from the
wagon. She walked back aways, among the clumps of mesquite. Suddenly she heard an angry rattle. She looked down,
and her right boot was planted square on the neck of a mad
five-foot diamondback rattler that had stretched out in the
shade to take a nap.

Before she could think what to do, she heard another
noise. She looked over to her left to see a mean little wild
hog. Its beady eyes glared, its sharp tusks quivered, and its
small hooves pawed the ground, getting ready to charge.

Quick as she could, Shirley stooped down, grabbed the snake careful like around the neck, and, using it as a whip, flipped its tail at the wild hog. That tail, rattle and all, wrapped itself tight about the neck of the hog.

But the hog was coming fast, and all Shirley could do was hang onto the snake and use all her strength to twirl the hog clear off his feet and round and around her head. With a zap she let go. The snake fell to the ground, done for. But the hog flew off, squealing and snorting and carrying on something awful.

Shirley's aim never was very good, so it happened that just as Claude climbed down from the wagon to see what was making the terrible racket, that hog sailed right past his face, nearly brushing the end of his nose.

Claude watched the hog until he was out of sight, way yonder past a far clump of mesquite, and he thought on it for a moment.

"Shirley," he called, "get back in the wagon. It seems to me a man has a right to set foot outside his wagon without gettin' bad-mouthed by a wild hog who wants the right of way. Especially," he added, "when that hog's in a place no hog ever ought to be. We're gonna have to move on."

Shirley climbed back into the wagon and gave a happy sigh of relief.

"If you say so, Claude," she said.

For the next few days Shirley and Claude headed east in that great state called Texas. The dusty trail rose and took them into land that was strewn with rocks and boulders of all sizes.

Claude pulled the stumbling, but good-natured, horses to a stop and said, "Shirley, I do believe this is the peaceful place we've been lookin' for."

Shirley gazed out at the ridges and rocks and the stubby trees whose roots clung to the patches of soil. And she said, "I hope not, Claude. This land is nothin' but bumpy-lumpy and makes me feel dry enough to spit cotton."

"Never mind. This place will grow on you, Shirley," Claude said. "For now, why don't you set things to right around here. I'll get our sleepin' pallets out of the wagon and tend to the horses."

So Shirley unfolded her long legs, stuck her feet in her boots, hiked up her skirts, and climbed down from the wagon. She strung a line between the rim of the wagon and a branch of a nearby tree, and on it she hung out to air Claude's long johns and his other shirt, and her petticoats and second-best, store-bought dress.

She was just finishing this chore when she heard a crackle of a broken twig. She turned around to see a large, mangy wolf creeping closer and closer. His eyes were narrow slits, his ears were laid back, and he was up to no good.

Shirley grabbed the nearest thing at hand, the frying pan that was hanging on the back of the wagon, and she let fly at the wolf.

Shirley's aim never was very good, so the frying pan hit the clothesline instead, sweeping it down, just as the wolf leaped forward.

Unfortunately for the wolf, he dove right inside the skirt and on up through the bodice of Shirley's second-best, store-bought dress. His head poked out of the sweetheart neckline, and his front paws were pinned so he couldn't use them.

Well, he set up a snarling and a yelping, meanwhile bouncing around on his back legs and making a terrible racket.

Just as Claude came around the front of the wagon to see what was going on, that old wolf bounced and leaped right on past him, carrying on something awful.

Claude watched the wolf until he disappeared around a far boulder, then he thought on it for a moment.

"Shirley," he said, "get back in the wagon. I don't know why that pointy-nose lady has got her dander up, but I sure don't want any near neighbors that mean and noisy. We're gonna have to move on."

Shirley gathered up their things, put them into the back of the wagon, and climbed up on the seat next to Claude. She gave a happy sigh of relief and said, "If you say so, Claude."

The trail into that great state called Texas curled east and southeast into its heartland. And as it rose it softened into rolling hills, with meadows cupped between. Splashes of blue and gold and red wildflowers dotted the grassy hillsides, and great oaks spread their branches to make deep pools of shade.

Upward they went, until they crested a gentle hill.

Shirley put a hand on Claude's arm and said, "Stop the wagon, Claude."

He pulled the tired, but good-natured, horses to a stop under a stand of oaks, and she said, "Take a look around us. Breathe in that pure air. How's this for a place of peace and quiet?"

"I don't know," Claude said. "Any place that looks this good is bound to get filled up with people afore long. And then we wouldn't remember what peace and quiet were all about."

"Down at the foot of the hill is a stream, probably just jumpin' with fish," Shirley said. "And you can look far enough in both directions goin' and comin' so you could spot a traveler and think on him two days afore he got here."

"I don't know," Claude said again. "Get down from the wagon, Shirley, and see what you can put together for supper. I'll get our sleeping pallets out of the wagon and tend to the horses."

Shirley unfolded her long legs, stuck her feet in her boots, hiked up her skirts, and climbed down from the wagon. She took out the stew pot and set it on the ground under an old and gnarled oak tree. Then she took down the

389

rifle. She was going into the woods to find some fresh meat for the table.

Suddenly she heard the rustle of small leaves, and she looked up to see a big bobcat on a branch near her head. His narrow eyes were gleaming, his lips were pulled back in a snarl, and his tail was twitching. Shirley knew he was getting his mind set to spring.

Well, Shirley stared that bobcat square in the eyes and said to him, "I've found my peaceful place, and you're not goin' to spoil it for me." She raised her rifle, aimed it dead center at the bobcat, and pulled the trigger.

Shirley's aim never was very good. The shot hit that old tree branch, snapping it with a crack that flipped the bobcat in an arc right over the wagon. He came down so hard against a boulder that the force knocked it loose, and it rolled down the hill, tearing up the turf.

Behind it came the screeching bobcat, all spraddle-legged, with every pointy claw digging furrows in the soil as he slid down the hill.

Splat! went the boulder into the stream, knocking two good-sized, unsuspecting trout up on the bank and damming up a nice little pond. The bobcat flew over the stream and ran off so fast that Shirley knew she'd seen the last of him.

Claude came running and said, "Shirley, what was makin' all that racket?"

"Nothin' much," Shirley said. "Just a few things gettin' done around here after a branch fell off that tree."

Claude peered at the tree. "Seems there's something oozin' out of that tree into our stew pot," he said.

"What pure good luck!" Shirley said. "Looks like when that branch broke, it opened a honey cache, Claude. You'll have somethin' good on your biscuits tonight."

She took his arm and pointed him toward the sloping hillside. "Take notice that my vegetable garden's already plowed, and there's two good-sized trout down by the stream that are goin' to be pan-fried for supper."

Claude thought on this a moment. Then he said, "Shirley, get back in the wagon and start pullin' out the stuff we'll need. If you can just learn to do your chores without makin' so much noise, then I think we've found us our place of peace and quiet."

Shirley leaned against the wagon and gave a happy sigh of relief. She looked down at the stream that was sparking with pieces of afternoon sunlight, and she gazed out over the hills and the meadows that were soft and pleasing to the eyes.

She gave Claude the biggest smile he'd ever seen anyone come up with, and she said, "If you say so, Claude."

Reader's Response ⁓ What do you think was the
funniest thing Shirley did? Explain your answer.

RIDDLE ME THIS

Pioneers like Shirley and Claude lived in isolated places without VCRs, televisions, and electric lights. Can you imagine what families did for fun without these modern inventions?

Telling riddles was one popular pastime. Test your skill on these folk riddles from America's past.

What is full of holes and holds water? (a sponge)

What has a mouth and does not speak,
a bed and does not sleep? (a river)

Look in my face I am somebody; look in
my back I am nobody. What am I? (a mirror)

What has four legs and a foot, but can't
walk? a head, but can't talk? (a bed)

What has teeth and can't bite? (a comb)

What runs around the garden without moving? (a fence)

Four fingers and a thumb, yet flesh and
blood I have none. What am I? (a glove)

A Sea of GRASS

by Duncan Searl

For six generations, the Davidson family has farmed the flat
and fertile soil of the Nebraska plains. With a fleet of trucks and
tractors, the family plants and harvests more than a thousand
acres of wheat each year. Barns, sheds, houses—the farm has
enough buildings for a small village. Miles of fences and farm
roads stretch in all directions to connect the pieces.

When twelve-year-old Keith Davidson scans the horizon, he wonders what the farm was like long ago, when the first Davidsons arrived on the land.

Grandpa Davidson has told him that the farm began as "a sea of grass and a hole in the ground."

The first time Keith heard this, he had to accompany his grandfather to a nearby creek to understand. There, Grandpa pointed toward a place in the streambank which appeared to have been scooped out. That, Grandpa told Keith, was where the Davidson farm began.

The Dugout

Early in April of 1872, the Davidsons' covered wagon rolled onto their 160-acre land claim in eastern Nebraska. There was no shelter waiting for them. Like most settlers on the Great Plains, the Davidsons had to build their own shelter. At first, the family lived in the covered wagon. That was all right for a while. But by fall, they needed more protection from Nebraska's cold and windy climate.

Back east, the Davidsons had lived in a wooden farmhouse. They would have liked to build a wooden house on the Plains, too. But there wasn't a tree in sight. Lumber for building wasn't available in Nebraska, even if the family had been able to afford it.

There wasn't time for building, anyway. As farmers, the Davidsons knew they had to get on with the all-important work of plowing and planting. Only then would their new land provide enough harvest to see them through the winter.

Rabbits and foxes dig their burrows and dens in hillsides, and that's what the Davidsons did too. The settlers chose the streambank location because it was conveniently close to water. There were no building materials to buy or skilled workers to hire. After two days of digging, the Davidsons' new home was ready.

Earth formed three walls, the roof, and the floor of the dugout. The fourth wall was the opening. The Davidsons covered it with canvas from the top of their covered wagon. A small hole dug overhead allowed smoke from the kitchen fire to escape.

Most people believe in the old saying, "There's no place like home." The Davidsons, however, might not have felt that way about their dugout. The cramped dwelling was damp and dark, even on sunny days. Dirt from the roof sifted down into bedding and food. Insects and snakes were constant house guests.

Hoping their new shelter would be a temporary one, the Davidsons began to plow and plant. But this wasn't as easy as they had expected. In the early 1870s, more than a foot of thick sod covered almost every inch of the territory. Held together by a mass of tangled roots, this sod was almost impossible to cut through. It could take weeks to plow a single acre. Settlers like the Davidsons became known as "sodbusters."

The sod's toughness gave the settlers an idea. Why not build with it? The new fields were covered with long ribbons of sod that had been plowed up. It would be a simple matter to cut these into smaller pieces and use them as building blocks. The settlers even had a nickname for this unusual building material—"Nebraska marble."

Building with Sod

At first, the Davidsons weren't sure whether they should build with sod. But a sudden summer rainstorm made up their minds. The downpour sent a wall of water racing along the side of their streambank. This flash flood poured into their dugout, sweeping away some of the family's few possessions. After rescuing what they could of their muddy clothing and food supplies, the Davidsons began work on a safer, better shelter.

The next home site was on a gently-sloping hillside far from the stream. Into the slope, the family dug a level floor about ten feet wide and twelve feet long. Fortunately, the Davidson children had found some cottonwood trees growing along a river a few miles away. From this precious wood, their father cut a few beams to use as a frame for their new house.

The frame of the house was simple. In front, two poles were sunk into the ground. A third beam was nailed across the tops of them. From this crosspiece, other beams were stretched back to the hillside to form the frame of a roof.

The whole family worked to cut and move the heavy blocks of prairie grass. To form walls, the sod was stacked like bricks. Each "brick" was about two feet long, one foot wide, and six inches thick. Loose dirt was used between the layers to keep them level. Every fourth layer was laid crosswise of the others to bind the wall more firmly.

The Davidsons used sod for the front of their house and on each side to fill the triangular space between the roof and the slope of the hillside. The roof was also sod, laid atop a layer of branches and poles that stretched across the roof beams. The rear part of the house was dug out. The front was sod. So the house was called a dugout soddy.

When building the front of their new home, the Davidsons included a frame for a door and a window. There weren't enough boards for a wooden door, though. So the family used a flap of

deerskin instead. Plate glass for windows was a luxury few settlers could afford. So the Davidsons used a piece of oiled paper
to fill the window opening. It let in light but kept wind and
water out.

The dugout soddy was an improvement of a plain dugout. It
was drier and airier than the dugout. It was larger and more
comfortable. Outside, wildflowers and grass grew out of the
roof, giving the home a happy, carefree appearance.

The Davidsons lived in their dugout soddy for almost ten
years. During this time, they struggled to improve their farm.
They plowed more land and planted more crops. They built a
sod barn for their horses and cow. They bought some new farm
equipment. The family enjoyed good harvests and even saved
money from the crops they sold.

But everyday life in a dugout soddy was difficult. Chunks of dirt fell from the walls and ceiling, making house-cleaning an impossible chore. Mice and insects lived in the walls. During heavy rains, the roof was sure to leak. The Davidsons often had to drape a sheet of canvas next to the ceiling to catch the dripping rain and mud. Wet and muddy, the roof beams soon began to rot. Part of the roof almost caved in one winter under the weight of the snow.

About this time, many of the Davidsons' neighbors were building free-standing sod houses to replace their dugouts. The Davidsons thought about building one of these roomy and sturdy sod houses, too. But they all had their hearts set on another kind of shelter. Without speaking about it, everyone in the family knew what they were saving for.

A New House

In the late spring of 1881, three wagonloads of lumber from the East arrived at the Davidson farm. That was just enough for a one-room house, about twenty feet long and sixteen feet wide.

The family built it themselves, using stones from a nearby river for the foundation. The house had a wooden door and three glass windows.

Inside, the fireplace was the center of the house. It provided warmth, light, and heat for cooking. In the evening, the family would gather around this hearth to talk, read, sew, and plan for the future.

The house was furnished simply with homemade chairs and tables. Two sleeping lofts were built below the roof. There was no plumbing in the building. Until the well was dug, water had to be carried from the nearby stream. By today's standards, the house was small and rough. But after living in a dugout soddy, the Davidsons thought the new house was a palace.

Eventually, that "new house" became only one room in the modern-day Davidson farmhouse. As the family and farm grew, so did the farmhouse. Rooms were added to meet the needs of each generation. But it all started with that one room, called the "family room" by the Davidsons today. Not a bad name for a place where one family has lived for over 100 years!

DAKOTA DUGOUT

written by Ann Turner
illustrated by Ronald Himler

AMERICAN

LIBRARY

ASSOCIATION

1985

Tell you about the prairie years?
I'll tell you, child, how it was.
When Matt wrote, "Come!"
I packed all I had,
cups and pots and dresses and rope,
even Grandma's silver boot hook,
and rode the clickety train

to a cave in the earth,
Matt's cave.
Built from sod, you know,
with a special iron plow
that sliced the long earth strips.
Matt cut them into bricks,
laid them up, dug into a hill
that was our first home.

I cried when I saw it.
No sky came in that room,
only a paper window
that made the sun look greasy.
Dirt fell on our bed,
snakes sometimes, too,
and the buffalo hide door
could not keep out the wind
or the empty cries in the long grass.

The birds visited me,
there was no one else,
with Matt all day in the fields.
A hawk came, snake in its claws,
a heron flapped by with wings like sails,
and a sparrow jabbered the day long
on a gray fence post.
I jabbered back.
Winter came sudden.

Slam-bang! the ground was iron,
cattle breath turned to ice,
froze their noses to the ground.
We lost twelve in a storm
and the wind scoured the dugout,
whish-hush, *whish*-hush.
Spring, child, was teasing slow
then quick,
water booming in the lake,

geese like yarn in the sky,
green spreading faster than fire,
and the wind blowing
shoosh-hush, *shoosh*-hush.
First summer we watched the corn grow,
strode around the field clapping hands.
We saw dresses, buggies, gold in that grain
until one day a hot wind baked it dry
as an oven, *ssst-ssst, ssst-ssst.*

405

willows our roof under the earth.
I pasted newspaper on the walls,
set bread to bake on the coals,
and the wind was quiet.
Corn grew finally,
we got our dresses, buggies, some gold,
built a clapboard house
with windows like suns,
floors I slipped on,
and the empty sound of too many rooms.
Didn't think I'd miss
the taste of earth in the air.
Now the broom went *whisp*-hush,
and the clock tocked like a busy heart.
Talking brings it near again,
the sweet taste of new bread
in a Dakota dugout,
how the grass whispered like an old friend,
how the earth kept us warm.
Sometimes the things we start with
are best.

Matt sat and looked two whole days,
silent and long.
Come fall we snugged like beavers
in our burrow, new grass on the floor,

Reader's Response ∾ In your opinion, what was most difficult about living in a pioneer home?

Library Link ∾ *Would you like to know more about life on the prairie? Try* My Prairie Year *by Brett Harvey or* Chancy and the Grand Rascal *by Sid Fleischman.*

AMAZING DISCOVERY

One winter day in 1975, Joanna Stratton made an amazing discovery. Joanna was a junior at Harvard University in Cambridge, Massachusetts, and was spending her winter vacation at her grandmother's house in Topeka, Kansas. She decided to explore the attic where she had often played as a child. This time she noticed several old filing cabinets tucked far under the eaves. She opened one of the drawers and saw file after file of papers that had turned yellow with age.

She began to read the papers and soon realized that they were the stories of over 800 pioneer women. Joanna's great-grandmother had collected the stories many years earlier by interviewing some of the women and asking others to write their stories. Joanna eventually published a book called *Pioneer Women* which has helped us to understand better what life was like for pioneer families.

These pictures show us how difficult life must have been for the brave people who chose to "Go West."

Which photograph speaks to you of the hardness of pioneer life?

A FAMILY HOME

from Katie John
by Mary Calhoun

READERS'
CHOICE
AWARD

The whole family is very excited about the book Katie John's father is writing. Katie John's enthusiasm turns to misery, however, when she learns that they will have to sell their big, old family home. The proceeds from the sale will support the family until her father can finish and sell his book.

It was November-cold as Katie John walked home from the library. Dusk had sifted down from the gray sky, and the street lights were already lit. The wind, whipping through bare branches, made Katie huddle deep into her coat. She clutched a pile of library books to her chest, smiling at the warm feeling she got from them. She'd picked out such good ones this time. Another one about Jane, a new book of fairy tales, and a book about a girl in Revolutionary War times that looked

exciting. She could hardly wait to curl up in the big chair and start reading. Which one, though? They all looked so good. The one about Jane, she decided. The Moffats were so cozy, just right for a cold winter evening.

Katie rounded the corner onto her block, and the wind pushed straight at her now. At the end of the block, at the top of the hill, she could see her house, one light shining yellow out of an upstairs window. The tree branches around the house flung about in the wind, but the house itself rose square and solid above them.

It's like a ship, riding out a storm, Katie thought. No, more like a great lighthouse, standing steady as a rock with all the storm swirling around it. And the light is a beacon for me.

In a spurt against the wind, Katie ran up the hill and into the house. She pushed the door shut and stopped in the hall. How quiet the house was, after the noise of the wind outside. So still and warm. Yet alive with a murmur of little sounds. Katie stood there, holding her books, soaking in the warmth, listening. That soft rumble under her feet was the stoker in the furnace coming on. That distant tap-tap-tap was her father working at his typewriter upstairs . . . tap-tap-tap, ping, went the bell faintly. A rattle of a pan lid said Mother was back in the kitchen. Katie sniffed. Oh good! Hamburgers and onions, with mashed potatoes and gravy, her favorite supper.

Now in the stillness she heard the tock-tock of the old marble clock in the parlor. It's like the sound of the house, ticking away at its business, she thought. She turned to look in at the clock on the mantelpiece. Why, it had been ticking there for almost a hundred years, ever since Great-Grandpa brought it home in the wheelbarrow.

Lovingly, Katie looked at all the signs of the Clark family, gleaming in soft lamplight or shadowy in corners— the polished dark woods, the vases and china collected over the years, Great-Grandfather's paintings on the walls, Great-Aunt Emily's crocheted doilies on Katie's reading chair. Her fingers smoothed the yellow wood of the door-frame. The good house that Great-Grandfather built. The good home.

Suddenly Katie John knew why Aunt Emily had never left this house, never gone away for new adventure when it was clear that she wouldn't marry.

Because this was home.

As simple as that. Because this was where she belonged.

The next thought came as surely as summer follows spring: *This is where I belong, too.*

Katie felt such a spreading in her chest that she wanted to stretch out her arms. Oh, she loved this house! She loved Barton's Bluff. She even loved Miss Crackenberry and that crazy Prince. Because they were all a part of living here.

She dropped her books on the big chair and tossed her coat at the hall hatrack as Dad came clattering down the stairs.

"Oh, Dad!" She ran to him. The words for all that she wanted to say choked in her throat. "Dad, come quick!"

She pulled him back to the kitchen. She had to say it to both of them.

"Dad, Mother, the house—let's stay! Let's not sell the house. Let's just stay here. Let's live here always!"

"Oh now, Katie," Dad began, laughing.

But Mother looked at her with a sad little smile. "I know, Katie. I know. If only we could—"

Dad wasn't laughing now. "I'd like to stay, too. It's a good house, and we're happy here. I don't have to live in New York to write. But—"

The facts hadn't changed. They still needed the sale money from the house to live on until he started earning money from his books.

Dad rubbed his face. "There's something else. This is a bad time to tell you. But we'll just have to face it."

Someone wanted to buy the house. It was the fat man who had wanted to turn it into a rooming house.

Katie's mind spun back to the day he'd come, the day she had learned so much about Aunt Emily. He had spit on the fire screen. He wanted to squeeze in lots of roomers. Make some money from the house before it fell apart, he said.

"He made a pretty good offer," Dad was saying. "Came near our asking price. I'm afraid we'll have to—"

"No!" Katie cried. "No no no!"

He wouldn't take care of the house. He said he didn't want to spend money on repairs. And an old house needed lots of care. Dad had said the house needed a new roof. With all those people, the place would get rattletrap and dirty, start to fall apart. She'd seen some of the old homes that were now rooming houses, boardinghouses. Crumbling steps, broken windows, paint cracked, washing flapping on the porches. No!

Katie argued. She begged. At last she cried. She stopped when she saw that Mother and Dad looked almost ready to cry, too.

All through the miserable supper that no one ate, Katie's thoughts wound drearily. So they'd leave the house. Go live in some dinky little New York apartment. Oh, a person could be happy anywhere. Sure. But this was home. And then to think of that man spitting on the house, the hordes of people moving in and out and none of them loving it, and it crumbling away.

The hamburger tasted like soggy cardboard in her mouth, and she could hardly swallow it. Money. Hateful, horrible stuff. Where could they get some money, so they could stay?

If only she and Sue could have found a sack of gold hidden away somewhere in the house when they were looking for secret places. Or if Great-Aunt Emily had left some money.

But all she'd left was the house. And old houses were so big and expensive to keep up, they weren't good for anything any more but to rent out rooms.

Oh, if only the fat man even loved the house, Katie thought in despair. Then at least he might take care of it.

Wait. What was that? Rent out rooms but take care of the house. Ye-es-s, yes! Why couldn't they do it instead of that man?

Katie started to blurt it out. Then she stopped. Dad might say, "No, Katie," and not really understand the idea. Better to think it all out and then tell them.

After supper Katie hurried right off to bed, leaving her parents sighing because they thought she was so unhappy. But she had to be alone, now, and in bed was the best place for thinking things through. Now she must be careful. She couldn't go whizzing at this idea in her usual way. This was serious business. Their last chance. She had to get it just right, so it would make sense to grownups.

As Katie threw off her clothes, though, she felt a doubt. Was it worth it? Would it be the same, would the house still be home with renters in it? She didn't want to share her home with a lot of other people.

It's better than nothing, she told herself firmly. It will still be our house.

She scrambled under the covers and began to figure. Now it was clear they'd have to rent out most of the house, if they were to make enough money to live on. They must live on just the first floor. She'd have to give her pretty bedroom to her folks, she realized with a twinge of regret. She could sleep in the little room off the kitchen.

Then they could rent all the rooms on the second and third floors. And the basement, too. Yes, the little servants' apartment, where the dumbwaiter ended up, would be nice for someone. And oh, what a lucky thing that Aunt Emily had put in so many bathrooms!

But would anyone want to rent rooms in an old house? They should get nice people who would take care of their rooms. What could be special about the rooms?

Why, the fireplaces! Every room had a fireplace. So far Dad had lit the little fireplace in the kitchen, and Katie loved dressing before the open brick hearth on cold mornings.

Everyone loves a fireplace, she reasoned, and here they could have one of their own even in a rented room. Some of the fireplaces were really beautiful, too, with carving around the edges and lacy iron or painted fire screens. Yes, the fireplaces could be the drawing card.

Katie John was getting sleepy now; her plans were fuzzy at the edges. Tomorrow she'd tell Mother and Dad about it . . . so good to know things were working out. So good that the house had bathrooms and fireplaces and big rooms for renters. The house would save itself, after all . . . or maybe it was Great-Grandfather who was saving it, because of the way he'd built the house, she thought drowsily. And Aunt Emily. All the Clarks had put so much into the house. Because they loved it.

And what had she herself put into the house? The thought waked her up a little. Nothing, really. Well, she was probably the only person outside of the builder who knew what the inside of the dumb-waiter walls looked like. But that wasn't doing anything. She would, she promised herself. Someday she'd do something for the old house.

The next morning Katie decided not to tell her folks yet. It was a good plan. But grownups had such a habit of saying "No, Katie" to good plans.

Better if they could actually see it working out. Upon waking up, it had been quite plain what she must do: find a renter.

What's more, she knew just the person. Her teacher, Miss Howell. Not long ago Miss Howell had been saying that soon she and her sister must move into town from their farm for the winter. They lived out on a hill above the river in their old homeplace. Now that she understood so much more, Katie guessed they must love their house as she did hers. But it was too cold and icy for two old ladies to live out there alone in the winter. So, as Miss Howell had been telling her when she was helping after school the other day, every winter they moved into an apartment in town. And they hadn't found one yet.

As Katie walked to school she grew more and more excited as she figured how a little kitchen could be put in one of the rooms upstairs, so that Miss Howell could have a big two-room-and-bath apartment. She was so wrapped up in plans that she forgot to stop for Sue. Later at school she explained to Sue that she had something very big brewing, and she'd tell her tonight if it worked out.

Katie almost burst before recess time. When the bell rang she stayed in the room and told Miss Howell all about it. About loving the house and wanting to stay and renting out rooms. Then she was afraid it sounded as though she were begging. So as not to put Miss Howell on the spot, she said hastily:

"Of course, you mustn't do it just to help us out. You shouldn't rent the apartment unless you really like it." And couldn't help adding honestly, "But I hope you do."

Miss Howell, who had listened carefully, smiled now. "I understand, Katie John. Of course I want to help you. But I promise you I won't rent it unless it will suit Julia and me. After all, we're the ones who will have to live there all winter."

Miss Howell pointed out that it would also depend on how much the rent would be. She thought that Katie should talk it over with her parents first. But Katie had her plans fixed.

"Please, just look at the rooms first," she said. "Then if you're already interested, Mother and Dad will think about it more seriously."

So Miss Howell said that she'd come home with Katie after school. Katie could hardly keep her mind on schoolwork for the rest of the day. She made all the circles in penmanship slant the wrong way because she was thinking about the one last important detail. How would she work out that part? Maybe she shouldn't—it might make Mother and Dad mad . . . . But it would make everything so perfect. Katie pushed at her bangs. She just had to do it. If only her folks would be out, just once, when she got home from school.

As it happened, Miss Howell had to stay after school for a parent conference. She said she'd drive down to Katie's house afterward. But that was fine. It would give Katie plenty of time to finish that last detail.

"Got to hurry," she told Sue after school. "I'll run on ahead and see you later. Tell you all about it then."

Sue looked disappointed but nodded patiently. Oh, what a joy it was to have a good friend like Sue! Another reason for staying in Barton's Bluff. Let Miss Howell like the rooms, Katie prayed, as she ran.

Mother and Dad were just coming out the front door when Katie got home. They were going down to Mr. Follensbee's real estate office to talk over plans for selling the house to the fat man.

"You're not going to sign anything already?" Katie cried.

Dad shrugged unhappily. "Honey, you know it's got to be done. But no, we won't be signing anything today. We'll be right back."

"Be sure you don't," Katie said. "We may not have to sell the house yet!"

She heard Mother say as they went down the walk, "Poor child. She's hoping for a miracle." And Katie giggled, almost about to burst with excitement. Little did they know!

She ran down to the basement for the things she needed and took them upstairs. When she had that all ready, she set about making the apartment look as handsome as possible, dusting, opening curtains, taking dust covers off the furniture. She'd chosen two big rooms with a connecting bathroom. The front room overlooked the river, and the back room could be partitioned into a bedroom and kitchen, she'd decided. It already had a washbowl that could be used for washing dishes.

The doorbell rang. It must be Miss Howell. Katie did the last important thing. Then she raced down the stairs and brought her teacher in.

"Mother and Dad went to the real estate office, but they'll be right back," Katie told her. "I'll show you the apartment."

Katie's hands were suddenly cold and she clasped them in front of her as she led Miss Howell up the stairs. Miss Howell's warm voice was saying nice things about how beautiful the house was, but now Katie couldn't answer. The important thing was, what would she think of the apartment?

Along the hall . . . open the door . . . Katie gasped.

Smoke! Black smoke billowed in the room and poured out the doorway.

"The house is on fire!" Katie screamed. "Quick! Water!"

She ran to get water from the bathroom somehow. And then she saw that the room wasn't on fire, after all. The wretched black smoke was pouring from the fireplace—the beautiful fireplace, where she'd worked so hard laying wood. That had been the important thing that was to make it all perfect. She wanted Miss Howell to be greeted by a homey blaze when she looked into the room. Just before she'd run downstairs she'd lit the fire.

And now look! Smoke filled the room, and more was coming out all the time. The wood was burning, but the smoke wasn't going up the chimney.

"We must put out the fire quickly!" Miss Howell scooped up the empty coal bucket from the hearth and ran to the bathroom for water.

Katie ran after her, sobbing and getting in the way.

"No, you open the windows," Miss Howell said, hurrying back to the fireplace.

Fortunately, the fire hadn't gotten well started yet, and the blaze died under the water.

"Oh, look at the room!" Katie wailed. "It'll be black with smoke!"

She beat at the smoke, trying to push it out the window before it settled on the walls and the white curtains. The fire reduced to wet black ashes, Miss Howell rushed to help Katie, fanning the smoke with a sheaf of school papers.

"What in the world!"

Katie turned and saw her horrified parents coming into the room.

"It's all my fault!" she cried in despair. "I wanted to make a nice fire, but the smoke didn't go up the chimney."

"Because the chimney is capped! All of them are except the one for the kitchen." Dad's face was angry. "Young lady, I—"

"Oh, wouldn't you know!" Katie sobbed. "Everything I do goes wrong!"

"Let's get the smoke out of here first," Mother suggested.

She and Dad joined Miss Howell in fanning smoke out the windows while Katie poured out the whole story.

"I knew I shouldn't have lit that fire," she ended miserably, "but it seemed like such a wonderful idea. And now look."

She stared at the soupy mass of ashes in the fireplace.

"Well," Dad said slowly," of course you shouldn't have lit the fire without a grownup around—you do get carried away with your ideas, Katie. But basically you had a pretty good plan, at that."

In fact, he'd been thinking about renting out apartments, too, he said. He'd figured that from the rents they could pay for the upkeep of the big house and have a little left over.

"We can't do it, though, Katie," he added quickly. "I soon realized that running an apartment house would throw entirely too much work on your mother. And we couldn't afford to hire help."

Then Mother made a confession. She too had been thinking about renting, had even checked on rental regulations. But, according to fire laws, they couldn't have women and children on the third floor, only men. So that meant she'd have to do all the weekly cleaning and laundry for those rooms, plus all the general work of taking care of an apartment house.

"I just don't see how I could do it all alone," she sighed, "and I won't have you leave your writing to do it," she told her husband.

He shook his head sadly. "I could do the repair work and take care of the furnace. But it would still leave too great a burden on you. We'll just have to forget it."

Katie had been looking from one parent to another. Well, for goodness' sakes! So she had been on the right track, with her idea about renting. For once she'd thought something through

almost like a grownup would! Her chest stopped feeling so tight.

But still, it didn't do any good. They had to leave, just the same. Renting rooms meant too much work for Mother. Katie sighed. It was just too bad that she wasn't big enough to help.

And then Katie began to get all hot inside, the way she always did when she was about to have a wonderful idea. Just how big did she have to be to help? How big, to sweep down the

stairs that renters would dirty, to make beds, hang sheets on the line, dust furniture, vacuum floors? She could do those things.

But all that work! Katie shuddered. I'm just a little girl. I hate

housework. It would take so much time.

"I could do it," she heard herself saying. "I could help. I could work after school and on Saturdays."

Mother smiled but shook her head. "It's really sweet of you, Katie. But you're just a little girl. I have to stand over you even to get you to dust your room."

"I know! I know!" Katie cried desperately. "But I can change! Now I want to work. If only we can stay here!"

She had to make them understand. To make them know how much she wanted to stay, enough to do all that work. The words tumbled out until Mother interrupted.

"Why, you've really made up your mind, haven't you!" She laughed. "And I know you, Katie John. When you set your mind on something, you stick to it. I do believe I can depend on you!" She turned to Dad. "Dear, let's try it!"

Dad looked from Mother to Katie John. He threw up his hands and laughed. "It's all right with me. You women will be doing all the work!"

All the tensely held breath went out of Katie. "Oh, Daddy!" She flung herself at him.

While he hugged her he said that after he started earning money from his book they could hire a cleaning woman. And Mother said they'd get things organized so Katie wouldn't have to work all the time. But Katie hardly heard. All she could think was: We're staying! We're staying!

Miss Howell had been wandering around the rooms, and now she came back to the Tuckers.

"May I have the honor of being your first renter?" she asked with a twinkle in her smile.

Despite the smoky fireplace, she said—and Dad hastily said he'd uncap the chimneys—she liked the rooms and was sure her sister would, too.

That made things perfect, but all Katie could do was reach out and squeeze her teacher's hand. Dad and Mother and Miss Howell went off to the second room to discuss how they could partition it and put in a stove and refrigerator. Katie walked out into the hallway.

And so they would stay. The old Clark house would go on, with the Tucker family in it. And the renters, too. Wonder who they'd be? Why, it could be fun, Katie realized with a little prick of excitement, having all sorts of people—nice ones and maybe ornery ones—coming to live here. And she and Mother would take care of them.

A warm, satisfied feeling spread through Katie, clear down to her stomach, because everything had worked out so well. Even the answer to that question that had been bothering her last night: What could she do for the old house to match the loving care of Great-Grandfather and Great-Aunt Emily? Her work. All that pesky housework that would help them keep the house.

Katie John looked up the stairwell to the top of the house, then down to the hall below. She started down the stairs, sliding her fingers along the banister.

"Hello, home," she said softly.

Reader's Response ~ Do you think Katie's behavior was selfish or unselfish? Why did you choose your answer?

Victoriana

round turrets
or many steep
gabled roofs

tall windows
or windows
with stained
glass panels

fancy, carved
woodwork on
the outside of
the house called
"gingerbread"

wide curving
porches and
balconies

Katie John shares a love of
Victorian homes with many
people. Do you know what makes
these homes so special and why
they are called Victorians?

The original Victorian homes
were built from about 1830 to
1900, during the reign of Queen
Victoria of England. The styles
popular during this time are
generally called Victorian.

Some common details of this
style of architecture in America are
noted in this drawing.

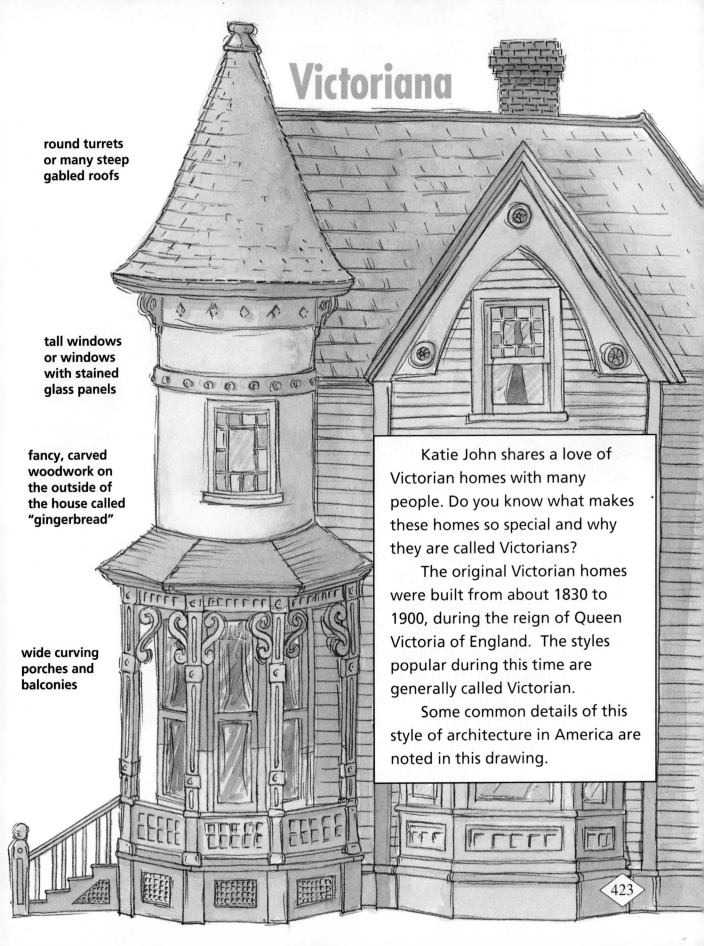

AWARD
WINNING
AUTHOR

There Is an Island

by Jean Fritz

Once long ago in the far, far north, there lived a giant who had such long legs that he could cross from one continent to another in a single step. So one day he put his left leg firmly on the coast of Siberia. Then he stretched his right leg—and stretched and stretched it until his foot came down on North America. And there he was straddling the Bering Sea! Below him he saw the sea—big but empty. What it needed was an island. So reaching down, the giant scooped up a handful of mud from the bottom of the sea and began squeezing the water out of it. He squeezed and squeezed until it was as dry as any island could be. Then he planted it in the emptiness. Not in the middle. No, he placed it closer to his left leg, close to Siberia. Later the island was called St. Lawrence Island, but the people who live there have always called it *Sivuqaq*,[1] which in their language means "squeezed dry."

[1]Sivuqaq (sē vō′ kähk)

The people in the "squeezed dry" place are Yupik Eskimos. And although their island belongs to America, they live so close to Siberian Yupiks that they speak the same language, share the same customs, and often have the same names. Over the years they have visited back and forth as if they were part of one big family. They

have sung together, hunted together, danced together, and traded together—American chewing tobacco and walrus hides in return for reindeer pants, alder bark, and wolf-skin ruffs.

And every June and July, the men from St. Lawrence and the men from Siberia would get together to race and wrestle with each other. The races started as soon as the people from Siberia arrived in Gambell, the town perched on the tip of the island closest to Siberia. The men ran around a circular track, around and around, until one by one they had to drop out, and at last only the winner was left.

Then a St. Lawrence man took off his parka and went to the center of the circle and squatted. This meant that it was time for wrestling and he took on anyone who challenged him. One by one,

they entered the ring. But as soon as a man was knocked down, he had to quit. The champion was the last one left on his feet.

All year the men trained for this event, each man wanting to prove his strength. The training for the competition was so fierce that one might expect fights to break out. But they didn't. The people of St. Lawrence honored peace above all else, and the elders on the island made sure that peace was kept. The elders were used to settling arguments whenever they occurred, winter or summer. They ordered the contestants to wrestle or vie with each other in lifting heavy rocks, and soon arguments were forgotten and hasty words forgiven.

It was the same during the competition when the Siberians were there. If tempers began to get out of hand, the elders had only to say, "Enough!" So everyone stayed in good spirits, and at the end of the contests, all were ready for the feasting and fun to begin. They played games, ate and danced together—men and women, boys and girls. And they sang. Long, long into the summer twilight they sang the old songs they all knew.

The elders were considered the wisest and most important people on the island. After all, they were the ones who had "seen the sun first" and welcomed it back most often. What could be more special than that? So the elders were the ones who made sure that all the ceremonies were carried out properly. On an island

where the sun goes down and stays down for most of the eight months of the winter—and comes up and stays up for most of the four months of summer—and where life itself depends on what can be taken from the sea, people have to make sure that they please the gods.

Because whales are most important to the survival of the Yupik people, there are special songs of petition to the gods before a whale hunt begins, certain rituals to be followed when a whale is captured, and when it is finally beached. Some of the whale must be returned to the ocean, some water from the ocean must be brought to the whale; for like all life, whales have spirits and must be honored. Indeed, Yupiks feel a kinship with the whale, the walrus, and the seal. Do they not

all share the same cold waters, fight the same storms, know when the ice comes and when it goes?

Of course some things changed over the years. The islanders, who in the early days lived in caves dug into the hillsides, moved to houses made of walrus skins, and finally to small wood houses provided by the government. Once, after a famine, the islanders brought reindeer over from Siberia, and reindeer herders started a new town which they called Savoonga. Airplanes came to the island, and an airstrip was built to receive them.

In countries far away there were wars. And finally, in the early 1940s, there was a world war with warships even in their own sea, and with their own men signing up for the National Guard. Yet the Yupiks remained a peaceful people. One thing they thought would never change: Nothing could stop them from visiting back and forth with relatives and friends in Siberia.

Yet there were changes in Siberia too. The day came when Gambell men visiting Siberia found Russians, white men, in the Yupik villages. Some were policemen dressed in uniform

who walked about with rifles and billy clubs. The Siberians told their island friends not to worry. When they saw a policeman, they should shout, "*Trastuwu!*"[2] In Russian this is *Zdrasteuite*[3] and is simply a greeting, but to the islanders it sounded like a password. "*Trastuwu*," they would shout, no matter how far away they were.

This seemed to keep them safe, and they visited as they always had.

World War II was over in 1945, but the Siberian Yupiks and the St. Lawrence Yupiks may not have paid much attention to the fact that their two countries were not friendly. Then one day in 1948, the schoolteacher, the only person on St. Lawrence who had a radio, heard some astounding news that had to be passed on quickly to the islanders. The Russian government had passed a law which denied anyone the right to enter Siberia or even Siberian waters. Furthermore, no one from Siberia could leave Siberia.

At first the people on St. Lawrence could not believe such news. How could it be? Had someone forgotten to say the password? Had the teacher heard wrong?

²Trastuwu (träs tōo′ wōo)
³Zdrasteuite (zdräv stvoo tye)

But it was true. The international date line, an imaginary line that runs between Siberia and St. Lawrence, was the point that no one was allowed to cross. Some St. Lawrence men claimed that they could tell where that line was. The water was ruffled at that point, they said, as though currents were crossing each other. And when it was Monday on one side of the line, it was Tuesday on the other side. But from now on they would be stuck in St. Lawrence time and the Siberians would be stuck in Siberian time, with never a word of greeting between them. It was like telling the spring birds not to return next year.

All they could hope for was change, but change did not come. Instead, there were military units in Alaska with their guns ready to turn on Siberia if necessary. And in Siberia, they supposed, it must have been the same. After a while, the islanders gave up racing and wrestling for basketball. Still, on clear days when they looked across the water to the Siberian hills, they were heartsick.

Ten years passed. Twenty. Thirty. Now only grandparents and the elders remembered what it was like in the old days, but they told the young ones. Then as forty years approached, everyone agreed that this was just too long. Soon even memories would go. What could they do? Some of the islanders had already joined Eskimos from northern Alaska, from Canada, and from Greenland in an Arctic Eskimo organization—

the Inuit (Eskimo) Interpolar Conference—to try to persuade the world to make the Arctic a nuclear-free, nonmilitary zone. They knew it might be impossible, but sometimes people had to work for the impossible, didn't they? Still, they needed the Siberian Eskimos to work with them.

Many people in Alaska agreed to help. They wrote letters to the Russian government. They talked to people who talked to other people who in turn talked to people in important places who could say yes or no. Alaskan children wrote notes to Siberian children, attached them to helium balloons, and let them loose over the water, hoping they would float over the international date line into the next day.

Finally the Russian government said yes. One plane load of Eskimos could come for one day to the town

of Provideniya on the Siberian coast. It was to be called Friendship Flight One, and surely that meant there would be a Friendship Flight Two and Three, until maybe people could stop counting.

On Tuesday, June 14, 1988, the flight took off. Of course everyone was excited. Ora Gologergen, a seventy-two-year-old elder from St. Lawrence, hoped to meet a friend she had played with as a girl in Gambell. Darlene Orr, who was in her twenties and too young to have met any Siberians, knew she had relatives somewhere in the area. In Provideniya, not just Eskimos (who made up a small part of the population) were celebrating but the whole town.

Russian school children waited for the Friendship Flight, waving American and Russian flags and holding up banners with messages of peace and pictures of doves.

Ora found her childhood friend, but they laughed and cried so much that later she couldn't remember what they had said. Darlene and her aunt, Nancy Walunga, who also went, discovered that their relatives had been relocated to the nearby village of Sirenki and they couldn't go there. Instead, they were invited to tea with a group of local Yupik women. Darlene's aunt had brought tapes of Yupik dances, and when she played these, the women clapped in delight. Although the kitchen where they were sitting was small, the women jumped to their

feet, lined up, and danced the old dances together. Then they sat down for a bowl of reindeer meat and a dish of raw fish.

From beginning to end, the day was a success, but best of all, there was a promise of more. Perhaps soon the Siberians could bring a plane of Eskimos to Alaska. Perhaps St. Lawrence islanders could make the trip to Siberia by boat right over the international date line. And yes, perhaps the Siberian Eskimos would be allowed to send representatives to the Interpolar Conference.

For Darlene Orr, the good news was that she would be invited to Sirenki for their annual whale hunt. Later in the summer when she arrived, she found that she was

suddenly part of a huge family, all with the same last name. And there they were on a Siberian beach, all of them speaking the same Yupik language as if they had grown up together.

To make everything perfect, the whale hunters got their whale on their first day out. Nothing can bring Yupiks more joy than catching their whale. Not only is it their food for the winter; it is their victory over life in a place where life is hard to live. And when the whale boats came to shore, towing the whale behind them, the crew sang the whale-catch cry together as Yupiks had always done. *"Uu-huk! Uu-huk!"* The very sound of the cry rang with triumph.

Standing on the beach with her new family, watching the traditional ceremony of bringing water to the beached whale and returning part of the whale to the water, Darlene felt lifted beyond herself. She was one with these people, one with all people, one with the land and the sea and the sky which all people shared. At a time like this, one could believe that anything was possible. Not only peace throughout the Arctic, but peace throughout the world.

Reader's Response ∼ What are some of the feelings you had as you read this story? What caused you to have them?

Arctic Games

The Yupiks of St. Lawrence Island share their love of games and sports with Eskimos everywhere. Long indoor hours during months of winter darkness are filled with games for people of all ages. In summer, outdoor games are popular community activities.

A favorite indoor game is the two-legged high kick. The jumper has to hit a hanging object with both feet at the same time and then land back on the floor with both feet. Men have hit the target at ten feet above the ground and women at over six feet.

In summer, the blanket toss is by far the most spectacular sport. The "blanket" is actually several walrus hides sewn together with holes for hand grips all around the edge. With twelve people holding on, a person gets into the blanket. Suddenly the holders pull the blanket tight—sending the person high into the air. Women are the best "fliers" and some go as high as thirty-three feet. On the way down they perform somersaults and twists while the others cheer them on.

435

On My Way Home

by Jean Fritz
from *Homesick: My Own Story*

Jean Guttery was an American who enjoyed growing up in China. Her parents taught the Chinese about American ways. Jean especially loved Lin Nai-Nai, who helped raise her. In 1927, the Gutterys crossed the Pacific Ocean on a journey to America with their friend, Mrs. Hull, and her children, Andrea, David, and Edward.

It took twenty-eight days to go from Shanghai to San Francisco, and on that first morning I thought I'd be content to lie on my deck chair and stare at the ocean and drink beef tea the whole time. Not Andrea. She thought the ocean was one big waste. We should be watching the people, she said, and sizing them up as they went by. So we did. We found that mostly they fit into definite types. There were the Counters, for instance: fast-walking men, red-cheeked women, keeping score of how many

NEWBERY
HONOR
1983

times they walked around the deck, reveling in how fit they were. Then there were the Stylish Strollers, the Huffers and Puffers, the Lovebirds, leaning on each other, the Queasy Stomachs who clutched the railing and hoped for the best.

"You notice there's no one our age," Andrea said.

That was true. We had seen young people who were probably in their twenties, children who were Edward's age, and of course the majority who were our parents' age or older. But not one who might be in seventh or eighth grade or even high school.

Andrea jumped from her chair. "I'm going to explore."

Normally I would have gone with her but I hadn't had a chance yet to get my fill of the ocean. It was the same ocean as I'd had in Peitaiho,[1] and I looked and looked. I walked up

[1]Peitaiho (bā dī' hō): a city in China where Jean and her family usually spent the summer.

feeling disappear. This is the place, a kind of imaginary line in the ocean, where all ships going east add an extra day to that week and all ships going west drop a day. This is so you can keep up with the world turning and make time come out right. We had two Tuesdays in a row when we crossed the line and after that when it was "today" for me, I knew that Lin Nai-Nai was already in "tomorrow." I didn't like to think of Lin Nai-Nai so far ahead of me. It was as if we'd suddenly been tossed on different planets.

On the other hand, this was the first time in my life that I was sharing the same day with my grandmother.

Oh, Grandma, I thought, ready or not, here I come!

It was only a short time later that Edward saw a couple of rocks poking out of the water and yelled for us to come. The rocks could hardly be called land, but we knew they were the beginning of the Hawaiian Islands and we knew that the Hawaiian Islands were a territory belonging to the United States. Of course it wasn't the same as one of the forty-eight states; still, when we stepped off the *President Taft* in Honolulu (where we were to stay a couple of days before going on to San Francisco), we

wondered if we could truthfully say we were stepping on American soil. I said no. Since the Hawaiian Islands didn't have a star in the flag, they couldn't be one-hundred-percent American, and I wasn't going to consider myself on American soil until I had put my feet flat down on the state of California.

We had a week to wait. The morning we were due to arrive in San Francisco, all the passengers came on deck early, but I was the first. I skipped breakfast and went to the very front of the ship where the railing comes to a point. That morning I would be the "eyes" of the *President Taft*, searching the horizon for the first speck of land. My private cere- mony of greeting, however, would not come until we were closer, until we were sailing through the Golden Gate. For years I had heard about the Golden Gate, a narrow stretch of water connecting the Pacific Ocean to San Francisco Bay. And for years I had planned my entrance.

Dressed in my navy skirt, white blouse and silk stockings, I felt every bit as neat as Columbus or Balboa and every bit as heroic when I finally spotted America in the distance. The decks had filled with passengers by

now, and as I watched the land come closer, I had to tell myself over and over that I was HERE. At last.

Then the ship entered the narrow stretch of the Golden Gate and I could see American hills on my left and American houses on my right, and I took a deep breath of American air.

" 'Breathes there the man, with soul so dead,' " I cried,

" 'Who never to himself hath said, This is my own, my native land!' "

I forgot that there were people behind and around me until I heard a few snickers and a scattering of claps, but I didn't care. I wasn't reciting for anyone's benefit but my own.

Next for my first steps on American soil, but when the time came, I forgot all about them. As soon as we were on the dock, we were jostled from line to line. Believe it or not, after crossing thousands of miles of ocean to get here, we had to prove that it was O.K. for us to come into the U.S.A. We had to show that we were honest-to-goodness citizens and not spies. We had to open our baggage and let inspectors see that we weren't smuggling in opium or anything else illegal. We even had to prove that we were germ-free, that we didn't have smallpox or any dire disease that would infect the country. After we had finally passed the tests, I expected to feel one-hundred-percent American. Instead, stepping from the dock into the city of San Francisco, I felt dizzy and unreal, as if I were a made-up character in a book I had read too many times to believe it wasn't still a book. As we walked the Hulls to the car that their Aunt Kay had driven up from Los Angeles, I told Andrea about my crazy feeling.

"I'm kind of funny in the head," I said. "As if I'm not really me. As if this isn't really happening."

"Me too," Andrea agreed. "I guess our brains haven't caught up to us yet. But my brains better get going. Guess what?"

"What?"

"Aunt Kay says our house in Los Angeles is not far from Hollywood."

Then suddenly the scene speeded up and the Hulls were in the car, ready to leave for Los Angeles, while I was still stuck in a book without having said any of the things I wanted to. I ran after the car as it started.

"Give my love to John Gilbert," I yelled to Andrea.

She stuck her head out the window. "And how!" she yelled back.

My mother, father, and I were going to stay in a hotel overnight and start across the continent the next morning, May 24, in our new Dodge. The first thing we did now was to go to a drugstore where my father ordered three ice-cream sodas. "As tall as you can make them," he said. "We have to make up for lost time."

My first American soda was chocolate and it was a whopper. While we sucked away on our straws, my father read to us from the latest newspaper. The big story was about America's new hero, an aviator named Charles Lindbergh who had just made the first solo flight across the Atlantic Ocean. Of course I admired him for having done such a brave and scary thing, but I bet he wasn't any more surprised to have made it across one ocean than I was to have finally made it across another. I looked at his picture. His goggles were pushed back on his helmet and he was grinning. He had it all over John Gilbert, I decided. I might even consider having a crush on him—that is, if and when I ever felt the urge. Right now I was coming to the bottom of my soda and I was trying to slurp up the last drops when my mother told me to quit; I was making too much noise.

The rest of the afternoon we spent sight-seeing, riding up and down seesaw hills in cable cars, walking in and out of American stores. Every once in a while I found myself smiling at total strangers because I knew that if I were to speak to them in English, they'd answer in English. We were all

Americans. Yet I still felt as if I were telling myself a story. America didn't become completely real for me until the next day after we'd left San Francisco and were out in the country.

My father had told my mother and me that since he wasn't used to our new car or to American highways, we should be quiet and let him concentrate. My mother concentrated too. Sitting in the front seat, she flinched every time she saw another car, a crossroad, a stray dog, but she never said a word. I paid no attention to the road. I just kept looking out the window until all at once there on my right was a white picket fence and a meadow, fresh and green as if it had just this minute been created. Two black and white cows were grazing slowly over the grass as if they had all the time in the world, as if they knew that no matter how much they ate, there'd always be more, as if in their quiet munching way they understood that they had nothing, nothing whatsoever to worry about. I poked my mother, pointed, and whispered, "Cows." I had never seen cows in China but it was not the cows themselves that impressed me. It was the

whole scene. The perfect greenness. The washed-clean look. The peacefulness. Oh, *now*! I thought. Now I was in America. Every last inch of me.

By the second day my father acted as if he'd been driving the car all his life. He not only talked, he sang, and if he felt like hitching up his trousers, he just took his hands off the wheel and hitched. But as my father relaxed, my mother became more tense. "Arthur," she finally said, "you are going forty-five."

My father laughed. "Well, we're headed for the stable, Myrtle. You never heard of a horse that dawdled on its way home, did you?"

My mother's lips went tight and thin. "The whole point of driving across the continent," she said, "was so we could see the country."

"Well, it's all there." My father swept his hand from one side of the car to the other. "All you have to do is to take your eyes off the road and look." He honked his horn at the car in front of him and swung around it.

At the end of the day, after we were settled in an overnight cabin, my father took a new notebook from his pocket. I watched as he wrote: "May 24. 260 miles." Just as I'd suspected, my father was out to break records. I bet that before long we'd be making 300 miles or more a day. I bet we'd be in Washington, P.A., long before July.

The trouble with record breaking is that it can lead to Narrow Squeaks, and while we were still in California we had our first one. Driving along a back road that my father had figured out was a shortcut, we came to a bridge with a barrier across it and a sign in front: THIS BRIDGE CONDEMNED. DO NOT PASS. There was no other road marked DETOUR,

444

so obviously the only thing to do was to turn around and go back about five miles to the last town and take the regular highway. My father stopped the car. "You'd think they'd warn you in advance," he muttered. He slammed the door, jumped over the barrier, and walked onto the bridge. Then he climbed down the riverbank and looked up at the bridge from below. When he came back up the bank, he pushed the barrier aside, got in the car, and started it up. "We can make it," he said.

It hadn't occurred to me that he'd try to drive across. My mother put her hand on his arm. "Please, Arthur," she begged, but I didn't bother with any "pleases." If he wanted to kill himself, he didn't have to kill Mother and me too. "Let Mother and me walk across," I shouted. "Let us out. Let us OUT."

My father had already revved up the motor. "A car can have only one driver," he snapped. "I'm it." He backed up so he could get a flying start and then we whooped across the bridge, our wheels clattering across the loose boards, space gaping below. Well, we did reach the other side and when I looked back, I saw that the bridge was still there.

"You see?" my father crowed. "You see how much time we saved?"

All I could see was that we'd risked our lives because he was so pigheaded. Right then I hated my father. I felt rotten hating someone I really loved but I couldn't help it. I knew the loving would come back but I had to wait several hours.

There were days, however, particularly across the long, flat stretches of Texas, when nothing out-of-the-way happened. We just drove on and on, and although my father reported at the end of the day that we'd gone 350 miles, the scenery was the same at the end as at the beginning, so it didn't feel as if we'd moved at all. Other times we ran into storms or into road construction and we were lucky if we made 200 miles. But the best day of the whole trip, at least as far as my mother and I were concerned, was the day that we had a flat tire in the Ozark Mountains. The spare tire and jack were buried in the trunk under all our luggage, so everything had to be taken out before my father could even begin work on the tire. There was no point in offering to help because my father had a system for loading and unloading which only he understood, so my mother and I

445

set off up the mountainside, looking for wildflowers.

"Watch out for snakes," my mother said, but her voice was so happy, I knew she wasn't thinking about snakes.

As soon as I stepped out of the car, I fell in love with the day. With the sky—fresh, blotting-paper blue. With the mountains, warm and piney and polka-dotted with flowers we would never have seen from the window of a car. We decided to pick one of each kind and press them in my gray geography book which I had in the car. My mother held out her skirt, making a hollow out of it, while I dropped in the flowers and she named them: forget-me-not, wintergreen, pink, wild rose. When we didn't know the name, I'd make one up: pagoda plant, wild confetti, French knot. My mother's skirt was atumble with color when we suddenly realized how far we'd walked. Holding her skirt high, my mother led the way back, running and laughing. We arrived at the car, out of breath, just as my father was loading the last of the luggage into the trunk. He glared at us, his face streaming with perspiration. "I don't have a dry stitch on me," he said, as if it were our fault

that he sweat so much. Then he looked at the flowers in Mother's skirt and his face softened. He took out his handkerchief and wiped his face and neck and finally he smiled. "I guess I picked a good place to have a flat tire, didn't I?" he said.

The farther we went, the better mileage we made, so that by the middle of June we were almost to the West Virginia state line. My father said we'd get to Washington, P.A., the day after the next, sometime in the afternoon. He called my grandmother on the phone, grinning because he knew how surprised she'd be. I stood close so I could hear her voice.

"Mother?" he said when she answered. "How about stirring up a batch of flannel cakes?"

"Arthur!" (She sounded just the way I knew she would.) "Well, land's sakes, Arthur, where are you?"

"About ready to cross into West Virginia."

My grandmother was so excited that her words fell over each other as she tried to relay the news to my grandfather and Aunt Margaret and talk over the phone at the same time.

The next day it poured rain and although that didn't slow us down, my mother started worrying. Shirls

Avenue, my grandparents' street, apparently turned into a dirt road just before plunging down a steep hill to their house and farm. In wet weather the road became one big sea of mud which, according to my mother, would be "worth your life to drive through."

"If it looks bad," my mother suggested, "we can park at the top of the hill and walk down in our galoshes."

My father sighed. "Myrtle," he said, "we've driven across the Mohave Desert. We've been through thick and thin for over three thousand miles and here you are worrying about Shirls Avenue."

The next day the sun was out, but when we came to Shirls Avenue, I could see that the sun hadn't done a thing to dry up the hill. My father put the car into low, my mother closed her eyes, and down we went, sloshing up to our hubcaps, careening from one rut to another, while my father kept one hand down hard on the horn to announce our arrival.

By the time we were at the bottom of the hill and had parked beside the house, my grandmother, my grandfather, and Aunt Margaret were all outside, looking exactly the way they had in the calendar picture. I ran right into my grandmother's arms as if I'd been doing this every day.

"Welcome home! Oh, welcome home!" my grandmother cried.

I hadn't known it but this was exactly what I'd wanted her to say. I needed to hear it said out loud. I was home.

Reader's Response ～ If you had been Jean, what would have been the best memories of the trip for you?

Library Link ～ *"On My Way Home" is one chapter from a book about Jean. To find out how Jean enjoys life in Pennsylvania, read* Homesick: My Own Story *by Jean Fritz.*

CHARLES LINDBERGH MAKES FIRST SOLO FLIGHT ACROSS ATLANTIC

Volume 5 Number 4   World Wide Tribune

Nineteen twenty-seven was an important year in Jean Fritz's life. Finally she was making the trip home she had always dreamed about. We don't know how much time she had to read the newspapers. But if she did, she read about some very exciting events.

IN THE NEWS...

Transatlantic Telephone Service Established
The Jazz Singer Is First Successful Talking Picture
First Public Long-Distance Television
Transmission in United States
Mechanical Cotton Picker Invented
Tornado Devastates St. Louis, Missouri in 5 Minutes!

IN SPORTS...

Babe Ruth's 60 Home Runs Set New Record
The Harlem Globetrotters Basketball Team Is Organized
New York Yankees Win World Series

Which of these things most surprised you?
Which one would you like to learn more about?

This Is My Rock

This is my rock,
And here I run
To steal the secret of the sun;

This is my rock,
And here come I
Before the night has swept the sky;

This is my rock,
This is the place
I meet the evening face to face.

David McCord

To Dark Eyes Dreaming

Dreams go fast and far
  these days.
They go by rocket thrust.
They go arrayed
  in lights
    or in the dust of stars.
Dreams, these days,
  go fast and far.
Dreams are young, these days,
  or very old.
They can be black
  or blue or gold.
They need no special charts,
  nor any fuel.
It seems, only one rule applies,
  to all our dreams—
They will not fly except in open sky.
  A fenced-in dream
    will die.

Zilpha Keatley Snyder

Today's Immigrants

by Luz Nuncio Schick

From the earliest years of this country's existence, immigrants have been coming to the United States. Today, immigrants continue to come to America, and they share the same dream as immigrants of the past—to make a new home and a better life for themselves and their children.

On the weekend of July 4, 1986, all Americans were invited to New York City for a special birthday party. The Statue of Liberty, one of the city's most famous monuments, was turning one hundred years old. Six million people came, and many million more across the United States watched the celebration on television. For four days and nights, people enjoyed concerts, parades, speeches, and fireworks in honor of the newly renovated statue. That special Fourth of July weekend became known as "Liberty Weekend."

During the celebration, Americans were not just honoring the statue's age or beauty. They were especially proud of what the Statue of Liberty stands for. For the last century, the Statue of Liberty was the first glimpse of America for the millions of immigrants entering the country through New York harbor. With her torch raised high, the Statue of Liberty symbolizes a welcome to immigrants from all over the world. It symbolizes a chance to make a better life in the United States.

Early Newcomers

Immigrants have been coming to the United States from the time of its founding. During the first century of immigration, most of the newcomers were English, Irish, Scottish, German, and Scandinavian.

During this time, people were also brought to the United States from Africa against their wishes. Blacks have been in the United States since colonial times and have served their country and contributed to its culture like other groups of newcomers. But until the end of the Civil War, most blacks were slaves. They were not free to make a better life for themselves and their children. Like other newcomers, they had their own hopes and dreams of freedom. But unlike European immigrants, blacks had no opportunity when they were brought here to make those dreams come true.

Later Immigrants

During the second century of the United States' existence, especially from 1880 until 1920, most immigrants to the United States were Italian, Greek, or eastern European. A small but important wave of Chinese and Japanese immigrants was recruited to come to America from the 1850s until the end of the nineteenth century. They worked as miners, farm laborers, and for the fishing and railroad industries. In fact, much of the Western link of the Transcontinental Railroad was built by Chinese workers.

The European immigrants came to America to escape poverty or violence in their own countries. They survived hard and often heartbreaking journeys to make America their new home. When they arrived, life for nearly all of them was very difficult and different from the life they had known in their old homelands. America was a country of big cities and new ways. Many of the immigrants came from farms and villages where ways of life had not changed much over time.

All immigrants struggled to adapt themselves to their new home. They learned English and worked hard to make life better and easier for their children. They *assimilated*, which means that they changed some of their ways and ideas to blend into the ways and ideas of people in their new home.

But in changing themselves to become American, these immigrants also changed America. They brought with them not only different foods and different music from their homelands, but talent, special knowledge, and skills. They brought the best of their old home to their new home for everyone to share.

Today's Immigrants

Like immigrants before them, some recent immigrants have had to suffer a long, dangerous voyage across an ocean in order to reach America. But most immigrants today come by plane. Others come by train, car, or by foot. When they arrive, many of them are not as surprised at what they find in America as earlier immigrants were. Modern means of transportation and communication have made the world a smaller place, so many of today's immigrants already know something about American culture when they arrive.

Today's immigrants are different from earlier immigrants in another way. Most of the immigrants who came to the United States over the last two centuries were western, southern, or eastern European. They were, for example, from England and Germany, Italy and Greece, and Poland and Romania. Today, most of the immigrants come from non-European countries. They come mostly from countries in Latin America and Asia.

Immigrants from Latin America

Today's immigrants from Latin America come mainly from Mexico and countries in Central America such as Guatemala and El Salvador. They also come from islands in the Caribbean such as

Cuba and Puerto Rico, and from South American countries such as Argentina and Peru. However, the number of South American immigrants is not as great as that of immigrants from Mexico, Central America, and the Caribbean.

Although most Latin American immigrants see themselves as Hispanics sharing the same Spanish language and culture, there are many differences among Hispanic groups. Some Hispanic immigrants choose to come to the United States. Others come because war, economic hardship, or political trouble in their own countries leaves them no choice but to leave. Some have visited the United States before and may have friends or relatives in this country. Others come to settle in America sight unseen, knowing nobody.

Hispanic immigrants also come from different economic backgrounds. Many immigrants come to the United States for whatever jobs they can find, no matter how low the pay and how hard the work. But other immigrants have received much training for the work that they do. These immigrants are doctors, lawyers, professors, or business people. They come to the United States because they believe it is a better place to carry on their work. Some of these immigrants also come because of civil war or other political unrest in their countries.

One Hispanic Immigrant

Teresa Fraga[1] had worked as a migrant worker in the farms and ranches of the United States for years before coming to settle in Chicago in 1966. She had come to the United States at a time when Mexicans were being encouraged by the American government to come and fill the demand for migrant farm workers and other kinds of laborers.

As a migrant worker, Teresa worked in the fields, caring for and harvesting fruit and vegetable crops. She received very low pay, and the workday was long and hard. Her husband also worked in the fields. They could only work for a few weeks at each place,

[1]Teresa Fraga (te re′ sä   frä′ gä)

456

Teresa Fraga, at left, enjoys talking with her family in the dining room of their Chicago home.

since that was how long it took to complete the work. When they finished working on one farm or ranch, they would move on to another. They never knew where they would find work next, or how long it would last, or what it would pay.

Teresa and her family decided to go to Chicago to find work that would last more than just a few weeks. They settled in the Mexican neighborhood in the Pilsen-Little Village area of Chicago. Teresa's husband found a job as a construction worker, and their family grew.

The Pilsen-Little Village area where Teresa and her family settled is a large and established Mexican neighborhood in Chicago. It has been home for Mexicans coming to Chicago since the beginning of this century. Like the European immigrants before them, Mexican immigrants have made their first home in communities where their language is spoken and where friends and relatives may already live.

In spite of the harsh Chicago winters, Teresa and her family felt at home in the Pilsen-Little Village neighborhood. The streets in this neighborhood are lined with Mexican restaurants and bakeries. There are also several supermarkets and grocery stores that sell food and newspapers from Mexico. These restaurants and stores are usually decorated with piñatas and streamers in the colors of the Mexican flag: red, white, and green. Murals on the outside walls of buildings portray scenes from Mexican history or famous Mexican patriots.

Above, Teresa joins in a celebration in front of one of the colorful murals in her neighborhood. *Left*, Teresa greets a former student.

As the years passed for Teresa and her family in the Pilsen-Little Village part of Chicago, Teresa became more involved in efforts to improve her neighborhood. She joined groups that were pressing to have a new high school built in the area because the schools they had were old and overcrowded. She became a member of the neighborhood council.

Many Mexican immigrants dream of returning to their homeland. Others dream of staying in the United States but moving closer to Mexico, to one of the southwestern states that borders on Mexico and has a large Mexican population. These immigrants miss the warm weather and the ways of their culture.

Teresa and her family shared this dream. For years they went to Texas each winter, to check on the house that they were having built. But when the house was finally finished, it stood empty for eleven years. The Fraga family did not go.

Somehow, over the twenty years the Fraga family had lived in Chicago, they had quietly decided to stay. The Fraga children had grown up and gone to school in their neighborhood in Pilsen-Little Village. Teresa had worked hard to make it a neighborhood that made her feel proud. Her husband had found a good job to support the family.

The Fraga family made friends and found a stable life in the city after traveling up from Mexico through the fields of the United States as migrant workers. They came to America looking for work, but they found a home.

Immigrants from Asia

Like Latin American immigrants, Asian immigrants coming to the United States today are from different countries, social classes, and backgrounds. They also come for different reasons.

Many recent Asian immigrants, such as those from Vietnam, Cambodia, and Laos, fled their countries during the period from 1960 to the late 1970s because of war and violence there. Many were fishermen or farmers in tiny Asian villages. For these immigrants, the journey and the process of getting used to a new life in America have been very hard. Other Asian immigrants who came to the United States during this time were professionals. They came to the United States also seeking to escape the violence and to further their careers in American universities, medical centers, and technical fields.

One Asian Immigrant

Nghi Lu[2] came to the United States from Vietnam in 1984, when she was seventeen. She had lived in the small town of Bac Lieu,[3] in South Vietnam, with her father, mother, four brothers, and three sisters.

A few years earlier, one of Nghi Lu's sisters had come to the United States and had settled in Chicago. As soon as she was able, Nghi Lu's sister applied to the American Immigration and Naturalization Service as a *sponsor* to help the rest of her family come to the United States. A *sponsor* is someone who asks the United States government to allow other people who are not United States citizens to come live in the United States. Usually, a sponsor is a member of the family of the future immigrants. The sponsor agrees that he or she will provide for the immigrants and help them make their new life in America.

Nghi Lu remembers clearly the day when she arrived in Chicago. The weather was bitterly cold and there was snow on the ground. Nghi Lu and her family were not prepared for the harsh winter weather. They were wearing the same light clothes they had worn at home in Vietnam. But Nghi Lu's sister was prepared. She met her family at the airport with coats, sweaters, scarves, and gloves. The only thing she forgot, laughs Nghi Lu, was boots!

Nghi Lu remembers hurrying to get out of the cold, feeling the sharp sting of the wind, but also feeling very happy and excited at having her family together again.

The first few months in Chicago were hard for Nghi Lu and her family. They not only had to get used to the cold weather, but to a new way of life. In Vietnam, Nghi Lu and her family had lived in an airy, two-story building with the living quarters on the upper floor and a variety store on the lower floor. Nghi Lu and her brothers and sisters went to a school with large classrooms that held up to seventy students.

In Chicago, Nghi Lu's family lived in a brick apartment building

460   [2]Nghi Lu (ngē l$\overline{oo}$)   [3]Bac Lieu (bäk ly$\overline{oo}$)

Above, new stores open as Nghi Lu's neighborhood attracts more immigrants from Southeast Asia. *Right*, a recent photo shows Nghi Lu.

on a busy street. At school, the classes Nghi Lu and her brothers and sisters attended were smaller, but they were made up of students from all over the world who had also just come to America. Like these students, Nghi Lu and her brothers and sisters took classes both in English and their native language.

Nghi Lu felt the most homesick the first time her family

461

celebrated Chinese New Year in Chicago. Like many of their neighbors in Vietnam, Nghi Lu's family had adopted Chinese holidays. Although Nghi Lu and her family were able to find most of the things they needed for their celebration in Chicago's Chinatown, New Year was just not the same as it had been in Vietnam. Like other immigrants they loved their new country, but their old home remained a part of them, and they still missed it very much.

Today, Nghi Lu speaks three languages: Vietnamese, Chinese, and English. Although it was hard for Nghi Lu to learn English and to get used to her school in the big city, she worked very hard and was helped by her teachers and counselors. In June 1987, she graduated from high school. Because of her hard work, she earned tenth place in a class of 490 students. Nghi Lu plans to go on to college, where she will study nursing.

Nghi Lu says that she would like to return to Vietnam some day. She would like to see aunts and uncles who are still there. She would also like to spend time using her education to help her people. Nghi Lu believes that the freedom she has found here to keep learning, the chance to get a good education, and her own hard work will open many new doors for her. Nghi Lu has her family in America, and little by little, she is making America her home.

Today's immigrants are like all previous immigrants in one very important way. Their coming to America, no matter how difficult or painful, is a celebration of the chance to make a better life and a new home in America.

Reader's Response ～ What is the most important new fact or idea you learned about immigrants from reading this article?

Let's Dance

Folk dance is one way that Americans celebrate their ethnic heritage. Immigrants from around the world have brought their native dances with them to America. These dances help all of us to share in the diverse cultures that make up the American mosaic.

The Jarana from Mexico combines Spanish movements with Mayan rhythms.

The Ribbon Dance from China has its roots in the Han dynasty, almost 2,000 years ago.

These folk dancers celebrate their Ukrainian heritage in traditional costumes.

A Good Chance

by Ianthe Mac Thomas

The train was coming. Luke could hear it whistling and rumbling through the tunnel that cut into the side of the mountain. Clouds of thick, black smoke dotted the sky behind it. It was coming fast.

As on other days, the train made Luke feel like running. He liked to race with the train, no matter how far away. To him, the train was movement and excitement, a part of the world whizzing past.

But today was different. Today Luke was going places, but not with the train. After running only a short distance, he gave up. He reached the point where the tracks curved around his family's old peach orchard. Then, gasping for breath, he threw himself on the grass. He lay there for some time, breathing in the sweetness of the blades around him.

"Luke?" It was his father's voice. "We're ready."

Luke got up slowly and walked to the driveway with his dad. Today he and his parents were moving out of Esperanza, the little town they had always called home. His friends Jesse and Alberta had come to see him off, but he couldn't even bring himself to wave goodbye to them. He tried to lift his hand, but it felt *so* heavy! As he quickly ducked into the waiting station wagon, he felt his heart jump in his chest.

Once in the car, Luke closed his eyes. He could picture the streets they'd be taking out of town. He knew every one of them by heart. He could see the small cluster of one-story shops that seemed to hug each other along the four blocks of Main Street.

Everything he had ever needed was close by: Colby's Fish Market, where Mr. Colby had saved fish heads for Luke's cat; Sara's Bake Shop, where all the cakes for his family's special events had been baked. Even the Old Lawson house, now the town's public library, held special memories for Luke. Luke had spent many happy times reading there last summer.

Across the street from these places was the town square. It had green park benches, clipped hedges and a two-hundred-year-old oak tree. Luke and Jesse loved that tree. Luke's dad had once helped them hang a swing from it, and all the little kids in town still used that swing.

Most of the town's buildings, stores, and houses were small and old, but each was painted and neat. Every sidewalk, though cracked, was carefully swept each morning. Luke knew every crack, every lawn, every swinging gate, every scraggly rosebush in town.

Now it seemed to Luke that his dad was taking too much time driving out of town. The car moved more slowly than he expected. Soon, though, the ride became smooth, and Luke knew they were on the highway. Luke kept his eyes pressed shut, as if in this way he could also shut out his parents' conversation.

"I hope—" he heard his mother say, "I just hope it won't be too hard for me to find a place to park every morning. And . . . oh," her voice trailed off.

"I know," said Luke's father. "There will be so much to do! Moving to a new place is never easy. But how could we pass up a good chance?"

Luke remembered the Friday night when his father had come home with a big smile on his face. He had grabbed

Luke's mother around the waist and they had put on music and done a dance called the "tango" across the living room floor.

Luke still couldn't believe it. He felt his whole life had turned upside down the moment his father began telling about his big promotion. The family would have to move to San Francisco, his dad had said. Shortly after that, his mother had also landed a good job there. All was set. The family was going to move to San Francisco.

From the very first, Luke had said he wouldn't move. He couldn't even *imagine* it. What would a day be like without his friends Jesse and Alberta?

And what would his life be like if he didn't wake up in his old room? For one thing, he'd miss the brown carpet with the horse design on it. It was tacked down in his room and too old, his mother had said, so they wouldn't be taking it.

Luke loved that carpet. He liked to pretend that the horses came to life at night and visited wonderful new places he had read about. Sometimes he dreamed they were galloping across some wide prairie, sometimes through deep canyons. But his horses were always there in the morning when he woke up.

Now it was Luke who was going to a new place, and going away for good. As the car rolled down the highway, he could feel his father looking at him in the rearview mirror. The next time his father spoke, Luke felt that his dad was trying hard to explain something not just to him, but to himself as well.

"We knew it wouldn't be easy," his father continued, "but how could I *not* accept the promotion?" He turned to his wife. "How could *you* turn down your new job? It's not just *one* good chance, but *two*, and we have to take advantage—"

"Yes . . . I guess so," Luke's mother said. Her words came out slowly, almost sadly.

On hearing this, Luke straightened up in the back seat. His ears tingled as he waited for what she might say next, what he hoped she would say. His mouth felt dry. His hands were damp.

He wanted his mom to tell his father to turn around and go back to Esperanza. Maybe his father would agree. Maybe this whole move would become nothing more than a bad dream.

But it wasn't anything like a dream when Luke heard his mother's next words. "Yes, you're right," she continued. "Sometimes I think how much I'll miss my friends and the town and . . . well, everything. Things will be *so* different! But you're right. We couldn't pass up a good chance like this."

When she said this, the matter seemed settled. Luke sank back against the seat. He felt all his energy seep out of him. All his hope was gone.

Luke's mom turned in her seat and gently squeezed his chin. "You awake, honey?" she said. "Luke?"

He kept his eyes closed, but he could feel her fingers stroking his cheek.

"It's not going to be so bad, Luke, you'll see. San Francisco is beautiful. It has that fantastic Golden Gate Bridge, remember? And, Luke . . . Luke?" Her voice was playful and soft, almost pleading.

It took all of Luke's effort to keep his eyes shut. He knew his mom was trying to cheer him up, but he didn't care. He only wanted to go back home where he felt comfortable, where he knew everyone and everyone knew him. He turned his face away from her and looked out the open window. The wind whipped his face, and he soon fell asleep.

"Hey, move it, mister!" someone called out to Luke's father. Luke awakened to the man's sharp voice. He rubbed his eyes and looked out the car window.

So *this* was their welcome to the big city, thought Luke. He had never seen so many buildings in his life. They seemed to crowd over them, too close for comfort. They seemed like monsters about to swallow people whole. A police or ambulance siren screamed somewhere in the distance. The traffic inched its way into the city.

Luke could see that both his parents were concentrating hard as they drove through the traffic. He thought they looked a little like new kids at school trying to find their classroom. He shook his head and smiled. He didn't know why, but then and there he decided he would be easier on them.

As Luke looked around, he caught sight of flower boxes on the balconies of modern apartment buildings, high above the street. It shocked him to see them. They looked so pretty against the concrete and steel.

The next sight surprised Luke even more. Beyond a cluster of buildings Luke could see the tops of trees. Trees!

For the first time that long day, Luke said something to his parents: "Hey, there are trees here."

The remark made them all laugh. His father answered, "Yeah, trees! And a park where we can ride horses. Not so bad, huh?"

When they reached the apartment building that was to be their new home, Luke tried not to look very interested. Yes, the place *was* big, but it hadn't swallowed them whole, as Luke had expected. Its bigness seemed to promise something, but just what, Luke couldn't imagine.

Luke and his parents were standing at a door exactly like all the others, except this one had a name plate with their last name printed on it. His father had just inserted the key in the lock when another door down the hall opened.

A woman stuck her head out, smiling cheerfully. She said, "Welcome, I'm your neighbor, Mrs. . . .", but she didn't get a chance to finish her sentence. A boy about Luke's own age pushed past her.

"Excuse me, Ma," he said. Then he saw Luke and said, "Hi, I'm Mark. What's your name?"

Luke looked at him and answered shyly, "I'm Luke."

Mark said, "Do you play stickball? There's a game going on over in the park. Want to come?"

Luke shuffled his feet, which already seemed to be answering for him. He looked at his father. His father laughed and said, "Go ahead. We'll wait for the movers in the meantime. Just be careful crossing the streets."

Luke decided that it was much easier to hit a ball with a bat instead of the sawed-off broomstick they'd given him. But he did manage to bunt the ball once with the stick, and he soon found himself absorbed in the game.

He, Mark, two girls with bright red hair, and a boy with a bandage on his knee were one team. The park had a real, regulation baseball diamond with canvas bases and a slate scoreboard. Luke's side lost, but when he and Mark were leaving, the other kids shouted after them, "Hey, Mark, you and the new kid coming back tomorrow? We'll beat you again." Luke laughed, surprised at this sudden invitation to return for another game.

When Luke got back to the apartment, his father was opening a large pizza carton. His mother was standing in the living room amid some partially unpacked boxes. She looked tired and confused.

"Come and get it!" Luke's father said. He held the box of steaming pizza out for her to see. "Leave that for now. Let's eat!"

His mother looked at his father and sat down on one of
the boxes. "I'm almost too tired to eat," she said.

To Luke, her voice sounded like she really meant it. Suddenly he wasn't upset with his mother *or* father anymore.
He thought maybe they were feeling more scared about all
the "newness" than he was.

At that moment, Luke thought he understood what his
parents meant when they talked about not missing a good
chance. Sometimes, reaching for a good chance might mean
having to give something up—even something you loved.

Luke walked over to his mother and put his arm around
her shoulders. "Come on, Mom," he said, and led her to the
table.

They all sat in silence for a minute, munching on their
slices of pizza. When his mother asked him how he'd liked
the game in the park, Luke answered slowly, "It's okay. But
they don't have real bats, just sticks."

Then he remembered how he and his friend Jesse had
sanded their own bats and used cardboard for bases back

home. Thinking of Jesse made Luke feel sad. Suddenly he didn't feel like eating anymore.

But that pizza smelled *so* good! Luke finished his slice, then ate two more. He couldn't help it. The pizza was delicious.

That night, as Luke lay in bed, the noises of the city drifted up to his window. He couldn't hear any crickets, but someone in their building was playing a recording. He perked his ears and recognized the song, one of his favorites. Alberta used to sing it while they gathered fallen peaches in the orchard. Luke turned in bed and hummed a few bars of the song.

He thought about the two red-haired girls. They must be twins, he decided. They were good at stickball. Not better than Alberta, but they were good.

Luke's thoughts continued to pile up. It didn't seem possible that the day was over. His eyelids felt so heavy, he had to close his eyes. Tired as he was, he couldn't sleep. He wondered if Jesse was sleeping.

He remembered the delicious pizza he'd had that day. Jesse would have loved it. "Jesse *will* love it," Luke corrected himself, "when he comes to visit."

"Yes, Jesse, Mark, and me," Luke murmured as he fell asleep.

Reader's Response ~ If you had been in Luke's situation, would you have felt the same way he did? Why or why not?

Moving

Some statistics on moving:

- One out of five families moves each year.
- Forty million people move each year.
- Summer is the most popular time of the year to move.

Some tips on moving:

Keep a journal to write about the way you are feeling as you get closer to the day you will move.

Get a camera and take pictures of your friends, your house, and your neighborhood. Your pictures will help you to remember the people and places you are leaving behind.

Get a notebook and have your friends write their names, addresses, and phone numbers. Then you can write to them when you get to your new home. Give them your new address and ask them to write to you.

July 8th

I can't believe I'm moving in two weeks! My mom says that I'll like our new home but I'm not sure. I don't think Domino (my cat) wants to move because he'll miss his friends, too. I hope my friends, Emma and Sam, will write to me especially about how our baseball team is doing.

MY OLD HOUSE →

MY FRIENDS ↓

NEWBERY
MEDAL
1986

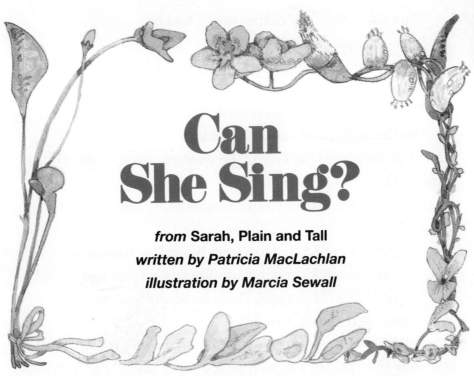

Can She Sing?

from **Sarah, Plain and Tall**

written by Patricia MacLachlan

illustration by Marcia Sewall

"Did Mama sing every day?" asked Caleb. "Every-single-day?"
He sat close to the fire, his chin in his hand. It was dusk, and the
dogs lay beside him on the warm hearthstones.

"Every-single-day," I told him for the second time this week.
For the twentieth time this month. The hundredth time this year?
And the past few years?

"And did Papa sing, too?"

"Yes. Papa sang, too. Don't get so close, Caleb. You'll
heat up."

He pushed his chair back. It made a hollow scraping sound
on the hearthstones, and the dogs stirred. Lottie, small and
black, wagged her tail and lifted her head. Nick slept on.

I turned the bread dough over and over on the marble slab
on the kitchen table.

"Well, Papa doesn't sing anymore," said Caleb very softly. A
log broke apart and crackled in the fireplace. He looked up at me.
"What did I look like when I was born?"

477

"You didn't have any clothes on," I told him.

"I know that," he said.

"You looked like this." I held the bread dough up in a round pale ball.

"I had hair," said Caleb seriously.

"Not enough to talk about," I said.

"And she named me Caleb," he went on, filling in the old familiar story.

"*I* would have named you Troublesome," I said, making Caleb smile.

"And Mama handed me to you in the yellow blanket and said . . ." He waited for me to finish the story. "And said . . .?"

I sighed. "And Mama said, 'Isn't he beautiful, Anna?' "

"And I was," Caleb finished.

Caleb thought the story was over, and I didn't tell him what I had really thought. He was homely and plain, and he had a terrible holler and a horrid smell. But these were not the worst of him. Mama died the next morning. That was the worst thing about Caleb.

"Isn't he beautiful, Anna?" Her last words to me. I had gone to bed thinking how wretched he looked. And I forgot to say good night.

I wiped my hands on my apron and went to the window. Outside, the prairie reached out and touched the places where the sky came down. Though winter was nearly over, there were patches of snow and ice everywhere. I looked at the long dirt road that crawled across the plains, remembering the morning that Mama had died, cruel and sunny. They had come for her in a wagon and taken her away to be buried. And then the cousins and aunts and uncles had come and tried to fill up the house. But they couldn't.

Slowly, one by one, they left. And then the days seemed

long and dark like winter days, even though it wasn't winter. And Papa didn't sing.

Isn't he beautiful, Anna?

No, Mama.

It was hard to think of Caleb as beautiful. It took three whole days for me to love him, sitting in the chair by the fire, Papa washing up the supper dishes, Caleb's tiny hand brushing my cheek. And a smile. It was the smile, I know.

"Can you remember her songs?" asked Caleb. "Mama's songs?"

I turned from the window. "No. Only that she sang about flowers and birds. Sometimes about the moon at nighttime."

Caleb reached down and touched Lottie's head.

"Maybe," he said, his voice low, "if you remember the songs, then I might remember her, too."

My eyes widened and tears came. Then the door opened and wind blew in with Papa, and I went to stir the stew. Papa put his arms around me and put his nose in my hair.

"Nice soapy smell, that stew," he said.

I laughed. "That's my hair."

Caleb came over and threw his arms around Papa's neck and hung down as Papa swung him back and forth, and the dogs sat up.

"Cold in town," said Papa. "And Jack was feisty." Jack was Papa's horse that he'd raised from a colt. "Rascal," murmured Papa, smiling, because no matter what Jack did Papa loved him.

I spooned up the stew and lighted the oil lamp and we ate with the dogs crowding under the table, hoping for spills or handouts.

Papa might not have told us about Sarah that night if Caleb hadn't asked him the question. After the dishes were cleared and washed and Papa was filling the tin pail with ashes, Caleb spoke up. It wasn't a question, really.

"You don't sing anymore," he said. He said it harshly. Not because he meant to, but because he had been thinking of it for so long. "Why?" he asked more gently.

Slowly Papa straightened up. There was a long silence, and the dogs looked up, wondering at it.

"I've forgotten the old songs," said Papa quietly. He sat down. "But maybe there's a way to remember them." He looked up at us.

"How?" asked Caleb eagerly.

Papa leaned back in the chair. "I've placed an advertisement in the newspapers. For help."

"You mean a housekeeper?" I asked, surprised.

Caleb and I looked at each other and burst out laughing, remembering Hilly, our old housekeeper. She was round and slow and shuffling. She snored in a high whistle at night, like a teakettle, and let the fire go out.

"No," said Papa slowly. "Not a housekeeper." He paused. "A wife."

Caleb stared at Papa. "A wife? You mean a mother?"

Nick slid his face onto Papa's lap and Papa stroked his ears.

"That, too," said Papa. "Like Maggie."

Matthew, our neighbor to the south, had written to ask for a wife and a mother for his children. And Maggie had come from Tennessee. Her hair was the color of turnips and she laughed.

Papa reached into his pocket and unfolded a letter written on white paper. "And I have received an answer." Papa read to us:

"Dear Mr. Jacob Witting,

"I am Sarah Wheaton from Maine as you will see from my letter. I am answering your advertisement. I have never been married, though I have been asked. I have lived with an older brother, William, who is about to be married. His wife-to-be is young and energetic.

"I have always loved to live by the sea, but at this time I feel a move is necessary. And the truth is, the sea is as far east as I can go. My choice, as you can see, is limited. This should not be taken as an insult. I am strong and I work hard and I am willing to travel. But I am not mild mannered. If you should still care to write, I would be interested in your children and about where you live. And you.

"Very truly yours,
"Sarah Elisabeth Wheaton

"P.S. Do you have opinions on cats? I have one."

No one spoke when Papa finished the letter. He kept looking at it in his hands, reading it over to himself. Finally I turned my head a bit to sneak a look at Caleb. He was smiling. I smiled, too.

"One thing," I said in the quiet of the room.

"What's that?" asked Papa, looking up.

I put my arm around Caleb.

"Ask her if she sings," I said.

Caleb and Papa and I wrote letters to Sarah, and before the ice and snow had melted from the fields, we all received answers. Mine came first.

Dear Anna,

Yes, I can braid hair and I can make stew and bake bread, though I prefer to build bookshelves and paint.

My favorite colors are the colors of the sea, blue and gray and green, depending on the weather. My brother William is a fisherman, and he tells me that when he is in the middle of a fogbound sea the water is a color for which there is no name. He catches flounder and sea bass and

bluefish. Sometimes he sees whales. And birds, too, of course. I am enclosing a book of sea birds so you will see what William and I see every day.

Very truly yours,
Sarah Elisabeth Wheaton

Caleb read and read the letter so many times that the ink began to run and the folds tore. He read the book about sea birds over and over.

"Do you think she'll come?" asked Caleb. "And will she stay? What if she thinks we are loud and pesky?"

"You *are* loud and pesky," I told him. But I was worried, too. Sarah loved the sea, I could tell. Maybe she wouldn't leave there after all to come where there were fields and grass and sky and not much else.

"What if she comes and doesn't like our house?" Caleb asked. "I told her it was small. Maybe I shouldn't have told her it was small."

"Hush, Caleb. Hush."

Caleb's letter came soon after, with a picture of a cat drawn on the envelope.

Dear Caleb,

My cat's name is Seal because she is gray like the seals that swim offshore in Maine. She is glad that Lottie and Nick send their greetings. She likes dogs most of the time. She says their footprints are much larger than hers (which she is enclosing in return).

Your house sounds lovely, even though it is far out in the country with no close neighbors. My house is tall and the shingles are gray because of the salt from the sea. There are roses nearby.

Yes, I do like small rooms sometimes. Yes, I can keep a fire going at night. I do not know if I snore. Seal has never told me.

Very truly yours,
Sarah Elisabeth

"Did you really ask her about fires and snoring?" I asked, amazed.

"I wished to know," Caleb said.

He kept the letter with him, reading it in the barn and in the fields and by the cow pond. And always in bed at night.

One morning, early, Papa and Caleb and I were cleaning out the horse stalls and putting down new bedding. Papa stopped suddenly and leaned on his pitchfork.

"Sarah has said she will come for a month's time if we wish her to," he said, his voice loud in the dark barn. "To see how it is. Just to see."

Caleb stood by the stall door and folded his arms across his chest.

"I think," he began. Then, "I think," he said slowly, "that it would be good—to say yes," he finished in a rush.

Papa looked at me.

"I say yes," I told him, grinning.

"Yes," said Papa. "Then yes it is."

And the three of us, all smiling, went to work again.

The next day Papa went to town to mail his letter to Sarah. It was rainy for days, and the clouds followed. The house was cool and damp and quiet. Once I set four places at the table, then caught myself and put the extra plate away. Three lambs were born, one with a black face. And then Papa's letter came. It was very short.

Dear Jacob,

    I will come by train. I will wear a yellow bonnet. I am plain and tall.

Sarah

"What's that?" asked Caleb excitedly, peering over Papa's shoulder. He pointed. "There, written at the bottom of the letter."

Papa read it to himself. Then he smiled, holding up the letter for us to see.

Tell them I sing was all it said.

Sarah came in the spring. She came through green grass fields that bloomed with Indian paintbrush, red and orange, and blue-eyed grass.

Papa got up early for the long day's trip to the train and back. He brushed his hair so slick and shiny that Caleb laughed. He wore a clean blue shirt, and a belt instead of suspenders.

He fed and watered the horses, talking to them as he hitched them up to the wagon. Old Bess, calm and kind; Jack, wild-eyed, reaching over to nip Bess on the neck.

"Clear day, Bess," said Papa, rubbing her nose.

"Settle down, Jack." He leaned his head on Jack.

And then Papa drove off along the dirt road to fetch Sarah. Papa's new wife. Maybe. Maybe our new mother.

Gophers ran back and forth across the road, stopping to stand up and watch the wagon. Far off in the field a woodchuck ate and listened. Ate and listened.

Caleb and I did our chores without talking. We shoveled out the stalls and laid down new hay. We fed the sheep. We swept and straightened and carried wood and water. And then our chores were done.

Caleb pulled on my shirt.

"Is my face clean?" he asked. "Can my face be *too* clean?" He looked alarmed.

"No, your face is clean but not too clean," I said.

Caleb slipped his hand into mine as we stood on the porch, watching the road. He was afraid.

"Will she be nice?" he asked. "Like Maggie?"

"Sarah will be nice," I told him.

"How far away is Maine?" he asked.

"You know how far. Far away, by the sea."

"Will Sarah bring some sea?" he asked.

"No, you cannot bring the sea."

The sheep ran in the field, and far off the cows moved slowly to the pond, like turtles.

"Will she like us?" asked Caleb very softly.

I watched a marsh hawk wheel down behind the barn.

He looked up at me.

"Of course she will like us." He answered his own question. "We are nice," he added, making me smile.

We waited and watched. I rocked on the porch and Caleb rolled a marble on the wood floor. Back and forth. Back and forth. The marble was blue.

We saw the dust from the wagon first, rising above the road, above the heads of Jack and Old Bess. Caleb climbed up onto the porch roof and shaded his eyes.

"A bonnet!" he cried. "I see a yellow bonnet!"

The dogs came out from under the porch, ears up, their eyes on the cloud of dust bringing Sarah. The wagon passed the fenced field, and the cows and sheep looked up, too. It rounded the windmill and the barn and the windbreak of Russian olive that Mama had planted long ago. Nick began to bark, then Lottie, and the wagon clattered into the yard and stopped by the steps.

"Hush," said Papa to the dogs.

And it was quiet.

Sarah stepped down from the wagon, a cloth bag in her

hand. She reached up and took off her yellow bonnet, smoothing back her brown hair into a bun. She was plain and tall.

"Did you bring some sea?" cried Caleb beside me.

"Something from the sea," said Sarah, smiling. "And me." She turned and lifted a black case from the wagon. "And Seal, too."

Carefully she opened the case, and Seal, gray with white feet, stepped out. Lottie lay down, her head on her paws, staring. Nick leaned down to sniff. Then he lay down, too.

"The cat will be good in the barn," said Papa. "For mice."

Sarah smiled. "She will be good in the house, too."

Sarah took Caleb's hand, then mine. Her hands were large and rough. She gave Caleb a shell—a moon snail, she called it— that was curled and smelled of salt.

"The gulls fly high and drop the shells on the rocks below," she told Caleb. "When the shell is broken, they eat what is inside."

"That is very smart," said Caleb.

"For you, Anna," said Sarah, "a sea stone."

And she gave me the smoothest and whitest stone I had ever seen.

"The sea washes over and over and around the stone, rolling it until it is round and perfect."

"That is very smart, too," said Caleb. He looked up at Sarah. "We do not have the sea here."

Sarah turned and looked out over the plains.

"No," she said. "There is no sea here. But the land rolls a little like the sea."

My father did not see her look, but I did. And I knew that Caleb had seen it, too. Sarah was not smiling. Sarah was already lonely. In a month's time the preacher might come to marry Sarah and Papa. And a month was a long time. Time enough for her to change her mind and leave us.

Papa took Sarah's bags inside, where her room was ready

with a quilt on the bed and blue flax dried in a vase on the night table.

Seal stretched and made a small cat sound. I watched her circle the dogs and sniff the air. Caleb came out and stood beside me.

"When will we sing?" he whispered.

I shook my head, turning the white stone over and over in my hand. I wished everything was as perfect as the stone. I wished that Papa and Caleb and I were perfect for Sarah. I wished we had a sea of our own.

The dogs loved Sarah first. Lottie slept beside her bed, curled in a soft circle, and Nick leaned his face on the covers in the morning, watching for the first sign that Sarah was awake. No one knew where Seal slept. Seal was a roamer.

Sarah's collection of shells sat on the windowsill.

"A scallop," she told us, picking up the shells one by one, "a sea clam, an oyster, a razor clam. And a conch shell. If you put it to your ear you can hear the sea." She put it to Caleb's ear, then mine. Papa listened, too. Then Sarah listened once more, with a look so sad and far away that Caleb leaned against me.

"At least Sarah can hear the sea," he whispered.

Papa was quiet and shy with Sarah, and so was I. But Caleb talked to Sarah from morning until the light left the sky.

"Where are you going?" he asked. "To do what?"

"To pick flowers," said Sarah. "I'll hang some of them upside down and dry them so they'll keep some color. And we can have flowers all winter long."

"I'll come, too!" cried Caleb. "Sarah said winter," he said to me. "That means Sarah will stay."

Together we picked flowers, paintbrush and clover and prairie violets. There were buds on the wild roses that climbed up the paddock fence.

"The roses will bloom in early summer," I told Sarah. I looked to see if she knew what I was thinking. Summer was

when the wedding would be. *Might* be. Sarah and Papa's wedding.

We hung the flowers from the ceiling in little bunches. "I've never seen this before," said Sarah. "What is it called?"

"Bride's bonnet," I told her.

Caleb smiled at the name.

"We don't have this by the sea," she said. "We have seaside goldenrod and wild asters and woolly ragwort."

"Woolly ragwort!" Caleb whooped. He made up a song.

"Woolly ragwort all around,
Woolly ragwort on the ground.
Woolly ragwort grows and grows,
Woolly ragwort in your nose."

Sarah and Papa laughed, and the dogs lifted their heads and thumped their tails against the wood floor. Seal sat on a kitchen chair and watched us with yellow eyes.

We ate Sarah's stew, the late light coming through the windows. Papa had baked bread that was still warm from the fire.

"The stew is fine," said Papa.

"Ayuh." Sarah nodded. "The bread, too."

"What does 'ayuh' mean?" asked Caleb.

"In Maine it means yes," said Sarah. "Do you want more stew?"

"Ayuh," said Caleb.

"Ayuh," echoed my father.

After dinner Sarah told us about William. "He has a gray-and-white boat named *Kittiwake*." She looked out the window. "That is a small gull found way off the shore where William fishes. There are three aunts who live near us. They wear silk dresses and no shoes. You would love them."

"Ayuh," said Caleb.

"Does your brother look like you?" I asked.

"Yes," said Sarah. "He is plain and tall."

At dusk Sarah cut Caleb's hair on the front steps, gathering his curls and scattering them on the fence and ground. Seal batted some hair around the porch as the dogs watched.

"Why?" asked Caleb.

"For the birds," said Sarah. "They will use it for their nests. Later we can look for nests of curls."

"Sarah said 'later,'" Caleb whispered to me as we spread his hair about. "Sarah will stay."

Sarah cut Papa's hair, too. No one else saw, but I found him behind the barn, tossing the pieces of hair into the wind for the birds.

Sarah brushed my hair and tied it up in back with a rose velvet ribbon she had brought from Maine. She brushed hers long and free and tied it back, too, and we stood side by side looking into the mirror. I looked taller, like Sarah, and fair and thin. And with my hair pulled back I looked a little like her daughter. Sarah's daughter.

And then it was time for singing.

Reader's Response ∾ What quality would you look for in a person who was going to play an important role in your life?

Library Link ∾ *To enjoy more episodes about Sarah, read the rest of the book* Sarah, Plain and Tall *by Patricia MacLachlan.*

BROWSING FOR BOOKS

Your Own Library

How many books are there in your house that are your own? You probably have many more than you think, especially if you count all your picture books, and the early readers that you read when you were very young.

In fact, you may even have enough books to start your own library. The most important thing about a library isn't to have lots of books. It's having just a few good books that you really like. If you have those, there are only two other things you need for a library. The first is a place to keep your books. A shelf or even a space at the back of your desk could be a fine place to start. Or, perhaps you could stack some boxes in a convenient corner. It doesn't have to be fancy as long as it is your own special place—a place that says, ''These are my books. This is my library.''

The second thing you need is a way to organize your books—some categories to keep the different kinds of books separate. For one person, that could mean different sections for baseball, football, and basketball stories. For another, there would be books by each of several science-fiction writers.

A question you might have is, ''Why start my own library?'' One good reason is that it's fun, and it's an easy way to start a collection. So, if you've always wanted to have a collection but didn't know what to collect or how to get started, or if you didn't think you could afford to collect expensive coins, stamps, or dolls, try starting a library. With just a few books and a place to keep them, your collection will be well on the way. And the books will always be there to remind you of the great experience you've had reading them.

Jem's Island

by Kathryn Lasky

It came back to him in the winter night—that rhythm. Lying on the top bunk, Jem raised his arms toward the ceiling and gripped the imaginary double-blade paddle. Dropping his left wrist, he rotated it one quarter turn in the other hand, feathered, and dipped silently into the water. The room was thick with sleep and the soft snores of his younger brother in the lower bunk. But Jem was awake and paddling in the top bunk. Through a winter night the summer rhythms came back, the strokes that his father had taught him, the strokes that drew the kayak through the water. Slender and like a polished mahogany needle, the boat they called *Wasso* slipped through that water. He did not hear his brother in the lower bunk. The framework of the double-decker beds melted into darkness, and Jem saw instead wings of spray flying in silver symmetry off the bow as *Wasso* sliced through the chop of the bay.

That's the way it would be next summer, when he and his dad took their camping trip. If he could only wait! But summer was five months away. Deer Isle and Penobscot Bay seemed a million miles from Cleveland. Why, Jem muttered, did I have to be born in Cleveland?

If he had to wait five months for his first overnight kayak trip to an island, he could at least read about his dad's trip of twenty years ago—the big trip, the voyage. Voyage? Trip? *Wasso* would take Jem and his father no more than twenty-five miles to and from an island, round trip. But the same kayak had carried his dad and his uncle Peter a thousand miles from Skagway, Alaska, to Seattle, Washington. A thousand miles is a voyage. Twenty-five miles is a trip, Jem guessed. But still, he could hardly wait. And it would be just he

492

and his dad. Not Michael, not Jessica, not his mom.
Just he and his dad. He turned on the lamp and opened
the faded loose-leaf notebook. First there was the picture, the wobbly diagram of the kayak, an aerial view
of the boat without its deck, showing stowage space.
The drawing was captioned "The World's Largest
Three-Dimensional Jigsaw Puzzle." It was like assem-
bling a jigsaw puzzle to fit in all the gear that the two
brothers needed for sixty days in the wilderness.
Cooking utensils, sleeping bags, food, books, charts,
tools, cameras, spare parts. Two hundred pounds of
gear in all had to fit into the twenty-foot kayak. Jem
and his father would need only a fraction of this gear.
Fitting it in would be no problem, but still Jem loved
studying this diagram because if you had a plan, even
things that seemed impossible could become adventures. Real adventures, he had decided, had plans.

Everyone had said twenty years ago that Ben Gray and his brother Peter couldn't do it, would never survive the thousand-mile journey along the rugged and desolate coast with its treacherous tides that could suck them straight out to sea. But the southeast coast of Alaska was the ultimate challenge for expert kayakists like the two brothers. And twenty years ago Ben and Peter Gray were the first to attempt it, at least in recorded history.

Jem opened the journal and began to read. The journal was full of wonderful, true stories, like the one about the killer whales that trailed the kayak for ten minutes. And it was full of great places with names like Tracy Arm, Meyer's Chuck, and Taku Harbor. And there were people in the journal, too, whose names were stories in themselves: Lonesome Pete and Halibut Pete and Tiger Olsen. There were true tales of a coastline where hundreds of eagles still flew, of fantastically shaped icebergs, of ghost towns and gold panners.

Jem's trip this summer would be no voyage; he didn't kid himself about that. There were no killer whales in Penobscot Bay. But there were dolphins, and it was beautiful. Hurry up and wait!

Jem shut the book and turned off the light.

Jem poured over chart number 309 of East Penobscot Bay on the porch of their cabin that foggy summer morning. Stinson's Neck on the chart looked more like a witch riding a broomstick than an island. And Pickering Island looked like a seagull plunging out of the sky for a fish. Some of the islands, like Saddleback and Great Spoon, looked like what they were called. But Jem wondered about other islands that had been named for reasons apart from their shapes. These were the "Once-upon-a-time" islands. That's what his mom had said. They had real stories and almost real stories connected with them, and that is how they came by their names.

Deer Isle, where Jem and his family spent the summer, was a once-upon-a-time island, for once there had been more deer than people on the island. But the high ledge on which the Gray family cabin perched had been named the Giant's Chair. The cabin was on the top of the chair back. Thirty feet below, a slab of pink rock formed the seat which slid into the sea. Hog Island, to the east of Deer Isle, certainly didn't look like a hog. There must be a story there, Jem thought. But the south part of the island was called Devil's Head, and if you looked at it a certain way—Jem cocked his head so that his eyes read it northeast to southwest—it did look a little like a devil's head.

"Do you think that looks like a devil's head, Michael?"

"No. I think it looks like an atomic starblaster."

"Is that all you ever think about—galactic warfare?"

"Well, all you think about is kayak trips to islands!"

The screen door opened. "Fog bored or fog bound?"

"I'm not bored, Mom. I find Michael boring!"

"And I find you boring, with all your plans for your big trip. You'd think you were going to Alaska or something. Well, you're not!"

Liza Gray saw the hurt in Jem's eyes. "Come on, Michael. Come with me. We'll go pick blueberries."

"You can't see them in the fog."

"Come on, Michael." She took his shoulders and steered him firmly inside.

Michael turned as he went through the screen door. "Just remember," he yelled, "you're only going overnight. It's no big-deal trip!"

Jem returned to chart 309. Michael was jealous. He knew that, but he was still mad at his brother. He looked at the chart. He had to figure out where he and his dad would go tomorrow. His father was letting him do most of the planning. He could choose the island. It could be any island as long as they could get there and back within two days. Next year they would take a longer trip, but for this year two days and a night was the limit.

Heart Island was too close. They could come and go in a morning even with the wind against them. It was blowing southeast now. Southeast always brought in the fog. But it would probably turn around to northwest by tomorrow. Northwest was the clearing wind. After eleven summers on Deer Isle, Jem knew something about the ways of the wind on this coast. Northwest would be a following wind, perfect for Isle au Haut[1] or Kimball Island. At twelve miles that was the farthest Jem could imagine going. The kayak's speed was just over three miles an hour. With a following wind it might be closer to four. So they had to plan on four hours to get there. Getting back, if it was still blowing northwest, would take a lot longer, for the wind would be against them, "hard on the nose." A closer choice might be Dagger or Sheep Island, especially if it blew northeast. Jem lined up his hand on the northeast axis of the chart. On the chart these islands didn't appear very interesting. Too round, Jem

[1]Isle au Haut (īl ə hō')

thought, not enough dents and wiggles in the shoreline. The islands with jagged contours and deep clefts, where the sea furrowed inland, making narrow bays, coves, and miniature fjords, were always the most exciting to explore.

If, however, a northerly wind didn't come, and it blew southwest instead, what then? Maybe Pickering? Too close, Jem thought. Or Hog? Or Chatto? Not Chatto. Chatto was too close to the mainland. He hoped it would blow northwest. Northwest was a good wind. It was crisp and cool, and it cleared.

As Jem was folding up the chart, his little sister Jessica walked out on the porch.

"Are you taking the Pop-Tarts, Jem? Because there's only one left and I want it!"

"No, we're not taking Pop-Tarts."

"Why not? You always eat Pop-Tarts. You've eaten Pop-Tarts for breakfast every morning since you were born."

"Well, I'm not going to eat them on this trip. There's no way to bake them. Besides, they might get soggy. We'll be eating hardtack. That's what sailors eat at sea on long voyages, and Grand Banks fishermen. It doesn't get soggy. Come on, I'll show you."

On the floor of the kitchen under a shelf was a curved-bottom storage case. Jem flipped up the lid. Inside, among other stores, was a box labeled Grimson's Hardtack Bread. Jem opened the box and took out a biscuit. "Here." He handed it to Jessica.

"Ooooh! It's like a little stone muffin. Are you sure you can bite it?"

"Once you crack it open, you can."

"With a hammer?"

"No, a rock will do!" said their father, who had just walked in. "Or you can soak it a bit in salt water."

"I thought you didn't want anything soggy. Why don't you take cereal?"

"We don't want anything that gets soggy before we want it to," Jem said.

"Besides," said Ben, "cereal is for breakfast tables, for everyday. We're going camping."

"Yeah," said Jem, nodding at his plain-speaking dad. He wished his dad had been there when Michael was bugging him.

"What else you got there, Jem?"

"Jam, sugar, coffee for Dad . . . "

"What will *you* drink?"

"Water."

"That's all?"

"Maybe some of that instant grape stuff that you can mix with water, as long as we can get it in a can and not a bag. We got cheese, too."

"That's not cheese," Jessica said.

"It is, too. It's Vermont cheddar."

"Not all cheese is flat and comes in individual cellophane wrappers, Jess," her father said. "Here, try some." Ben unwrapped the hunk of cheddar and cut a small piece for Jessica. She took a tiny nibble and crinkled her nose.

"Yuck!"

"It's great! Here, give me some, Dad." Jem ate a wedge of the cheese. "It probably tastes even better with hardtack."

"What will you have for dinner?" Jessica asked.

"Fish or clams—whatever we can catch or dig up or pick. Plenty of berries now, and mackerel are running," Ben said.

"I think you need to take a steak, just in case."

That evening Jem and his father checked over the lists that Jem had printed neatly on two pieces of paper. There were two lists—one for food and one for equipment.

FOOD

hardtack	apples
jam	butter
sugar	coffee
peanut butter	instant grape juice
cheese	chocolate bars
oranges	

It looked pretty short to Jem. He hoped his father was right about the clams, the mackerel, and the berries. The gear list was much longer.

GEAR

fishing tackle	tool kit
clam spade	camera
cooking pot	sleeping bags
skillet	tent
two forks, two spoons	tarp
Swiss army knife	compass
first aid kit	chart
canteens	rain gear
water jugs	books
spare rudder	games?
spare paddle	

"Should we bring cards?" asked Jem.

"Should we?" said his father. "I don't know."

"I guess maybe it's like cereal. We do it all the time here. So maybe I won't take a deck to the island."

"I bought something in town that you might want to take." Jem's dad reached toward the mantle. "Here you go."

He tossed Jem a leather book with a dolphin carved on the front. Inside the book, bound like a notebook with leather thongs instead of rings, were hundreds of blank pages. A book with hundreds of pages is for a voyage, Jem thought, not just a trip. What was his dad thinking?

"Come on. Open it up. Here's a pencil. Time for your first navigation lesson. We need to chart out some possible courses. You say you're thinking about Duck Harbor on Isle au Haut and Kimball Island."

Ben lit another kerosene lamp and spread out chart 322. It looked just like the other chart except there were two compass roses—drawings of the face of a compass—in the parts of the chart that showed open water.

Jem hunched over the chart. His dad moved the lamp closer.

"You see this compass rose, Jem?"

"Um-hmm."

"The outside ring is the ring of true direction, of the geographic location of the North Pole. The inside ring is the magnetic direction. It shows the magnetic North Pole, the one that the compass needle points to. You always plot your course in reference to the inner circle, the magnetic direction. Now take these parallel rules. The first step is to lay them along the straightest sea line between Deer Isle and the island you want to go to. Where's that?"

"Isle au Haut or maybe Kimball's."

"Well, it will be the same line, so you can start."

Jem took the two straightedge transparent rulers. They were numberless and connected in parallel to one another by crosspieces that allowed one to slide in front of the other. He laid them down along the angle of the direction between Deer Isle and Isle au Haut.

"Okay, that's the angle of your course. Now draw a line along your course."

Jem drew a straight line between the two islands.

"Now step the rules toward the compass rose, but keep them at the same angle as your course."

Jem slid the two parallel strips of plastic back and

forth, and the rules moved sideways until they were over the compass rose.

"What does it read? Remember, read the inside circle for the magnetic direction. That's the one you want."

"180° south."

"Okay. Write that down along the line you've drawn, and in your notebook, too. Now you can measure the distance with the dividers."

This Jem knew how to do. He took sharp bronze needles that were joined at the top and opened them up to the three-mile length on the chart's scale. Holding the same width, he measured it off on his course line. "Twelve and a half miles," Jem said.

"Good," his father said. "Add on two miles for rounding Dunham Point. We can follow the coast until then, and then we'll pick up the compass course. To be on the safe side, chart a couple of other courses in case the wind is not northwest and we have to go in another direction."

Jem stayed up another hour charting courses to islands in every direction. He stepped his way with parallel rules across shoals and channels, through the bay to islands called Sparrow and Bear, Scraggy and Bumpkin, Brimstone and Shag, Otter and Colt, Rabbit Ear and Drunkard's Ledge. There was a kind of excitement that Jem felt when he drew these lines and knew that they really meant something, that they could actually guide him to new destinations. The lines turned winter dreams into something real.

There was no wind. There was only fog and the sound of lapping water. The summer house slept, but

Jem and his father were up carrying gear down to the shore. The kayak rested upside down on the small crescent of beach. It was as beautiful upside down as right side up. The Swedish boat builders who made it loved wood so much that they had seen to it that the grain of the wood was perfectly symmetrical—not just on top where it showed, but on the bottom, too. The boat was strong but light, not much more than fifty pounds unloaded. Jem and his father carried it across the beach and walked barefoot into the bone-aching cold water. Jem slid the curved stowage case into the stern. Its contours were identical to those of the hull. The fit was perfect. This and another stowage case like it had been made twenty years earlier by the brothers for their Alaska trip. In between the two seats, under the covered deck, was room for more storage. They packed in their sleeping bags, clothes, and a camera. In the bow, toward the point, the tent had been fitted; behind it, the repair kit and spare parts.

When the last piece of gear was stowed, Jem and his father pulled on their rubber spray skirts. This was the part that makes kayaking different from any other type of boating. This was the part that made it special for Jem. The spray skirts have an elastic hole to fit around the paddler's waist and an elastic outer edge that fits over the rim of the cockpit. It makes a seal between the paddler and the boat so that no water can get in. But the spray covers do more than keep a paddler dry. The spray skirt made Jem a part of the boat and the boat part of him. The outer and inner edges of the spray skirt formed a double ring. Maybe, Jem thought, it was like the double circle of the compass rose with its true direction and magnetic direction.

Jem and his father climbed into their cockpits.
There was always that thrilling first motion that Jem
felt when he lowered himself into the seat and felt the
water underneath the keel just inches away. It was in
that instant that the boat came alive for Jem, and he

felt an extraordinary connection with the most far-off places, for in the water world everything was one and everything seemed possible. In the stern cockpit Jem fitted his spray skirt over the rim, and his father did the same in the bow cockpit. The seal was made, and with one stroke they glided into deeper water. The white fog swallowed them. Only the dip of their paddles could be heard. There were no splashes. A V of ripples streamed back toward Jem as the bow sliced through the still water.

Jem and his dad paddled silently. The fog was so thick that they could not see the coast to follow it to Dunham Point. Instead, they had to use another compass course that Jem had plotted the night before. The compass was mounted on the deck just in front of his father, and Ben Gray steered by pushing with his feet on a bar that was beneath the deck and attached by wires to the rudder in the stern of the boat. Unless the fog lifted, there would be no way of visually knowing when they rounded the point to pick up the new compass course of 180° south. So Jem had worked out the mileage on this coastal course and knew that they had to paddle 250° west-southwest for exactly forty minutes to clear Dunham Point before turning onto their new course for Isle au Haut. It was Jem's job to keep track of the time and call the course change. Somewhere a lobsterman was hauling traps. Jem could tell that the lobsterman was hauling and not traveling by the rhythmic idling of the engine. But the fog blanketed everything, and the engine sounded like the throb of a great muffled heart.

It was an edgeless world they paddled through, without boundaries or perimeters. The water itself seemed almost the same colorless gray of the fog. It could have been either sky or space through which they moved. It was a timeless world, really, except for the forty minutes that Jem had ordered necessary. Now the throb of the engine was swallowed up too by the fog. There was no sound except for the twin dip of their paddles. Jem could listen to his own heart, his own breathing. His arms held strong. They did not tire as they had last summer. He felt he could paddle forever like this, with the paddle striking the rhythm between him and the sea.

Suddenly there was a raw tidal smell. Unmistakably, it was the strong and slightly sweet odor of wet rocks and seaweed exposed at low tide. It was the smell that scared the daylights out of sailors at night

or in fog, but in a kayak with its six-inch draft, or
depth, there was little need to fear going aground.

"I can smell the point," Ben said.

"Yep. We're right on schedule." Jem looked at his
watch. Thirty-eight minutes had passed, and Dunham
Point was off their left, or port, side, probably not
more than twenty yards. "We paddle straight for two
more minutes and then turn on to 180° south."

Exactly two minutes later, when Jem called, "New course," the fog thinned. The rocky point became softly visible, as if it were behind a screen or gauze. On top of one of the point's rocks, like a teacup on a saucer, a seal arched its back, yawked, and slid into the water.

"Seals all around here," Ben said.

As the fog lifted, Jem and his dad became more talkative. The muffled private world of the gray mist evaporated as the sun burned through, and a new world was revealed, with green islands set like small jewels in the sparkling water. Cormorants and seagulls cruised effortlessly over *Wasso*. Jem and Ben paddled on, picking up their pace, skimming close to steep-shored islands, under cliffs that cascaded with moss

and trees that grew straight out from sheer rock faces, defying gravity. With the shallow depth of the kayak, Jem and his father could glide close enough to touch the rock.

At lunchtime they slid into a slight curve of a beach on South Porcupine Island. Small stones, as smooth and round as coins and polished by a million years of lapping water, covered this beach. Jem and his dad sat down to eat their lunch.

"The hardtack looks just like the stone, Dad."

"Probably as hard, too."

Jem tried to crack a biscuit open. "It is. See? Not a crumb."

"Better find a sharper rock. Try over there." Ben pointed to a place at the edge of the beach.

Jem walked over and began looking. Just as he was picking up a sharp-edged rock from amid the debris of driftwood and seaweed, a wise, calm eye seemed to stare up at him. It was a flat piece of driftwood in the perfect contours of a whale's head, with the likeness of a whale's eye set within. Jem drew the wood from its rock ledge. A sculptor could not have carved it better. Gathered in a swirl of wrinkles, the eye was centered at precisely the right spot in the sea-silvered wood, which itself was shaped just like a whale from flukes to head. There were even the fine horizontal lines combing the lower half of the "body," just like the striations on the underside of a blue whale.

Jem munched his hardtack and cheese and looked at the driftwood whale. "For just two people alone on an island," he said, "this is a pretty noisy lunch. Hardtack has to be one of the noisiest foods going."

After lunch they dug some clams. It was near low tide then, and by evening it would be high tide, and they wouldn't be able to dig any. They picked a small pail of berries, too, and each ate a handful. Then they climbed back into *Wasso* and slid away, the driftwood whale tucked in under the spray skirt near Jem's leg. Mark, Scraggy, Sparrow, West Halibut slid by. Then came an island between Halibut and Kimball that had no name. Jem had hardly noticed it on the chart. They rounded its stubby headland, and on the underside a cove opened up, surprising Jem and his father. Long and crooked as an old person's finger, the cove appeared to channel far into the island.

"Let's go there," Jem said excitedly.

"Let's do!"

A cormorant seemed to be the only inhabitant of the cove. The following tide gave *Wasso* a slight boost. Jem and his father rested their paddles and coasted quietly up the cove that was full of blind corners and secret turns. It was when they passed the last "knuckle," just before the fingertip, that Jem decided that this was where they should camp. Suddenly Kimball Island and Isle au Haut seemed crowded in comparison to this no-name island with its surprise cove.

"I want to camp here, Dad. Is that okay with you?"

"Fine," Ben said and smiled to himself, remembering from twenty years ago that self-discovered things always seemed better and uncharted places more memorable than charted ones.

They coasted to the tip of the water finger. There was a sand beach. Pink ledges on either side sloped into the water, making shallow, tub-size pools just right for swimming. There was a rock just right for cast fishing and a cliff just right for climbing. It was a

place you got to and you knew exactly what you wanted to do. First Jem swam in the pools and then in the
larger part of the cove as the sea grass ribboned
through his legs. His dad watched from shore.

"How can you stand that cold water, Jem?"

"I just keep my feet on the bottom!" Jem whooped
and ducked.

After swimming Jem explored the shoreline. Besides
the big rock pools, there were several small tidal pools.
Glittering in the late afternoon sun, they looked like
oddly-cut jewels. Each pool was alive with small plants
and seaweeds and some with tiny minnows.

Jem and his father climbed the short cliff. On top
of the island was a thick grove of spruce. From the
water this grove of trees had looked like a crown on
the round flat top of the island. Through the trees and
out the other side of the grove the land turned brambly
with berry bushes. They picked blueberry, raspberry,
and blackberry, dropping them into Ben's hat because
they had forgotten the pail. Some islands were
"picked out" by hikers and boaters, but "No Name,"
as Jem had begun to call his island, was not lived on or
visited or picked from, except by cormorants and seagulls and whatever four-footed animals lived there.

"Lucky we dug those clams on Porcupine," Jem said,
as he watched his father pan-fry a ridiculously small mackerel which ordinarily they would have thrown back.

"This is just an hors d'oeuvre. Those clams will be
great!" Ben slid the fish onto a tin plate. It looked even
smaller. Jessica might have been right—a steak, just in
case. "Hand me the rest of the butter. We'll melt it for
the clams."

Jem wondered what Jessica, Michael, and his mother were doing now, that very moment. Eating dinner, he guessed. Maybe chowder, maybe hamburgers. He wondered if they wondered what he was doing. They must. Two places were empty at the table. They didn't have a table here. There was a slab of rock that did fine. They had pulled *Wasso* above the high tide line and turned her upside down, and now they sat leaning against her hull. The cove faced west, just like the Giant's Chair. Jem and his dad shared out the mackerel—all four bites of it—and a heap of clams, and watched the sun slide down behind the horizon like a thin gold coin. It was good thinking that he and his dad, and his mom and Jess and Michael were miles apart but watching the same sun slide on down—Jem and Ben from a beach on an island with no name and a rock for a table, the other Grays from a beach on an island called Deer with a pine table.

They had finished their berries. "Tell me a story, Dad. Tell me an Alaska story."

"An Alaska story? I've told you all of them a hundred times."

"I still like to hear them."

"Alaska was one adventure. This is Maine, another adventure. I'll tell you a Maine story."

"Is it true?"

"You bet."

"Good, let's hear it."

"Once upon a time, a long time ago, on Deer Isle . . . "

"Before the bridge to the mainland?"

"Yes, long before the bridge. If there had been a bridge, this story wouldn't have happened. No, it was before I was born and your grandfather was just a few years older than yourself, maybe seventeen or eighteen at the most. The winters were long on an island without a bridge, especially when it was the kind of winter cold enough to ice the channel but not cold enough to make the ice safe for walking across to the mainland. Too thin for feet, too thick for canoes. You think Cleveland is bad. You ought to try an out island in February. Well, March came, and the ice started to break right up, and your grandfather was sure that his charts from the Coast and Geodetic Survey Department had come. He wanted to pick them up."

"The ones for his trip out the St. Lawrence and around the Gaspé Peninsula?"

"That's it, the New England circumnavigation. He'd dreamed of it all winter. He'd ordered the charts just after Christmas, so he was sure they had arrived. That first morning when the ice had just cleared off, no sooner, a herd of low, dark clouds scudded in, and the channel water became choppy as a northeast wind whistled down. My grandfather, your great-grandfather, said 'Looks like a Northeaster, Pete. You going?' And your grandfather, his son, said he thought he could make it across and back before anything got nasty."

"He let him go?"

"Yes."

"Did he warn him or anything?"

"He asked him if he was going."

"So he just let him go like that?"

"Yes."

"What happened?"

"He made it across fine, but on the way back the wind started to build really fast, and by the time he was halfway across, the channel was boiling white—tops of waves blowing right off. My dad was paddling along. If he'd turned around to go back he would have been caught on the side, abeam, and swamped. He would have lived about two minutes in that water. He had no choice but to paddle right into the teeth of this thing. Somehow he made it. When he walked up from the beach to the old farmhouse where our family lived, his dad was standing there on the front porch. He'd watched him come back. His dad's cheeks were all wet, his eyes red. He'd been crying. He never thought his son would make it back."

"Did he kiss him?"

"No. He wasn't the kissy kind. I think Dad told me that he said something like 'Charts still dry, Pete?'"

"Huh." Jem thought a minute. "Do you think he was right to let him go?"

"You have to let go sometime."

"Would you have let me go?"

Ben paused. "I guess if I thought you were a good enough paddler, I really couldn't stop you."

"Did your parents try to stop you when you and Uncle Pete went to Alaska?"

"No, but all their friends in Cleveland thought they should have, thought they were crazy to let us go." Ben laughed softly. "Come on, let's you and me go for a night glide!"

"A 'night glide'? What's a 'night glide'?"

"You can only do it on a night like this. No wind, and the water is as still as a dark mirror."

They paddled out of the long cove and turned southwest, skimming close to the steep shore. Overhead a million stars chinked the night sky, and as they paddled Jem picked out Orion's Belt: the three bright studs all in a row and the silver point of the sword that dropped below the belt. There were stars, there was the slender mahogany needle, and there was the dip of the paddle. Jem felt part of it all. It was hard to tell where he left off and the boat began. Wood, water, paddler, and stars, they combined for night gliding around the island. Soon Jem noticed a stream of stars streaking back from the bow. Each paddle dip produced a galaxy of small, luminous specks, all sliding smoothly astern.

"Phosphorescence!" Ben said. "Stars in the sky! Stars in the water!"

Star paddler, Jem thought, as he dipped his paddle in the water.

They had just rounded the southeast tip of No Name Island when Jem felt the presence of something else in the water. Catching his breath, he saw, amid the galaxies of phosphorescence, a streaking in the night sea like licks of pale fire.

"Dolphins, Dad!" A pair of dolphins swam just off *Wasso*'s starboard (right) side. Amid the showering sparks of phosphorescence, Jem couldn't really see their shapes. Only the trail of watery fire that streamed around the dolphins was visible.

"They probably think we're a new fish in the neighborhood," said Ben. "Watch them play around us."

The dolphins dived and arced over one another, braiding the bright water, swimming alongside, just out of the dip of the paddles. A magical energy seemed to surround the kayak.

517

Jem and his dad did not put up their tent that night. The moon was riding high when they passed the last knuckle of the long-fingered cove. The night air was warm and they decided to sleep out instead of covering up the stars. Jem crawled into his sleeping bag feeling a little bit hungry. He realized suddenly that he had never gone to bed feeling a little bit hungry in his life. Tomorrow he would get up early and try to catch a bigger mackerel for breakfast. He didn't need food now, really. Besides, munching hardtack would be too noisy and he wanted to think about things—like his driftwood whale. Why had the sea made a perfect whale? How had it happened? What joining of water, wind, and current had modeled the wood into the unmistakable folds of a whale's eye? What accidental collision of natural forces had shaped the whale's body? Had it taken eleven years? An old person's lifetime? A century? Or a thousand years for wind and water to make the wooden whale? Jem fell asleep thinking of driftwood whales and paddling the stars.

Mist rose from the still water of the cove. It was the in-between time, just at the tail end of the last gray of a fading night, but before the first pink of dawn. His father still slept, while Jem stood on a rock with his fishing line. There was a reasonable-sized mackerel in the pail, but Jem was hungry enough that it seemed like a good idea to try for another one. There was a tug on the line. He reeled it in. A plump mackerel thrashed on the end, gilded by the sun that was just slipping up in the east.

Ben was up now, bending over the fire, poking in some kindling to bring it back to life. Jem cleaned the fish on the rock and brought them over to the fire.

"Roe!" That was the first word spoken that morning. "One of them has roe, Dad." Fish eggs were a favorite of Jem's. He usually liked them with bacon. But this wasn't usual, so he guessed he would like them without.

It would be time to go soon, to leave No Name Island, to paddle out of the long-fingered surprise of a cove. There was a part of Jem that wanted to go—to tell Michael and Jessica and his mother about the galaxies in the water, to show them the driftwood whale. But there was a bigger part that wanted to stay, that wanted the trip never to end.

They washed their dishes with sea water and sand. They packed up their sleeping bags, the fishing gear, their plates and pots and pans. The clam shells and fish-bones they returned to the sea. The orange peel and empty instant grape juice can they put in a bag to carry with them. They doused the fire with water and a paddleful of sand. Before they left, Ben set up the camera on self-timing and took a picture of the two of them standing with their paddles at the tip of the finger cove called Surprise on No Name Island.

Summer, which always seemed to gallop from August to Labor Day, had briefly stopped for Jem and his dad. Now they put on their spray skirts and slipped *Wasso* into the water. Jem didn't want to leave. It wasn't just the island he didn't want to leave, it was everything since yesterday morning.

Jem lowered himself into the stern seat. There was that first motion of water under the keel. The thrill was stronger. The boat came alive in a new way for Jem. Everything did seem possible. In that moment he knew that he was not leaving anything behind. None of it—not the peace of the island, not the magic of the dolphins, or the small water galaxies of the night glide, or the skill to chart a course. It was all part of him now, forever, and would be a part of his winter dreams.

As they paddled out of the long-fingered cove, past the first knuckle and the second, Jem began to dream a new dream—the dream for summers to come, when his parents would let go, when he and Michael would be old enough to paddle alone to another island for a day, a week, or maybe a summer of a thousand miles.

GLOSSARY

Full pronunciation key* The pronunciation of each word is shown just after the word, in this way: **abbreviate** (ə brē′vē āt).

The letters and signs used are pronounced as in the words below.

The mark ′ is placed after a syllable with a primary or heavy accent as in the example above.

The mark ′ after a syllable shows a secondary or lighter accent, as in **abbreviation** (ə brē′vē ā′shən).

SYMBOL	KEY WORDS	SYMBOL	KEY WORDS
a	ask, fat	b	bed, dub
ā	ape, date	d	did, had
ä	car, father	f	fall, off
		g	get, dog
e	elf, ten	h	he, ahead
er	berry, care	j	joy, jump
ē	even, meet	k	kill, bake
		l	let, ball
i	is, hit	m	met, trim
ir	mirror, here	n	not, ton
ī	ice, fire	p	put, tap
		r	red, dear
o	lot, pond	s	sell, pass
ō	open, go	t	top, hat
ô	law, horn	v	vat, have
oi	oil, point	w	will, always
o͝o	look, pull	y	yet, yard
o͞o	ooze, tool	z	zebra, haze
yo͝o	unite, cure		
yo͞o	cute, few	ch	chin, arch
ou	out, crowd	n̑g	ring, singer
		sh	she, dash
u	up, cut	th	thin, truth
ʉr	fur, fern	*th*	then, father
		zh	s in pleasure
ə	a in ago		
	e in agent	′	as in (ā′b′l)
	e in father		
	i in unity		
	o in collect		
	u in focus		

*Pronunciation key and respellings adapted from *Webster's New World Dictionary, Basic School Edition,* Copyright © 1983 by Simon & Schuster, Inc. Reprinted by permission.

A

a·bide (ə bīd′) *verb.* to put up with: I really can't *abide* carrots. **abided, abiding.**

ab·so·lute (ab′sə lōōt) *adjective.* **1.** whole, complete, perfect. **2.** pure, untainted: The blackness out the spaceship window was *absolute.* **3.** unlimited by rules or conditions. **4.** certain; definite.

ab·sorb (əb zôrb′ *or* ab zôrb′) *verb.* **1.** to suck up. **2.** to take one's full attention: The book *absorbed* me so much I didn't hear the doorbell. **absorbed, absorbing.**

ac·claim (ə klām′) *verb.* to greet with praise or applause. —**acclaimed** *adjective.* recognized as a special talent: The crowd mobbed the *acclaimed* singer.

a·dapt (ə dapt′) *verb.* **1.** to change something so it fits. **2.** to change oneself to life in a new situation: I expect to *adapt* quickly to my new school.

air pres·sure (er′ presh′ər) *noun.* the force that the earth's atmosphere exerts on everything on the earth.

al·le·vi·ate (ə lē′vē āt) *verb.* to relieve, lessen, or ease: I removed the splinter to *alleviate* the pain in my finger.

a·maze·ment (ə māz′mənt) *noun.* great surprise: Imagine my *amazement* when the dog began to sing!

an·ces·tor (an′səs tər) *noun.* a person who lived before you in your family line: My *ancestors* came from Ireland. **ancestors.**

an·ni·ver·sary (an′ə vur′sər ē) *noun.* **1.** the date on which an event happened in an earlier year: Yesterday was my parents' fifteenth wedding *anniversary.* **2.** the celebration of such an event.

an·noy (ə noi′) *verb.* to bother: The loud noises *annoyed* me as I studied. **annoyed, annoying.**

ap·plause (ə plôz′) *noun.* the act of clapping one's hands to show approval.

ar·chi·tect (är′kə tekt) *noun.* a person who draws plans for and oversees construction of buildings and other structures.

ar·gu·ment (är′gyə mənt) *noun.* **1.** a discussion or dispute in which people disagree: The Eskimos wrestled to settle *arguments.* **2.** a reason given for or against something. **3.** a brief report of the main points in a book, article, etc. **arguments.**

as·sis·tant (ə sis′tənt) *noun.* a person who helps someone: The zookeeper's *assistant* held the panda cub.

as·ton·ish·ment (ə ston′ish mənt) *noun.* wonder; great surprise: Our *astonishment* grew as the circus act continued.

as·tound (ə stound′) *verb.* to surprise so much as to confuse or make speechless: They were shocked by the *astounding* news. **as·tound·ing.**

at·mos·phere (at′məs fir) *noun.* **1.** the air that surrounds the earth. **2.** the gases around any planet or star. **3.** the general feeling of a place or thing.

at·trac·tive (ə trak′tiv) *adjective.* very pleasing, charming, pretty, delightful, etc.: He thought using a new toothpaste would make him more *attractive.*

au·di·tion (ô dish′ən) *noun.* a time when an actor or musician gives a short performance to try to get a job. —*verb.* to take part in an audition: She plans to *audition* for a major part in the school play.

au·thor·ize (ô′thə rīz) *verb.* to allow: The club treasurer *authorized* us to buy the supplies. **authorized.**

a·wak·en (ə wāk″n) *verb.* to arouse; to wake someone up. **awakened, awakening.**

ax·is (ak′sis) *noun.* a real or imaginary line around which something turns: The earth's *axis* goes through the North and South Poles.

architect

Absorb comes from a Latin word that means "to swallow or soak up."

Atmosphere comes from two Greek words, *atmos* meaning "vapor" and *sphaera* meaning "sphere."

B

beacon

Boardinghouse is a combination of the root words *board* and *house*. Board refers to the daily meals that could sometimes be purchased in a house that rented rooms. This use of the word *board* goes back to a time when meals were served on rough planks of wood, or boards. In time, the meals themselves came to be known as *board*.

burrow

bag·gage (bag′ij) *noun.* suitcases taken on a trip; luggage: We had too much *baggage* to fit in the car's trunk.

bal·co·ny (bal′kə nē) *noun.* **1.** a platform that sticks out from the side of a building. **2.** an upper floor of a theater. **balconies.**

ban·is·ter (ban′əs tər) *noun.* a railing for people to hold on to, often along a staircase.

bar·ri·er (bar′ē ər) *noun.* something that blocks the way: The piles of rocks were *barriers* across the path. **barriers.**

bash·ful·ness (bash′fəl nəs) *noun.* a feeling of shyness: The baby always shows *bashfulness* with strangers.

bea·con (bēk″n) *noun.* **1.** a strong light used for warning or guarding. **2.** a tower with beams of light.

bed·rock (bed′rok′) *noun.* the solid rock that lies under the soil on the earth's surface: They dug down to *bedrock* when they built this building.

bleak (blēk) *adjective.* **1.** not sheltered; bare: We looked out at the *bleak,* harsh plains. **2.** gloomy.

bliz·zard (bliz′ərd) *noun.* a heavy snowstorm with strong winds.

board·ing·house (bôrd′iṅg hoʊs′) *noun.* a house where people pay to live and eat their meals: Some of the large homes on our street have been turned into *boardinghouses.* **boardinghouses.**

bod·ice (bod′is) *noun.* the upper part of a woman's dress.

boul·der (bōl′dər) *noun.* a large rock made smooth by the wind and water.

bow (boʊ) *noun.* the front section of a seagoing vessel: We stood in the *bow* of the ship and watched the water ahead.

Braille *or* **braille** (brāl) *noun.* a system of printing and writing used by blind people. Letters, numbers, etc., are formed by patterns of raised dots that are traced with the fingers: She could read any book she wanted with the help of *braille.*

brand (brand) *noun.* **1.** a piece of burning wood. **2.** a mark burned on the skin or hide with a hot iron. **3.** a specific kind or make: We always used the same *brand* of toothpaste.

bunk·house (buṅgk′hoʊs) *noun.* a building on a ranch or in a camp where people sleep. **bunkhouses.**

bunt (bunt) *verb.* to hit a baseball lightly, on purpose, so that it does not go far: The coach told me to *bunt.* —*noun.* a baseball hit so lightly, on purpose, that it does not go out of the infield.

bur·row (bur′ō) *noun.* a hole that an animal digs in the ground: Some rabbits live in *burrows.* **burrows.**

C

ca·ble (kā′b'l) *noun.* **1.** a thick wire made of other wires twisted together: The bridge is held up by *cables.* **2.** the wires through which electricity can be sent. **cables.**

cache (kash) *noun.* **1.** a place where things are hidden or stored: The pirate had a secret *cache* of gold. **2.** anything hidden like this.

cal·cu·la·tion (kal′kyə lā′shən) *noun.* **1.** the act of finding out an answer through arithmetic. **2.** the answer found through arithmetic: Our *calculations* show that the club lost money this year. **calculations.**

cam·ou·flage (kam'ə fläzh) *noun.*
1. the act of hiding soldiers, etc.,
from the enemy by painting or
covering them with leaves or
branches. **2.** a natural disguise such
as the green color of insects that live
on leaves and grass. **3.** anything used
to hide or mislead. —*verb.* to hide by
means of disguise. **camouflaged.**

cap·i·tal (kap'ə t'l) *noun.* **1.** the form
of a letter used to begin a sentence.
2. the city or town where the
government is located.

cap·tive (kap'tiv) *noun.* someone or
something caught and kept as a
prisoner. —*adjective.* held as a
prisoner: The *captive* fish struggled
against the net.

car·bon di·ox·ide (kär'bən dī ok'sīd)
noun. a gas made up of carbon and
oxygen: People breathe in oxygen and
breathe out *carbon dioxide.*

cast (kast) *verb.* **1.** to throw or toss.
2. to choose actors for a play. —*noun.*
1. a throw. **2.** a stiff form made of
plaster which is placed on a broken
arm or leg to keep it in place while it
heals. **3.** the actors in a play.

ca·the·dral (kə thē'drəl) *noun.* **1.** the
principal church of a district, headed
by a bishop. **2.** any large, important
church. **cathedrals.**

cel·e·bra·tion (sel'ə brā'shən) *noun.* a
special party in honor of an event: In
November, we begin to plan our New
Year's *celebration.*

cen·sus (sen'səs) *noun.* an official
count in a country or area to find out
how many people there are, and their
sex, ages, occupations, etc.: Officials
take a *census* every ten years.

cen·ten·ni·al (sen ten'ē əl) *adjective.*
1. lasting one hundred years.
2. happening once in one hundred
years. **3.** of a hundredth anniversary.
—*noun.* a hundredth anniversary or
its celebration.

chan·nel (chan'l) *noun.* **1.** a riverbed
or streambed. **2.** the part of a harbor
or other body of water where the
water is deeper.

chuck·le (chuk'l) *verb.* to laugh softly:
We *chuckled* at the puppy's silly
behavior. **chuckled, chuckling.**

clap·board (klab'ərd *or* klap'bôrd)
noun. a thin board used as siding for
a wooden house. —*adjective.* of thin
board.

clap·per (klap'ər) *noun.* the tongue of
a bell that claps against the side of
the bell to cause the ringing sound.

clat·ter (klat'ər) *noun.* **1.** sharp, loud
sounds. **2.** noisy talking. —*verb.* to
make a clatter: The students *clattered*
through the halls at noon. **clattered,
clattering.**

cle·ver (klev'ər) *adjective.* **1.** quick in
thought or learning; smart;
intelligent: They had to be *clever* to
think up so many poems for the
greeting cards. **2.** skillful. **3.** showing
skill or clear thinking.

clus·ter (klus'tər) *noun.* a number of
things growing or seen together: A
cluster of flowers grew at the edge of
the lake.

com·e·dy (kom'ə dē) *noun.* **1.** a story
that is funny. **2.** a funny event: The
mix-up of the packages turned out to
be a real *comedy* in the end.

com·mis·sion·er (kə mish'ə nər) *noun.*
a member of a group chosen to do a
certain thing: Ten *commissioners* were
appointed by the governor.
commissioners.

com·mu·ni·ca·tor (kə myoo'nə kāt'ər)
noun. one who passes on
information: He was a powerful
communicator.

com·pel (kəm pel') *verb.* to make
someone do something: The guards
compelled everyone to leave the
museum at 5:00. **compelled,
compelling.**

a fat	ɔi oil	ch chin
ā ape	oo look	sh she
ä car, father	oo tool	th thin
e ten	ou out	*th* then
er care	u up	zh leisure
ē even	ur fur	ng ring
i hit		
ir here	ə = a *in* ago	
ī bite, fire	e *in* agent	
o lot	i *in* unity	
ō go	o *in* collect	
ô law, horn	u *in* focus	

Clapboard is a variation on the
German word *klappholtz.*
Klappen means "to fit together,"
and *holtz* means "wood."

clapper

525

Congress

Congress comes from a Latin word that means "a coming together; a friendly meeting."

contestant

com·pe·ti·tion (kom′pə tish′ən) *noun.* the act of competing; rivalry, or athletic match.

com·plain (kəm plān′) *verb.* **1.** to express annoyance with something or show pain or displeasure: He *complained* that there were no birthday cards for stepparents. **2.** to make a charge about something bad. **complained.**

com·pli·cat·ed (kom′plə kāt′id) *adjective.* not simple; difficult to solve, understand, etc.: Starting a business was more *complicated* than we thought.

con·cen·trate (kon′sən trāt) *verb.* to gather all one's efforts: You must *concentrate* on keeping your eyes on the ball.

con·dense (kən dens′) *verb.* **1.** to become thicker or denser: Steam will *condense* into water drops on a cold window. **2.** to make shorter.

con·fuse (kən fyōōz′) *verb.* to mix up in one's mind: He was *confused* by the difficult instructions. **confused, confusing.**

Con·gress (koñg′grəs) *noun.* the group of people in the government of the United States that makes laws: *Congress* is made up of the Senate and the House of Representatives.

con·scious·ness (kon′shəs nis) *noun.* awareness of one's own feelings or of what is happening around one: Her *consciousness* of all the nighttime noises kept her awake for hours.

con·sul·ta·tion (kon′səl tā′shən) *noun.* a meeting to talk over a problem.

con·test·ant (kən tes′tənt) *noun.* one who takes part in a game, race, etc.: The *contestant* challenged the giant, but did not win. **contestants.**

con·ti·nent (kont″n ənt) *noun.* any of the large land areas on earth: Asia is the largest *continent.*

con·va·les·cent (kon′və les″nt) *adjective.* regaining strength and health after an illness: a *convalescent* child. —*noun.* one who is recovering from an illness: The *convalescent* needed rest and healthy foods to get well.

crum·ble (krum′b'l) *verb.* to break into small pieces. —**crumbling** *adjective.* breaking into crumbs.

cu·bic (kyōō′bik) *adjective.* **1.** shaped like a cube. **2.** having measure in three directions: A *cubic* inch is the volume of a cube that is one inch long, one inch wide, and one inch high.

cul·ture (kul′chər) *noun.* **1.** the use of soil for crops. **2.** improvement by study of the mind or manners. **3.** the ideas, skills, arts, and tools of a certain people; way of life: We studied the *culture* of the Native Americans during the 1700s.

cus·tom·er (kus′tə mər) *noun.* a person who buys, especially on a regular basis: The *customers* were lined up at the door when the store announced a sale. **customers.**

D

dan·der (dan′dər) *noun.* **1.** tiny bits from feathers or hair that may cause allergies. **2.** anger or temper. —**get one's dander up.** to become angry: They were rude, and that *got her dander up.*

daunt·less (dônt′lis) *adjective.* without fear; not to be frightened or discouraged: The *dauntless* astronauts ventured into the unexplored blackness.

daz·zle (daz″l) *verb*. **1.** to be so wonderful as to cause admiration: We were *dazzled* by the cellist's brilliant playing. **2.** to make nearly blind with a bright light. **dazzled.** —**dazzling** *adjective*. nearly blinding.

de·ceit·ful (di sēt′fəl) *adjective*. lying or misleading: I think he was *deceitful* about the missing money.

def·i·nite·ly (def′ə nit lē) *adverb*. **1.** clearly: Say *definitely* what you need. **2.** certainly; surely.

de·ject·ed·ly (di jek′tid lē) *adverb*. unhappily; in a discouraged way: She frowned *dejectedly* when she heard the bad news.

del·i·cate (del′i kit) *adjective*. **1.** pleasant because of its lightness or mildness. **2.** easily hurt; not strong: Be careful of the *delicate* glassware.

de·ny (di nī′) *verb*. **1.** To say that something is not true. **2.** to refuse to give: They were *denied* the right to enter the country. **denied.**

de·scend·ant (di sen′dənt) *noun*. a person who comes after you in your family: My children and grandchildren will be my *descendants*. **descendants.**

de·scent (di sent′) *noun*. the act of moving down to a lower place: Be careful on your *descent* from the top of the tower.

de·scribe (di skrīb′) *verb*. **1.** to give a picture of in words: She *described* her idea to me in detail. **2.** to trace an outline of. **described.**

de·sert (di zurt′) *verb*. to leave someone or something when one should not. **deserting.** —**deserted** *adjective*. abandoned.

de·serve (di zurv′) *verb*. to have a right to; be one who has earned something: After studying so hard I *deserve* a break.

de·sign (di zīn′) *verb*. to think of and draw plans to make: She is *designing* all her own clothes. **designed, designing.**

de·spair (di sper′) *verb*. to give up hope: I *despaired* of ever finding my lost keys. **despaired, despairing.**

des·ti·na·tion (des′tə nā′shən) *noun*. the place where a person or thing is going: Their *destination* was the outer edges of the galaxy.

des·tin·y (des′tə nē) *noun*. **1.** fate; that which is bound to occur. **2.** that which seems to make things turn out the way they do: *Destiny* led me to my life as a space pioneer.

de·tain (di tān′) *verb*. to hold back: I must *detain* you for a few more minutes.

de·tour (dē′tŏŏr) *noun*. **1.** a turning aside from the direct route. **2.** a route used when the usual route is closed to traffic. —*verb*. to use or have to use a detour. **detours.**

di·a·mond (dī′mənd *or* dī′ə mənd) *noun*. **1.** a very hard, valuable, clear stone. **2.** a four-sided figure having four equal sides and equal opposite angles. **3.** a baseball playing field.

di·gest (di jest′ *or* dī jest′) *verb*. to change food into a form that the body can use: The snake ate the mouse whole; it would be *digested* later. **digested.** —*noun*. a short summary or report of a longer story, article, etc.

di·lem·ma (di lem′ə) *noun*. a problem in which someone must choose between two things that are equally unpleasant or dangerous: We faced the *dilemma* of continuing on even though we were lost, or stopping and waiting in the bitter cold.

dis·grace (dis grās′) *noun*. shame; loss of respect: I am in *disgrace* due to my bad behavior.

dis·tract (dis trakt′) *verb*. **1.** to draw someone's thoughts or attention from one thing to another: José was *distracted* by thoughts of the new guitar. **2.** to make unable to think clearly; confuse; bewilder. **distracted.**

a fat	ɔi oil	ch chin
ā ape	ŏŏ look	sh she
ä car, father	ōō tool	th thin
e ten	ou out	*th* then
er care	u up	zh leisure
ē even	ur fur	ng ring
i hit		
ir here	ə = a *in* ago	
ī bite, fire	e *in* agent	
o lot	i *in* unity	
ō go	o *in* collect	
ô law, horn	u *in* focus	

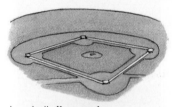
baseball **diamond**

Detour is based on the French word *destorner* which means "to divert."

Dumbwaiter came into being because people wanted to be able to have dinner without the services of a waiter. *Dumb,* in this case, means "silent" or "speechless." Dumbwaiters, unlike human servants, were silent and also could not listen in on their employer's conversations.

eaglets

doc·u·ment (dok′yə mənt) *noun.* a printed or written record, often used to prove something: Birth certificates are important *documents.* **documents.**

dom·i·nant (dom′ə nənt) *adjective.* most important or most powerful; ruling, controlling: Among wolves, the strongest male is the *dominant* one in the pack.

doom (do͞om) *verb.* to destine or condemn to a bad or tragic end: The expedition was *doomed* when supplies ran out.

dou·ble-bit·ted axe (dub″l bit″d aks) *noun.* a tool for chopping wood, having two blades pointing in opposite directions on the end of the handle.

doze (dōz) *verb.* to nap; to lightly sleep: I had just begun to *doze* when the thunder awakened me. **dozed.**

dra·mat·ic (drə mat′ik) *adjective.* **1.** having to do with the theater or drama. **2.** like a drama or play; vivid and exciting: The last minute goal provided a *dramatic* ending to the soccer game.

dread (dred) *verb.* to look forward to fearfully. —*noun.* great fear of an event that is about to happen: I feel real *dread* about tomorrow's test.

drow·sy (drou′zē) *adjective.* **1.** half asleep; sleepy. **2.** making one sleepy. **drowsier, drowsiest.**

dug·out (dug′out) *noun.* a shelter that is dug in the ground.

dumb·wait·er (dum′wāt′ər) *noun.* a small elevator used to send food and small things from one floor to another.

dune (do͞on *or* dyo͞on) *noun.* a small hill made of sand. **dunes.**

dusk (dusk) *noun.* the part of twilight just before the night's full darkness.

dwell·ing (dwel′iñg) *noun.* a house; home: Some Native Americans lived in a kind of *dwelling* called a "hogan."

E

ea·glet (ē′glit) *noun.* a young eagle. **eaglets.**

e·co·nom·ic (ē′kə nom′ik *or* ek′ə nom′ik) *adjective.* having to do with managing money: We studied the president's *economic* policy.

ed·i·tor (ed′ə tər) *noun.* **1.** someone who prepares pieces of writing for publication by correcting and changing them. **2.** someone who is in charge of a newspaper or magazine and decides what will be printed in it.

ee·rie (ir′ē) *adjective.* giving a feeling of fear or mystery; weird: The moon shining through the fog gave the road an *eerie* look.

el·der (el′dər) *noun.* **1.** a person who is older. **2.** certain church, temple, or town officials: The *elders* of the village make the rules. **elders.**

el·e·vate (el′ə vāt) *verb.* to raise or lift up: Our spirits were *elevated* by the play. **elevating.** —**elevated** *adjective.* raised up.

em·brace (im brās′) *verb.* to hold closely in one's arms in order to show love; to hug. **embraced, embracing.**

en·cir·cle (in sur′k′l) *verb.* to make a circle around; to surround. **encircled, encircling.**

en·dure (in do͝or′ *or* in dyo͝or′) *verb.* **1.** to put up with; to hold up under difficulties: She *endured* the long, lonely winter. **2.** to last; to continue to exist. **endured, enduring.**

en·gi·neer (en′jə nir′) *noun.* **1.** a person who is trained in the science of building machinery, roads, bridges, etc. **2.** a person who drives a railroad locomotive.

en·rich (in rich′) *verb.* to give more value, quality, etc.: My experiences in the jungle will *enrich* my life.

en·zyme (en′zīm) *noun.* a protein produced in animal and plant cells that causes chemical reactions: The *enzymes* in our stomachs help to digest food. **enzymes.**

e·qua·tor (i kwāt′ər) *noun.* an imaginary circle around the middle of the earth, exactly halfway between the North and South Poles: Tropical rain forests are located along the *equator.*

es·cort (es′kôrt) *verb.* to go along with someone for protection: She *escorted* the small boy home. **escorted, escorting.**

ex·ag·ger·ate (ig zaj′ə rāt) *verb.* to make something seem greater than it really is: She always *exaggerates* the size of the fish she caught. **exaggerates.**

ex·ec·u·tive (ig zek′yə tiv) *noun.* any of the people who manage the business of an organization. —*adjective.* having to do with managing: She has strong *executive* talents and runs the business well.

ex·hi·bi·tion (ek′sə bish′ən) *noun.* a public show: We went to the art *exhibition.*

ex·ile (eg′zīl *or* ek′sīl) *verb.* to require that a person leave his or her own country and live somewhere else: They made space their new home after they were *exiled* from earth.

ex·pec·ta·tion (ek′spek tā′shn) *noun.* **1.** something expected or looked forward to for good reasons: He has *expectations* of getting a raise in his salary. **2.** the act of looking forward to something. **expectations.**

ex·pert (ek′spərt *or* ik spurt′) *adjective.* **1.** having a great deal of special knowledge and experience; very skillful. **2.** from an expert. —*noun.* expert person; authority: We didn't need to be *experts* to start our new business.

ex·plo·sion (ik splō′zhən) *noun.* **1.** the act of exploding, or blowing up with a loud noise. **2.** any noisy outburst. **3.** a rapid and great increase: The population *explosion* is a worldwide problem.

ex·te·ri·or (ik stir′ē ər) *adjective.* of or on the outside. —*noun.* the outside or outer part: The *exterior* of the building is painted white.

ex·tinc·tion (ik stiṅgk′shən) *noun.* the state of being or becoming extinct, or dying out: Because its forest homes are being destroyed, the ctenosaur lizard is close to *extinction.*

F

false·hood (fôls′hood) *noun.* a lie: If you get caught in a *falsehood*, you will be punished.

fam·ine (fam′ən) *noun.* **1.** a lack of food so great it causes starvation in a wide region. **2.** a great lack of anything.

fan·tas·tic (fan tas′tik) *adjective.* **1.** very strange or weird. **2.** seeming to be beyond belief: The hero in the story had *fantastic* strength.

fer·tile (fur′t′l) *adjective.* able to grow much fruit or large crops: The land along the river was very *fertile.*

fidg·et (fij′it) *verb.* to move around in a restless or nervous way: She *fidgeted* in her chair while waiting for the dentist. **fidgeted.**

flash flood (flash′ flud′) *noun.* a sudden overflowing of water after a heavy rain.

a fat	ɔi oil	ch chin
ā ape	oo look	sh she
ä car, father	ōō tool	th thin
e ten	ou out	*th* then
er care	u up	zh leisure
ē even	ur fur	nĝ ring
i hit		
ir here	ə = a *in* ago	
ī bite, fire	e *in* agent	
o lot	i *in* unity	
ō go	o *in* collect	
ô law, horn	u *in* focus	

explosion

Famine is based on the Latin word *fames*. It means "hunger."

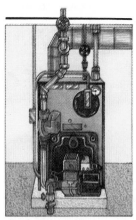

furnace

guitar

flush (flush) *verb.* **1.** to become red in the face: Her cheeks were *flushed* from the heat. **2.** to empty out with water. **flushed, flushing.**

folk·lore (fōk'lôr) *noun.* the stories and beliefs told by a people: We listened for hours to Grandma's Finnish *folklore.*

for·age (fôr'ij) *verb.* to search or look for food: The squirrel came down the tree to *forage* for food.

for·bid (fər bid') *verb.* to order that something not be done: Customers are *forbidden* to go behind the counter. **forbade, forbidden, forbidding.**

for·mu·la (fôr'myə lə) *noun.* **1.** a phrase that is used frequently in a certain way so that its actual meaning is almost lost. **2.** a set of directions for doing or making something: It was easy to figure out the *formula* for making toothpaste.

foun·da·tion (foun dā'shən) *noun.* the bottom part that supports a building: A house with a solid *foundation* will stand for a long time.

found·ry (foun'drē) *noun.* a place where metal is melted and poured into molds to cool.

free (frē) *verb.* not having; without: Six weeks after I broke my leg, the doctor *freed* my leg from the cast.

frost·bit·ten (frôst'bit''n) *adjective.* damaged by exposure to extreme cold.

fu·ri·ous (fyoor'ē əs) *adjective.* very angry: He was *furious* at the mistake.

fur·nace (fur'nəs) *noun.* a structure in which heat is produced for warming a building.

fur·row (fur'ō) *noun.* a long, thin, shallow trench made in the dirt by a plow: The tractor made all the *furrows,* and we planted corn seeds in them. **furrows.**

G

gear (gir) *noun.* **1.** a part of a machine having wheels with teeth that fit into each other. **2.** tools and equipment needed to do something: I packed my camping *gear* in the car.

gen·er·ous (jen'ər əs) *adjective.* willing to give; not selfish.

ge·nius (jēn'yəs) *noun.* **1.** great natural talent: His paintings showed his artistic *genius.* **2.** a person who has such a talent. **3.** a person with a very high IQ.

gi·gan·tic (jī gan'tik) *adjective.* very big; huge: An elephant is *gigantic* when compared to a mouse.

good·will (good'wil') *noun.* a feeling of kindness or friendliness: There is a feeling of *goodwill* during the holiday season.

grat·i·tude (grat'ə tōod *or* grat'ə tyōod) *noun.* being grateful or thankful for a favor.

grief (grēf) *noun.* a deep sorrow: He had many *griefs* in his long life. **griefs.**

grim·y (grī'mē) *adjective.* very dirty; covered with dirt or grime: The old coin was *grimy* from being on the street.

guilt (gilt) *noun.* **1.** the state of having committed a crime. **2.** the feeling that one has done something wrong or is to blame for something: He could not ignore the *guilt* he felt after telling his sister a lie. **3.** a wrong act; crime; sin.

guise (gīz) *noun.* **1.** a costume. **2.** the way something looks, often a false appearance: In the story, the prince appears in the *guise* of a poor man.

gui·tar (gi tär') *noun.* a musical instrument having six strings: You play the *guitar* by plucking the strings.

H

hail (hāl) *verb.* to welcome with a shout: We *hailed* the arrival of the president. **hailed, hailing.**

hard·ship (härd'ship) *noun.* something hard to bear; trouble or pain. **hardships.**

hard·wood (härd'wood) *noun.* a wood such as oak, walnut, or maple that is hard and closely grained. **hardwoods.**

harsh (härsh) *adjective.* **1.** rough; not pleasing. **2.** cruel: The punishment was unusually *harsh.*

hatch·et (hach'it) *noun.* a small axe; a tool for chopping or splitting wood.

ha·ven (hā'vən) *noun.* **1.** a harbor. **2.** a safe place.

hearth (härth) *noun.* **1.** the brick or stone floor of a fireplace. **2.** the life of the home.

heart·land (härt'land') *noun.* a central area of a country, especially one that is thought to be very important to the country.

heart·sick (härt'sik) *adjective.* very unhappy or sad.

hem·i·sphere (hem'ə sfir) *noun.* **1.** half of a sphere or globe. **2.** one of the halves into which the earth is divided in geography.

her·ald (her'əld) *noun.* a person in earlier times who made public announcements.

he·ro·ic (hi rō'ik) *adjective.* **1.** like a hero: The legend speaks of many *heroic* men and women. **2.** showing great bravery.

her·o·ine (her'ə win) *noun.* **1.** a woman or girl who has done something brave. **2.** the most important woman or girl character in a play or story: She was cast as the *heroine*, which was the most important role in the play.

hi·ber·nate (hī'bər nāt) *verb.* to spend the winter in a state of sleep, in which the body temperature is lower than normal. —**hibernation** *noun.* the state of a kind of sleep with lower than normal body temperature: The bear came out of *hibernation* in the spring.

his·tor·i·cal (his tôr'i k'l) *adjective.* **1.** having to do with history: Many *historical* records are stored in this library. **2.** actually happened in history; not fictional.

hob·by (hob'ē) *noun.* something that a person likes to do in his or her spare time: My *hobby* is collecting stamps.

home·site (hōm'sīt) *noun.* a place where a house is or will be built: The pioneer family chose a flat area for its *homesite.* **home site.**

hor·i·zon·tal (hôr'ə zon't'l) *adjective.* parallel to the horizon; not vertical; flat and even; level.

hor·ri·fy (hôr'ə fī) *verb.* **1.** to fill with fear. **2.** to disgust. —**horrified** *adjective.* shocked. **horrifying.**

hud·dle (hud''l) *verb.* **1.** to crowd close together: We *huddled* under the umbrella. **2.** to hunch oneself up. **huddled, huddling.**

hur·tle (hurt''l) *verb.* to throw or move with a lot of speed: The wagon *hurtled* down the path, frightening its passengers. **hurtled, hurtling.**

a fat	ɔi oil	ch chin
ā ape	oo look	sh she
ä car, father	ōo tool	th thin
e ten	ou out	th then
er care	u up	zh leisure
ē even	ur fur	ng ring
i hit		
ir here	ə = a *in* ago	
ī bite, fire	e *in* agent	
o lot	i *in* unity	
ō go	o *in* collect	
ô law, horn	u *in* focus	

Western Hemisphere

Hobby first referred to a small or mid-sized horse. Then in 1818, a riding toy with a carved horse's head became popular. It was called a *hobby horse. Riding your hobby* came to mean any favorite pastime, done purely for pleasure. Finally, the *riding* was dropped, and *hobby* now refers to anything people like to do in their spare time.

I

i·den·ti·cal (ī den'ti k'l) *adjective.* exactly the same: The two chairs are *identical.*

Immigrant is based on the word *migrate*, which comes from Latin. It means "to move from one place to another."

immigrants

id·i·o·ma·tic (id′ē ə mat′ik) *adjective.* using phrases that have meanings different from what the words usually mean, such as "Drop everything," to mean "Stop what you are doing": The character's *idiomatic* speech was enjoyable to hear.

il·le·gal (i lē′gəl) *adjective.* against the law: It is *illegal* to drive a car without a license.

il·lit·er·ate (i lit′ər it) *adjective.* **1.** uneducated; not knowing how to read or write. **2.** showing a lack of education. —*noun.* a person who does not know how to read or write.

ill·ness (il′nis) *noun.* a sickness or disease: He could not play in the baseball game because of *illness.*

il·lus·tra·tion (il′ə strā′shən) *noun.* **1.** a picture used to explain or decorate: I liked the colorful *illustrations* in the book. **2.** an example. **illustrations.**

im·mi·grant (im′ə grənt) *noun.* a person who comes to a new country to live.

im·print (im′print) *noun.* a mark that is made by pressing: When she awoke, her face had the *imprint* of the wrinkled blanket on which she had slept.

im·prov·i·sa·tion (im prov′ə zā′shən) *noun.* something that is made up as one goes along, as with a speech, song, or act: Because the play was not written ahead of time, it was presented as *improvisation.*

in·de·pen·dence (in′di pen′dəns) *noun.* freedom: The colonists wanted their *independence.*

in·ef·fi·cient (in′ə fish′ənt) *adjective.* **1.** lacking the skill to do what is needed: The worker was *inefficient* the first day on the job. **2.** not bringing the desired result without wasting energy, time, or material: The rusty motor was *inefficient.*

in·fec·tious (in fek′shəs) *adjective.* **1.** as a result of infection: Measles is an *infectious* disease. **2.** likely to spread to others: His cheerful mood was *infectious.*

in·fi·nite (in′fə nit) *adjective.* **1.** without beginning or end; no limits: The spaceship did not need *infinite* speed. **2.** vast; very great — *noun.* something infinite.

in·gen·ious (in jēn′yəs) *adjective.* **1.** cleverly planned and made: She had an *ingenious* idea for a science project. **2.** clever; skillful in making or inventing things.

in·scrip·tion (in skrip′shən) *noun.* something written or carved on a coin, statue, building, or book: We read the *inscription* in the stone above the doorway.

in·sert (in surt′) *verb.* to put something into something else: He *inserted* the key into the lock. **inserted, inserting.**

in·sig·nif·i·cant (in′sig nif′ə kənt) *adjective.* of no importance: I forget *insignificant* facts quickly.

in·te·ri·or (in tir′ē ər) *noun.* the inner part or inside of something. —*adjective.* inner; inside: The *interior* lining of the box is red velvet.

in·ter·rup·tion (in tə rup′shən) *noun.* **1.** a break, pause, or stopping: I finished my homework quickly because there weren't any *interruptions.* **2.** anything that causes a break in talk or action. **3.** the act of breaking in on talk or action.

in·val·id (in′və lid) *noun.* **1.** one who is injured or sick, especially one who is likely to be so for some time: The *invalids* ate only broth until they were well. **2.** of or for invalids. **invalids.**

in·val·u·a·ble (in val′yo͞o wə b'l *or* in val′yə b'l) *adjective.* priceless; with value too great to measure: The dictionary, with its vast information, was *invaluable* to the students.

in·ven·tor (in ven′tər) *noun.* someone who invents: He is the *inventor* of a cheaper brand of toothpaste.

in·vest·ment (in vest′mənt) *noun.* **1.** an investing of time, money, etc. with the hope of receiving something in return: The paper, paints, and markers we bought were our first *investment* in the new business. **2.** the sum of money invested.

in·vi·ta·tion (in′vi tā′shən) *noun.* **1.** the asking of someone to come somewhere or do something. **2.** a special letter asking someone to come somewhere: I mailed him an *invitation* to visit us.

J

jour·nal·ist (jʉr′n′l ist) *noun.* a person who works on a magazine or newspaper as a writer or editor.

jour·ney (jʉr′nē) *noun.* a trip.

K

kelp (kelp) *noun.* a large, coarse brown seaweed: The beach was covered in *kelp* washed to shore by the storm.

kin·ship (kin′ship′) *noun.* **1.** family relationship. **2.** relationship; close connection: His *kinship* with his friends got him through the tough times.

L

land·scape (land′skāp) *noun.* **1.** an area of scenery: The mountain *landscape* stretched out in front of her. **2.** a picture showing such a view.

lean-to (lēn′tōō′) *noun.* **1.** a simple shelter sometimes built against a tree or post, usually open on one of its long sides. **2.** a small building with a slanted roof built against the side of another building.

lec·tor (lek′tər) *noun.* **1.** a person who reads the Scripture lessons in a church service: John listened to the *lector* as he sat in church. **2.** a college or univeristy lecturer, esp. in Europe.

li·brar·i·an (lī brer′ē ən) *noun.* **1.** the person who runs a library. **2.** a person who has had special training to work in a library: The *librarian* helped me find the books for my research paper.

Li·brar·y of Con·gress (lī′brer′ē uv koñg′gres) *noun.* the United States national library in Washington, D.C.

li·cense (lī′s″ns) *verb.* to give permission to; allow by law: Mary was *licensed* to drive a car. **licensed, licensing.** *British spelling: lisensed.*

lit·er·a·ture (lit′ər ə chər) *noun.* **1.** the writings of a certain country, time, etc.; especially, novels, poems and plays thought to have lasting value. **2.** the work or profession of writing such things. **3.** all the writings on a subject such as medical *literature*.

log·ger (lôg′ər) *noun.* a person who works at cutting down trees and taking the logs to a sawmill: Paul Bunyan was supposed to have been a *logger*.

lone·ly (lōn′lē) *adjective.* unhappy because of being alone: He felt *loneliest* at night, although he was alone all day as well. **lonelier, loneliest.**

a fat	oi oil	ch chin
ā ape	o͝o look	sh she
ä car, father	o͞o tool	th thin
e ten	ou out	*th* then
er care	u up	zh leisure
ē even	ur fur	ñg ring
i hit		
ir here	ə = a *in* ago	
ī bite, fire	e *in* agent	
o lot	i *in* unity	
ō go	o *in* collect	
ô law, horn	u *in* focus	

invitation

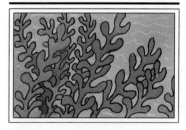

kelp

loy·al·ty (loi'əl tē) *noun.* quality of being faithful to one's family, country, etc.: He proved his *loyalty* to his country by defending it.

lux·u·ry (luk'shə rē *or* lug'zhə rē) *noun.* anything that gives comfort or pleasure but that one does not need to survive: A new dress is a *luxury* that I can't afford.

M

mal·a·dy (mal'ə dē) *noun.* a disease or sickness: Many explorers before them had died from the mysterious *malady.*

mal·func·tion (mal fuñgk'shən) *verb.* to not work as it should —*noun.* an instance of this failure: The crew of the ship died from an oxygen *malfunction.*

mam·mal (mam'əl) *noun.* any animal with glands in the female that produce milk for feeding its young: The whale is the largest *mammal* on Earth. **mammals.**

man·sion (man'shən) *noun.* a large house.

mar·vel (mär'v'l) *noun.* a wonderful thing. —*verb.* to wonder; be astonished: We *marveled* at the athlete's skill. **marveled, marveling.**

mar·vel·ous (mär'v'ləs) *adjective.* **1.** causing astonishment, wonder. **2.** splendid; very good: I thought his ideas were *marvelous.*

mas·ter·piece (mas'tər pēs) *noun.* **1.** something made with great skill. **2.** the finest thing a person has ever done: Many people consider the ''Mona Lisa'' to be Leonardo da Vinci's *masterpiece.*

match·stick (mach'stik) *noun.* a slender piece of wood coated at one end with a chemical that catches fire when scratched.

me·di·um (mē'dē əm) *noun.* a way of communicating with the public: Television is today's most popular *medium.*

mem·oirs (mem'wärz) *plural noun.* the story of a person's life written by that person; autobiography: I read the *memoirs* of a famous artist.

mem·o·ry (mem'ər ē) *noun.* **1.** the ability to remember. **2.** something that is remembered: I have good *memories* of my visits to your house. **3.** the part of a computer that stores information. **memories.**

mile·age (mīl'ij) *noun.* **1.** the total number of miles: The *mileage* from San Francisco to Los Angeles is less than from San Francisco to Phoenix. **2.** the average number of miles a car will go on a gallon of fuel.

mil·i·tar·y (mil'ə ter'ē) *adjective.* of, by, or for an armed force, soldiers. —*noun.* the army; soldiers: There were units of the *military* on the island.

min·strel (min'strəl) *noun.* in earlier times, an entertainer who sang, played an instrument, and recited poems.

mir·a·cle (mir'ə k'l) *noun.* **1.** something that seems to go against the laws of nature. **2.** a surprising or remarkable thing: It will be a *miracle* if we win.

mis·sion (mish'ən) *noun.* **1.** special errand or duty that a group or person is sent to do, as by the government, church, etc.: We needed enough supplies for a ten-year *mission.* **2.** the special task that a person seems to be meant for in life; a calling: His *mission* in life was to be a poet.

mod·ern·ist (mod'ərn ist) *noun.* **1.** one who likes modern things, practices, or ideas. **2.** in recent architecture, one who designed buildings in a spare, simple style: Many buildings in New York City were designed by *modernists.* **modernists.**

Memoirs is an English word that has its roots in two languages. From the Latin *memoria* and from the French *mémoire*, it means *memory.* Today we use it to mean a written record of events that are worth remembering.

mansion

monk (mungk) *noun*. a man belonging to a religious group of men who live according to very strict rules.

mo·not·o·nous (mə not'n əs) *adjective*. **1.** sameness of tone or pitch: The speaker's *monotonous* voice lulled me to sleep. **2.** having little or no change; boring or tiresome.

mon·u·ment (mon'yə mənt) *noun*. a statue or building put up in honor of a famous person or event: Washington, D.C., has *monuments* that honor past presidents. **monuments.**

moor (moor) *verb*. to tie a boat in place with ropes or anchors: We *moored* the boat at the dock. **moored, mooring.**

mus·cu·lar (mus'kyoo lər) *adjective*. **1.** made up of, of, or performed by a muscle or muscles. **2.** with well developed muscles; strong: His father was *muscular* from lifting boxes in the warehouse.

mu·si·cian (myoo zish'ən) *noun*. someone skilled in music, such as a composer or one who plays a musical instrument or sings, especially for a living: She dreamed of being a *musician* some day.

N

na·tion·al (nash'ə n'l) *adjective*. having to do with the whole nation: We have a *national* election for president every four years.

na·tive (nāt'iv) *adjective*. **1.** having to do with the place where someone was born: The United States is my *native* land. **2.** born in or belonging to a certain country. —*noun*. a person born in a certain place.

neg·lect (ni glekt') *verb*. **1.** to fail to do something because of carelessness. **2.** to pay too little attention to: He *neglected* to water the dying plant. **neglected, neglecting.**

nu·cle·ar (noo'klē ər *or* nyoo'klē ər) *adjective*. **1.** of or having to do with a nucleus or nuclei. **2.** of, involving, or using the nuclei of atoms. **3.** of or involving atomic bombs or other nuclear weapons. **nuclear-free.**

nu·tri·ent (noo'trē ənt *or* nyoo'trē ənt) *noun*. any of the substances in food that are required for health, such as minerals, proteins, vitamins, etc.: Lizards get all their *nutrients* from the leaves and flowers they eat. **nutrients.**

O

ob·ser·va·tion (ob'zər vā'shən) *noun*. **1.** the act or power of seeing or noticing. **2.** the fact of being seen or noticed. **3.** the noting and writing down of some fact: It was our *observation* that there were no good greeting cards.

of·fi·cial·ly (ə fish'əl lē) *adverb*. in a formal way; in the manner of someone who has authority or power: We were told *officially* by the committee about the plans for the new building.

o·men (ō'mən) *noun*. an event that is supposed to be a sign of something good or bad to come: I took the dark clouds as an *omen* that I would have a bad day.

o·pin·ion (ə pin'yən) *noun*. **1.** a belief not based on certainty, but on what one thinks is likely or true: She thought about both sides of the question before giving her *opinion*. **2.** what a person thinks about the value or good of something. **3.** judgment by an expert.

a fat	oi oil	ch chin
ā ape	oo look	sh she
ä car, father	oo tool	th thin
e ten	ou out	*th* then
er care	u up	zh leisure
ē even	ur fur	ng ring
i hit		
ir here	ə = a *in* ago	
ī bite, fire	e *in* agent	
o lot	i *in* unity	
ō go	o *in* collect	
ô law, horn	u *in* focus	

the Washington **Monument**

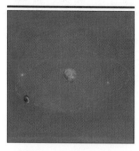

orbit

pavilion

pedestal

or·bit (ôr′bit) *noun.* the path followed by a planet or moon around another planet or the sun: The earth completes an *orbit* around the sun every 365 days.

or·di·nance (or′d′n əns) *noun.* **1.** a law, usually made by the local government: The traffic *ordinance* is strictly enforced. **2.** an order, rule, or regulation.

or·tho·dox (ôr′thə doks) *adjective.* keeping to the usual or traditional beliefs or customs in religion or politics.

P

pal·let (pal′it) *noun.* a bed or mattress of straw that is used on the floor. **pallets.**

par·tial·ly (pär′shəl lē) *adverb.* not totally: The work is *partially* done.

par·ti·tion (pär tish′ən) *noun.* a wall that separates two rooms. —*verb.* to divide into parts: We *partitioned* the attic to make small bedrooms. **partitioned, partitioning.**

pa·vil·ion (pə vil′yən) *noun.* a building used for exhibits at a fair or park.

peace·ful (pēs′fəl) *adjective.* **1.** free from noise; quiet: I love the *peaceful* seashore at dawn. **2.** not fighting.

ped·es·tal (ped′is t′l) *noun.* the base that holds up a statue or lamp.

per·ma·frost (pʉr′mə frôst′) *noun.* soil under the earth's surface that is always frozen.

per·mis·sion (pər mish′ən) *noun.* the act of allowing: I have received *permission* to go on the trip.

per·son·al·i·ty (pʉr′sə nal′ə tē) *noun.* **1.** the special qualities which make a person unique. **2.** qualities in a person that attract others; energy, charm,

cleverness: His sense of humor added to his *personality.* **3.** an unusual or famous person.

pe·ti·tion (pə tish′ən) *noun.* a formal request signed by a number of people: We sent the governor a *petition* for more funds.

phi·los·o·phy (fi los′ə fē) *noun.* the study of human thought about what is right and wrong: The more they read, the more their *philosophy* deepened.

pit·y (pit′ē) *noun.* a feeling of sadness for someone's troubles: It was a *pity* to see the hungry animals. —*verb.* to feel sorry for. **pitied, pitying.**

plain (plān) *adjective.* **1.** open; clear. **2.** without luxury. **3.** simple; easy. **4.** not good-looking. **5.** not fancy. —*noun.* a large area of flat land: The pioneers crossed the *plains.* **plains.**

plank (plañgk) *noun.* a long, wide board. **planks.**

play·wright (plā′rīt) *noun.* a writer of plays: We congratulated all the *playwrights* on the success of the drama festival. **playwrights.**

plead (plēd) *verb.* to request in a serious way; beg. —**pleading** *adjective.* in a begging and serious manner: She used a *pleading* voice to ask her father's permission.

plot·ter (plot′ər) *noun.* a person who makes secret plans with other people: The crew caught the *plotters* before they could capture the ship. **plotters.**

plumb·ing (plum′ing) *noun.* **1.** the pipes, sinks, and drains of a building's water or gas system. **2.** the work of a plumber.

po·lar (pō′lər) *adjective.* **1.** near the North or South Pole. **2.** near either end of a sphere like the earth or other planets: They studied the *polar* areas of Mars.

po·lit·i·cal un·rest (pə lit′i k′l un rest′) *noun.* a condition in which people are unhappy with their government and are struggling to change it.

pon·der (pon′dər) *verb*. to think deeply and carefully about: He was *pondering* their offer of a new job. **pondered, pondering.**

por·trait (pôr′trit *or* pôr′trāt) *noun*. a drawing or painting of a person: The President will sit for his official *portrait* next week.

pov·er·ty (pov′ər tē) *noun*. being poor or not having enough to live on: Many people live in *poverty*.

prai·rie (prer′ē) *noun*. a large, flat area of grassy land with few trees.

prance (prans) *verb*. **1.** to spring from the hind legs in a spirited way, particularly while moving. **2.** to move along with strutting, lively steps: Hank was so happy he *pranced* all the way home. **pranced.**

prank·ster (praṅk′stər) *noun*. someone who plays tricks, often causing mischief: A *prankster* must have put soap in the fountain.

pre·cau·tion·ar·y (pri kô′shə ner′ē) *adjective*. using care beforehand to prevent danger from occurring: Locking doors is a *precautionary* measure to stop thieves from entering.

pre·cious (presh′əs) *adjective*. **1.** having great value. **2.** much loved: The grandmother's ring was *precious* to her granddaughter.

pri·va·cy (prī′və sē) *noun*. **1.** the state of being away from the company of others; seclusion: She went to her room for *privacy*. **2.** secrecy.

pro·claim (prō klām′) *verb*. to announce: The governor *proclaimed* a special holiday. **proclaimed, proclaiming.**

prof·it (prof′it) *noun*. **1.** the sum of money gained in business deals after subtracting expenses: Their *profits* were low the first month since they spent so much on supplies. **2.** gain of any kind; benefit; advantage. **profits.** —*verb*. to be of advantage to.

pro·jec·tion (prə jek′shən) *noun*. something that sticks out: The cat sat on a *projection* near the top of the wooden fence.

pro·mot·er (prə mō′tər) *noun*. one who helps increase the popularity, growth, or sales of something: Our coach is a *promoter* of regular exercise for children.

pro·mo·tion (prə mō′shən) *noun*. a raising to a higher rank or grade: He received a *promotion* from clerk to supervisor.

pros·per·i·ty (pro sper′ə tē) *noun*. being wealthy or successful: We wish for peace and *prosperity* throughout the world.

pro·test (prə test′) *verb*. to speak out against; object to: She *protested* that her grade was unfair. **protested, protesting.**

pro·voke (prə vōk′) *verb*. **1.** to make angry or annoy: His constant teasing *provoked* me. **2.** to arouse or call forth.

pu·ma (pyōō′mə *or* pōō′mə) *noun*. a large animal of the cat family, with a slender, tan body and a long tail; another name for cougar.

a fat	oi oil	ch chin
ā ape	oo look	sh she
ä car, father	ōō tool	th thin
e ten	ou out	*th* then
er care	u up	zh leisure
ē even	ur fur	ṅg ring
i hit		
ir here	ə = a *in* ago	
ī bite, fire	e *in* agent	
o lot	i *in* unity	
ō go	o *in* collect	
ô law, horn	u *in* focus	

Puma came to our language from the Inca Indians of Peru. The Spanish conqueror Pizarro learned the Inca name for this American cougar when he came to Peru in the 1500s.

Q

quar·an·tine (kwôr′ən tēn) *noun*. **1.** keeping a diseased person, animal or plant away from others so the disease does not spread: The robbers were kept in *quarantine* because they had the measles. **2.** a place where such persons, plants or animals are kept.

puma

537

R

rab·bi (rab′ī) *noun.* the spiritual leader of a Jewish temple or synagogue: The *rabbi* led his congregation in prayer.

rack·et (rak′it) *noun.* loud noise or clatter: Skateboards make a *racket!*

rag·ged (rag′id) *adjective.* **1.** shabby. **2.** rough and uneven: The paper tore, leaving a *ragged* edge.

rav·e·nous·ly (rav′ə nəs lē) *adverb.* in a very hungry way: We ate the meal *ravenously.*

raw·hide (rô′hīd) *noun.* cattle hide that is not yet tanned into leather.

re·al es·tate (rē′əl ə stāt′ *or* rēl′ ə stāt′) *noun.* a piece of land and whatever is on it, such as buildings or trees.

re·al·ize (rē′ə līz) *verb.* **1.** to understand completely: He *realized* the bike had a flat tire when he tried to ride it. **2.** bring into being; to make real. **realized.** *British spelling: realise.*

re·cep·tion (ri sep′shən) *noun.* **1.** a receiving or being received. **2.** a party at which guests are received: We went to the wedding *reception* after the ceremony.

reck·on (rek′ən) *verb.* **1.** to count. **2.** to think of as being. —**reckoned with.** to have thought about; considered: We *reckoned with* her probable reaction as we made our plans.

re·cruit (ri kro͞ot′) *verb.* to get new members: We *recruited* members for the soccer team. **recruited, recruiting.**

re·cy·cle (rē sī′k′l) *verb.* to use over and over, as a single supply of water, paper, etc.: *Recycling* newspapers is easy. **recycling.**

ref·er·ence (ref′ər əns *or* ref′rəns) *noun.* **1.** the act of referring. **2.** a source of information: We used the dictionary as a *reference.*

Renovate has its roots in the Latin prefix *re* meaning "again," and the Latin word *novus* meaning "new."

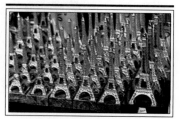

replicas

Resemble is an English word that is based on the Latin word *similare*, "to copy," and the French word *resembler*, "to seem, to be like."

reg·u·la·tion (reg′yə lā′shən) *noun.* a rule or law. —*adjective.* done according to rules: We wore our *regulation* scout uniforms on our hikes.

re·lay (rē′lā *or* ri lā′) *verb.* to receive and pass on: We will *relay* the message to her.

re·lief (ri lēf′) *noun.* **1.** lessening of pain, trouble, or worry: The people came inside to get *relief* from the cold. **2.** help given to victims of disasters.

re·lo·cate (rē lō′kāt) *verb.* **1.** to find again. **2.** to move to another location: Her relatives were *relocated* to another village. **relocated.**

rem·e·dy (rem′ə dē) *noun.* **1.** a treatment that cures or relieves a disease: We have no perfect *remedy* for the common cold. **2.** anything that corrects a problem.

ren·o·vate (ren′ə vāt) *verb.* to make like new; repair: We *renovated* the old house. **renovated, renovating.**

rent·er (rent′ər) *noun.* someone who pays money at regular times to live in a house or apartment: This house is occupied by a *renter.*

rep·li·ca (rep′li kə) *noun.* an exact copy of something, such as a painting.

rep·re·sen·ta·tive (rep′rə zen′tə tiv) *noun.* someone who represents others: The people send *representatives* to Congress to voice their concerns. **representatives.**

re·search (ri surch′ *or* rē′surch) *noun.* patient, careful study in order to find out facts about some subject: We had to *research* what type of people buy greeting cards. —*verb.* to do research.

re·sem·ble (ri zem′b′l) *verb.* to look like: Two houses on the block *resemble* our house, but both are smaller.

re·sign (ri zīn′) *verb.* to give up a membership or job: I will *resign* as club president after this meeting.

re·sound (ri zound′) *verb.* **1.** to echo over and over. **2.** to become filled with sound. **resounded, resounding.**

rid·dle (rid′′l) *noun.* a puzzle, often in the form of a question with a tricky meaning or answer.

rit·u·al (rich′oo wəl) *adjective.* of, like, or done as a rite: The Eskimos followed certain *rituals* when a whale was captured. **rituals.**

riv·er·bed (riv′ər bed′) *noun.* the bottom of a river: The water had dried up, leaving behind a cracked and dusty *riverbed.*

rot (rot) *verb.* to spoil from dampness or other causes: The tomatoes will *rot* on the vine if the rain continues.

rum·bus·ti·cal (rəm′bəs tə kəl) *adjective.* robust, robustious: They played in a loud and *rumbustical* manner. *Usually British.*

rus·tle (rus′′l) *verb.* to move with a soft, rubbing sound. —*noun.* a soft, rubbing sound: We heard the *rustle* of her long, silk dress.

S

sand·spit (sand′spit′) *noun.* a ridge of sand formed in a river or along the seashore.

scale (skāl) *noun.* **1.** an instrument or machine for weighing. **2.** one of the thin, small plates covering the body of a fish or reptile. **3.** a series of spaces marked off by lines and used for measuring distances or amounts. **4.** a system for grouping or classifying by size, importance, or perfection: The director always made his movies on a very grand *scale.*

scav·enge (skav′inj) *verb.* to look for food or items, especially that which is thrown away: The vultures were

scavenging around the campground. **scavenged, scavenging.**

sce·ner·y (sē′nər ē) *noun.* **1.** the view in an outdoor area: We love mountain *scenery.* **2.** the painted background used for a play: The *scenery* made the stage look like an ancient castle.

scent (sent) *noun.* **1.** smell: I love the *scent* of lilacs. **2.** the sense of smell. **3.** a smell that an animal leaves.

script (skript) *noun.* **1.** handwriting. **2.** a copy of a play, movie, or television show, used by the cast of the play, movie, or show.

sea·wall (sē′ wôl) *noun.* a wall built to protect an area of shoreline from being washed away by the waves.

seep (sēp) *verb.* to leak slowly through small openings; ooze: Water was *seeping* from that old hose into the ground. **seeped, seeping.**

self-re·li·ance (self′ri lī′əns) *noun.* trust in one's own efforts, judgment, and abilities: Because she had always taken care of herself, she had great *self-reliance.*

sen·sa·tion (sen sā′shən) *noun.* **1.** a feeling that comes from the senses, the mind, or the body: The minty taste gave my mouth a tingling *sensation.* **2.** a feeling of excitement among people. **3.** something that stirs up such feeling.

ser·pent (sur′pənt) *noun.* a large snake.

set (set) *noun.* **1.** scenery and furniture used on a theater stage: Our drama club has several *sets* to use for different plays. **2.** a group of things that go together. **3.** a number of parts put together in a cabinet, as in a television set. **4.** a group of six or more games in tennis won by a margin of two or more games. **5.** in mathematics, any group of units, numbers, etc. **sets.**

shim·mer (shim′ ər) *verb.* to shine with a flickering light or gleam faintly: The silk dress *shimmered* in the sunshine. **shimmered, shimmering.**

a fat	oi oil	ch chin
ā ape	oo look	sh she
ä car, father	oo tool	th thin
e ten	ou out	*th* then
er care	u up	zh leisure
ē even	ur fur	ng ring
i hit		
ir here	ə = a *in* ago	
ī bite, fire	e *in* agent	
o lot	i *in* unity	
ō go	o *in* collect	
ô law, horn	u *in* focus	

sandspit

seawall

Stash probably was given to the English language by American hoboes. It is thought to be a combination of *store* and *cache*. Hoboes said they *stashed* away their few things so that others wouldn't find them and steal them.

snowshoes

sod

shrug (shrug) *verb.* to pull up one's shoulders to show that one does not care or does not know something: He only *shrugged* when we asked where she was. **shrugged, shrugging.**

shuf·fle (shuf″l) *verb.* **1.** to walk or dance with a dragging motion of the feet: He *shuffled* slowly along the hall. **2.** to mix playing cards. **shuffled, shuffling.**

shuf·fle·board (shuf″l bôrd) *noun.* a game in which long sticks are used to push pucks onto numbered sections of a triangle painted on the ground or some other surface.

siege (sēj) *noun.* the surrounding of a city or other place by an army trying to capture it.

skill·ful·ly or **skil·ful·ly** (skil′fəl lē) *adverb.* in an expert way; in a well-trained or practiced manner.

slab (slab) *noun.* a flat, broad, thick piece: There were big *slabs* of marble in the artist's studio. **slabs.**

smidge (smij′) *or* **smidg·en** (smij′ən) *noun.* a little bit.

snarl (snärl) *verb.* **1.** to growl fiercely, showing the teeth: The dog was *snarling* at the man at the gate. **2.** to speak in an angry voice. **snarled, snarling.**

snout (snout) *noun.* the nose and jaws projecting from the head of an animal, as on a pig. **snouts.**

snow·shoe (snō′shoo) *noun.* a wooden frame with leather strips that is worn on the shoes to keep a person from sinking into the snow. **snowshoes.**

snug (snug) *verb.* **1.** to cause to fit closely: We *snugged* like beavers in our burrow. **2.** to make snug. **snugged, snugging.**

soar (sôr) *verb.* to fly high in the air: The eagle *soared* above the clouds. **soared, soaring.**

sod (sod) *noun.* the top layer of earth that contains grass and its roots: The pioneers' plows broke the *sod*.

sod·bus·ter (sod′bus′tər) *noun.* a farmer on the frontier in the American West who broke through the sod to plant a crop. **sodbusters.**

so·lar sys·tem (sō′lər sis′təm) *noun.* a sun and all the planets, moons, and other bodies that move around it.

span (span) *noun.* **1.** the part of a bridge between two supports: The main *span* of the bridge is more than ninety yards long. **2.** a certain period of time. **spans.**

spar (spär) *verb.* **1.** to box in a skillful way: He put up his fists and began to *spar* with his brother. **2.** to argue; exchange remarks.

spe·cies (spē′shēz) *noun.* **1.** a collection of animals or plants that are alike in certain ways. **2.** a type or kind: The black rhino is an endangered *species*.

spec·i·fi·ca·tion (spes′ə fi kā′shən) *noun.* a detailed description.
—**specifications** *plural noun.* a description of all the necessary details for something, including sizes and materials: The engineer had the *specifications* for the new building.

splen·dour or **splen·dor** (splen′dər) *noun.* **1.** great brightness. **2.** the quality of being beautiful in a grand way: We admired the *splendour* of the room.

spout (spout) *verb.* to shoot out in a forceful way: Spray was *spouting* from the whale's airhole. **spouted, spouting.**

sta·bil·i·ty (stə bil′ə tē) *noun.* steadiness; firmness: I don't trust the *stability* of that chair.

star·va·tion (stär vā′shən) *noun.* the condition of dying or suffering from lack of food: Deer may die of *starvation* in a cold, snowy winter.

stash (stash) *verb.* to hide in a secret, safe place. **stashed, stashing.**

ster·i·lize (ster′ə līz) *verb.* making sterile: We had to *sterilize* the jars before putting food in them. **sterilized.**

strand (strand) *noun.* **1.** a thread or wire twisted together with others to make a rope or cable. **2.** something that is like a string or rope: She twisted a *strand* of her hair as she talked. **strands.**

stren·u·ous (stren′yōō wəs) *adjective.* **1.** requiring much energy or effort: Running is a *strenuous* exercise. **2.** very active.

struc·ture (struk′chər) *noun.* something that is built, such as a house or building.

suc·cess (sək ses′) *noun.* favorable outcome: We felt our business was a *success* when we got over 100 orders for cards in the first week.

suc·cess·ful (sək ses′fəl) *adjective.* **1.** turning out well; achieving success: With orders pouring in, we felt *successful* at our new business. **2.** fortunate; prosperous.

sup·port (sə pôrt′) *verb.* **1.** to hold up. **2.** to provide money for. —*noun.* **1.** being supported. **2.** a person or thing that holds up. —*adjective.* weight carrying.

sur·vey (sər vā′) *verb.* **1.** to look over carefully. **2.** to measure the size or shape of a piece of land using special instruments. **surveyed.** —*noun.* **1.** a study of the general facts. **2.** a measurement of size and location of land. —**surveying** *adjective.* measuring the land: The *surveying* task was made difficult by the hilly land.

sur·vi·val (sər vī′v′l) *noun.* the act of continuing to exist: We depended on the abundant fish for our *survival.*

sus·pen·sion (sə spen′shən) *noun.* **1.** something held by support from above. **2.** the act of keeping out or away from because of unacceptable behavior.

sus·pi·cious·ly (sə spish′əs lē) *adverb.* acting in a way that shows a lack of trust or confidence: The detective looked *suspiciously* at the man in the trenchcoat.

swamp (swomp) *noun.* a piece of damp land; bog.

sway·backed (swā′bakt) *adjective.* having a spine that sags in the middle: The old horse was *swaybacked.*

sym·bol·ize (sim′b′l īz) *verb.* to stand for something: The flag *symbolizes* the United States. **symbolizes, symbolized, symbolizing.**

sym·met·ri·cal (si met′ri k′l) *adjective.* balanced; right half like the left half.

T

tem·po·rar·y (tem′pə rer′ē) *adjective.* lasting for a short time; not permanent: The rainy weather will be *temporary.*

ten·e·ment (ten′ə mənt) *noun.* an apartment house that is old and crowded.

text (tekst) *noun.* **1.** the words on a page, not including pictures. **2.** the actual words a writer uses in a book, speech, or other writing: He read the *text* of his speech one last time.

thaw (thô) *verb.* to melt: The ice on the lake will *thaw* by spring.

the·o·ret·i·cal (thē′ə ret′i k′l) *adjective.* **1.** based on theory rather than practice or experience: *Theoretically,* the ship could fly through the Light Barrier, but it had never before been done. **2.** worked out or planned from thinking, not from experience: The detective was good at *theoretical* thinking. —*adverb.* **theoretically.**

a fat	oi oil	ch chin
ā ape	o͞o look	sh she
ä car, father	o͞o tool	th thin
e ten	ou out	*th* then
er care	u up	zh leisure
ē even	ur fur	ng̅ ring
i hit		
ir here	ə = a *in* ago	
ī bite, fire	e *in* agent	
o lot	i *in* unity	
ō go	o *in* collect	
ô law, horn	u *in* focus	

strand

suspension bridge

Thrive, which comes from Norwegian, has a selfish early meaning, which was "to seize or grasp for oneself." Perhaps in times gone by, if people didn't *seize* what they needed, they didn't *thrive.*

vessel

the·o·ry (thē′ə rē) *noun.* **1.** an explanation of why something happens. **2.** the general rules followed in a science or an art. **3.** an idea, guess, or opinion. **theories.**

thrive (thrīv) *verb.* **1.** to become successful; to do well. **2.** to grow in a strong and healthy way: The baby *thrived* on homemade baby food. **thrived, thriving.**

tilt (tilt) *verb.* to tip to one side: The flowers *tilt* toward the sun.

toil (toil) *verb.* to work hard. —*noun.* hard work: We read about the workers' *toils* in building the railroad. **toils.**

toll·booth (tōl′ booth) *noun.* a booth or gate at which money is collected before or after going over a bridge, toll road, turnpike, or through a tunnel.

tra·di·tion·al (trə dish′ən′l) *adjective.* handed down from older people to younger ones: We sang the *traditional* holiday songs.

trag·e·dy (traj′ə dē) *noun.* **1.** a serious play that has a sad ending. **2.** something that is very sad: The loss of his dog was a *tragedy* to him.

turf (tʉrf) *noun.* the top layer of the ground; sod.

turn·pike (tʉrn′pīk) *noun.* **1.** a large road that has a gate where money is paid. **2.** a gate where a toll is paid. **3.** any main highway.

U

un·con·scious (un kon′shəs) *adjective.* **1.** unable to feel and think: He fainted and was *unconscious* for a minute. **2.** not aware of something.

un·in·hab·it·ed (un′in hab′it id) *adjective.* not lived in; not inhabited: When the space explorers found no signs of life, they reported that the planet appeared *uninhabited.*

V

vast (vast) *adjective.* very large: Our universe is *vast.*

ven·ture (ven′chər) *noun.* an activity in which there is some risk of losing something: The orange juice stand is a new *venture* for its owner.

ver·dict (vʉr′dikt) *noun.* **1.** the jury's decision about a court case. **2.** any judgement or opinion: It was the crew's *verdict* that the ship would make it through the rough seas.

ves·sel (ves″l) *noun.* **1.** any hollow utensil for holding something as a pot, bowl, etc. **2.** a boat or ship, especially a large one. **3.** any of the body's tubes through which blood flows.

ves·tige (ves′tij) *noun.* a part or mark left from something that is no longer there: The snowbank was the last *vestige* of the big storm.

vi·brate (vī′brāt) *verb.* to move back and forth quickly.

vie (vī) *verb.* to challenge; to compete with others for an honor or reward: She was determined to *vie* with me for first place.

view·point (vyoo′point) *noun.* the position from which one thinks about something; attitude: His *viewpoint* was completely different from hers. **viewpoints.**

vig·il (vij′əl) *noun.* a time when someone stays awake to watch at night.

vil·lain (vil′ən) *noun.* **1.** an evil character in a story or play. **2.** a wicked person: We were afraid the *villain* would rob us. **villains.**

vi·o·la·tor (vī′ə lāt′ər) *noun.* a person who breaks a law, rule, or agreement: Traffic *violators* will be fined. **violators.**

vi·o·lence (vī′ə ləns) *noun.* **1.** a force used to hurt or cause damage: The demonstrators protested without *violence.* **2.** great strength.

vol·un·teer (vol ən tir′) *noun.* a person who offers to do something without being forced to do so: We asked for several *volunteers* to clean up after the party. **volunteers.**

voy·age (voi′ij) *noun.* **1.** a trip by water: We went on an ocean *voyage.* **2.** a trip through the air or outer space.

W

wade (wād) *verb.* to walk through water, mud, or anything that slows one down. **waded, wading.**

wea·ry (wir′ē) *adjective.* very tired; worn out.

wist·ful·ly (wist′fəl lē) *adverb.* in a manner showing a wish or a longing: She looked *wistfully* at the toys in the store window.

worth (wʉrth) *noun.* **1.** the quality that makes something have merit. **2.** the value of something: She sold the car for less than it's *worth.*

Y

yank (yańgk) *noun.* a sudden, strong pull. —*verb.* to pull or jerk. **yanked, yanking.**

year·book (yir′bʊok) *noun.* a book published at the end of a year that tells about events during that year.

a fat	oi oil	ch chin
ā ape	ōo look	sh she
ä car, father	ōō tool	th thin
e ten	ou out	*th* then
er care	u up	zh leisure
ē even	ur fur	ŋ ring
i hit		
ir here	ə = a *in* ago	
ī bite, fire	e *in* agent	
o lot	i *in* unity	
ō go	o *in* collect	
ô law, horn	u *in* focus	

wade

543

ABOUT THE
Authors & Illustrators

BARBARA AIELLO

✳ Barbara Aiello is a nationally recognized educator and puppeteer. The book series The Kids on the Block started as a puppet program to introduce young audiences to the topic of children with disabilities. She has won numerous awards for her work including the Surgeon General's Medallion for Excellence in Public Health. Ms. Aiello lives with her husband, daughter, and two cats on top of a hill in Westminster, Maryland.

GENEVIEVE BARLOW

■ Genevieve Barlow was born in Gardena, California, where she still lives. In addition to being a writer, she has also been a schoolteacher and a translator for the Red Cross in Puerto Rico. Her book *Latin American Tales* was chosen as a Junior Literary Guild selection. *(Born 1910)*

QUENTIN BLAKE

▲ Quentin Blake is an award-winning illustrator of children's books. He has published numerous books in the United States and in his native England. Mr. Blake is well known for illustrating many of Roald Dahl's books. He received the Kate Greenaway Medal in 1980 for outstanding illustration in a children's book. *(Born 1932)*

544

CLAIRE BOIKO

✳ Claire Boiko has been actively involved in theater for more than thirty years as a producer, director, and writer. She is a regular contributor to the magazine *Plays: A Drama Magazine for Young People*. Ms. Boiko presently makes her home in California.

DAVID BUDBILL

◼ David Budbill is a playwright, poet, and author of stories for young people. He, his wife, two children, and several pets live in a small town in Vermont in a house that he and his wife built. His wife, Lois Eby, paints and has illustrated some of her husband's books of poetry. David Budbill has received the Dorothy Canfield Fisher Award for *Bones on Black Spruce Mountain*. *(Born 1940)*

CLYDE ROBERT BULLA

▲ Although Clyde Robert Bulla never had any formal training in writing, he learned his art by reading. "Reading was a kind of magic . . ." he says. "By the time I was ready for the third grade, I had read most of the books in our school library." From the time he was a young boy, Bulla wanted to be a writer. When he was in the fourth grade, he won a prize for a story he had written. As an adult, he has continued to win prizes and awards for his writing. *(Born 1914)*

EVE BUNTING

❋ Eve Bunting was born in Ireland, but now lives in California. Her literary awards include the Golden Kite Award. Eve Bunting has said, "I like to write, and I particularly like to write about Ireland. As an immigrant, although I appreciate the ever-blue skies of California, I sometimes long for the misty grays of Ireland." *(Born 1928)*

MARY CALHOUN

■ Mary Calhoun says that her books grow out of her enthusiasms. When she became interested in folklore, the result was five picture book stories about elves in European countries. "Some of my earlier books," she says, "were the result of an enthusiasm plus nostalgia. The *Katie John* books developed from my happy memories of childhood in the big old brick house my great-grandfather built on a bluff above the Mississippi." One of her stories, *Cross-Country Cat*, has won several awards. *(Born 1926)*

VICTORIA CHESS

▲ Victoria Chess loves being an illustrator. More than twenty-five years after illustrating her first book, the artist says that she can "still get up every morning happy, and eager to get on with whatever assignment I have at the moment." Ms. Chess was born in Chicago, raised in Connecticut, and attended schools in Rhode Island, Switzerland, and Massachusetts. She hopes that "children will enjoy my pictures, and learn to laugh at the world and not take themselves too seriously." One of her books, *Bugs*, won an American Institute of Graphic Arts Book Show Award in 1976. *(Born 1939)*

ADRIAN FORSYTH

✳ Adrian Forsyth is a noted biologist, an award-winning nature writer, and photographer. He spends the winter months working in the tropical rain forests of South America and summers on his farm in Ontario, Canada. *Journey Through a Tropical Jungle* is Mr. Forsyth's first book for children. *(Born 1951)*

JEAN FRITZ

■ Jean Fritz was born in Hankow, China, where her parents were missionaries. She returned to the United States when she was thirteen years old. One reason she likes to write historical fiction is "to bridge the distance between past and present . . . to say 'Don't forget.'" Her children, she says, have been her most helpful critics. They have also given the titles to a number of her books. Among the many honors she has received for her work are a Newbery Honor, the American Book Award, and the Boston Globe-Horn Book Award. *(Born 1915)*

JAMES CROSS GIBLIN

▲ James Giblin says his interest in writing goes back to his childhood. "When I was five, I loved the 'Blondie' comic strip and drew and wrote strips of my own." He wrote a highly successful one-act play when he was in college and continues to use dramatic techniques in his writing of nonfiction books. His goal is to write books that he would have enjoyed when he was the age of his readers. James Giblin has won both the American Book Award and the Golden Kite Award. *(Born 1933)*

RONALD HIMLER

Ronald Himler is an author and award-winning illustrator of children's books. He was born and raised in Cleveland, Ohio and began painting at an early age. Before becoming a children's illustrator, Mr. Himler was a technical sculptor for General Motors and a toy designer and sculptor for a New York company. Mr. Himler is married and has two children, Daniel and Anna. He has received numerous awards for his work, including American Institute of Graphic Arts awards for *Baby* and *Rocket in My Pocket*. *(Born 1937)*

NORTON JUSTER

Norton Juster grew up in Brooklyn, New York, and now lives on a farm in northwestern Massachusetts. He was trained as an architect and continues to practice and teach architecture. He says, "Writing and architecture work well together; one acts as a relaxation from the other..." The writing of *The Phantom Tollbooth* began as a way to relax from a difficult planning project and was intended to be a short story. The book was made into a full-length cartoon and released in 1970. *(Born 1929)*

RUDYARD KIPLING

Rudyard Kipling was born in Bombay, India. He was sent to school in England and continued to live there. He wrote political essays, novels, poetry, and books for young people. Two of his best-known and most popular books are *The Jungle Book* and *Just So Stories*. He received many honors and awards for his writing including the Nobel Prize in literature. Rudyard Kipling is buried in the Poets' Corner at Westminster Abbey in London, England. *(1865–1936)*

KATHRYN LASKY

✳ Kathryn Lasky said that when she was growing up she was always thinking up stories but she did not want anybody to know about them. Later, she showed them to her parents, and still later to her husband. Then she showed them to others. She says "I write directly from my own experiences." Her husband has illustrated two of her books. *A Baby for Max* uses her husband's photographs of their son to tell the story. Kathryn Lasky has won both the Boston Globe-Horn Book Award and the Newbery Honor Book award. *(Born 1944)*

PATRICIA LAUBER

■ Patricia Lauber used to find it difficult to answer the question "How did you become a writer?" She says, "Finally I realized what the problem was: I don't think that I 'became' a writer; I think I was born wanting to write." She likes to write about many different things. Several of her books have been Junior Literary Guild selections, and *Volcano* is a Newbery Honor book. *(Born 1924)*

MYRON LEVOY

▲ Myron Levoy worked as a chemical engineer before beginning his career as a writer. He has earned a number of awards and honors, both in the United States and in other countries. One of his books was selected as a Boston Globe-Horn Book Honor Book. His international awards include the Dutch Silver Pencil Award and the Austrian State Prize for Children's Literature.

PATRICIA MACLACHLAN

Patricia MacLachlan was born in Wyoming and has lived in Minnesota, Connecticut, and Massachusetts. She has written several award-winning books for young adults. One of her best-loved novels, *Sarah, Plain and Tall*, won many awards including a Newbery Medal. In addition to her career as a writer, Ms. MacLachlan teaches and lectures on children's literature. She presently makes her home in western Massachusetts with her husband and children. *(Born 1938)*

MARGARET MAHY

Margaret Mahy grew up in a small town in New Zealand as the oldest of five children. Her mother read stories to Margaret and her siblings as they were growing up. Her father sang songs and told them original stories. The stories that most stirred her imagination were about a huge black-maned lion. She never forgot that lion, and wrote her first book, *A Lion in the Meadow*, about him. That book won an award in New Zealand for children's literature. Ms. Mahy has also received the Carnegie Medal for two of her books. A former children's librarian, she is now a full-time writer. *(Born 1936)*

DAVID MCCORD

David McCord was born in New York City. When he was twelve, his family moved to a ranch in southern Oregon. He said, "This was frontier country then; no electric lights, oil, or coal heat. We pumped all our water out of a deep well and pumped it by hand. I didn't go to school for three years, but I learned the life of the wilderness, something about birds, animals and wild flowers, trees and geology, and self-reliance." His poetry has won a number of awards. *(Born 1897)*

JEAN MERRILL

✳ Jean Merrill's favorite childhood memories are of being outdoors on her parents' farm in upstate New York. With her two sisters she built huts, dams, and rafts, tumbled in hay lofts, swam, and tobogganed. She also found time to read, and the pleasure of reading inspired her to write. Many of her books are about growing up on a farm. Others, like *The Pushcart War,* are set in New York City, where she still lives for the six months each year when she is not on her farm in Vermont. She has won many awards for her books and stories. *(Born 1923)*

NICHOLASA MOHR

■ Nicholasa Mohr has had a varied career as a graphic artist, television producer and writer, teacher, and novelist. Her design for the jacket of her award-winning story, *Nilda,* won a Citation of Merit from the Society of Illustrators. Ms. Mohr's stories reflect her experiences growing up in New York City as a member of the Puerto Rican community. She is the mother of two grown sons, and presently lives in Brooklyn, New York. *(Born 1935)*

JOAN LOWERY NIXON

▲ When Joan Lowery Nixon decided to write fiction, her two oldest daughters, who were in the second and sixth grades, told her, "If you're going to write a book, it has to be for children, and it has to be a mystery, and you have to put us in it." She did what they asked. Since then, she has written books in which her other two children appear. In addition to her own writing, she collaborates with her husband on nonfiction books, two of which were chosen as Outstanding Science Trade Books for Children. Among the numerous awards Ms. Nixon has earned is the Edgar Allen Poe Award from the Mystery Writers of America. *(Born 1927)*

SCOTT O'DELL

Scott O'Dell was born in Los Angeles when it was still a frontier town with "more horses than automobiles, more jack rabbits than people." He said, "The very first sound I remember was a wildcat scratching on the roof as I lay in bed." The frontier and the sea are the setting for many of the stories he has written for young people. Several of his books have been chosen as Newbery Honor books. Scott O'Dell was a recipient of the Newbery Medal and the Hans Christian Andersen Award. *(1903–1989)*

LILLIE PATTERSON

Lillie Patterson has been a librarian and a teacher, as well as an author. She has written a number of biographies and a book of poetry. She says, "I grew up on the beautiful island of Hilton Head [South Carolina] under the care of a grandmother . . . a great reader and singer. From my grandmother I captured a sense of the power of words. It was natural that I would follow a career . . . in writing." Her biography of Martin Luther King, Jr., won the Coretta Scott King Award.

JACK PRELUTSKY

Jack Prelutsky is a singer, actor, translator, and poet. He graduated from the High School of Music and Art in New York City. A friend who liked his nonsense verse and his drawings of imaginary animals persuaded him to try to get them published. He did. Since then he has written many books of poetry. He has also translated several books of poetry from German. He says that all of his characters contain parts of people he knows and parts of himself. Several of his books have been chosen as Junior Literary Guild selections. *(Born 1940)*

THEODORE ROETHKE

✳ Theodore Roethke, born in Saginaw, Michigan, was both a poet and a teacher. As a young child, he spent many hours working and playing among the acres of flowering plants and vast greenhouses owned by his family. In later years, he incorporated the experiences of his childhood into his poetry. He taught English at several colleges. As a poet he received numerous awards, including the 1954 Pulitzer Prize in poetry for *The Waking: Poems 1933–1953*. *(1908–1963)*

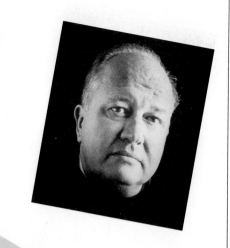

MARCIA SEWALL

▇ Marcia Sewall was born and raised in Providence, Rhode Island, but now lives near Boston, Massachusetts. She taught art in high school before becoming a full-time illustrator. Many of her books have won awards including the New York Times Best Illustrated Book and several were named Newbery Honor books. *(Born 1935)*

JEFFREY SHULMAN

▲ Jeffrey Shulman is the co-author with Barbara Aiello of *Business Is Looking Up*. He has written several children's books on a variety of issues including drug education, the environment, and family issues. In addition to writing, he is the publisher of Twenty-First Century Books, a children's book company based in Frederick, Maryland. Mr. Shulman makes his home in Maryland with his wife Gretchen, three daughters, one goldfish, two hermit crabs, and four cats.

ZILPHA KEATLEY SNYDER

❋ When she was eight, Zilpha decided she was "cut out to be a writer." Growing up on a farm in southern California, her life was centered on animals and books. She especially loved to read. When she began to write professionally, her students and her own children came to mind, and writing stories for them came easily. Her book *The Egypt Game* was a runner–up for the Newbery Medal. *(Born 1928)*

IANTHE MAC THOMAS

▦ Ianthe Mac Thomas is not only a writer but also a sculptor who has shown her wrought iron and steel pieces in exhibitions. In her writings, Ianthe Mac Thomas tries to emphasize the importance of caring for others. The *Interracial Books for Children Bulletin* said that her book *Hi, Mrs. Mallory!* was "a book about love and caring and sharing. . . ." *(Born 1951)*

ANN TURNER

▲ In addition to being a writer, Ann Turner has been a high school English teacher. She has said: "I grew up being interested in different peoples and cultures. . . . I am concerned with the things that make each culture individual, and the traits that hold us together. . . . I feel we must know the Eskimos, the Aborigines, the ancient Chinese, and Paleolithic man." *(Born 1945)*

WALT WHITMAN

※ During the Civil War, Walt Whitman volunteered as a hospital nurse and cared for sick and wounded soldiers. His experiences affected him deeply and are reflected in many of his poems. Other poems, however, celebrate the joy and beauty of nature. Although Walt Whitman's poetry was not appreciated during his lifetime, he is now considered among the great American poets. *(1819–1892)*

ROSEBUD YELLOW ROBE

■ Rosebud Yellow Robe lived in New York City, but she was born in Rapid City, South Dakota. She was the daughter of Chief Chauncey Yellow Robe, chief of the Lakota-oyate tribe. She was descended from two famous leaders of the Dakota Sioux nation, Iron Plume and Sitting Bull. Rosebud Yellow Robe gave talks in libraries and public schools in the New York area about the history of Native Americans. She wrote several books, including *An Album of the American Indian.*

JANE H. YOLEN

▲ Jane Yolen was born in New York City and moved to Westport, Connecticut, when she was thirteen. She said that there were so many writers and artists in Westport that "I just assumed that when you grew up, you became a writer." She has two pieces of advice for young people interested in writing: "Read and write. Read and read and read. It's the only way you will discover what great stories have been told and what stories you want to tell better. Write every day because writing is like a muscle that needs to be flexed." Jane Yolen's books have earned many honors. *(Born 1939)*

AUTHOR INDEX

Grateful acknowledgment is made to the following publishers, authors, and agents for their permission to reprint copyrighted material. Every effort has been made to locate all copyright proprietors; any errors or omissions in copyright notice are inadvertent and will be corrected in future printings as they are discovered.

"The Brooklyn Bridge: Emily's Triumph" by Charnan Simon, © 1989 by Silver, Burdett & Ginn Inc.

"Business Is Looking Up" excerpt from *The Kids on the Block* Book Series by Barbara Aiello and Jeffrey Shulman, copyright © 1988. Text reprinted by permission of Twenty-First Century Books, a Division of Henry Holt & Co., Frederick, Maryland. Fee donated to the National Federation of the Blind.

"Can She Sing?" excerpt from *Sarah, Plain and Tall* by Patricia MacLachlan, jacket art © 1985 by Marcia Sewall. Text and illustrations reprinted by permission of the American publisher, Harper*Collins* Publishers and of the British publisher, Julia MacRae Books, a division of Walker Books Ltd.

Dakota Dugout by Ann Turner and illustrated by Ronald Himler is reprinted by permission of the publishers, Macmillan Publishing Company, and of the author's agent, Curtis Brown Ltd. Text copyright © 1985 by Ann Turner. Illustrations copyright © 1985 by Ron Himler.

Day of the Earthlings by Eve Bunting, copyright © 1978 by Creative Education, Inc. Text reprinted by permission of Creative Education, Inc.

"Designing Washington, D.C." from *Benjamin Banneker: Genius of Early America* by Lillie Patterson. Copyright © 1978 by Lillie Patterson. Published by Abingdon Press. Text reprinted by permission of the author.

The Emperor and the Kite by Jane Yolen, text copyright © 1967 by Jane Yolen. Reprinted by permission of the publisher, Philomel Books, and of the author's agent, Curtis Brown Ltd.

"Ezra, the Baseball Fan" from *Baseball Fever* by Johanna Hurwitz. Text copyright © 1981 by Johanna Hurwitz. Reprinted by permission of William Morrow & Company, Inc./Publishers, New York.

"A Family Home" excerpt from *Katie John* by Mary Calhoun. Text copyright © 1960 by Mary Calhoun. Reprinted by permission of Harper*Collins* Publishers.

"A Good Chance" by Ianthe Mac Thomas, © 1989 by Silver, Burdett & Ginn Inc.

If You Say So, Claude by Joan Lowery Nixon, illustrated by Lorinda Bryan Cauley. Text Copyright © 1980 by Joan Lowery Nixon. Illustrations copyright © 1980 by Lorinda Bryan Cauley. Reprinted by permission of Viking Penguin Inc., of the author's agent, Writer's House Inc., and of the artist's agent, Florence Alexander.

Jem's Island by Kathryn Lasky. Text copyright © 1982 Kathryn Lasky. Reprinted with the permission of the publisher, Charles Scribner's Sons, an imprint of Macmillan Publishing Company, and of the author's attorney, Sheldon Fogelman.

"Journey Through a Tropical Jungle" excerpt from *Journey Through a Tropical Jungle* by Adrian Forsyth, illustrated by Julie Wootten. Copyright 1988. Text and illustrations reprinted with permission of the American publisher, Simon & Schuster Books for Young Readers, a division of Simon & Schuster Inc. and of the Canadian publisher, Greey de Pencier Books, Toronto.

"Keplik, the Match Man" from *The Witch of Fourth Street and Other Stories* by Myron Levoy. Text copyright © 1972 by Myron Levoy. Reprinted by permission of HarperCollins Publishers.

"Lee Bennett Hopkins Interviews Isaac Bashevis Singer" by Lee Bennett Hopkins. Text reprinted by permission of Curtis Brown Ltd. Copyright © 1974 by Lee Bennett Hopkins. Updated interview specially prepared for Silver, Burdett & Ginn Inc. by Lee Bennett Hopkins.

"The Liberty Bell" from *Fireworks, Picnics, and Flags* by James Cross Giblin. Text copyright © 1983 by James Cross Giblin. Reprinted by permission of Clarion Books/Ticknor & Fields, a Houghton Mifflin Company.

"The Librarian and the Robbers" from *The Great Piratical Rumbustification & the Librarian and the Robbers* by Margaret Mahy, illustrated by Quentin Blake. Copyright © 1978 by Margaret Mahy. Text and illustrations reprinted by permission of American publisher, David R. Godine, Publisher and of the British publisher, J M Dent & Sons Ltd. Publishers, a division of Weidenfeld (Publishers) Ltd.

"Mars: A Close-up Picture" excerpt from *Journey to the Planets* by Patricia Lauber. Text copyright © 1982 by Patricia Lauber. Reprinted by permission of Crown Publishers, Inc.

"Night Journey" copyright 1940 by Theodore Roethke. From *The Collected Poems of Theodore Roethke* by Theodore Roethke. Text reprinted by permission of the American publisher, Doubleday, a division of Bantam Doubleday Dell Publishing Group, Inc., and of the British publisher, Faber & Faber Ltd.

"The No-Guitar Blues" from *Baseball in April and Other Stories*, copyright © 1990 by Gary Soto. Text reprinted by permission of Harcourt Brace Jovanovich, Inc.

"Odysseus and the Sea Kings" excerpt from *The Voyage of Odysseus: Homer's Odyssey Retold by James Reeves*. Copyright © 1973 by James Reeves. Text reproduced with permission of Blackie & Sons, Ltd., Glasgow and London.

"On My Way Home" by Jean Fritz. Excerpt of text reprinted by permission of the publishers, G. P. Putnam's Sons, and of the author's agent, the Gina Maccoby Literary Agency, from *HOMESICK: My Own Story* by Jean Fritz, copyright © 1982 by Jean Fritz.

"Philbert Phlurk" from *The Sheriff of Rottenshot* by Jack Prelutsky. Illustrations by Victoria Chess. Text copyright © 1982 by Jack Prelutsky. Illustrations copyright © 1982 by Victoria Chess. Reprinted by permission of Greenwillow Books, a division of William Morrow, Inc./Publishers, N. Y.

"The Popcorn Blizzard" from *Paul Bunyan Swings His Axe* by Dell J. McCormick, copyright 1936 by The Caxton Printers, Ltd. Text reprinted by permission of The Caxton Printers, Ltd.

"A Sea of Grass" by Duncan Searl, © 1989 by Silver, Burdett & Ginn Inc.

"The Search for the Magic Lake" from *Latin American Tales: From the Pampas to the Pyramids of Mexico* retold by Genevieve Barlow. Copyright © 1966 by Rand McNally & Company. Text reprinted by permission of Eiko Tien, Conservator for the Estate of Genevieve Barlow.

"Snowshoe Trek to Otter River" excerpt from *Snowshoe Trek to Otter River* by David Budbill. Text copyright © 1976 by David Budbill. Reprinted by permission of Dial Books for Young Readers, and of the author.

"Star Fever" by Claire Boiko. Text reprinted by permission of Plays, Inc. from *Children's Plays for Creative Actors*, copyright 1967.

"The Thanksgiving Play" from *Felita* by Nicholasa Mohr. Text copyright © 1979 by Nicholasa Mohr. Text reprinted by permission of Dial Books for Young Readers, and of the author. Accompanying excerpt from "An Interview with Author Nicholasa Mohr" by Myra Zarnowski, © 1991, from *The Reading Teacher*, October 1991. Text reprinted with permission of Myra Zarnowski and the International Reading Association.

"There Is an Island" by Jean Fritz, Copyright © 1990 by Jean Fritz. Originally published in *The Big Book for Peace*, edited by Ann Durell and Marilyn Sachs, published by Dutton Children's Books, a division of Penguin Books USA Inc. Text reprinted by permission of Gina Maccoby Literary Agency.

"This Is My Rock" from *One at a Time* by David McCord. Copyright 1929 by David McCord. First appeared in *The Saturday Review of Literature*. Text reprinted by permission of Little, Brown and Company.

"Through the Tollbooth" excerpt from *The Phantom Tollbooth* by Norton Juster, illustrations by Jules Feiffer. Text copyright © 1961 by Norton Juster, illustrations copyright © 1961 by Jules Feiffer. Reprinted by permission of the American publisher, Alfred A. Knopf, Inc., a Division of Random House, Inc., and of the British publisher, Collins Publishers.

"A Time to Talk" by Robert Frost. Copyright 1916 and renewed 1944 by Robert Frost. Reprinted from *The Poetry of Robert Frost* edited by Edward Connery Lathem, by permission of the Estate of Robert Frost in care of the British publisher, Jonathan Cape Ltd.

"To Dark Eyes Dreaming" from *Today Is Saturday* by Zilpha Snyder, © 1969 by Zilpha Keatley Snyder. Published by Atheneum Press. Text reprinted by permission of the author.

"Today's Immigrants" by Luz Nuncio, © 1989 by Silver, Burdett & Ginn Inc.

"Tonweya and the Eagles" from *Tonweya and the Eagles and Other Lakota Indian Tales* retold by Rosebud Yellow Robe. Text copyright © 1979 by Rosebud Yellow Robe Frantz. Text reprinted by permission of Dial Books for Young Readers.

"The Toothpaste Millionaire" excerpt from *The Toothpaste Millionaire* by Jean Merrill. Copyright © 1972 by Houghton Mifflin Company. Text reprinted with permission of Houghton Mifflin Company.

"Voyage by Canoe" excerpt from *Island of the Blue Dolphins* by Scott O'Dell. Copyright © 1960 by Scott O'Dell. Text reprinted by permission of the American publisher, Houghton Mifflin Company, and of the British publisher, Penguin Books Ltd. All rights reserved.

"What Is an American?" by Loren Gary, © 1989 by Silver, Burdett & Ginn Inc.

"When Shlemiel Went to Warsaw" from *When Shlemiel Went to Warsaw & Other Stories* by Isaac Bashevis Singer. Translated by the author and Elizabeth Shub. Copyright © 1968 by Isaac Bashevis Singer. Text reprinted by permission of Farrar, Straus and Giroux, Inc.

"The White House" from *The Spice of America* by June Swanson. Text Copyright © 1983 by June Swanson. Reprinted by permission of Carolrhoda Books, 241 First Avenue North, Minneapolis, MN 55401.

"Working with Al" excerpt from *Shoeshine Girl* by Clyde Robert Bulla. Copyright © 1975 by Clyde Robert Bulla. Text reprinted by permission of Harper*Collins* Publishers and the author's agent Bill Berger Associates, Inc.

COVER ILLUSTRATION: Michael McGurl

ILLUSTRATION: 1-11, Tamar Haber-Schaim; 16-24, Don Weiler; 25, Susan Tyrrell; 26-40, Kathleen Howell; 41, Carol Schweigert; 58-72, Quentin Blake; 73, Judy Filippo; 74-84, Andy San Diego; 86, Robert Roth; 87, Lindy Burnett; 88-107, Loel Barr; 108-118, Matt Faulkner; 119, Margery Mintz; 120-121, Victoria Chess; 131, Daniel Clifford; 132-147, Carol Vidinghoff; 152-162, Robert Freeman; 163, Fabio Deponte; 182, Andrea Grassi; 194-208, Lydia Dabcovich; 209, Debby Barrett; 210-216, Floyd Cooper; 218-219, David Frampton; 220-224, Wally Niebart; 225, Fabio Deponte; 226-244, Allen Schrag; 245, Ruby Shoes Studio; 246-257, Christopher Denise; 262-276, Betsy Day; 277, Kathey Parkenson; 283, Peter Bianco; 284-296, Teresa Fasolino; 297, Debby Barrett; 300-310, Rae Ecklund; 311, Sara Deponte; 312-324, Mike Eagle; 325, Fabio Deponte; 326-334, Robert Casilla; 335, Susan Tyrrell; 336-350, Jules Feiffer; 351, Susan Tyrrell; 352-353, Robert M. Cunningham; 361, Fabio Deponte; 362-377, Alan Cober; 382-392, Lorinda Bryan Cauley; 393, Daniel Clifford; 395-401, Brian Callanan; 394, Robert Hynes; 402-406, Ronald Himler; 408-422, Jim Lamarche; 423, Fabio Deponte; 424-434, Toni Goffe; 435, Debra Pagano; 436-448, Donald Cook; 449, Greg Lamb; 450-451, Annouchka Galouchko; 464-474, Allen Eitzen; 475, Sara Deponte; 476, Marcia Sewall; 476-489, borders, Rosekrans Hoffman; 491-521, Jeffrey Terrison; 523, Marcy Ramsey; 524, (t) Meg Kelleher Aubrey; 524, (b) Marcy Ramsey; 525, Meg Kelleher Ramsey; 526, (b) Marcy Ramsey; 527, Marcy Ramsey; 529, Marcy Ramsey; 530, (t) Claudia Sargent; 530, (b) Melinda Fabian; 531, Richard Kolding; 533, (t) Marcey Ramsey; 533, (b) Richard Kolding; 536, (t) Beverly Benner; 539, (b) Marcy Ramsey; 540, (t) Debbe Heller; 540, (b) Cheryl Kirk Noll; 541, Marcy Ramsey; 544-555, Tamar Haber-Schaim.

PHOTOGRAPHY: 12-13, Jerry Howard/Positive Images; 13, LES CONSTRUCTEURS, 1950, oil on canvas by Fernand Léger, (1881-1955), French. Musée Léger, Biot/Bridgeman Art Library/Art Resource, New York; 42, © Gregory G. Dimijian/Photo Researchers, Inc.; 44, Michael Fogden/DRK Photo; 45, Michael & Patricia Fogden; 46, © Gregory G. Dimijian/Photo Researchers, Inc., (inset) Turid Forsyth; 47, Bruce Lyon; 48, Michael & Patricia Fogden; 49, Michael Fogden/Animals, Animals; 50, Michael & Patricia Fogden; 51, Andre Bartschi/Adrian Forsyth; 53-55, Michael & Patricia Fogden; 56, Bruce Lyon; 57, G. I. Bernard, Oxford Scientific/Earth Scenes/Animals, Animals; 85, courtesy, Gary Soto; 122, BROOKLYN BRIDGE © 1982 by Milton Bond, courtesy Jay Johnson Gallery; 124, Rensselaer Polytechnic Institute Archive; 126-127, New York Public Library; 129, Culver Pictures; 148-149, Paul Marrow/FPG International; 149, JOHNS, Jasper. FLAG (1954-55; dated on reverse 1955). Encaustic, oil and collage on fabric mounted on plywood, 42 1/4 x 60 5/8". Collection, The Museum of Modern Art, New York. Gift of Phillip Johnson in honor of Alfred H. Barr, Jr. Photograph © 1989 The Museum of Modern Art, New York; 150, Ken O'Donoghue; 163, © Art Source; 164, (t) © 1993 Chuck Fishman/Woodfin Camp & Associates, (b) UPI/Bettmann Newsphotos; 166, (l) The Bettmann Archive, (r) Robert Frerck: TSW/Chicago; 167, (l) Jay Lurie/Bruce Coleman, (r) Phil Matt/Gamma Liaison; 168, Norman McGrath; 169, (t) Leslie A. Kelly, (b) Alan L. Graham, f/Stop; 170, (tl) Richard W. Browne, (tr) Richard W. Browne, f/Stop, (m) © 1993 David Burnett/Contact Press Images/Woodfin Camp & Associates; 171, © 1993 Chuck Fishman/Woodfin Camp & Associates; 173, The Anthony Blake Photo Library/Roax Brothers/Gerritt Buntrock; 174, Library of Congress; 176, Rich Frasier, courtesy St. John's Church, Washington, D. C.; 177, (l) National Portrait Gallery/Smithsonian Institution, (r) The Pennsylvania Academy of Fine Arts; 178, Library of Congress; 181, The Granger

Collection; 183-184, Science Museum, England/Michael Holford; 189, The Maryland Historical Society, Baltimore; 190, Robert Llewellyn; 191, BUILDING THE FIRST WHITE HOUSE, Washington, D. C., 1798, by N. C. Wyeth, © Smithsonian Institution; 192-193, Charles Krebs/The Stock Market; 209, © Phil Cantor; 217, © Russ Finley; 245, NASA; 258-259, E. R. Degginger; 259, LAILA AND MAJNUN AT SCHOOL, leaf from a 16th century Persian manuscript, artist unknown. Folio 129 recto. © The Metropolitan Museum of Art, New York. Gift of Alexander Smith Cochran, 1913. (13.288.7); 261, Ken O'Donoghue; 278-281, Susan Greenwood/Gamma Liaison; 298-299, Julius Fekete/The Stock Market; 351, From FEIFFER: JULES FEIFFER'S AMERICA FROM EISENHOWER TO REAGAN by Jules Feiffer, edit., Steven Heller Copyright © 1982 by Jules Feiffer. Reprinted by permission of Alfred A. Knopf, Inc.; 354-361, NASA; 378-379, Scott Nielsen/Imagery, 379, CRAZY QUILT BEDCOVER, quilt, c. 1850-1900 by Celestine Bacheller. American. Quilt made of pieced, appliquéd and embroidered silk and velvet. 74 1/4 x 57". Gift of Mr. & Mrs. Edward J. Healy in Memory of Mrs. Charles O'Malley. Courtesy, Museum of Fine Arts, Boston. 63.655; 381, Ken O'Donoghue; 407, Kansas State Historical Society; 453, © 1993 Wesley Frank/Woodfin Camp & Associates; 457-461, Brent Jones; 463, (tr) © D. Donne Bryant, (ml) © Jack Vartoogian, (br) Michael P. Gadomski/Bruce Coleman; 526, (t) © 1993 John Ficara/Woodfin Camp & Associates; 528, Dr. Scott Nielson/Bruce Coleman; 532, The Bettmann Archive; 534, Ruth Lacey; 535, Martin Rogers/Stock, Boston; 536, (m, b) Tom Pantages; 537, W. T. Hall/Bruce Coleman; 538, © Frank Siteman 1988; 539, (t) Tom Pantages; 542, © Frank Siteman 1988; 543, Mike Mazzaschi/Stock, Boston; 544, (t) provided by the author, (m) courtesy of Eiko Tien, (b) By Vrooland, courtesy of A. P. Watt Ltd.; 545, (t) provided by the author, (m, b) Lois Eby; 546, (t, m) H. W. Wilson Company, (b) courtesy of Little, Brown and Company; 547, (t) Turid Forsyth, (m) H. W. Wilson Company © Clarion Books; 548, (t) courtesy Macmillan Publishing Co., (m) courtesy Hampshire College, (b) The Bettmann Archive; 549, (t) Christopher Knight, (m) H. W. Wilson Company; 550, (t) Dick Carnes, Harper & Row Publishers, Inc., (m) provided by the author, (b) H. W. Wilson Company; 551, (t) by Ronni Solbert, (b) Delacroix Press; 552, (m) provided by the author; 553, (t) The Bettmann Archive; 554, (t, m) provided by the author, (b) Houghton Mifflin Company; 555, (t) Clarion Books, (m) The Bettmann Archive, (b) Delacroix Press.